Children must learn to act appropriately, in ways that differ from society to society and from context to context. How best to socialize children so they can function successfully is a crucial question that has fascinated educators and psychologists for centuries.

In a world where children exhibit unchildlike levels of violence, matters concerning child rearing take on an immediacy for parents and psychologists. Does physical punishment prevent violent behavior? Are there ways to influence children so that punishment will not be necessary?

Drawing upon rich, longitudinal data, the contributors to this volume examine benefits and costs of coercion and punishment, considering such topics as mental health, antisocial and criminal behavior, substance abuse, and issues related to measurement and prediction. They look at coercion among peers, aggressive behavior in boys and girls, different parenting styles, and effects of home context. The volume brings together evidence that has appeared in disparate literatures, and questions the easy assumptions that have been made about coercion and punishment.

Coercion and punishment in long-term perspectives

Coercion and punishment in long-term perspectives

Edited by

JOAN McCORD
Temple University

Published by the Press Syndicate of the University of Cambridge
The Pitt Building, Trumpington Street, Cambridge CB2 1RP
40 West 20th Street, New York, NY 10011-4211, USA
10 Stamford Road, Oakleigh, Melbourne 3166, Australia

First published 1995

Printed in the United States of America

Library of Congress Cataloging-in-Publication Data
Coercion and punishment in long-term perspectives / edited by Joan
McCord.
p.   cm.
Includes bibliographical references.
ISBN 0-521-45069-1
1. Discipline of children – Psychological aspects.   2. Child
psychology.   I. McCord, Joan.
HQ770.4.C64   1995
649'.64 – dc20   94-12724
                                                                      CIP

A catalog record for this book is available from the British Library.

ISBN 0-521-45069-1 Hardback

Contents

Contributors

Jacqueline Barnes-McGuire
Department of Psychiatry
Harvard Medical School of Public
   Health

John E. Bates
Department of Psychology
Indiana University

Frankie Bernèche
Research Unit on Children's Psycho-
   Social Maladjustment
University of Montreal

Michel Boivin
School of Psychology
Laval University

Judith S. Brook
Community Medicine
Mt. Sinai School of Medicine

Pierre Charlebois
Research Unit on Children's Psycho-
   Social Maladjustment
University of Montreal

Patricia Cohen
Columbia College of Physicians &
   Surgeons
Columbia University School of Public
   Health

John D. Coie
Department of Psychology – Social
   and Health Sciences
Duke University

Wendy Craig
Department of Psychology
Queen's University, Kingston

Kelly R. Damphousse
Department of Sociology
Texas A&M University

Nancy Darling
Department of Psychology
Temple University

Kenneth A. Dodge
Department of Psychology and
   Human Development
Vanderbilt University

Jean E. Dumas
Department of Psychological Sciences
Purdue University

Felton Earls
Department of Maternal & Child
   Health
Harvard School of Public Health

Anne C. Fletcher
Carolina Consortium of Human
    Development
Center for Developmental Science
University of North Carolina, Chapel
    Hill

Claude Gagnon
Research Unit on Children's Psycho-
    Social Maladjustment
University of Montreal

Harald Janson
Department of Psychology
University of Stockholm

Denise B. Kandel
Department of Psychiatry and School
    of Public Health
Columbia University and
New York State Psychiatric Institute

Howard B. Kaplan
Department of Sociology
Texas A&M University

Kate Keenan
Department of Psychology
University of Pittsburgh

Ingrid Klackenberg-Larsson
Department of Psychology
University of Stockholm

Peter J. LaFreniere
Child Studies Department
Maine University

Serge Larivée
Research Unit on Children's Psycho-
    Social Maladjustment
University of Montreal

John H. Laub
College of Criminal Justice
Northeastern University and
Murray Research Center
Radcliffe College

Marc Le Blanc
School of Psycho-Education
University of Montreal

John Lochman
Duke University Medical Center and
    Department of Psychology

David Magnusson
Department of Psychology
University of Stockholm

Barbara Maughan
MRC Child Psychiatry Unit
Institute of Psychiatry, London

Joan McCord
Department of Criminal Justice
Temple University

Gerald R. Patterson
Oregon Social Learning Center,
    Eugene

Debra J. Pepler
Department of Psychology
York University

Patricia Peters
Centre for Research in Human
    Development
Concordia University

Gregory S. Pettit
Department of Family and Child
    Development
Auburn University

Andrew Pickles
MRC Child Psychiatry Unit
Institute of Psychiatry, London

David Quinton
MRC Child Psychiatry Unit
Institute of Psychiatry, London

William L. Roberts
Department of Psychology
Cariboo College

Robert J. Sampson
Department of Sociology
University of Chicago and
Ogburn-Stouffer Center, NORC

Alex E. Schwartzman
Centre for Research in Human
  Development
Concordia University

Lisa A. Serbin
Centre for Research in Human
  Development
Concordia University

Daniel S. Shaw
Department of Psychology
University of Pittsburgh

Håkan Stattin
Department of Psychology
University of Stockholm

Laurence Steinberg
Department of Psychology
Temple University

Murray A. Straus
Family Research Laboratory
University of New Hampshire

Robert Terry
Department of Psychology
Duke University

Richard E. Tremblay
Research Unit on Children's
  Psychosocial Maladjustment
University of Montreal

Pierrette Verlaan
Centre for Research in Human
  Development
Concordia University

Frank Vitaro
School of Psycho-Education
University of Montreal

Ping Wu
Department of Psychiatry
Columbia University

Audrey Zakriski
Department of Psychology
Duke University

Acknowledgments

The chapters in this volume are based on presentations at the Society for Life History Research Conference, which took place in Philadelphia, Pennsylvania, April 29 to May 2, 1992. I wish to thank the participants at the conference. Their questions and discussions helped to make the research reported in these essays both challenging and interesting.

I would like also to acknowledge the willing and valuable assistance of Ingrid Farally and Kevin Conway. They were able to keep this volume on schedule and in good order. Finally, I owe a special debt to Carl A. Silver for his encouragement and cogent criticisms.

1 Introduction: coercion and punishment in the fabric of social relations

JOAN McCORD

Democracy depends heavily on consensus. Persuasion, coercion, and fear provide the means for bringing about that consensus and jointly account for much of the education or training of children to participate in society. Children must be taught to act appropriately – in ways that differ from society to society and from context to context. How they are taught remains something of a mystery.

This book developed from the ways in which researchers responded to the mystery. Successful socialization can be viewed as subtle coercion, possibly making punishment unnecessary. The question of how best to socialize children so that they function well is a large and crucial question that has fascinated parents, educators, philosophers, and psychologists for centuries.

Persuasion seems a natural adversary of punishment from the perspective of a teacher or a parent. If children can be persuaded to do as the adult wishes, no punishment need be considered. A child persuaded to help clean the home need not be punished for having failed to do so. Although a threat of punishment might be persuasive, the boundaries between persuasion and punishment remain reasonably clear.

Coercion can be less clearly identified. Conceptually, coercion implies forcing people to do what they would not otherwise have done. For example, when an individual is forced at gunpoint to do something he or she would not otherwise choose to do, the action can be described as one of coercion. Alexis de Tocqueville (1839/1945) noted that the public

among a democratic people, has a singular power, which aristocratic nations cannot conceive; for it does not persuade others to its beliefs, but it imposes them and makes them permeate the thinking of everyone by a sort of enormous pressure of the mind of all upon the individual intelligence. (p. 11)

Tocqueville thus asserts that public opinion can be coercive.

To learn how to eat with utensils as is done in Western societies, for example,

1

children must be taught complicated processes of holding forks, knives, and spoons. They come to expect to have the utensils for certain types of meals. Social customs, including some that involve when to eat and sleep — perhaps even when to be hungry or tired — are formed by weapons that appear to be as powerful as guns in creating uniform behavior.

Coercion implies forcing individuals to choose to do things that they might not otherwise do were choice more broadly allowed. It need not imply either threat or resistance. Actions that at one time are coerced can become voluntary at another, showing no apparent difference in their circumstance. I argue that from this point of view, socialization necessarily requires coercion.

Voluntary actions have historically been distinguished from those performed with coercion by identifying what Aristotle considered a "moving principle" of action. When the moving principle is within the agent, when the agent knows what he or she is doing and wants to do that thing, the action is voluntary. Persuasion can lead a person to want to do something, and therefore, to do it voluntarily.

Punishments can be justified only on condition that the agent who is punished should have done a different thing. Importantly, then, the use of punishment implies a belief that the punished person *could* have done a different thing. Therefore, punishments are inappropriate when actions are coerced.

Threats of punishment can lead to voluntary choice. Threats of punishments are often used by parents, teachers, or by society to persuade people to behave in acceptable ways. If the threats fail to be persuasive, punishments may follow.

Threats of punishments can also be coercive. Punishments can restrict choice, thus rendering actions involuntary. When a person fears punishment, he or she may not perceive possibilities for choice that would be evident in the absence of such fears. From this perspective, coercion may be seen as beneficial through providing a means for avoiding punishment. And yet the right to resist coercive action seems to be a right for which many are willing to fight and even to die.

This volume considers mental health, antisocial and criminal behavior, and substance abuse in relation to a variety of types of coercive interactions and punishments. It includes evidence gathered in families, schools, and penal institutions. The authors scrutinize methods for gathering data as well as substantive issues.

Some chapters suggest that subtle coercion can be powerful in shaping behavior. Dumas and LaFreniere (Chapter 2), for example, show how anxious and aggressive children tend to coerce their parents into behaving aversively. By exchanging children in laboratory situations, they show also that mothers of the aggressive and the anxious children were capable of behaving with positive affect. This evidence raises questions about designing interventions to teach parents techniques for positive interaction with children — techniques they may already know but fail to use with their own children.

Patterson suggests that a considerable amount of experience "goes by unnoticed." Among the little-noticed experiences discussed in the chapters to follow are those linked with classroom seating. Charlebois, Bernèche, Le Blanc, Gagnon, and Larivée (Chapter 12) found that 85% of the boys they traced between the ages of 9 and 11 years were sitting in roughly the same classroom locations in different years. Both teachers' and the boys' behavior reflected this placement: aggressive children seated in middle rows became less disruptive than their previously similarly aggressive classmates seated elsewhere. The fact that teachers were less intrusive in their interactions with children sitting in middle rows may provide a clue to understanding this result.

Coercion by peers can be subtle. Boivin and Vitaro (Chapter 11) captured differences between aggressive boys involved in networks and those who were loners. The affiliated aggressive boys tended to be more aggressive than the unaffiliated ones. Furthermore, within networks, those who were less aggressive than their peer associates tended to become more aggressive. Both discoveries raise a question about whether training aggressive boys to have more social skills might be useless or even counterproductive. A part of the answer might be given in the evaluation study by Pepler, Craig, and Roberts.

Pepler, Craig, and Roberts (Chapter 13) studied effects of social skills training on children in Grades 1 through 6. The training seemed to increase the children's social skills: They were better liked by their peers, and their teachers rated them as having fewer behavior problems than they had prior to the training. Yet their aggressive behavior on the playground had not been reduced.

Coie, Terry, Zakriski, and Lochman (Chapter 14) considered networks in sixth and eighth grade. To their surprise, the researchers discovered that aggressive deviant cliques tended to be perceived as socially preferred. In a second study, they also found that having deviant peer associates had a positive effect on social status for boys, although not for girls.

Using a different set of measures and different groups of children, Schwartzman, Verlaan, Peters, and Serbin (Chapter 21) also found that aggressive children were approved by their peers. Although both boys and girls preferred their same-sex peers to be nonaggressive in first grade, boys preferred aggressive girls and girls preferred aggressive boys by the time they reached seventh grade.

Bates, Pettit, and Dodge (Chapter 7) examined children's shifts in aggressiveness between kindergarten and first grade. They were unsuccessful in discovering links to harsh prior discipline, changes in discipline, or stressful events. Their findings raise issues about why aggressive behavior changes.

Evidence from several chapters suggests that punishment typically operates to increase aversive behaviors of children and to aggravate other forms of social problems. Straus (Chapter 4) presents evidence, for example, that punishment in childhood increases the probability of subsequent depression. Tremblay (Chapter 8) discovered that disciplining techniques based on power were more likely to lead to delinquency than were techniques based on attachment. Kaplan and Damphousse (Chapter 18) found that negative sanctions tended to increase deviance especially when these were used without also using personal and social restraints.

The coercive model proposed by Patterson (Chapter 5) includes bidirectional influences between parents and their children. On this account, parents become increasingly reluctant to intrude, giving children expanding domains for selecting theft or other antisocial forms of behavior as sources of stimulation.

Kandel and Wu (Chapter 6) investigated the bidirectional interacting coercion process from the mother's perspective, finding that punitive discipline tends to produce aggressive behavior, which in turn reduced closeness and supervision. Cohen and Brook (Chapter 9) also investigated bidirectional coercion processes. Their focus was on patterns of the relationship between conduct disorder and punishment from infancy through adolescence. The results of their analyses suggest that although lack of closeness between mothers and their children independently contributes to conduct disorder, use of punishments also should be considered an influence contributing to developing conduct problems.

Laub and Sampson (Chapter 15) considered both informal and formal sanctions to investigate consequences of punishment. Their analyses showed that harsh discipline increased the likelihood of serious criminal behavior during adolescence, but after adolescence had residual effects only when mediated by prior delinquency. In addition, they found that by decreasing the probability of job stability, longer incarceration increased recidivism. Le Blanc (Chapter 17) also considered both formal and informal sanctions in his models. Although his data are only weakly predictive, they suggest that beliefs formed early influence criminal behavior.

Etiological differences between aggression of girls and that of boys showed up in a study of infants observed with their mothers at 12, 18, and 24 months of age. Keenan and Shaw (Chapter 10) found that aggressive boys became more aggressive by the age of 2 years if their mothers were unresponsive, whereas aggressive girls became more aggressive if their mothers were depressed. Fletcher, Darling, and Steinberg (Chapter 16) report sex-related differences in the etiology of drug use as well. Among teenagers, they found that together with peer use of drugs, teenagers' perceived absence of parental monitoring tended to increase the likelihood that girls – but not boys – would begin to use drugs. In their multigenerational study, Stattin, Janson, Klackenberg-Larsson, and Magnusson (Chapter 19) showed that mothers' tolerance for annoyance, as well as their experiences in terms of discipline, influenced their disciplinary behavior. The fathers' tolerance for annoyance and experiences in terms of discipline, however, had little impact on their disciplinary behavior.

In addition to the focus on substantive issues, chapters address methodological problems with using common measures of interactive processes. Maughan, Pickles, and Quinton (Chapter 3), for example, compare retrospective and prospective data. They discuss several interpretations of the results showing that retrospective reports evidence links not revealed through prospective ones. Stattin and his coworkers show the extent of discrepancy between contemporaneous and retrospective reports of physical punishment, and Barnes-McGuire and Earls (Chapter 20) indicate the difficulties of crossing cultural lines while attempting to assess interaction in families.

Evidence from several studies, based on data from various age groups, using disparate measures gathered from different cultures, suggests that fear — at least as related to punishments — fails to lead to successful socialization. In addition, evidence from these studies provides grounds for questioning the assumptions justifying teaching parents of aggressive children how to use more positive discipline and teaching aggressive children how to be more socially skillful. In sum, the authors of these chapters have provided food for thought.

Each chapter, of course, contains far more material than has been described here. The authors explore new territories as well as scrutinize familiar terrains. Coming from several disciplines, they have created a base of evidence on which new research should be built. Perhaps even more significantly, they have raised important questions about the effects of punitive policies.

REFERENCES

Aristotle. (1941). *Ethica Nicomachea* (Book 3, Chapter 1, lines 22–24) (translated by W. D. Ross). In R. McKeon (Ed.), *The basic works of Aristotle.* New York: Random House.
Tocqueville, Alexis de. (1839/1945). *Democracy in America,* Vol. 2. New York: Random House.

I   Mental health, coercion, and punishment

2   Relationships as context: supportive and coercive interactions in competent, aggressive, and anxious mother–child dyads

JEAN E. DUMAS AND PETER J. LAFRENIERE

In 1622 William Gouge published an early treatise on education written in English. In it he warned parents about the many "vices" of children, of which one is "stubbornnesse, when children pout, swell, and give no answer at all to their parents. This is too common a fault in children, and many parents are much offended and grieved thereat" (p. 248).

It obviously did not take social scientists to discover that oppositional, defiant, or otherwise coercive behaviors can be a major source of stress for parents of young children. Descriptive studies of family interactions have shown that mothers commonly attempt to manage their preschoolers by commanding or disapproving once every 3 to 4 minutes and that instances of child noncompliance or defiance, which are very common at that age, tend to elicit more parental attention than instances of positive behavior (Forehand, King, Peed, & Yoder, 1975; Johnson, Wahl, Martin, & Johansson, 1973). Clinical and laboratory evidence suggests that such increases in attention are commonly associated with corresponding increases in both aversive and indiscriminate responding on the part of parents and play a key role in differentiating between functional and dysfunctional family interactions (e.g., Dumas & Wahler, 1985; Patterson, 1982; Sawin & Parke, 1979; Snyder, 1977). For example, in a careful laboratory study, Snyder found that when compared with functional families, dysfunctional families (1) exhibited displeasing behaviors at a much higher rate than do functional families, (2) provided fewer positive and more aversive consequences for pleasing behaviors and fewer aversive and more positive consequences for displeasing behaviors, and (3) were less responsive to all consequences than were functional families. Although aversive and indiscriminate responding clearly play a role in the development and maintenance of dysfunctional child behavior in general, and coercion in particular, the processes that may account for this association remain a source of debate.

Applied researchers and clinicians commonly assume that aversive and indiscrimi-

9

nate patterns of family relationship reflect a lack of effective parenting skills and seek to account for such skill deficit at least partly by looking at the socioemotional context in which families operate (Patterson, 1982). Coercive family processes have thus repeatedly been linked to the presence of adverse contextual factors (for reviews, see Dumas, 1989a, 1994; Griest & Forehand, 1982; Wahler & Dumas, 1987). Generally speaking, adverse factors such as maternal emotional distress or depression (Brody & Forehand, 1986; Dumas, Gibson, & Albin, 1989; Hops et al., 1987), marital discord (Fantuzzo et al., 1991; Jouriles, Murphy, & O'Leary, 1989), social isolation (Dumas 1986a; Dumas & Wahler, 1985), and socioeconomic disadvantage (Dumas & Wahler, 1983; Webster-Stratton, 1985) are associated with elevated probabilities of behavioral dysfunction in children (especially aggressive or antisocial behaviors), as well as with child-rearing difficulties in parents. For example, Dumas (1986a) found that mothers were more likely to act in an aversive and indiscriminate manner toward their children when they had experienced a large proportion of aversive contacts with adults in the 24-hour period preceding a home observation than when they had not, even though their children's behavior did not differ under these two conditions. Social and economic adversity has also been related to the effectiveness of therapeutic interventions with dysfunctional families (Dumas, 1984; Dumas & Wahler, 1983; Wahler, 1980). Dumas and Wahler (1983) found that families burdened by socioeconomic disadvantage and social isolation were unlikely to benefit from a standardized program designed to train parents in effective child management skills.

Adverse contextual factors must clearly play a major role in any comprehensive understanding of child and family functioning. However, Dumas (1989b) noted that most studies of contextual factors conceptualize them as external entities that are characteristic of a person's or family's environment (e.g., unsupportive community contacts) and argued that this conceptualization was too narrow. As clinical and developmental evidence shows (Dumas & LaFreniere, 1993; Hinde, 1987; Kochanska, 1992), contextual factors include external, environmental factors, as well as interactional factors that reflect a person's relational history with other persons. In this perspective, we assume that family relationships, whether they are supportive or coercive in nature, are part of behavioral repertoires of responses that characterize the manner in which family members interact (see Voeltz & Evans, 1982; Wahler & Dumas, 1989). Specifically, these repertoires are transactional in nature, such that patterns of interaction established in the past between two or more persons tend to influence the manner in which these persons are likely to keep interacting (Olson, 1992; Sameroff & Emde, 1989). For example, the likelihood that a mother's command to her child will end up in immediate compliance, rather than in a protracted coercive episode, depends on the stimuli that both of them exchange (e.g., the clarity of the command), on the presence of external contextual events (e.g., child involvement in a competing activity), *and* on the interactional history that child and mother have acquired over the years. In other words, it depends in part on the repertoire of responses they have acquired as a function of living together, that is, on their *relationship*. As we have argued elsewhere (Dumas,

LaFreniere, Beaudin, & Verlaan, 1992), coercive family processes may reflect two different sources of stress, one that originates in unfavorable environmental conditions (*environmental stress*) and the other in dysfunctional patterns of interaction (*relationship stress*).

A growing body of findings supports a relationship approach to stress, pointing to transactional influences both within and across contexts (Dumas et al., 1989; Dumas & Gibson, 1990; Hart, Ladd, & Burleson, 1990; Kochanska, 1992; van Aken & Riksen-Walraven, 1992). For example, Dumas and colleagues (1989, 1990) found that maternal depressive symptomatology was systematically related to the behavior of conduct disorder children, not only toward their own mothers but also toward other family members. Thus, conduct disorder children tended to be more compliant and less aversive toward their mothers when the latter were depressed than when they were not. However, the same children were less compliant and more aversive toward their fathers and siblings when their mothers were depressed than when they were not, suggesting that maternal dysfunction was related in a complex manner to the children's relationships with their mothers *and* other family members. Similarly, Hart et al. (1990) found that children whose mothers relied on power assertive methods of discipline were less likely to be accepted by peers and more likely to resort to coercive methods to resolve peer conflict than were children whose mothers were authoritative and supportive in their discipline.

This chapter describes a series of studies conducted to compare supportive and coercive patterns of interaction in socially competent and dysfunctional children and their mothers, as well as to specify the implications that reliable differences may have for prevention of long-term behavior disorders. Although the behavior of dysfunctional, in particular aggressive, children and their mothers has received considerable attention, our research differs from previous work in two important respects. First, we assessed mother–child interactions in the course of a laboratory task that was purposely selected to elicit low levels of conflict and high levels of interest and cooperation from all children. This choice allowed us to determine the extent to which dysfunctional children and their mothers differ in their interactions from competent dyads when they are observed under optimal, rather than typical conditions. Second, we compared three groups of children – socially competent, anxious, and aggressive – in interaction with their mothers. Using a newly designed instrument (see later), we selected these groups on the basis of independent teacher ratings so as to assess the extent to which the children's behavior in one context would be predictive of their relationships with their mothers in a different context. The competent group was selected to provide a direct comparison of patterns of interaction in functional and dysfunctional dyads, while the anxious and aggressive groups were selected to contrast such patterns in dyads in which children present clearly distinguishable sets of behavioral and emotional difficulties. Coercive family processes have been extensively studied in aggressive, conduct disorder children and their families, but not in families in which children present a different set of behavioral difficulties. Anxious children and their mothers were selected as a comparison group because children who display behaviors that are symptomatic of anxiety and withdrawal represent the second most prevalent form of childhood dysfunction after aggressive and conduct problems (Achenbach & Edelbrock, 1981) and because empirical evidence suggests that these two forms of dysfunction are associated with different parental practices.

Considerable evidence shows that parents of aggressive children can be described as emotionally distant from their children, toward whom they take a "permissive" stance characterized by low levels of control and a pattern of indiscriminate responding. This contrasts with parents of anxious children, who also show little warmth but tend to be "authoritarian," displaying elevated levels of control and a predominantly discriminate but aversive pattern of responding (Baumrind, 1967; Maccoby & Martin, 1983). The characterization of parents as "permissive" or "authoritarian" derives from an early model of child development, in which parents are viewed as molding the child through their parenting style. However, as we have argued elsewhere (LaFreniere & Dumas, 1992), a transactional model recasts the child as an active agent and assumes that patterns of parent–child interaction reflect each partner's ongoing contribution to the relationship. Specifically, we hypothesize that coercive family processes may result in very different outcomes for the child, depending on the "relative balance of power" in the parent–child relationship. In aggressive dyads, this balance has shifted to the child and the mother is unable to exercise appropriate control, whereas in anxious dyads the shift favors the mother, leaving the child with insufficient opportunities to assert a developmentally appropriate degree of autonomy.

The three studies described here address this hypothesis from different perspectives. These studies, which are part of an ongoing, large-scale evaluation of socioemotional development in the preschool years, relied on the same experimental paradigm (outlined later). In the first one, we compared conditional probabilities of positive and aversive maternal and child responsiveness to establish the extent to which the three groups differed when observed under the same experimental conditions. In the second study, we focused specifically on control–compliance sequences as a measure of coercion in the three groups. Finally, in the last study, we compared patterns of mother–child interactions when children in the three groups completed the experimental task with their own and with an unfamiliar mother, in an attempt to disentangle the effects of maternal and child characteristics (individual effects) from the effects of cumulative past interactions between mothers and their own children (relationship effects).

Study 1

Participants

A random-stratified sample of 42 competent (22 girls, 20 boys), 42 anxious (22 girls, 20 boys), and 42 aggressive (25 girls, 17 boys) children was selected on the basis of standardized teacher ratings (see later) from a representative sample of 994 children of French-Canadian background recruited from 60 different preschool classrooms in the Montreal metropolitan area. Children ranged in age from 33 to 74 months. The mean age of girls was 52.2 months (SD = 10.1, range 34–74) and the mean age of boys was 47.8 months (SD = 9.6, range 33–69). Eighteen percent of the mothers had not completed high school, 35% had completed high school, and 47% had some college education or a college degree. Family incomes ranged from welfare to Can\$9,999 (21% of families), 10,000 to 19,999 (18%), 20,000 to 39,999 (23%), and 40,000 and above (38%). There were trends for mothers in the anxious and aggressive groups to have less education and lower incomes than mothers in the competent group. However, only one significant group difference was found, indicating that dyads in the anxious group had lower family incomes than their counterparts in the competent group, overall $F(2, 123) = 4.38$, $p < .05$. With the exception of 6 families of Asian or Haitian origins, all families were Caucasian.

Procedures and measures

Teacher evaluations. Children were evaluated by two classroom teachers toward the end of the fall session (1989 or 1990) using the Preschool Socioaffective Profile (PSP; LaFreniere, Dumas, Capuano, & Dubeau, 1992). The PSP is a new instrument designed specifically to provide reliable and valid differentiation between social competence, anxiety-withdrawal, and anger-aggression in the preschool years. The PSP is a standardized 80-item rating scale that provides measures of adjustment via scores on three factors labeled Social Competence (SC), Anxiety-Withdrawal (AW), and Anger-Aggression (AA). The first factor describes a broad range of adaptive qualities, rather than specific behavioral competencies. The second factor describes anxious, depressed, isolated, and withdrawn behaviors, and the third factor describes angry, aggressive, selfish, and oppositional behaviors. Each factor contains items tapping affective characteristics (e.g., sad, worries, doesn't smile or laugh) and social characteristics (e.g., remains apart, inactive, watches others play, defiant when reprimanded) involving peers or adults.

LaFreniere and colleagues (1992) reported that interitem reliability of the three PSP factors was uniformly high (.86, .85, .83), as were internal consistency (Cronbach's alpha .92, .90, .85) and 2-week test–retest reliability (.86, .82, .78). Intercorrelations among factor scores showed that the anxiety-withdrawal and anger-aggression scales were orthogonal ($r = .02$), and that the social competence scale was negatively correlated with the anxiety-withdrawal ($r = -.38$) and anger-aggression ($r = -.37$) scales. Direct comparisons with the extensively validated Child Behavior Checklist-Teacher Report Form (Achenbach & Edelbrock, 1981) provided strong evidence of concurrent validity for the PSP, and direct observation and peer sociometric measures demonstrated the discriminant validity of all three factors.

Table 2.1. *PSP scale Z score means and (standard deviations) by group*

PSP scale	Competent	Anxious	Aggressive
Social competence	1.44 (0.32)	− 1.12 (0.72)	− 0.81 (0.75)
Anxiety-withdrawal	− 1.07 (0.49)	1.73 (0.70)	− 0.07 (0.73)
Anger-aggression	− 1.08 (0.55)	0.04 (0.76)	1.61 (0.65)

Table 2.1 presents the PSP scale Z scores (means and standard deviations) by group. Groups were formed on the basis of separate gender norms. The competent group consisted of children whose scores were 1.0 SD or more above the mean on the social competence scale and less than 0.25 SD above the mean on the anxiety-withdrawal and anger-aggression scales. The anxious group consisted of children whose scores were 1.0 SD or more above the mean on the anxiety-withdrawal scale and at least 0.5 SD higher than their score on the anger-aggression scale. Similarly, the aggressive group consisted of children whose scores were 1.0 SD or more above the mean on the anger-aggression scale and at least 0.5 SD higher than their score on the anxiety-withdrawal scale.

Experimental procedure and task. Each mother–child dyad was invited to come to a university laboratory to participate in a "grocery task" game. This task, which we have described in detail elsewhere (e.g., LaFreniere & Dumas, 1992), is based on a paradigm developed by Gauvin and Rogoff (1989) and adapted by us for use with preschool children. It consists of planning an efficient route through a miniature grocery store laid out as a three-dimensional board game on a 71×61 cm table that a 3- to 4-year-old can easily reach while standing. Fifty-six miniature items of general use are arranged on six shelves on each side of three rows and on four shelves along the inside of the store's outer walls. The task, which is explained to child and mother through verbal instructions, modeling, and practice, requires the child to move a small toy "shopper" through the store to "buy" items on a "shopping list." Each list consists of five 8×12 cm cards with easily identifiable pictures of items available in the store. The child is asked to follow three simple rules: (1) make the "shopper" take the shortest path to the item; (2) do not allow the "shopper" to fly over the store to reach an item; and (3) do not allow the "shopper" to buy items not on the shopping list. After making sure that both child and mother understand the task, the experimenter gives the child different lists of five items each for up to five separate trials, but makes no further intervention except to verify that the child recognizes all five items on the list before each new "shopping trip." After completion of three trips or 18 minutes, the experimenter asks the mother to complete a different task on an adjacent table and the child to continue the grocery task alone, with the understanding that child can ask mother for help at any time. Children then complete two shopping trips alone or work on the task for another 6 minutes.

Observational measures. Mother–child interactions during the grocery task were videotaped through a one-way mirror and later coded and analyzed with the INTER-ACT coding and software systems (1987). The coding system consists of five categories of codes (actor, behavior, setting, adverb, and valence) that are combined according to specific syntactical rules to form discrete observation strings to summarize commonly occurring instances of parent–child interactions. Following coding of each videotape, raw data are stored on a desktop computer for cleanup, verification, and analysis.

Individual behavior codes were collapsed to form comparable clusters of mother and child behaviors: (1) *positive* consisted of laughter, helping, approving, and affectionate behavior; (2) *aversive* consisted of critical, punishing, disapproving, or aggressive behavior, and of intrusive/coercive commands; (3) *control* consisted of clearly stated requests or instructions with which the person could immediately comply or refuse to comply; (4) *compliance* consisted of compliance within 10 seconds of a preceding control attempt; (5) *noncompliance* consisted of active refusal to comply within 10 seconds of a preceding control attempt; (6) *positive affect* consisted of the expression of positive emotions (e.g., smiling) that accompanied any coded behavior; and (7) *aversive affect* consisted of the expression of negative emotions (e.g., loud or sarcastic tone of voice) that accompanied any coded behavior.

The reliability of the coding system was assessed by having two observers code 40% of observations simultaneously but independently. For each behavior cluster, the software computed a 2×2 matrix of agreements and disagreements, which reflected the extent to which both observers recorded the same event within 10 seconds of each other, and calculated percentage agreement, a liberal measure of inter-observer agreement, and Cohen's kappa, a more stringent measure of agreement that controls for chance agreement. Measures were obtained for each observation and then averaged across observations. Percentage agreements ranged from .95 to .99 ($M = .97$) and kappas from .55 to .89 ($M = .71$). The combination of high percentage agreement with low kappa for some clusters (e.g., noncompliance) reflected low occurrence, a situation in which high levels of agreement are difficult to obtain when controlling for chance agreement.

The behavioral observations were used to calculate conditional probabilities of occurrence of specific behavior cluster combinations so as to assess the extent to which mothers and children responded contingently to each other's immediately preceding (i.e., within 15 seconds) behaviors and matched each other's affect. Specifically, conditional probabilities of positiveness and aversiveness in response to preceding positiveness, aversiveness, compliance, or noncompliance, as well as conditional probabilities of positive or aversive affect in response to positive or aversive affect, were calculated separately for mother and child and then averaged by group. To assess the degree of mother and child responsiveness toward each other, each conditional probability was compared to its relevant base rate or expected probability on the basis of a time-based procedure described in Moran, Dumas, and Symons (1992). These comparisons, which relied on a z statistic that controls for autocorrelation (Dumas, 1986b), provided tests for the significance of each measure of responsiveness. To reduce the probability of Type I error (i.e., rejecting the null hypothesis when in fact it is true), z statistics are reported only if they were significant at the $p = .01$ level or higher.

Maternal and child responsiveness

Detailed comparisons of mother–child interactions in this sample can be found in Dumas, LaFreniere, Beaudin, and Verlaan (1992) and LaFreniere and Dumas (1992). We report here only the results of the analyses that compared supportive and coercive responsiveness within groups. Table 2.2 shows that competent children and their mothers maintained a supportive interaction style characterized by a coherent pattern of behavioral and affective reciprocity. Mothers of competent children generally matched their children's behavior and affect. They responded positively by issuing contingent praise or affection immediately after child positiveness and compliance, but not after child aversiveness and noncompliance. The same mothers did not respond with increased aversiveness to child positiveness and compliance, but responded aversively by issuing contingent criticism and disapproval to child aversiveness and noncompliance. A similar pattern of contingent responsiveness was seen in competent children, who responded positively to immediately preceding maternal positiveness and aversively to maternal aversiveness, and who matched positive affect with positive affect and aversive affect with aversive affect. The same children were also observed to respond positively to maternal aversiveness, a reaction that may serve to reduce the likelihood of coercive escalation associated with negative reciprocity.

Although anxious dyads were also observed to be reciprocal in their interaction style, mothers of anxious children displayed a pattern of negative reciprocity that contrasted sharply with that of mothers in the competent group. They failed to respond positively to positive child behavior or affect but responded aversively to aversive child behavior and affect. This overall negativity was also seen in these mothers' tendency to respond with increases in aversiveness to both compliance and noncompliance on their children's part. Mothers in the aggressive group more often displayed an indiscriminate than a negative pattern of reciprocity. They did not respond with increased positiveness to child positiveness or with increased aversiveness to child noncompliance. However, they responded with increased positiveness to child compliance *and* aversiveness, as well as with increased aversiveness to child aversiveness *and* child compliance.

Like their competent peers, anxious and aggressive children were contingently responsive to their mothers' behavior and affect. They responded positively to immediately preceding maternal positiveness (but not aversiveness) and aversively to maternal aversiveness, and matched maternal positive and aversive affect.

These results, which extend earlier findings (e.g., Baumrind, 1967; Snyder, 1977), show that even under conditions designed to elicit cooperation rather than

Table 2.2. *Conditional probabilities of mother and child responsiveness by groups*

Behavior	Factor[a]	Mother behavior			Child behavior		
		$p(A)$[b]	$p(A/B)$	Z score	$p(A)$	$p(A/B)$	Z score
Positiveness/ positiveness	SC	.107[c]	.201	3.52**	.031	.131	13.01***
	AW	.088	.114	0.81	.020	.095	8.85***
	AA	.083	.127	1.27	.016	.064	7.25***
Positiveness/ aversiveness	SC	.101	.111	0.39	.028	.059	2.34*
	AW	.061	.076	0.93	.020	.020	0.01
	AA	.067	.127	2.73*	.017	.020	0.43
Positiveness/ compliance	SC	.109	.169	4.40***			
	AW	.067	.055	− 1.28			
	AA	.078	.134	5.63***			
Positiveness/ noncompliance	SC	.098	.025	− 1.56			
	AW	.046	.053	0.39			
	AA	.078	.048	− 0.91			
Aversiveness/ positiveness	SC	.039	.039	− 0.03	.033	.028	− 0.59
	AW	.088	.063	− 0.79	.050	.069	1.37
	AA	.054	.032	− 0.79	.031	.021	− 1.06
Aversiveness/ aversiveness	SC	.055	.133	3.99***	.043	.183	8.45***
	AW	.146	.290	5.72***	.061	.172	10.37***
	AA	.070	.151	3.55**	.034	.120	7.63***
Aversiveness/ compliance	SC	.037	.050	1.54			
	AW	.120	.171	4.09***			
	AA	.060	.103	4.82***			
Aversiveness/ noncompliance	SC	.076	.375	6.81***			
	AW	.159	.343	5.59***			
	AA	.077	.095	0.54			
Positive affect/ positive affect	SC	.246	.422	6.45***	.070	.131	7.46***
	AW	.222	.327	1.75	.019	.078	9.31***
	AA	.232	.467	5.15***	.030	.092	8.79***
Aversive affect/ aversive affect	SC	.043	.129	4.05***	.038	.190	7.44***
	AW	.156	.310	4.53***	.039	.133	11.05***
	AA	.088	.216	3.68**	.023	.057	3.37**

[a] SC, social competence; AW, anxiety-withdrawal; AA, anger-aggression.
[b] $p(A)$ corresponds to the base rate probability of A (e.g., maternal positiveness), and $p(A/B)$ corresponds to the conditional probability of A given that B occurred in the immediately preceding 15 seconds (e.g., maternal positiveness given child compliance).
[c] Readers may notice small discrepancies in base rates across measures. This reflects the fact that the number of cases for any given analysis varied as a function of the number of subjects exhibiting the criterion behavior, since the computation of any conditional probability requires the presence of two specific events in the behavioral record (e.g., the probability of mother positiveness given child compliance cannot be computed if the child was never observed to comply).
$*p < .01; **p < .001; ***p < .0001$.

conflict, clear differences emerge in the dyadic interactions of mothers and their competent children on the one hand, and of mothers and their anxious or aggressive children on the other. These differences were explored in greater detail in Study 2, which focused exclusively on control–compliance sequences in the three groups.

Study 2

Observational measures

Study 2 made use of the same data set as Study 1 but derived different measures from the observations of mother–child interactions. The observational data were analyzed sequentially to isolate all control exchanges initiated by mother or child, to determine the proportion of these exchanges that were accompanied by positiveness or positive affect, or by aversiveness or aversive affect, and to calculate the probabilities that exchanges in general, and positive and aversive exchanges in particular, would end in mother or child compliance. This yielded six measures for each mother and child – three of control (overall, positive, aversive) and three of compliance (overall compliance and compliance to positive and aversive control).

In addition, a summary index of maternal discriminate behavior was calculated for each dyad to assess the extent to which mothers in the three groups made clear distinctions in the proportion of positive versus aversive control they used and in the proportion of compliance they gave to child positive versus aversive control. This index was defined as follows:

$$\frac{\Sigma(\text{maternal positive control} + \text{compliance to child positive control})}{\Sigma[(\text{maternal positive} + \text{aversive control}) + (\text{compliance to child positive} + \text{aversive control})]}$$

The index can range from 0 to 1. Mothers with scores below .5 would tend to be aversively discriminate (i.e., likely to rely on aversive control of child and to comply to aversive child control), while mothers with scores above .5 would tend to be positively discriminate and those with scores around .5 to be indiscriminate (i.e., as likely to rely on positive as on aversive control of child and to comply to positive as much as aversive child control).

Mother–child control–compliance sequences

Figure 2.1 illustrates the differences found in analyses of covariance and in corresponding analyses of cell means. These analyses were conducted to compare the three groups on the measures of maternal control and child compliance, as well as to control for child age, child gender, and family socioeconomic status (SES) when significant.

Overall control and compliance. There were significant group differences in overall maternal control [$F(2, 120) = 7.12$, $p < .001$]. Mothers of competent children

MATERNAL CONTROL

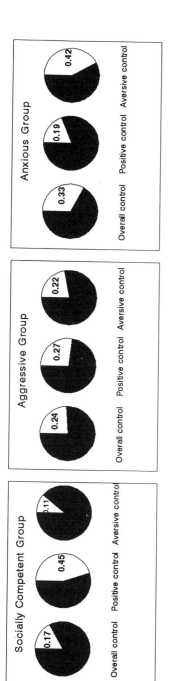

Socially Competent Group

Overall control — 0.17
Positive control — 0.45
Aversive control — 0.11

Aggressive Group

Overall control — 0.24
Positive control — 0.27
Aversive control — 0.22

Anxious Group

Overall control — 0.33
Positive control — 0.19
Aversive control — 0.42

CHILD COMPLIANCE

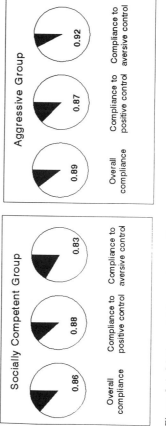

Socially Competent Group

Overall compliance — 0.86
Compliance to positive control — 0.88
Compliance to aversive control — 0.83

Aggressive Group

Overall compliance — 0.89
Compliance to positive control — 0.87
Compliance to aversive control — 0.92

Anxious Group

Overall compliance — 0.74
Compliance to positive control — 0.9
Compliance to aversive control — 0.78

Figure 2. 1. Mother–child control–compliance sequences.

initiated a smaller proportion of control sequences than did mothers of aggressive children, who in turn initiated fewer control sequences than did mothers of anxious children. Maternal control was also related to SES, as mothers with elevated levels of socioeconomic disadvantage made more attempts to control their children than did other mothers [$t(120) = 3.69$, $p < .0001$]. Although children complied with the majority of maternal control attempts in all groups, group differences emerged [$F(2, 123) = 6.22$, $p < .01$], with anxious children generally complying less than their competent or aggressive counterparts.

Positive and aversive control and compliance. Group differences were also found in the extent to which maternal control attempts were accompanied by positive [$F(2, 120) = 4.20$, $p < .02$] or aversive [$F(2, 120) = 8.59$, $p < .0001$] behavior or affect. Mothers of competent children initiated a larger proportion of positive control sequences than all other mothers, while mothers of anxious children initiated a larger proportion of aversive control sequences than all other mothers. Paired t tests conducted to compare proportions of within-group positive and aversive control indicated that mothers of competent children made more positive than aversive control attempts [$t(41) = 5.07$, $p < .0001$], that mothers of aggressive children made comparable numbers of positive and aversive control attempts [$t(41) = .69$, ns], and that mothers of anxious children made more aversive than positive control attempts [$t(41) = -2.59$, $p < .05$]. SES was again related to these findings, as mothers with elevated levels of socioeconomic disadvantage issued fewer control exchanges accompanied by positive behavior [$t(120) = -3.16$, $p < .01$] or affect and more control exchanges accompanied by aversive behavior or affect [$t(120) = 2.91$, $p < .01$]. No significant differences were found in the extent to which children complied to positive and aversive control attempts.

Child–mother control–compliance sequences

Figure 2.2 illustrates the differences found in the analyses of child control and maternal compliance.

Overall control and compliance. Significant group differences emerged also in overall child control [$F(2, 123) = 4.72$, $p < .01$]. Like their mothers, competent children initiated a smaller proportion of control sequences than did aggressive or anxious children. Although all mothers showed lower levels of compliance than their children, group differences were found [$F(2, 120) = 7.38$, $p < .001$], showing that mothers of competent children complied to 47% of their children's control attempts, while mothers of aggressive children complied to 35% of such attempts and mothers of anxious children to fewer than 20%. Maternal compliance was related to child age and gender, as mothers were more likely to comply to older than to younger children [$t(120) = 2.21$, $p < .05$] and to girls than boys [$t(120) = -3.07$, $p < .01$].

CHILD CONTROL

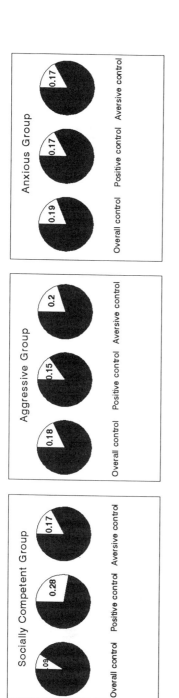

Socially Competent Group

Overall control · Positive control · Aversive control

Aggressive Group

Overall control · Positive control · Aversive control

Anxious Group

Overall control · Positive control · Aversive control

MATERNAL COMPLIANCE

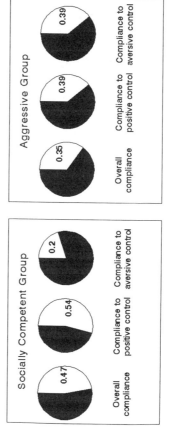

Socially Competent Group

Overall compliance · Compliance to positive control · Compliance to aversive control

Aggressive Group

Overall compliance · Compliance to positive control · Compliance to aversive control

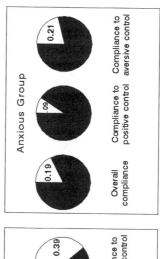

Anxious Group

Overall compliance · Compliance to positive control · Compliance to aversive control

Figure 2.2. Child–mother control–compliance sequences.

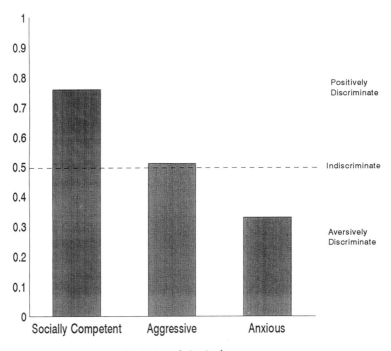

Figure 2.3. Index of maternal discriminate behavior by group.

Positive and aversive control and compliance. No significant group differences were found in the extent to which children's control attempts were accompanied by positive or aversive behavior or affect. Mothers of aggressive children were observed to be more likely to comply to children's aversive control attempts than were all other mothers, but this difference failed to reach statistical significance.

Index of maternal discriminate behavior

The group differences just described were confirmed by the summary index of discriminate maternal behavior reported in Figure 2.3. Results indicated that the overall group effect was significant [$F(2, 109) = 10.21$, $p < .0001$] and that each group differed significantly from the other two, with mothers of competent and anxious children being respectively positively and aversively discriminate, and mothers of aggressive children being indiscriminate. This measure was also related to socioeconomic disadvantage, with disadvantaged mothers presenting higher levels of indiscriminate behavior than less disadvantaged mothers [$t(109) = -2.38$, $p < .05$].

Integrating results from Studies 1 and 2

In keeping with the results of Study 1, mothers in the competent group exhibited a coherent, authoritative, and positively responsive control style. They made relatively few control attempts and, when they did so, were much more likely to accompany them with positive than with aversive behavior or affect. Their children tended to act in a similar manner and to see many of their control attempts succeed, especially when these attempts were positive in nature. In contrast, mothers of anxious children were more controlling and more likely to accompany their control attempts by aversive behavior or affect than were all other mothers. In addition, mothers of anxious children complied more often to aversive than to positive child control attempts, thus providing their children with a generally discriminate but aversive control environment. Finally, mothers of aggressive children differed from their counterparts in the other two groups by being generally indiscriminate. These mothers exhibited comparable levels of positive and aversive control attempts and were as likely to comply to positive as to aversive control attempts on the part of their children, thus making it impossible for their children to find a signal value in the manner in which they either issued their instructions or responded to child instructions.

These results suggest that processes involving both maternal compliance and predictability may be involved in dysfunctional mother and child control–compliance sequences. In keeping with previous research (Sansbury & Wahler, 1992; Wahler & Dumas, 1986; Wahler, Williams, & Cerezo, 1990), our findings show that aggressive children are most likely to have mothers who comply to a high level of children's control attempts, whether positive or aversive in nature. However, the fact that aggressive children appear to succeed regularly in their attempts to control their mothers does not seem enough to account for their status, as their competent counterparts were just as likely to see their control attempts reinforced. The findings indicate that aggressive status is most likely to be associated with high levels of maternal compliance *and* indiscriminate responding, that is, with exercising control in a context in which the child is unable to readily differentiate between positive and aversive maternal signals. In contrast to their competent and aggressive peers, anxious children rarely succeed in their attempts to control their mothers. Rather, they have mothers who not only are excessively controlling but also exercise control in a discriminate, aversive fashion.

Considered together, the results of Studies 1 and 2 offer tentative support for the concept of relationship stress introduced earlier, by suggesting that when assessed under the same conditions for competent dyads, aggressive and anxious dyads may behave in ways that reflect a long-standing history of relationship difficulties, rather than the stressful demands of the immediate environment. Indeed, from a transactional perspective, the most salient dimension of the environment lies in the dyad's relationship pattern. If this is correct, relationship difficulties within the family may act as a chronic source of stress, in addition to commonly acknowledged stressors, such as socioeconomic disadvantage. This interpretation must be made cautiously, however, as it is limited by the fact that the studies did not assess mother–child interactions over an extended period of time or manipulate the mother–child relationship experimentally. We turn now to Study 3, which was set up to provide an experimental manipulation of this relationship.

Study 3

Participants

A subsample of the mother–child dyads who participated in the first two studies took part in this study also. This subsample was obtained in the same manner as described for Study 1. However, when mothers were invited to come with their child to the laboratory, appointments were made at the same time for two mother–child dyads who did not know each other (with children of the same gender and less than 12 months apart in age, and of the same PSP classification). These requirements limited the size of the subsample to 30 dyads in each of the competent, aggressive, and anxious groups.

Experimental procedure

Upon arrival, each dyad was briefly introduced to the research task. One child was then taken to the experimental room, either with his or her own mother or the unfamiliar mother, while the other child and mother participated in a different research activity nearby. Approximately 30 minutes later, mothers and children were given a 10-minute break and snack, followed by another data collection period in which the mother and child who had not completed the experimental task did so. The order in which children completed the task and whether they did so with their own or the unfamiliar mother first was counterbalanced.

Maternal responsiveness to own and unfamiliar child

A complete report of the results of this study can be found in Dumas and LaFreniere (1993). We focus here only on those results of direct relevance to supportive and coercive processes. Conditional probabilities of maternal responsiveness in each condition are reported in Table 2.3. Mothers of competent children responded in a coherent fashion across conditions. Matching their behavior to the immediately preceding child behavior, they responded to child positive behavior, positive affect, or compliance with positive behavior or affect of their own. The increase in their base rate of positive affect was only significant in their interactions with their own children, probably because of the very high base rate of positive affect they displayed toward unfamiliar children. The pattern of reciprocity of mothers of competent

Table 2.3. *Conditional probabilities of mother responsiveness to own child and unfamiliar child by group*

Behavior toward	Factor[a]	Own child			Unfamiliar child		
		$p(A)$[b]	$p(A/B)$	Z score	$p(A)$	$p(A/B)$	Z score
Positiveness/	SC	.093	.153	1.79*	.073	.189	2.73**
positiveness	AW	.087	.132	1.18	.096	.333	3.19***
	AA	.092	.146	1.32	.079	.167	1.80*
Positiveness/	SC	.094	.105	0.34	.057	.056	−0.02
aversiveness	AW	.056	.065	0.52	.055	.000	−1.69*
	AA	.076	.144	2.68**	.056	.089	0.98
Positiveness/	SC	.099	.144	2.66**	.096	.267	7.71***
compliance	AW	.063	.054	−0.84	.055	.095	3.32***
	AA	.082	.142	4.99***	.061	.123	4.42***
Aversiveness/	SC	.039	.081	2.03*	.012	.056	1.69*
aversiveness	AW	.161	.351	7.11***	.051	.167	3.64***
	AA	.065	.154	3.73***	.038	.111	2.54**
Aversiveness/	SC	.027	.038	1.09	.010	.028	2.36**
compliance	AW	.128	.165	2.29*	.041	.070	2.61**
	AA	.058	.112	5.23***	.027	.071	4.59***
Aversiveness/	SC	.050	.312	4.74***			
noncompliance	AW	.165	.383	6.04***			
	AA	.064	.029	−0.82			
Positive affect/	SC	.224	.430	6.05***	.302	.390	1.62
positive affect	AW	.236	.297	0.87	.194	.500	2.87**
	AA	.217	.461	5.35***	.140	.364	3.71***
Aversive affect/	SC	.031	.087	2.62**			
aversive affect	AW	.179	.313	3.32***			
	AA	.049	.176	4.16***			

[a] For abbreviations, see Table 2.2.
[b] See note *b*, Table 2.2.
*$p < .05$; **$p < .01$; ***$p < .001$.

children was far from indiscriminate, however, as they responded aversively to child aversive behavior, aversive affect, and noncompliance.

Although mothers of anxious children were generally discriminate also, their pattern of results provided particularly striking differences across conditions: they responded in a strictly aversive fashion to their own, but not to unfamiliar children. Mothers of anxious children did not respond positively to their children's positive behavior or affect, but displayed the highest levels of positive responsiveness of all groups when interacting with unfamiliar children. The same mothers did not reinforce compliance in their own children but reinforced it in unfamiliar children, although their level of positiveness was lower in that condition than that of the

other mothers. As was found in the first two studies, absence of positive responsiveness to their own children was aggravated in mothers of anxious children by
evidence of systematic aversive responsiveness toward them.

Differences between conditions were also found for mothers in the aggressive
group. These mothers displayed a generally indiscriminate pattern of responses to
their own, but not to unfamiliar children. Like mothers of competent children,
they responded positively to positive affect and compliance across conditions. However, when interacting with their own children, mothers of aggressive children
failed to reciprocate positive behavior and were the only mothers who responded
with increased positiveness to child aversiveness and without increased aversiveness
to child noncompliance.

Child responsiveness to own and unfamiliar mother

Conditional probabilities of child responsiveness can be found in Table 2.4. Matching their behavior with the immediately preceding maternal behavior, competent
children generally responded in a coherent fashion across conditions. They were
positive in response to maternal positive behavior or affect, and aversive in response
to maternal aversive behavior or affect. Unlike other children, however, competent
children generally responded positively to their mothers' aversiveness. We believe
that this form of positive responsiveness may serve to reestablish a regular pattern
of positively toned interactions when mothers threaten to disrupt such a pattern by
being aversive. This is supported by the fact that whenever competent children
behaved positively, their mothers were likely to immediately reciprocate positively
also, breaking the chain of negative reciprocity in the short term and shaping
competent behavior in the child in the long term.

Anxious and aggressive children generally behaved like their counterparts in
interaction with their own mothers by responding positively to positive behavior or
affect and aversively to aversive behavior or affect. However, anxious children
displayed higher levels of aversive responsiveness (both behavior and affect) than all
other children. In contrast to their pattern of responsiveness toward their own
mothers, anxious and aggressive children rejected the positive overtures of unfamiliar mothers. Anxious children responded to positiveness on the part of unfamiliar
mothers by being aversive, and aggressive children by being both positive and
aversive. Similarly, the two groups responded to positive affect on the part of
unfamiliar mothers with both positive and aversive affect of their own. Finally,
anxious and aggressive children ignored all aversiveness on the part of unfamiliar
mothers, rather than responding in kind as they did when interacting with their
own mothers.

Discussion

Results of this last study show that competent, anxious, and aggressive mother–
child dyads can be distinguished on the basis of their patterns of responsiveness,

Table 2.4. *Conditional probabilities of child responsiveness to own and unfamiliar mother by group*

Behavior toward	Factor[a]	Own mother			Unfamiliar mother		
		$p(A)$[b]	$p(A/B)$	Z score	$p(A)$	$p(A/B)$	Z score
Positiveness/	SC	.024	.110	10.08***	.014	.052	5.50***
positiveness	AW	.019	.105	8.52***	.007	.012	0.96
	AA	.016	.056	5.12***	.011	.068	7.24***
Positiveness/	SC	.024	.062	2.26*			
aversiveness	AW	.019	.022	0.39			
	AA	.018	.023	0.50			
Aversiveness/	SC	.029	.030	0.09	.021	.012	−0.80
positiveness	AW	.051	.047	−0.28	.011	.115	5.05***
	AA	.035	.028	−0.60	.014	.069	3.50***
Aversiveness/	SC	.039	.137	4.54***	.020	.131	8.52***
aversiveness	AW	.067	.175	8.25***	.007	.000	−0.19
	AA	.039	.131	6.35***	.007	.000	−0.39
Positive affect/	SC	.060	.142	8.09***	.060	.111	5.40***
positive affect	AW	.022	.075	6.33***	.036	.097	3.23***
	AA	.036	.096	7.19***	.025	.068	3.98***
Aversive affect/	SC	.025	.024	−0.28	.032	.048	0.78
positive affect	AW	.050	.061	0.74	.017	.053	1.75*
	AA	.018	.025	1.17	.028	.055	2.15*
Aversive affect/	SC	.033	.127	3.71***			
aversive affect	AW	.046	.151	9.28***			
	AA	.012	.063	3.49***			

[a] For abbreviations, see Table 2.2.
[b] See note *b*, Table 2.2.
*$p < .05$; **$p < .01$; ***$p < .001$.

whether members of the dyads are familiar with each other or not. These findings, which extend earlier reports by Anderson, Lytton, and Romney (1986), Halverson and Waldrop (1970), and Landauer, Carlsmith, and Lepper (1970), support the conclusion that observed mother–child interactions in a laboratory situation such as the one we used reflect, to a large extent, the interactive history that mother and child share. Specifically, the results illustrate the supportive and coercive nature of relationships in competent and dysfunctional dyads. Competent dyads exhibited a coherent and supportive interaction style in both conditions, although they seemed to take particularly good "care" of their own relationship. For example, mothers of competent children displayed a very high level of unconditional positive affect toward the unfamiliar children. This is likely to have helped establish a temporary functional relationship with the unfamiliar child and to have facilitated completion of the task. However, unconditional positive affect would probably interfere with the development of competence in a lasting relationship and was not observed in the mothers' interactions with their own children. Similarly, when interacting with the unfamiliar mothers, competent children matched maternal aversiveness but made no attempt to respond to this aversiveness with positiveness also, as they did with their own mothers.

Although generally very positive and reciprocal, mothers of competent children were also observed to respond aversively to their children's aversive behavior, aversive affect, and noncompliance. In keeping with earlier work on authoritative parenting (Baumrind, 1967), our results suggest that childhood competence is associated, at least in part, with parenting practices in which maternal positive *and* aversive behavior and affect have high signal values. Specifically, it would appear that mothers of competent children are generally very positive with their children but will not hesitate to withdraw their positiveness and act in an aversive fashion when they disapprove of the child's behavior.

The results obtained with the anxious and aggressive dyads illustrate coercive and indiscriminate relationship patterns in one condition and supportive ones in the other. Thus, mothers of anxious children were consistently aversive toward their own children but very supportive toward the unfamiliar children. Of the three groups, mothers of anxious children displayed the highest levels of positiveness and positive affect in response to the unfamiliar children's positiveness and positive affect, but the lowest levels of positive responding when interacting with their own children. For their part, mothers of aggressive children behaved much like their competent counterparts toward the unfamiliar children. However, as was already seen in Study 1, these mothers failed to reciprocate their own children's positive behavior and were the only mothers who responded positively to children's aversiveness and did not actively disapprove of noncompliance. We believe that this pattern reflected a history of inconsistent discipline, characterized by a mismatch between mother and child behavior that was not seen when the same mothers interacted with unfamiliar children, with whom they obviously did not share the same relationship history.

It would appear that maternal behavior in the anxious and aggressive groups cannot be accounted for solely in terms of limited parenting skills. These mothers obviously had the necessary skills to behave positively and contingently. However, they did so only with the unfamiliar children. Similar differences across conditions have been reported by Anderson and colleagues (1986) in a study that involved an aggressive group. The same conclusion applies to the behavior of anxious and aggressive children, as these children had the skills to respond contingently but did not do so across conditions. However, their behavior was more dysfunctional when they interacted with the unfamiliar than with their own mothers. Anxious and aggressive children ignored, rejected, or responded in an ambivalent manner to the unfamiliar but not to their own mothers. This finding suggests that these children may not adapt readily to new social settings, such as the preschool. Having failed to acquire effective coping skills in interactions with their primary caregivers, anxious and aggressive children may attempt to deal with the demands of new social situations by rejecting or responding ambiguously to the positive overtures of other adults and by ignoring their aversive behaviors. This may provide these children with a short-term solution to social challenges. However, their failure to reciprocate positive interactions with new social partners is likely to deprive them of interactional experiences necessary to develop functional social skills across settings.

Conclusions

Results of our three studies highlight the nature of supportive and coercive processes in mother–child dyads, showing that mothers and children can reciprocally support each other or be perpetrators or victims of coercive processes of control. Specifically, the results throw light on three major aspects of interactive processes in mother–child dyads.

First, the results emphasize the essentially transactional nature of support and coercion in close relationships. Children were classified as competent, anxious, or aggressive on the basis of independent teacher ratings of their social and emotional adaptation in the preschool. In the laboratory, however, these ratings predicted maternal more than child behavior. This finding suggests that the patterns of mother and child responsiveness we observed reflected, at least in part, the presence or absence of a shared transactional history and the immediate and transient presence of various stimuli or the generalized personality characteristics of mothers or their children. The ratings distinguished maternal behavior in both conditions, showing that whereas mothers of competent children were supportive across conditions, mothers of anxious and aggressive children tended to be much more functional and supportive in their interactions with unfamiliar than with their own children.

Teacher ratings also distinguished child behavior, but only in interaction with the unfamiliar mothers. When interacting with their own mothers, the three groups of children tended to behave in a comparable manner. When interacting with the unfamiliar mothers, however, only competent children remained positive and reciprocal, whereas their aggressive and anxious counterparts generally ignored or rejected the unfamiliar mothers' overtures. This finding suggests a possible mechanism to account for the well-established linkage between disturbances in the mother–child relationship and subsequent problems in individual adaptation outside the home. What begins as a problem of dyadic regulation may over time become an enduring problem of the individual, as the child seeks to meet the demands of new social situations in ways that reflect what he or she has learned in the context of the home.

Second, the results highlight the differential "balance of power" that seems characteristic of aggressive and anxious dyads. This balance appears clearly to favor the child in aggressive dyads. As others found (Patterson, 1982; Snyder, 1977), our data show that aggressive children generally have mothers who are likely to comply to many of their control attempts, irrespective of the positive or aversive nature of such attempts. However, the fact that competent children are also regularly successful in their attempts to control their mothers indicates that maternal compliance is not enough to account for the coercive behavior of aggressive children. Rather, in keeping with clinical research on coercive family processes (Dumas & Wahler, 1985; Wahler et al., 1990), the results indicate that both maternal compliance and indiscriminate behavior play a role in the maintenance, if not in the development, of coercive behavior in aggressive children.

In contrast to their competent and aggressive peers, anxious children rarely succeed in their attempts to control their mothers. In these families, the balance of power is held by mothers who are not only excessively controlling but who also exercise this aversive control in a contingent fashion. If we accept that children need to be exposed to early patterns of interaction that allow for opportunities to exercise autonomy in a mutual give-and-take process (in which neither partner repeatedly dominates the other), these findings may hold the key to understanding why anxious children withdraw from social relationships and appear helpless in new contexts.

Finally, the finding that mothers demonstrated different parenting skills when interacting with unfamiliar children has implications for prevention and intervention efforts. Programs that are aimed at preventing or modifying coercive processes in families or peer groups commonly assume that participants lack skills that are associated with prosocial functioning. Although this may be a correct assumption, at least for some participants, evidence indicates that skills can vary considerably as a function of the conditions under which they are assessed and that failure to observe certain skills in one context does not necessarily imply that they are absent from a person's repertoire (e.g., Kazdin, Matson, & Esveldt-Dawson, 1981). It would be a mistake to conclude from our results that prevention and intervention programs should not teach skills. Rather, the results suggest that prior to any attempt to modify coercive processes, one should assess the conditions under which participants can or cannot perform certain skills so as to evaluate the extent to which training is required. In addition, the results indicate that the focus of prevention or intervention should be on the patterns of relationships that children and their parents, or children and their peers, have with each other, rather than on presumably intrapersonal skills. In this perspective, programs that seek to teach persons who regularly engage in coercive interactions to communicate in more effective ways (e.g., Dumas, Blechman, & Prinz, 1992) may be more promising than programs designed to impart specific skills.

Taken together, the results reported here suggest that direct observational studies of supportive and coercive interactions in mother–child dyads may provide a parsimonious means of accounting for known differences in child status in a different social context. Specifically, our data predict that supportive patterns of mother–child interaction are likely to be associated with the development of childhood competence, whereas coercive patterns predict the development of both anxiety and aggression, with mothers tending to be coercive in anxious dyads, and children in aggressive ones. If this is correct, differences in observed mother–child interaction patterns in the preschool years may become associated over time with the development of different forms of childhood disorder, suggesting that individual differences in social behavior in the early school years have observable roots in differential patterns of mother–child interaction in earlier years.

NOTES

The research reported here was supported by grants from the Social Sciences and Humanities Research Council of Canada to Jean E. Dumas and Peter J. LaFreniere and from the Medical Research Council of Canada to Jean E. Dumas. The authors wish to thank Pierrette Verlaan, Louise Beaudin, Catherine Gosselin, and France Capuano for their contributions to data collection, and Wendy Serketich, Rhonda Patterson, and Julie Martin for their contributions to data analysis.

Correspondence should be addressed to Jean E. Dumas, Department of Psychological Sciences, Purdue University, West Lafayette, Indiana 47907, U.S.A., or to Peter J. LaFreniere, Child Study Center, University of Maine, Orono, ME 04409.

REFERENCES

Achenbach, T. M., & Edelbrock, C. S. (1981). Behavioral problems and competencies reported by parents of normal and disturbed children aged four through sixteen. *Monographs of the Society for Research in Child Development, 46* (1).

Anderson, K. E., Lytton, H., & Romney, D. M. (1986). Mothers' interactions with normal and conduct-disordered boys: Who affects whom? *Developmental Psychology, 22,* 604–609.

Baumrind, D. (1967). Child care patterns anteceding three patterns of preschool behavior. *Genetic Psychology Monographs, 75,* 43–88.

Brody, G. H., & Forehand, R. (1986). Maternal perceptions of child maladjustment as a function of the combined influence of child behavior and maternal depression. *Journal of Consulting and Clinical Psychology, 54,* 237–240.

Dumas, J. E. (1984). Child, adult-interactional, and socioeconomic setting events as predictors of parent training outcome. *Education and Treatment of Children, 7,* 351–364.

Dumas, J. E. (1986a). Indirect influence of maternal social contacts on mother–child interactions: A setting event analysis. *Journal of Abnormal Child Psychology, 14,* 205–216.

Dumas, J. E. (1986b). Parental perception and treatment outcome in families of aggressive children: A causal model. *Behavior Therapy, 17,* 420–432.

Dumas, J. E. (1989a). Treating antisocial behavior in children: Child and family approaches. *Clinical Psychology Review, 9,* 197–222.

Dumas, J. E. (1989b). Let's not forget the context in behavioral assessment. *Behavioral Assessment, 11,* 231–247.

Dumas, J. E. (1994). Conduct disorder. In R. J. Corsini (Ed.), *Encyclopedia of psychology,* (2nd ed.) (pp. 289–293). New York: Wiley Interscience.

Dumas, J. E., Blechman, E. A., & Prinz, R. J. (1992). Helping families with aggressive children and adolescents change. In R. DeV. Peters, R. J. McMahon, & V. L. Quinsey (Eds.), *Aggression and violence throughout the life span* (pp. 126–154). Newbury Park, CA: Sage.

Dumas, J. E., Gibson, J. A. (1990). Behavioral correlates of maternal depressive symptomatology in conduct-disorder children: II. Systemic effects involving fathers and siblings. *Journal of Consulting and Clinical Psychology, 58,* 877–881.

Dumas, J. E., Gibson, J. A., & Albin, J. B. (1989). Behavioral correlates of maternal depressive symptomatology in conduct-disorder children. *Journal of Consulting and Clinical Psychology, 57,* 516–521.

Dumas, J. E., & LaFreniere, P. J. (1993). Mother–child relationships as sources of support or stress: A comparison of competent, average, aggressive, and anxious dyads. *Child Development, 64,* 1732–1754.

Dumas, J. E., LaFreniere, P. J., Beaudin, L., & Verlaan, P. (1992). Mother–child interactions in competent and aggressive dyads: Implications of relationship stress for behaviour therapy with families. *New Zealand Journal of Psychology, 21,* 3–13.

Dumas, J. E., & Wahler, R. G. (1983). Predictors of treatment outcome in parent training: Mother insularity and socioeconomic disadvantage. *Behavioral Assessment, 5,* 301–313.

Dumas, J. E., & Wahler, R. G. (1985). Indiscriminate mothering as a contextual factor in aggressive-oppositional child behavior: "Damned if you do, damned if you don't." *Journal of Abnormal Child Psychology, 13,* 1–17.

Fantuzzo, J. W., DePaola, L. M., Lambert, L., Martino, T., Anderson, G., & Sutton, S. (1991). Effects of interparental violence on the psychological adjustment and competencies of young children. *Journal of Consulting and Clinical Psychology, 59,* 258–265.

Forehand, R., King, H. E., Peed, S., & Yoder, P. (1975). Mother–child interactions: Comparison of a non-compliant clinic group and a non-clinic group. *Behaviour Research and Therapy, 13,* 79–84.

Gauvin, M., & Rogoff, B. (1989). Collaborative problem solving and children's planning skills. *Developmental Psychology, 25,* 139–151.

Gouge, W. (1622/1977). *Of domesticall duties.* New York: Walter J. Johnson.

Griest, D. L., & Forehand, R. (1982). How can I get any parent training done with all these other problems going on?: The role of family variables in child behavior therapy. *Child and Family Behavior Therapy, 4,* 73–80.

Halverson, C. F., Jr., & Waldrop, M. F. (1970). Maternal behavior toward own and other preschool children: The problem of "ownness." *Child Development, 41,* 839–845.

Hart, G. H., Ladd, G. W., & Burleson, B. R. (1990). Children's expectations of the outcomes of social strategies: Relations with sociometric status and maternal disciplinary styles. *Child Development, 61,* 127–137.

Hinde, R. A. (1987). *Individuals, relationships, and culture.* Cambridge University Press.

Hops, M., Biglan, A., Sherman, L., Arthur, J., Friedman, L., & Osteen, V. (1987). Home observations of family interactions of depressed women. *Journal of Consulting and Clinical Psychology, 55,* 341–346.

Johnson, S. M., Wahl, G., Martin, S., & Johansson, S. (1973). How deviant is the normal child? A behavioral analysis of the preschool child and his family. In R. D. Rubin, J. P. Brady, & J. D. Henderson (Eds.), *Advances in behavior therapy* (pp. 37–54). New York: Academic.

Jouriles, E. N., Murphy, C. M., & O'Leary, K. D. (1989). Interspousal aggression, marital discord, and child problems. *Journal of Consulting and Clinical Psychology, 57,* 453–455.

Kazdin, A. E., Matson, J. L., & Esveldt-Dawson, K. (1981). Social skill performance among normal and psychiatric inpatient children as a function of assessment conditions. *Behaviour Research and Therapy, 19,* 145–152.

Kochanska, G. (1992). Children's interpersonal influence with mothers and peers. *Developmental Psychology, 28,* 491–499.

LaFreniere, P. J., & Dumas, J. E. (1992). A transactional analysis of early childhood anxiety and social withdrawal. *Developmental Psychopathology, 4,* 385–402.

LaFreniere, P. J., Dumas, J. E., Capuano, F., & Dubeau, D. (1992). Development and validation of the Preschool Socioaffective Profile, *Psychological Assessment, 4,* 442–450.

Landauer, T. K., Carlsmith, J. M., & Lepper, M. (1970). Experimental analysis of the factors determining obedience of four-year-old children to adult females. *Child Development, 41,* 601–613.

Maccoby, E. E., & Martin, J. A. (1983). Socialization in the context of the family: Parent–child interaction. In E. M. Hetherington (Ed.), *Handbook of child psychology: Vol. 4. Socialization, personality, and social development* (pp. 1–101). New York: Wiley.

Moran, G., Dumas, J. E., & Symons, D. K. (1992). Approaches to sequential analysis and the description of contingency in behavioral interaction. *Behavioral Assessment, 14,* 65–92.

Olson, S. L. (1992). Development of conduct problems and peer rejection in preschool children: A social systems analysis. *Journal of Abnormal Child Psychology, 20,* 327–350.

Patterson, G. R. (1982). *Coercive family processes.* Eugene, OR: Castalia.

Sameroff, A. J., & Emde, R. N. (Eds.). (1989). *Relationship disturbances in early childhood.* New York: Basic.

Sansbury, L. L., & Wahler, R. G. (1992). Pathways to maladaptive parenting with mothers and their conduct disordered children. *Behavior Modification, 16,* 574–592.

Sawin, D. B., & Parke, R. D. (1979). Inconsistent discipline of aggression in young boys. *Journal of Experimental Child Psychology, 28,* 525–538.

Snyder, J. J. (1977). A reinforcement analysis of interaction in problem and non-problem families. *Journal of Abnormal Psychology, 86,* 528–535.

van Aken, M. A. G., & Riksen-Walraven, J. M. (1992). Parental support and the development of competence in children. *International Journal of Behavioral Development, 15,* 101–123.

Voeltz, L. M., & Evans, I. M. (1982). The assessment of behavioral interrelationships in child behavior therapy. *Behavioral Assessment, 4,* 131–165.

Wahler, R. G. (1980). The insular mother: Her problems in parent–child treatment. *Journal of Applied Behavior Analysis, 13,* 207–219.

Wahler, R. G., & Dumas, J. E. (1986). Maintenance factors in coercive mother–child interactions: The compliance and predictability hypotheses. *Journal of Applied Behavior Analysis, 19,* 13–22.

Wahler, R. G., & Dumas, J. E. (1987). Family factors in childhood psychopathology: Toward a coercion-neglect model. In T. Jacob (Ed.), *Family interaction and psychopathology: Theories, methods, and findings* (pp. 581–627). New York: Plenum.

Wahler, R. G., & Dumas, J. E. (1989). Attentional problems in dysfunctional mother–child interactions: An interbehavioral model. *Psychological Bulletin, 105,* 116–130.

Wahler, R. G., Williams, A. J., & Cerezo, A. (1990). The compliance and predictability hypotheses: Sequential and correlational analyses of coercive mother–child interactions. *Behavioral Assessments, 12,* 391–407.

Webster-Stratton, C. (1985). Predictors of treatment outcome in parent training for conduct-disordered children. *Behavior Therapy, 16,* 223–243.

3 Parental hostility, childhood behavior, and adult social functioning

BARBARA MAUGHAN, ANDREW PICKLES,
AND DAVID QUINTON

Introduction

Harsh and coercive parenting, even when it falls short of overt abuse, can have serious negative effects. To date, links with childhood conduct problems and delinquency have been most extensively explored (Loeber & Stouthamer-Loeber, 1986). Patterson (this volume) elegantly demonstrates how parental coercion feeds into the development of antisocial behaviors in childhood, and Cohen and Brook (this volume) trace the reciprocal patterning of these effects over time. Even in families where children are exposed to a range of problematic behavior from parents – where, for example, one or the other parent is psychiatrically ill – parental hostility appears to be among the most important risks (Rutter & Quinton, 1984).

There is mounting evidence that these processes have long-term effects. Early classic studies (McCord, 1979; Robins, 1966) demonstrated the impact of childhood family atmosphere on criminality in adulthood, and more recent reports suggest that long-term vulnerabilities may extend more widely. Holmes and Robins (1987), interviewing adults selected from the Epidemiological Catchment Area (ECA) samples, found that two very different types of adult psychiatric disorder – depression and alcohol problems – were both strongly associated with reports of unfair, harsh, and inconsistent discipline in childhood. In a similar way, Andrews, Brown, and Creasey (1990) found that adverse parenting (in this case abuse and neglect) showed strong links with disorder in the second generation more powerful than those from the parental disorder itself.

These findings raise important questions. From a theoretical perspective, we need a clearer understanding of how such long-term linkages come about and what they imply. Harsh parenting is likely to occur in families where children face other stressors, so one initial step is to establish that parental hostility does indeed carry an independent risk. Studies in childhood have reached different conclusions on whether harsh parent–child relationships or a more general atmosphere of family conflict may be most detrimental to development at that stage. Jouriles, Barling, and O'Leary (1987), for example, found that even in families facing severe marital violence, direct parent–child aggression still carried the greatest risk for children, while Jenkins and Smith (1991) argued for stronger effects of marital disharmony in a community sample. The implications of harsh parenting may thus differ in high-risk and general population groups. Fendrich, Weissman, Warner, and Mufson (1990) found that a range of family risk factors (poor marital adjustment, parent–child discord, affectionless control, and low family cohesion) were all more prevalent among children of depressed than nondepressed parents and that their impact varied in these two groups. To date, these more complex patternings of effects have been little explored in long-term studies.

A second series of questions concerns the pathways through which long-term consequences may come about. Holmes and Robins (1987), having ruled out a "third variable" explanation via low social class, proposed two other possible routes. First, effects might primarily be mediated through continuities in disorder in the child. If severe parenting is associated with disorder in childhood, continuities from that childhood disturbance may constitute the main direct link with problems later in life. Farrington and Hawkins (1991), studying criminal offending, provide an example of this kind. They found that harsh and erratic punishment was consistently associated with early-onset delinquency but showed few direct links with later persistence in crime. In their analyses, parental discipline seemed to have its effects early in the developmental sequence, with longer term links arising largely through continuities in boys' behavior.

An alternative model would suggest that harsh parenting sets the scene for more persisting vulnerabilities. Harshly treated children, even if they show no obvious disturbance in childhood, may still be at increased risk for disorder at a later point. Both of these pathways seemed important in the ECA analyses (Holmes & Robins, 1987). Especially in the case of depression, harsh discipline was a significant predictor even in the absence of childhood misbehavior. When respondents reported both childhood conduct problems and adult disorder, however, rates of harsh discipline were almost uniformly high. For different individuals, and possibly depending on the pattern of their later problems, different vulnerabilities seemed to apply.

Other questions concern the specificity of links with particular types of later outcome. Most studies suggest that conduct problems, antisocial behavior, and delinquency are the prime concomitants of hard parenting during childhood. Given the strong continuities in antisocial behavior (Robins, 1966, 1978), we might anticipate that the most severe adult outcomes would include antisocial personality disorder and crime. But adult vulnerabilities may also extend beyond severe difficulties of this kind to affect other aspects of individuals' functioning. Zoccolillo, Pickles, Quinton, and Rutter (1992), for example, found that childhood conduct disorder showed strong continuities with pervasive – though not necessarily severe – social problems among young adults reared in institutions. In these samples, previously conduct-disordered children had an increased risk of pervasive difficulties across a range of adult domains – in employment, marital and social relationships, and criminal offending. If similar effects are found in less disadvantaged samples, this wider legacy of adult difficulties might also flow from experiences of harsh parenting.

Finally, there is the issue of gender differences: are boys more likely to be exposed to hostile parenting than are girls, and do the sexes respond in different ways? Most studies have focused on boys or girls alone, so direct comparisons are limited. Somewhat to their surprise, Holmes and Robins (1987) found no significant sex differences in adults' reports of exposure to harsh discipline on any of their measures, either among subjects selected because of prior psychiatric problems or in a nondisordered comparison group. Longer term effects in adulthood also seemed largely independent of sex. Some studies in childhood have suggested that where hostility comes primarily from one parent, the same-sex child may be especially at risk (Rutter & Quinton, 1984). As far as we are aware, more complex patterns of this kind have not yet been examined from a long-term perspective.

Alongside these theoretical questions, important methodological issues also need to be addressed. Although some key studies have demonstrated long-term effects of harsh parenting using prospective designs, much evidence relies on retrospective accounts. Retrospective reports collected in adulthood, especially from individuals with recent difficulties, may well be open to bias. Depressive cognitions might color recollections of childhood, or memories might be subtly reconstructed to make sense of current problems. Brewin, Andrews, and Gotlib (1993), reviewing evidence on retrospective reporting, concluded that there was little reason to link psychiatric status with less reliable or less valid recall of early experience. Relatively few studies, however, have been able to assess the external validity of retrospective reports against independent criteria. Robins and colleagues (1985) compared accounts from siblings close in age, as well as retrospective reports with records made in childhood. Results from the sibling study were reassuring, showing no evidence of bias in recollections of childhood according to current psychiatric state or history of disorder. Levels of agreement were not always high, however, and the record study suggested some underreporting of childhood adversities by those with good adult outcomes.

We take up a number of these issues here. Our data come from two samples studied intensively in childhood (in the late 1960s and early 1970s), then recontacted as young adults. Both groups grew up in the same disadvantaged inner-city area, and both were similar in social background. Parenting styles and behavior problems in childhood were assessed in similar ways, as were adult outcomes. The samples differed in one important respect: the first, a high-risk group, focused on children of psychiatrically ill parents, while the second, stratified on child behavior problems, was drawn from the general population in the area. The high-risk sample provided the opportunity to examine whether parental deviance, psychiatric disorder, or parenting behaviors carried the greatest risk for long-term sequelae. Contrasting the two samples enabled us to explore how far patterns that emerged in the high-risk group were replicated for children growing up in difficult, but still less problematic, family circumstances.

The central concern of our analyses is with routes for long-term influences: does the impact of harsh parenting arise primarily via continuities from disorder in childhood, or are there later effects, mediated in other ways? In addition, as the adult phases of the studies included retrospective questioning on parental discipline and childhood problem behaviors, we have been able to compare prospective and retrospective measures on some key questions. Finally, throughout the analyses we have assessed the separate effects of hostile behavior from fathers and mothers, and examined how far the links that emerged were similar or different for boys and girls.

Samples

High-risk sample

The high-risk sample derives from a 4-year prospective study of the children of psychiatric patients conducted in inner London between 1965 and 1971 (Rutter & Quinton, 1984). The parents comprised a random selection from a consecutive series of patients with children under the age of 15, identified through the Camberwell Psychiatric Register (Wing & Hailey, 1972). Although the study was designed to investigate the impact of new parental disorders on children's behavioral development, half the families included one parent (patient or spouse) with a personality disorder. Chronic psychiatric problems were clearly common in this group.

One hundred and thirty-seven families were chosen for the original study. Parents were interviewed at the time of initial psychiatric contact and annually for the next 4 years. The adult follow-up, undertaken in the 1980s, focused on all children from these families who were aged 21 or older when the follow-up began, whose childhood psychiatric status had been assessed by parental interviews on at least two occasions, or who had participated in a substudy of childhood temperament (Graham, Rutter, & George, 1973). To examine the effects of hostility from either parent, we focus here on the 164 children meeting these criteria who were living in two-parent families at the time of the childhood assessments. Their mean age at follow-up was 27.3 years (SD = 3.21).

General population sample

The general population sample was derived from an epidemiological survey of 10-year-old children in the same inner London area, undertaken in 1970 (Rutter, Cox, Tupling, Berger, & Yule 1975). The total population of children in their last year of primary school ($N = 2,281$) was screened using the Rutter B(2) teacher rating scales (Rutter, 1967). Stratified samples were then selected for parental interview: a random sample of the full population ($n = 106$), enriched by a further 143 children with high (deviant) teacher behavior ratings. Parental interviews were successfully completed for 91.6% of selected children (228/249). The 198 children living with two parents at the time of the initial study formed the basis for the adult follow-up, undertaken when the subjects were in their late twenties ($M = 27.8$ years, $SD = 1.3$).

Measures

Both the childhood and adult follow-up phases of each study used an investigator-based interview method of known reliability and validity (Brown & Rutter, 1966; Rutter & Brown, 1966). In this approach coding rules are carefully specified, but the interviewer has the freedom to adapt the questioning to the respondent's conversational style and social circumstances. All the measures used here were collected and coded in the same way in the two studies.

Prospective measures

Childhood conduct disorder. Conduct disorder was assessed from the parental interview, which covered 33 symptomatic behaviors, rated for the degree of handicap caused in the child's social relationships and development. Clinical review of the interview protocols provided overall ratings of emotional, conduct, and mixed disorders. These were recoded into a binary measure of the presence or absence of conduct or mixed disorders.

The Rutter B(2) teacher rating scale, a 26-item questionnaire, provided a second prospective measure of behavior problems. High overall scores (≥ 9) were used to stratify the general population sample, and a binary variable reflecting scores above and below this cut-off was included in all logistic regression models to take account of this stratification. In addition, in the latent class analyses, a binary variable for the presence or absence of antisocial or mixed behavior problems among children scoring above the cut-off was used as one indicator of the latent class of conduct disorder.

Parental deviance and disorder. A clinical assessment of the severity and type of psychiatric disorder in each parent was rated from systematic accounts of 37 symptoms. This was recoded as a binary variable according to the presence of handicapping psychiatric symptomatology at the time of assessment. Accounts (but not official records) of paternal convictions for nontrivial offenses were coded in a similar way.

Parental marital relationships. Problems in parental marital relationships were assessed using a well-established interview measure (Quinton, Rutter, & Rowlands,

1975). Significant difficulties in the marriage could be characterized by apathy and dislike, or by open discord. The ratings were recoded as a binary measure reflecting the presence of significant open discord, the feature of parental relationships most consistently associated with conduct problems in children (Emery, Weintraub, & Neale, 1982).

Parenting behavior. Mothers gave detailed accounts of disciplinary methods and patterns of communication and interaction between themselves, their husbands, and the children in the 3 months preceding the interview. In addition, the mother's expressed positive and negative feelings toward the child were rated from the childhood interviews according to Camberwell Family Interview principles (Vaughn, 1989). These ratings were used to construct the measures of parenting behavior used here.

Mothers. Five measures of maternal behavior toward the child were factor analyzed to determine the dimensions to be used in the analyses: *warmth,* a 5-point overall rating of the degree to which the mother spoke about the child with a warm tone of voice; *positive remarks,* a 4-point measure of statements with an operationally defined positive content; *criticism,* a 4-point measure of negative expressed emotion; *irritability,* a 5-point measure of the frequency with which the mother snapped or shouted at the child; and *exposure to hostile behavior,* a 4-point summary rating of negative behaviors (including physical punishment) directed at the child. Principal components analyses using varimax rotation yielded a similar factor structure in both samples, with two clear factors, one of positive and one of negative/hostile behavior. The distributions of the factor scores in the random general population sample were used to define extreme levels of low positive and high negative maternal behaviors. Cut-offs (at the lowest 10% for positive behaviors and the highest 10% for negative) were applied in both samples to create binary variables for the presence of hostile, negative behaviors and marked lack of warmth in mother–child relationships.

Fathers. Comparable data for fathers covered accounts of irritability and hostile behavior. These were summed and dichotomized to reflect difficulties ranging from shouting or loss of temper on most days of the week to harsh and coercive discipline.

Retrospective measures

The prospective measures were detailed and reliable, but focused on specific and relatively brief periods in childhood. To provide more extensive coverage of both parent–child relationships and the subjects' behavior in childhood, retrospective accounts from the adult follow-up interviews were also examined. The retrospective sections of the interviews followed an approach previously used in a follow-up of young adults reared in institutions (Quinton & Rutter, 1988). Subjects were helped

Table 3.1. *Problems in adult social functioning: criteria*

Work
One or more of the following:
　Ever fired since age 18
　Walked out of three or more jobs since age 18
　Six or more jobs in past four years
　Persistent friction with work colleagues

Intimate relationships
One or more of the following:
　Two or more broken cohabitations
　Persistent discord in two or more cohabitations
　Violence in two or more relationships
　Two or more deviant partners (e.g., involved in alcohol, drugs, crime)
　Persistent problems in making or sustaining intimate relationships

Social relationships
One or more of the following:
　No confiding in family or friends
　Contacts with friends less than weekly
　Suspicious or lacking in trust

---

to recall childhood experiences through a careful historical reconstruction and encouraged to place events in relation to important personal markers to build up a coherent account. Like the other interview assessments, the retrospective measures were elicited using the investigator-based approach suggested by Brewin and colleagues (1993) as likely to improve the reliability of retrospective reporting. The measures used here are (1) *retrospective conduct disorder,* a binary variable coded positive if the subject described three or more conduct disorder symptoms from the DSM III criteria (American Psychiatric Association, 1980); and (2) *retrospective parental discipline,* a binary variable made separately for mothers and fathers and rated positive if the subject reported persistent disciplinary methods involving harsh physical punishments or parents being excessively hard, cold, belittling, or restrictive.

Outcome measures

Adult social functioning. In each study, later sections of the adult interviews provided detailed data on the subjects' functioning at work, in marriage or other intimate relationships, and in broader social relationships with friends and others. The ratings were designed to reflect the individual's contribution to difficulties and required evidence of a pattern of repeated problems over time. The specific items used to index problems in each domain are set out in Table 3.1: a positive rating on any item was taken to indicate difficulties in that domain. Official records of criminal convictions in adulthood provided a fourth measure of problems in social functioning.

Analyses: overview

The first stage of the analyses examined the cross-sectional associations between harsh parenting and problem behavior in childhood. Results from these analyses then formed the basis for examining possible long-term effects. Here we tested how far poor social functioning in adulthood could be explained in terms of continuity from childhood conduct problems, or whether parenting experiences added further to the models. For both cross-sectional and longitudinal analyses we began by exploring the data using logistic regressions. These provided a preliminary picture of the findings but, like all analyses based on observed variables, were potentially vulnerable to measurement error. Left uncorrected, the misclassification of subjects as a result of measurement error can either attenuate or inflate apparent associations among observed variables, so that the links identified in the logistic regression models may have been misleading. In attempting to overcome this, the main analyses were repeated using latent class analysis (LCA), a technique for categorical measures that is comparable to the structural equation modeling (SEM) used in many analyses of continuous measures. Like SEM, the latent class approach estimates relationships between latent categories, classes, or states that are not themselves observable, but are each indexed by a series of observed indicators. Here, we were concerned with two latent categorical variables, one of conduct problems in childhood, the second of difficulties in social functioning in adulthood. The relationships of the observed indicators to the latent classes are specified by a set of measurement equations, the parameters of which determine the probabilities of true and false positives and true and false negatives. A second set of equations specifies how the probability of being in the latent category of childhood problems relates to measured risk factors – such as the child's sex, and parental hostility – and also how such risk factors influence the continuity from the childhood latent categories to the corresponding categories in adulthood. A more complete description of the methodology is given in Zoccolillo and colleagues (1992). Finally, unlike logistic regression (which requires full data on all variables included in each model), LCA can use cases with only partial data (see, e.g., Winship & Mare, 1990).

Results

Sample characteristics

Prospective data for assessing the impact of parents' hostility in childhood in the latent class analyses were available for 121 subjects in the high-risk sample (74% of

Table 3.2. *Sample characteristics (percent)*

	High-risk (n = 83)	General population (n = 174)	
		Unweighted	Reweighted
Family characteristics			
Social class			
Nonmanual	33.8	20.8	19.2
Manual	66.5	79.2	80.7
Mother: psychiatric disorder	63.9	29.3	30.5
Father: psychiatric disorder	57.8	11.5	11.3
Father: criminality	33.7	16.1	12.7
Marital discord	44.6	12.4	8.5
Parent–child relations			
Mother: hostile	27.7	13.2	10.8
Mother: lack of warmth	22.9	13.8	13.0
Father: hostile	38.6	8.0	4.3
Child: conduct disorder			
Girls	21.1	8.8	9.0
Boys	28.9	13.2	4.1

those in two-parent families) and 177 subjects in the general population group (89%). The requirements of complete data for the logistic regressions resulted in some further minor losses in the general population sample (n = 174) and a more substantial reduction in the high-risk sample (n = 83). These losses were primarily due to structurally missing data (children being too young for teacher ratings at the phases at which parental hostility were assessed, or being selected for the study of temperament but not for parental accounts of disorder). Despite these reductions, comparisons within each sample showed no significant differences between full data cases and all original cases in two-parent families on any measure. Table 3.2 shows the characteristics of the samples with full childhood data. Measures for the community sample are presented in two ways: unweighted (reflecting the distributions in the enriched group) and reweighted to reflect distributions in the general population in the study area.

Children in both samples came from predominantly working-class homes; and even in the general population sample, levels of psychiatric symptomatology among mothers were relatively high. Rates of all types of family problems were much elevated in the high-risk group. On the measures of central interest here, maternal hostility to the child was over twice as common as in the community sample, and hostile father–child relations were much more prevalent. Figure 3.1 shows rates of exposure to hostile parenting separately for boys and girls. Although there were minor variations in the figures, there were no significant differences in either sample

Prospective parenting measures

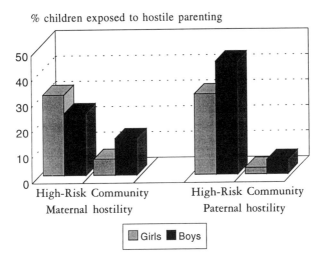

% children exposed to hostile parenting

Girls Boys

Retrospective reports of parenting

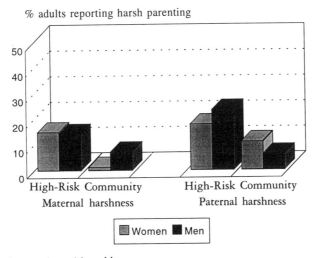

% adults reporting harsh parenting

Women Men

Figure 3.1. Harsh parenting: girls and boys.

in girls' and boys' exposure to hostile parenting or lack of maternal warmth. Levels of marital discord were also closely similar in the families of girls and boys (9.8 and 7.5%, respectively, in the general population sample, 39.5 and 48.9%, respectively, in the high-risk group).

Parental hostility and conduct problems in childhood

We began by exploring cross-sectional relations between the measures of parenting and other indicators of parent and family difficulties available from the childhood studies – parental psychiatric disorder, criminality in the children's fathers, and marital discord. As we had anticipated, there were very considerable overlaps, most marked in the high-risk sample, but following similar trends in the general population group. Hostile parenting was significantly more common among parents with handicapping psychiatric symptoms at the time of interview and was also strongly associated with marital discord. To illustrate, in the high-risk sample 60.4% of fathers with current psychiatric symptoms were rated as showing hostility to their children, by comparison with only 8.6% of those without disorder. In the general population sample, although absolute levels of harsh parenting were much lower, the contrasts were equally strong: 19.0% of fathers with disorder, but only 2.4% of those without, had hostile relationships with their children. In both samples parents were also more likely to show harsh parenting if marital relationships were discordant. Fathers' criminality, however, showed no direct links with hostile parenting once the effects of any overlap with disorder had been taken into account.

These findings echoed the patterns reported in other studies. On the one hand, neither parental psychopathology nor discordant marriages carried any necessary links with hostile parenting. When harsh parent–child relationships did occur, however, they were often embedded in a wider nexus of personal and interpersonal difficulties. In the high-risk group, where all children were by definition exposed to disorder in at least one parent, over 95% of children experiencing maternal hostility were also facing two or more other family stressors. Even in the general population sample, the overlaps were strong: all but 12.3% of children facing maternal hostility were experiencing at least one other difficulty, and over 50% faced two or more. Any examination of hostile parenting clearly needed to take these other stressors into account.

We turned next to examine associations between this range of family difficulties and conduct disorder in childhood. This was done first using linear logistic analyses, with conduct problems as the dependent measure and the indicators of parent–child relationships, parental characteristics, and marital discord as predictors. The design variables (psychiatric disorder in either parent and high teacher behavior ratings) were included in all the models, and the additional effects of other family factors were tested in turn. All factors with additional significant effects were then assessed jointly. Finally, sample × factor interaction terms were included to examine how far each factor appeared to operate similarly in the high-risk and general population groups. The significance of each effect was assessed by comparing the goodness-of-fit, as measured by the scaled deviance, of pairs of models including and excluding the factor of interest. This difference in scaled deviance is a likelihood ratio test statistic that is asymptotically chi-square distributed. The significance levels quoted for these chi-squares are for two-tailed tests.

Table 3.3. *Linear logistic models of childhood conduct disorder*

| | Odds ratio | Removing main effect | | |
		χ^2	df	p
Boys (n = 151)				
Design variables		11.84	3	.001
High teacher behavior rating	4.77			
Mother: disorder	4.13			
Father: disorder	0.59			
Additional factors				
Father: hostility	13.03	11.75	1	.001
Mother: hostility	3.37	4.46	1	.033
Father: criminality	3.19	4.05	1	.043
Girls (n = 106)				
Design variables		2.00	3	ns
High teacher behavior rating	0.60			
Mother: disorder	2.05			
Father: disorder	0.67			
Additional factors				
Mother: hostility	5.94	6.44	1	.001
Marital discord	3.77	3.12	1	.07

Table 3.3 summarizes the results, showing the chi-square value for the initial model including the design variables, odds ratios for each additional significant main effect, and the chi-square value for removing that effect from the model. For boys, all the design variables showed significant effects, and maternal hostility and lack of warmth as well as paternal hostility and criminality each made additional contributions when added singly to the models. Assessed jointly, maternal lack of warmth no longer contributed, but all the other factors remained significant. Testing interactions between each of these factors and sample, only the paternal hostility × sample term showed significant effects. The multivariate distributions within each sample suggested that this finding was based on some cells with rather small Ns, reflecting the low level of paternal hostility in the general population group. Considerable caution is thus required before concluding that this represented important differences between samples in the effects of father–child hostility. Overall, the main effects shown in Table 3.3, excluding this interaction, seemed to provide an adequate and more directly interpretable account of the findings.

These analyses suggested clear links between parental hostility and conduct problems in boys. Marital conflict between parents showed no additional effects on boys' conduct problems, but paternal criminality did. This might have indexed a variety of processes: direct modeling of parental antisocial behavior, other aspects of parenting not tapped by the hostility measures, or perhaps the boys' exposure to a more general culture of antisocial activities among both family and peers.

The models for girls showed fewer significant effects, and those that did emerge seemed more directly concerned with the quality of family relationships. The design variables were nonsignificant for girls, and maternal hostility was the only factor to show clear additional effects, with some suggestions of a trend for links with marital discord. Neither of these factors showed significant interactions by sample. In both the high-risk and general population groups, hostile mother–daughter relations seemed the most important correlates of conduct problems in girls.

Parental hostility and social adaptation in adulthood

These associations in childhood formed the backdrop for the longer term analyses that were our central concern. Full adult outcome data were available on 132 subjects from the general population sample (75.9% of those included in the childhood analyses) and for 79 cases in the high-risk group (95.2%). Retrospective reports of parental discipline were available for 110 subjects in the general population group and 75 in the high-risk sample. Table 3.4 gives details of the adult outcomes, showing the proportions of men and women in each group with good adaptation in adulthood, with problems in one domain of functioning, in two, and so forth. There were marked sex differences in the rates of poor social adaptation and also some differences between the high-risk and general population samples. As Table 3.4 suggests, the main sample differences were among women. Rates of harsh discipline reported retrospectively in the adult interviews were much lower than those suggested by the prospective accounts (see Figure 3.1). Once again, however, the rates of severe parenting reported by men and women in each sample were broadly similar.

We tested links between harsh parenting and adult outcomes in three steps. The first examined continuities between childhood conduct problems and adult social

Table 3.4. *Adult outcome: number of areas with problems in social adaptation (percent)*

No. areas of problems	High risk (n = 79)		General population (reweighted) (n = 132)	
	Women	Men	Women	Men
0	50.0	29.7	75.3	47.4
1	26.2	32.4	19.7	36.3
2	21.4	16.2	5.0	10.1
3	0	16.2	0	6.2
4	2.4	5.4	0	0

functioning. Next, we tested for additional effects of the prospectively measured family factors, assessed in the childhood studies. Finally, retrospective accounts of harsh parenting collected in the adult follow-ups were included in the analyses.

In the linear logistic analyses, problems in two or more domains of adult functioning were used to index poor adult outcome, and no problems or difficulties in a single area only reflected a lack of pervasive adult difficulties. For men, childhood conduct disorder showed strong links with poor adult functioning ($\chi^2 = 10.87$, 1 df, $p < .001$). Once this behavioral continuity had been included in the models, parental marital discord was the only prospective measure to show additional significant effects. The picture was rather different when retrospective measures of harsh parenting were included: then, reports of harsh discipline by both mothers and fathers showed clear links with adult functioning, and the prospective accounts of parental discord no longer remained significant.

Results for women were different in a number of respects. In particular, childhood conduct problems showed no clear continuities with adult functioning, nor did any of the prospectively measured childhood factors. Once again, however, retrospective accounts of harsh discipline did show an impact, centering only on harsh discipline from mothers.

These initial models suggested an interesting pattern. First, continuities from childhood conduct problems were strong for men but less marked for women. As Table 3.4 shows, relatively small proportions of women showed difficulties in two or more domains of functioning on the measures used here. Although our interest was in pervasive patterns of adult problems, this cut-off may have been too severe when applied to women in these samples. For both sexes, however, probably the more striking feature of the analyses, once links with childhood behavior had been taken into account, was the lack of associations between adult outcomes and harsh parenting assessed in childhood but the clear effects signaled by the retrospective reports.

Latent class analyses

LCA was used to examine this pattern further, allowing for differing levels of severity in outcome for men and women, and also taking account of measurement error. The model also generated (given the data available on each subject) a probability of his or her being in one latent category or the other in both childhood and adulthood. This allowed a form of *best estimate* contingency table to be constructed from the pooled information from the various childhood and adult indicators.

The general form of the models tested is shown in Figure 3.2. Childhood behavior problems were indexed by teacher-rated antisocial behavior, mothers' reports of conduct disorder, and the subjects' retrospective accounts of conduct problems. The four adult indicators of difficulties in intimate relationships, social relationships, work record, and crime indexed the adult problem category. The

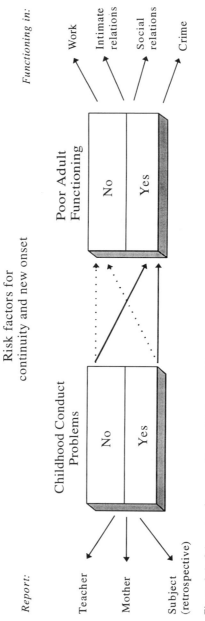

Report:

*Risk factors for
continuity and new onset*

Functioning in:

Childhood Conduct
Problems

| No |
| Yes |

Teacher

Mother

Subject
(retrospective)

Poor Adult
Functioning

| No |
| Yes |

Work

Intimate
relations

Social
relations

Crime

Figure 3.2. Schematic diagram of latent Markov model.

relationship of the childhood indicators to the latent categories was estimated by the same parameters for boys and girls, but the relationship of the adult indicators to the adult categories was estimated by separate parameters for men and women. In each case the adult classes reflected pervasive patterns of difficulty, but the nature of the adult outcome was allowed to differ both in severity and in the relative importance of problems in the four constituent domains for men and women. In all models, the prevalence of latent childhood problems, the rates of childhood-to-adult continuity, and the rate of onset of "new" adult problems were allowed to be different for boys and girls.

A sequence of models was then fitted to explore the impact of parental hostility on the prevalence of childhood conduct problems, on the rate of continuity in poor functioning between childhood and adulthood, and on the level of new onset adult difficulties. Each model included a dummy variable for sample, to check that the processes operating in the two samples were the same. In all cases the effects that were added or removed involved two parameters, a main effect and an interaction with sex, allowing different effects for boys and girls.

Table 3.5 shows the results of fitting the sequence of models using the prospective measures of parental hostility. Model A is the basic model, estimating the rates of problems at each time period and continuities between them, as already outlined. Models B to H show the effects of introducing the indicators of parental hostility at different points in the developmental sequence. Using the prospective measures, the effects of maternal hostility on contemporaneous childhood problems were highly significant $(A-B)$, and parameter estimates showed these to be rather greater for girls than for boys. Paternal hostility showed no additional effects $(B-C)$. Once the impact of maternal hostility on childhood problems had been taken into account, neither maternal nor paternal hostility had any impact on the continuity of problems into adulthood or on the occurrence of new problems in the early adult years. Although there were clear differences in the rates of adult difficulties between subjects who had and had not experienced maternal hostility in childhood, the prospective analyses suggested that these arose solely from continuities in disorder already established in childhood. The process also looked the same in both samples: though not tabulated, there were no significant differences in the prevalence of childhood conduct problems, in continuities to adulthood, or in rates of new onset between the samples, once the effects of maternal hostility were taken into account.

In a similar way, with maternal hostility included in the models, neither parental disorder, maternal lack of warmth, nor marital discord showed significant effects on the prevalence of childhood conduct problems, on continuity to adulthood, or on new onset adult difficulties. Paternal criminality did, however, show additional effects in childhood ($\chi^2 = 11.78$, 2 df, $p = .003$) and perhaps some marginal effects on continuity ($\chi^2 = 4.4$, 2 df, $p = .1$).

Table 3.6 shows the results from fitting a similar sequence of models using retrospectively rated parental hostility. The conclusions here differed in several

Table 3.5. *Latent class models fitted with mother and father prospectively measured harsh parenting (298 subjects)*

Model	Mother effects on — Childhood prevalence	Continuity into adulthood	New adult onset	Father effects on — Childhood prevalence	Continuity into adulthood	New adult onset	−log L		Likelihood ratio χ^2	df	p
A	—	—	—	—	—	—	799.99				
B	✓	—	—	—	—	—	785.08	(A − B)	29.82	2	.001
C	✓	✓	—	—	—	—	784.72	(B − C)	0.72	2	.7
D	✓	—	✓	—	—	—	784.53	(B − D)	1.10	2	.6
E	✓	—	—	✓	—	—	784.24	(B − E)	1.68	2	.4
F	✓	—	—	—	✓	—	784.82	(B − F)	0.52	2	.8
G	✓	—	—	—	—	✓	784.35	(B − G)	1.46	2	.5

Table 3.6. *Latent class models fitted with mother and father retrospectively measured harsh parenting (240 subjects)*

Model	Mother effects on — Childhood prevalence	Continuity into adulthood	New adult onset	Father effects on — Childhood prevalence	Continuity into adulthood	New adult onset	$-\log L$		Likelihood ratio χ^2	df	p
A	—	—	—	—	—	—	762.98				
B	✓	—	—	—	—	—	757.10	(A − B)	11.76	2	.002
C	✓	✓	—	—	—	—	753.48	(B − C)	7.24	2	.03
D	✓	—	✓	✓	—	—	753.42	(C − D)	0.12	2	.9
E	✓	—	—	✓	—	—	750.61	(C − E)	5.74	2	.06
F	✓	—	—	✓	✓	—	752.63	(C − F)	0.85	2	.7
G	✓	—	—	✓	—	✓	751.14	(C − G)	4.68	2	.1
H	✓	—	✓	✓	—	✓	748.76	(C − H)	9.44	2	.009

Table 3.7. *Distribution of subjects by sex and maternal harshness for latent behavioral histories (percent)*

	Prospectively measured maternal harshness			
	Girls		Boys	
	Harsh (*n* = 24)	Not harsh (*n* = 107)	Harsh (*n* = 34)	Not harsh (*n* = 133)
Childhood +, adult +	21	0	50	17
Childhood +, adult −	34	0	14	4
Childhood −, adult +	9	12	2	7
Childhood −, adult −	36	88	34	73
	Prospectively measured maternal harshness			
	Girls		Boys	
	Harsh (*n* = 11)	Not harsh (*n* = 104)	Harsh (*n* = 10)	Not harsh (*n* = 115)
Childhood +, adult +	25	3	58	29
Childhood +, adult −	19	1	0	0
Childhood −, adult +	40	0	17	0
Childhood −, adult −	16	96	25	71

Note: + denotes presence of disorder or problem; − denotes absence of disorder or problem.

respects. First, although the impact of maternal harshness in childhood remained important (A − B), some independent impact of parental hostility also appeared to be significant (B − C). Once again, the parameter estimates suggested that the effects for mothers were larger for girls, while those for fathers were smaller and similar for boys and girls. Second, maternal harshness (C − E), and to a lesser degree paternal hostility (C − G), both appeared to have an additional (marginally significant) impact in increasing the probability of new adult problems among subjects who had not shown conduct disorder in childhood. Refinement of the model (model H) to allow maternal hostility to influence new onset in girls only, and paternal hostility to influence new onset just in boys, suggested these effects might be sex specific. Again, once the effects of hostility had been accounted for, the process did not appear to differ between the samples.

To illustrate the pattern of effects Table 3.7 shows the distribution of the latent classifications of childhood and adult problem states by sex and maternal hostility categories. In all cases, around half of those with hostile mothers appear to have had childhood behavior problems. For boys, there was considerable continuity of problems in behavioral functioning, with persistence of childhood problems being shown by 80% in the prospective analysis and 100% in the retrospective. For girls, the continuity was lower, at 40% using prospective indicators and 65% using retrospective measures. The differences between prospective and retrospective measures were most striking in relation to the development of new adult problems. Using the prospective measures, a small proportion of both girls (12%) and boys (7%) not apparently exposed to maternal hostility in childhood showed new adult problems. Using the retrospective measures, no men or women without harsh parenting emerged as showing new problems in adulthood. For those exposed to maternal hostility, the pattern was reversed. Although continuity from childhood problems was still strong, 17% of men reporting harsh parenting retrospectively showed new adult problems, by comparison with only 2% in the prospective analyses, and the contrasts for women were even more marked — 40 versus 9%.

Accuracy of recall measures

The analyses thus suggested rather different interpretations of the role of parental hostility depending on whether prospective or retrospective measures of parenting were included. Models using the prospective measures suggested that the major effects of harsh parenting were on conduct problems in childhood; adding the retrospective accounts, there were suggestions of additional, later effects.

These differences might have arisen for a number of reasons. First, the retrospective measures might have been more accurate than the prospective: they covered longer periods in childhood and so may have tapped into more persistent harsh parenting or problems not present at the time the childhood data were collected. Alternatively, however, the retrospective accounts might have been biased by adult functioning, making subjects with adult difficulties more likely to remember, or to exaggerate, poor childhood circumstances, and/or those currently functioning well to forget or minimize them.

We would need contemporaneous measures of childhood environment from a number of sources, and covering a substantial period of time, to explore these possibilities fully. Some preliminary examination of the possibility of bias could, however, be made within our data, comparing contemporaneous childhood and retrospective accounts. To do this, we assessed agreement between the two sets of reports, taking the contemporaneous parental account as the criterion and the subjects' retrospective reports of the quality of parental discipline as the predictor or "test" (Fleiss, 1981).

Measures of agreement between the retrospective and prospective measures of parental hostility are given in Table 3.8. As a background, we should note that although the constructs underlying the measures taken in both childhood and adult studies were similar, they were not identical. In particular, the retrospective measures focused specifically on discipline, while the prospective accounts included this among a number of indicators of harsh parent–child relations.

The pattern of associations was broadly consistent across the measures. Overall,

Table 3.8. *Associations between prospective and retrospective measures: all subjects*

	False positives	False negatives	Sensitivity	Specificity	Kappa
Mother: hostile	.59	.15	.24	.93	.24
Father: hostile	.65	.18	.28	.88	.19

Table 3.9. *Associations between prospective and retrospective measures: comparing subjects with good and poor outcome*

Measure	n	Identified prospectively	Identified retrospectively	Sensitivity	Specificity
Mother hostility					
Outcome					
Good	168	27	9	.11	.96
Poor	53	14	12	.50	.87
Father hostility					
Outcome					
Good	162	29	19	.20	.90
Poor	46	17	13	.41	.79
Persistent hostility					
Outcome					
Good	62	16	6	.19	.93
Poor	23	10	6	.40	.84

the level of association was low, as reflected in the kappas, largely due to subjects' retrospectively reporting substantially fewer problems than were rated on the prospective accounts. The false negative rate was uniformly low, and the specificity of the reports high: when the subjects themselves reported an absence of parental hostility, the prospective measures generally concurred. In part, of course, this pattern is a function of the lower rate of retrospective reporting. On the other hand, the false positive rates were high on all three measures, suggesting much lower rates of agreement on positive accounts of harsh parenting. It was clearly important to know how far this reflected any systematic bias associated with subjects' later outcomes.

To explore this, Table 3.9 presents the figures separately for subjects with "good" adult outcomes (no difficulties, or problems in one domain only) and those with problems in two or more domains. As before, retrospective rates of reporting were always lower than prospective, but the differences were most marked in the good outcome group, resulting in sizable differences in sensitivity. There was little tendency for subjects with poor current functioning to overreport childhood problems; instead, a good deal of the lack of agreement between accounts reflected underreporting of childhood difficulties by those with good adult outcomes.

Differences in the persistence of harsh parenting might still, however, have affected the comparisons. The repeated childhood assessments in the high-risk sample allowed for some checks on this. These were used to construct an index of persistent maternal hostility, treated as present if moderate or high exposure to hostile parenting had been rated on at least two of the four assessments. Comparisons using this measure are presented on the last line of Table 3.9. The pattern of differences between subjects with good and poor adult outcomes remained essentially as before, suggesting that the differences in reporting were not to any major extent an artifact of persistence. Even where the prospective data suggested persistently poor mother–child relations, these were less likely to be reported by subjects with good later outcomes.

Bias in retrospective reporting has usually been assumed to arise from subjects with problems exaggerating past difficulties (to interviewers or indeed to themselves) to make sense of their situations. Our findings suggested that quite the opposite tendency was at work: like Robins and colleagues (1985), we found little evidence of exaggeration among those with poor adult outcomes, but instead a tendency for those in better current circumstances to forget – or possibly forgive – to a greater extent.

Conclusions

Against the background of studies demonstrating links between harsh parenting and both psychiatric problems and criminality in later life (McCord, 1979; Robins, 1966), we set out to explore the impact of these childhood experiences on a rather different adult outcome: a pattern of pervasive difficulties in social adaptation that though it fell well short of criteria for personality disorder, nonetheless seemed likely to be problematic for the individuals themselves, their families, and possibly the wider society. Our data enabled us to explore these issues in two different samples and to make comparisons between both processes and outcomes for men and women.

The first interesting feature of the findings concerned exposure to harsh parenting among boys and girls. Both prospective and retrospective accounts were in agreement here: although we might anticipate boys to be at greater risk of harsh parenting than would be girls, our data showed no consistent differences. Holmes and Robins (1987), in a more detailed examination of differing types of harsh discipline, also found girls and boys to be equally at risk. Their subjects were selected to reflect particular types of adult outcome. Our findings, on groups selected instead on the basis of childhood characteristics (individual and family), showed a similar pattern. Where parents used harsh disciplinary techniques, girls seemed quite as likely to be exposed to parental hostility as were boys.

The implications of this exposure also seemed broadly similar. In childhood, the associations between conduct problems and parental hostility were clear for both girls and boys. The logistic regression analyses suggested that parental hostility was among the most important family correlates, though they also identified additional effects of psychiatric disorder in mothers and criminality in fathers for the boys, as well as suggestions of effects of marital discord for girls. The latent class models identified maternal hostility as the most important link, with additional effects deriving from paternal criminality.

We then tested two possible routes of continued poor adult functioning: first, that the effects of harsh parenting arose largely in connection with childhood disorder and, second, that some longer term vulnerabilities might also be involved. The findings unequivocally supported the first of these pathways and offered some support for the second. For men, links from childhood conduct disorder were strong, though this pattern was less clear for women. Zoccolillo and colleagues (1992) found essentially similar levels of continuity for men and women in samples raised in institutional care. Although many of the subjects in the present analyses experienced a range of childhood adversities, these were arguably less severe than those found in an institutional upbringing. Subjects in the institutional samples may also have had more severe conduct problems than our subjects or have faced greater environmental adversities. Differences in any of these areas might account for the lower levels of continuity from childhood conduct problems that we found for the women studied here. For both sexes, however, harsh parenting appeared to be associated primarily with the occurrence of conduct disorder in childhood and had less impact on its likelihood of persisting or on the onset of new problems in adulthood.

Using prospective measures, our conclusions would broadly rest at this point. The introduction of the retrospective accounts raised the possibility of additional influences of harsh parenting, not reflected in the childhood conduct indicators, and having an apparently more direct effect on difficulties in functioning in adult life. As we have seen, there may be some elements of bias in these retrospective measures, largely in the direction of underreporting adverse childhoods among subjects with good later outcomes. It seems very likely, however, that they may still be signaling some additional effects of harsh parenting, operating not through childhood conduct problems but through other patterns of childhood difficulty or through later routes. Especially interesting here were the suggestions of some gender specificity in these processes, women being more vulnerable to hostile relations with mothers, and men with fathers. These differences might reflect variations in the recall of childhood or divergences in intervening mechanisms; both possibilities deserve further exploration.

NOTE

Early stages of these studies were supported by the Foundation for Child Development, the Social Science Research Council, and the W. T. Grant Foundation. Work on the adult follow-ups was supported by the Medical Research Council. We are most grateful to all the study members for sharing their experiences with us and to Christine Groothues, Lesley Gulliver, Ann Hagell, Rosanna Heal, Mary McNutt, Angela Park, Christina Shearer, and Frances Winder for interviewing in the adult follow-up studies.

REFERENCES

American Psychiatric Association. (1980). *Diagnostic and statistical manual of mental disorders* (3rd ed.). Washington, DC: American Psychiatric Association.

Andrews, B., Brown, G. W., & Creasey, L. (1990). Intergenerational links between psychiatric disorder in mothers and daughters: The role of parenting experiences. *Journal of Child Psychology and Psychiatry, 31,* 1115–1129.

Brewin, C. R., Andrews, B., & Gotlib, I. H. (1993). Psychopathology and early experience: A re-appraisal of retrospective reports. *Psychological Bulletin, 113,* 82–98.

Brown, G. W., & Rutter, M. (1966). The measurement of family activities and relationships: A methodological study. *Human Relations, 19,* 241–263.

Emery, R. E., Weintraub, S., & Neale, J. M. (1982). Effects of marital discord on the school behavior of children of schizophrenic, affectively disordered and normal parents. *Journal of Abnormal Child Psychology, 10,* 215–228.

Farrington, D. P., & Hawkins, J. D. (1991). Predicting participation, early onset and later persistence in officially recorded offending. *Criminal Behaviour and Mental Health, 1,* 1–33.

Fendrich, M., Weissman, M. M., Warner, V., & Mufson, L. (1990). Two year recall of lifetime diagnoses in offspring at high and low risk for major depression: The stability of offspring reports, *Archives of General Psychiatry, 47,* 1121–1127.

Fleiss, J. L. (1981). Statistical methods for rates and proportions (2nd ed.). New York: Wiley.

Graham, P., Rutter, M., & George, S. (1973). Temperamental characteristics as predictors of behavior disorders in children. *American Journal of Orthopsychiatry, 43,* 328–399.

Holmes, S. J., & Robins, L. N. (1987). The influence of childhood disciplinary experience on the development of alcoholism and depression. *Journal of Child Psychology and Psychiatry, 28,* 399–415.

Jenkins, J. M., & Smith, M. A. (1991). Marital disharmony and children's behaviour problems: Aspects of a poor marriage that affect children adversely. *Journal of Child Psychology and Psychiatry, 32,* 793–810.

Jouriles, E. N., Barling, J., & O'Leary, K. D. (1987). Predicting child behavior problems in maritally violent families. *Journal of Abnormal Child Psychology, 15,* 165–173.

Loeber, R., & Stouthamer-Loeber, M. (1986). Family factors as correlates and predictors of juvenile conduct problems and delinquency. In M. Tonry & N. Morris (Eds.), *Crime and justice: A review of research* (Vol. 7, pp. 29–149). Chicago: University of Chicago Press.

McCord, J. (1979). Some child-rearing antecedents of criminal behavior in adult men. *Journal of Personality and Social Psychology, 9,* 1477–1486.

Quinton, D., & Rutter, M. (1988). *Parenting breakdown: The making and breaking of intergenerational links.* Avebury: Gower.

Quinton, D., Rutter, M., & Rowlands, O. (1975). An evaluation of an interview assessment of marriage. *Psychological Medicine, 6,* 577–586.

Robins, L. N. (1966). *Deviant children grown up.* Baltimore: Williams & Wilkins.

Robins, L. N. (1978). Sturdy childhood predictors of adult antisocial behaviour: Replications from longitudinal studies. *Psychological Medicine, 8,* 611–622.

Robins, L. N., Schoenberg, S. P., Holmes, S. J., Ratcliff, K., Benham, A., & Works, J. (1985). Early home environment and retrospective recall: A test for concordance between siblings with and without psychiatric disorders. *American Journal of Orthopsychiatry, 55,* 27–41.

Rutter, M. (1967). A children's behaviour questionnaire for completion by teachers: Preliminary findings. *Journal of Child Psychology and Psychiatry, 8,* 1–11.

Rutter, M., & Brown, G. W. (1966). The reliability of measures of family life and relationships in families containing a psychiatric patient. *Social Psychiatry, 1,* 38–53.

Rutter, M., Cox, A., Tupling, C., Berger, M., & Yule, W. (1975). Attainment and adjustment in two geographical areas. I. The prevalence of psychiatric disorders. *British Journal of Psychiatry, 126,* 493–509.

Rutter, M., & Quinton, D. (1984). Parental psychiatric disorder: Effects on children. *Psychological Medicine, 14,* 853–880.

Vaughn, C. (1989). Expressed emotion in family relationships. *Journal of Child Psychology and Psychiatry, 30,* 13–22.

Wing, J. K., & Hailey, A. M. (1972). *Evaluating a community psychiatric service: The Camberwell Register, 1964–1971.* Oxford University Press.

Winship, C., & Mare, R. D. (1990). Log linear models with missing data: A latent class approach. *Sociological Methodology, 20,* 333–367.

Zoccolillo, M., Pickles, A., Quinton, D., & Rutter, M. (1992). The outcome of childhood conduct disorder: Implications for defining adult personality disorder and conduct disorder. *Psychological Medicine, 22,* 971–986.

4 Corporal punishment of children and adult depression and suicidal ideation

MURRAY A. STRAUS

Since the pioneering study of Elmer and Gregg (1967) there has been increasing recognition that the damage to children from physical "abuse" can involve more than broken bones and burns. There is compelling evidence that physically abused children also tend to suffer serious psychological injury and are at greater risk of engaging in crime (Egeland, Sroufe, & Erickson, 1983; McCord, 1988; Widom, 1989; Wolfe, 1987). However, the idea that ordinary and legal corporal punishment of a misbehaving child may also increase the probability of delinquency and later marital and psychological problems is seldom voiced in the United States. That should not be surprising because spanking and other forms of corporal punishment of children are routine events that are legal and for the most part expected of parents (Straus, 1991).[1] Moreover, there are deeply ingrained psychological and cultural reasons why the possible harmful effects of corporal punishment are not perceived (Carson, 1987; Greven, 1991; Straus, 1994).

As a result of this combination of legal and moral legitimacy and psychological commitment, the general public and social scientists assume that corporal punishment is *not* an important social or psychological problem. The underlying assumption of this chapter is the opposite. It is that corporal punishment puts a child at risk of serious injury, both physical and psychological. To the extent that this assumption is correct, the wide use of corporal punishment is a major problem of U.S. society. Evidence that corporal punishment increases the probability of later physical violence by the child was presented in a previous paper (Straus, 1991). This chapter takes the investigation of the harmful effects of corporal punishment one step further by testing the hypothesis that the more corporal punishment experienced as a child, the greater the probability of depression and suicidal thoughts as an adult.

59

Corporal punishment and depression

Depression is one of the most frequently occurring mental health problems. Depression that is serious enough to require clinical intervention is estimated to affect at least 1%, or about a million Americans (Charney & Weissman, 1988), and some estimates are 6% of the population (Holden, 1991). Less debilitating but still serious depression affects a much larger number. Although depression is a widespread and ancient human problem, as well as the subject of voluminous research, the relationship between corporal punishment and depression seems to have been ignored by psychologists, psychiatrists, and sociologists. Freud's essay "A Child Is Being Beaten" (1919), for example, is in a "Contribution to the Study of the Origin of Sexual Perversions," not the origin of depression. Moreover, the essay is about *fantasies* of being beaten. Freud denied the significance of actual beatings.[2] Nevertheless, Freud believed that "we have long known that no neurotic harbors thoughts of suicide which are not murderous impulses against others re-directed upon himself" (quoted in Greven, 1991, p. 129).

The lack of empirical research on the link between corporal punishment and depression is probably not accidental. It seems to be a case of "selective inattention," as was the lack of research on wife beating until the women's movement forced the issue into the public agenda. In the case of wife beating, the perceptual blinders were part of the selective perception of a male dominant society. In the case of corporal punishment, Greven (1991) suggests that the perceptual blinders are a result of the almost universal early experience with corporal punishment. On the basis of extensive historical data Greven (1991) concluded that corporal punishment has been ignored precisely because close to 100% of Americans are products of that system. He argues that the morality of corporal punishment is built into the deepest layers of personality by repeated exposure to it by persons the infant or toddler loves and depends on for survival. Ironically, the effect might be even more powerful for the fortunate few Americans whose parents stopped spanking after age 4 because experiences before age 3 or 4 are seldom part of conscious memory. The traumatic experience of being attacked by a parent as an infant or toddler might therefore tend to be an unconscious but powerful and continuing part of the psyche.

Corporal punishment also does not figure prominently in the thinking of the few sociologists who have studied children or even of child psychologists. My analysis of 10 of the leading child psychology textbooks found that they devoted an average of only half a page to corporal punishment despite the fact that it is an almost universal part of the socialization experience. In addition, little thought is given to the harm that corporal punishment might produce and the processes that might produce later harmful effects such as physical aggression and depression. In short, there has been no theory. The lack of empirical research on corporal punishment and depression therefore also reflects the fact that, until recently, there has been no theory positing such a relationship. However, Greven (1991) presents just such a theory.

Greven's theory holds that "depression often is a delayed response to the suppression of childhood anger . . . from being physically hit and hurt . . . by adults . . . whom the child loves and on whom he or she depends for nurturance and life itself" (Greven, 1991, p. 129). Greven's theory, and his most compelling evidence, involve the religious tradition of Calvinism and evangelical Protestantism. He provides abundant evidence that "melancholy and depression have been persistent themes in the family history, religious experience, and emotional lives of Puritans, evangelicals, fundamentalists and Pentecostals for centuries." Greven also provides extensive historical evidence on the frequency and severity of corporal punishment among these devout Protestants. He then argues:

The long-sustained persistence of melancholy and depression among twice-born Protestants is clearly no accident, since it has consistently been paralleled by the tradition of assault, coercion, and violence against children committed with the rod, the belt, the hand and other such instruments of parental discipline. . . . From all this historical evidence, it ought to be clear that depression is often the central mood characteristic of adults whose bodies were assaulted, whose wills were broken in childhood, and whose anger was forcibly suppressed. The rage and resentment never disappear; they just take more covert and dangerous forms, dangerous to the self, and potentially to others.

Depression rooted in anger remains so potent because it often begins so early – in the first three years of life, precisely the period corporal punishment advocates have always stressed as critical for the start of physical punishments. . . . The first assaults on children's bodies and spirits generally commences before conscious memory can recall them later. The unconscious thus becomes the repository of rage, resistance, and desire for revenge that small children feel when being struck by the adults they love. . . . Though they cannot remember consciously what happened to them during the first three or four years of life, the ancient angers persist while the adult conscience directs rage inward upon the self. These people hurt themselves just as their parents hurt them. (pp. 131–132)

Greven's theory is a highly plausible interpretation of the rich historical evidence he presents. However, although the evidence on the frequency of corporal punishment and depression among fundamentalists is clear, he does not provide empirical evidence showing that it is the corporal punishment that accounts for the depression, or even that the two are correlated. A test of Greven's theory using historical evidence is possible, at least in principle because even fundamentalist Protestants varied widely in their use of corporal punishment. Consequently, it might be possible to investigate whether depression occurred at a higher rate among those who experienced the most corporal punishment. Greven does not provide that type of data, and it may not be possible to do so. However, his theory can also be tested using data on contemporary families. The research reported in this chapter does that by examining the extent to which the experiences of people who participated in the 1985 National Family Violence Survey correspond to Greven's theory.

Method

Sample

A unique aspect of this study is that it is based on a large and nationally representative sample of U.S. couples interviewed for the 1985 National Family Violence Survey (Straus & Gelles, 1986, 1990). Interviews with the 6,002 respondents were conducted by telephone in the summer of 1985 (for information regarding the validity of telephone interviews in this survey, see Straus & Gelles, 1986, p. 472). To be eligible for inclusion, the respondent had to be age 18 or older and either (1) presently married, (2) presently living as a man–woman couple, or (3) a single parent with a child under 18 living with the parent, including divorced or separated parents. The response rate was 84%. Of the 6,002 respondents, between 4,745 and 5,700 had no missing data on the variables needed for the different analyses to be reported. Further information on the sampling design and the characteristics of the sample is given in Straus and Gelles (1986, 1990).

Measure of corporal punishment

Respondents were asked: "Thinking about when you yourself were a teenager, about how often would you say your mother or stepmother used corporal punishment, like slapping or hitting you? Think about the year in which this happened the most. Never, Once, Twice, 3–5 times, 6–10 times, 11–20 times, More than 20 times." This was followed by a parallel question asking about the corporal punishment the respondent experienced at the hands of his or her father. This is far from an ideal measure because the validity and reliability of recall data on events that took place many years earlier is questionable. Consequently, there is a need to consider the validity of the data.

Validity of the corporal punishment data

Selective recall. Selective recall could threaten the validity of the findings if those who develop psychological problems tend to remember more negative things about their childhood, such as having been hit as a teen, even though such punishment did not happen to them any more often than to those without psychological problems. That possibility is less likely because the percentage of people recalling being hit by a parent during adolescence is almost identical to the percentage of parents who reported hitting an adolescent during the year of the survey (Straus, 1983; Straus & Donnelly, 1993; Wauchope & Straus, 1990), and with corresponding percentages from studies based on interviews with teenage children reviewed in Straus and Donnelly (1993).

Statistically deviant. The data to be presented and those from previous studies indicate that half or more of adolescent children are hit by their parents. This indicates that the respondents in this study who were corporally punished during their teen years, since they are at least half of all American children, represent the modal situation, not a small and highly deviant subset of all teenagers.

Deviance in the normative sense. Many surveys show that over 80% of the population approves of corporal punishment, and many show approval rates in the 90% range (Straus, 1991). Unfortunately, the age of the child is not specified in those surveys and the approval rates are likely to be lower for hitting a 13- or 14-year-old. However, the New Hampshire child abuse survey (Moore & Straus, 1987) asked a representative sample of 914 New Hampshire parents if they agreed or disagreed with the statement "Sometimes it's a good idea for parents to slap their teenage child who talks back to them." Thirty-one percent agreed, 23% were neutral or "mildly disagreed," and only 46% strongly disagreed. I suggest that almost all of the 54% who did not "strongly disagree" really agreed at least somewhat. If this is correct, hitting a teenage child is far from a normatively deviant type of behavior.

The unique effects of corporal punishment of adolescents. It is possible that findings based on corporal punishment during adolescence may not apply to corporal punishment experienced as a toddler or young child. Concern over this potential source of error is somewhat mitigated by the results of previous research that indicates that corporal punishment of even very young children is associated with increased rates of such problematic behavior as physical aggressiveness and limited development of an internalized conscience (Sears, Maccoby, & Levin, 1957), as well as increased interpersonal problems with other children, delinquency, and aggression (Straus, 1991, in press; Vissing, Straus, Gelles, & Harrop, 1991).

Measures of depression

Depressive symptoms. Identifying who is depressed in a large cross-sectional sample of Americans is a difficult and controversial task. The method used in the 1985 National Family Violence Survey is based on the Psychiatric Epidemiological Research Instrument, or PERI (Dohrenwend, Kranoff, Askenasy, & Dohrenwend, 1976). The PERI provides data on a number of different psychiatric problems and is much longer than could be included in the half-hour interviews we conducted. The measure of depression that we used consists of the following four PERI items that Newman (1984) found to be most indicative of depression:

> Been bothered by feelings of sadness or depression.
> Felt very bad and worthless.
> Had times when you couldn't help wondering if anything was worthwhile anymore.
> Felt completely hopeless about everything.

Respondents were asked to indicate how often in the past year each of these things occurred using the following categories: Never = 0, Almost never = 1,

Sometimes = 2, Fairly often = 3, Very often = 4. These items were factor analyzed using the SPSS principal components program. The analysis found a single factor that accounted for 66% of the variance. The Depressive Symptoms Index used for this study is the factor-weighted sum of these four items and has an alpha coefficient of reliability of .82.

Suicidal ideation. Suicidal thoughts often accompany depression but are a separate phenomenon. Consequently we asked our respondents if they had "thought about taking your own life" in the previous 12 months. The response categories Yes and No were coded as 1 and 0.

Measurement of covariates

The analyses described later controlled for four variables that are known to be confounded with corporal punishment, depression, or both. Socioeconomic status (SES) was measured by factoring the following five items using the SPSS/PC principal components analysis: education of the wife and the husband, their occupational prestige scores, and the combined income of the couple. This resulted in one factor that explained 56% of the variance and has an alpha reliability coefficient of .80. *Heavy drinking* was measured by the top two categories of the *Drinking types* described in Kaufman Kantor and Straus (1987). Marital violence was coded as being present if, in response to the violence scale of the Conflict Tactics Scales (Straus, 1979, 1990), the respondent reported one or more violent incidents in the 12 months prior to the interview. Witnessing violence between parents was measured by asking respondents, "Now, thinking about the whole time when you were a teenager, were there occasions when your father/stepfather hit your mother/stepmother or threw something at her?" If the respondent answered affirmatively, he or she was then asked to indicate "How often did that happen" using the following response categories: once, twice, 3–5 times, 6–10 times, 11–20 times, and more than 20 times. This question was then repeated for witnessing violence by the mother or stepmother and the two scores were summed.

Specification of the model to control for confounding with other variables

Many risk factors, such as SES and gender, have been linked to depression in addition to the hypothesized effect of corporal punishment. Unless such variables are controlled, the findings might be spurious. For example, low-SES parents use somewhat more corporal punishment (Straus, 1994), and low-SES persons also have a higher rate of most types of psychological problems (Dohrenwend et al., 1992). This confounding could produce an association between corporal punishment and depression even if corporal punishment does not increase the probability of depression. Consequently, a 7×2 analysis of covariance was used. The 7-level variable is corporal punishment ranging in frequency from never to 20 or more times. The two-level variable is gender of the subject. For the reasons already noted, the following four covariates were included: heavy drinking, marital violence, witnessing violence between parents, and SES.

Four analyses of covariance were computed. The first used scores on the Depressive Symptoms Index as the dependent variable and the frequency of being corporally punished by the father as the main independent variable. The second repeated this but with corporal punishment by the mother as the independent variable. The third and fourth analyses were identical except that the dependent variable was the percentage who thought about committing suicide during the preceding 12 months.

Eight other analyses of covariance were computed. They follow the same pattern but the dependent variables were the four indicators making up the Depressive Symptoms Index.

Replication using logistic regression

The hypotheses concerning *depressive symptoms* and *suicidal ideation* were replicated using logistic regression or "logit" (Aldrich & Nelson, 1984). These replications provide information on the robustness of the findings and also a somewhat different approach to the measure of depressive symptoms. The approach is different because the logit analysis used as the dependent variable a dichotomized version of the Depressive Symptoms Index. A division point at the 90th percentile was chosen because, as noted by Jacobson and Revenstorf (1988), the important issue, both theoretically and clinically, is the occurrence of a high or chronic level of depressive symptoms. The results were graphed using the conditional-plotting technique developed by Hamilton (1990).

Prevalence and chronicity of corporal punishment

Prevalence

The percentages in the top row of Table 4.1 headed "By either" show that about half of all Americans can recall corporal punishment during their teen years and that more teenage sons are hit than daughters. The remaining percentages in the top row show that more sons are hit than daughters, regardless of whether the hitting is done by the mother or the father.[3] As previously noted, these rates are very close to those obtained by interviewing parents of teenage children (Straus & Donnelly, 1993; Wauchope & Straus, 1990).

Table 4.1 also shows that there is little difference in the percentage of mothers and fathers who hit a teenage son. However, when it comes to hitting daughters, 26.7% of fathers did so, compared with 35.6% of mothers, which is a 33% higher rate.[4]

Table 4.1. *Prevalence and chronicity of corporal punishment of teens by gender of parent and child*

Frequency	Corporal punishment					
	By either		By mother		By father	
	Daughter	Son	Daughter	Son	Daughter	Son
Annual prevalence						
Percent hit once						
or more	44.0	58.2	35.6	43.5	26.7	44.8
N	3,337	2,099	3,504	2,216	3,434	2,171
Annual chronicity						
Descriptive statistics						
Mean	6.6	8.1	5.6	6.5	4.6	5.4
SD	7.5	8.0	6.9	7.1	6.3	6.6
Median	4.0	4.0	2.0	4.0	2.0	2.0
Percentage distributions						
Once	23.2	17.3	28.8	20.6	41.5	30.9
Twice	19.8	15.8	22.5	19.3	21.6	20.0
3–5 times	25.0	23.6	22.9	28.8	17.3	24.1
6–10 times	13.5	17.8	10.6	12.9	8.1	10.9
11–20 times	7.8	11.6	7.0	9.3	5.2	7.0
21+ times	10.8	13.8	8.3	9.1	6.3	7.1
N for chronicity	1,474	1,213	1,270	970	895	952

Chronicity. Among those who experienced corporal punishment, the section headed "Annual chronicity" in Table 4.1 shows that in the majority of the cases it occurred more than once during the referent year. Twenty-six percent of the women recalled six or more incidents of having been hit by their mother and 20% having been hit this often by their father. Thirty-one percent of the men recalled having been hit as a teen six or more times by their mother and a quarter having been hit this often by their father.

Corporal punishment and depressive symptoms

Corporal punishment by mothers

Table 4.2 gives the results of the analyses of covariance to test the hypothesis that the more corporal punishment, the higher the Depression Symptom Index score, and Figure 4.1 plots the findings. As with many other studies, the women's

Table 4.2. *Depressive Symptoms Index by corporal punishment, analysis of covariance*

| Source of variance | df | Corporal punishment by | | | |
| | | Mother | | Father | |
		F	$p<$	F	$p<$
Main effects					
Corporal punishment	6	10.54	.001	5.57	.001
Gender of respondent	1	108.81	.001	113.33	.001
Interaction effect					
Corporal punishment by					
gender	6	1.05	.391	1.83	.089
Covariates					
Socioeconomic status	1	37.02	.001	38.37	.001
Husband-to-wife violence	1	167.66	.001	163.32	.001
Heavy drinking	1	0.02	.899	0.29	.594
Violence between					
respondent's parents	1	42.74	.001	40.55	.001

Depressive Symptoms Index score is higher than the men's. For the men, there is a clear tendency for depressive symptoms to increase with each increment of corporal punishment. For the women in this sample, the slope starts out even more steeply than that for the men, but then declines for the highest categories of corporal punishment. Rather than attempting to interpret that decrease, it seems more plausible to regard it as the result of small *n* fluctuations and to interpret the findings as evidence that is consistent with the hypothesis.

Component items

The analyses just described were repeated separately for each of the four items making up the depression index. All four depressive symptoms were found to be significantly related to corporal punishment, but the relationships were not as regular or as strong as those based on the combined effect of all six indicators in the form of the depression index. This is probably because single indicator measures are generally less reliable and less valid measures of an underlying latent construct.

Interaction and partial effects

The third row of Table 4.2 provides data on whether the relation between corporal punishment and depression is different for sons and daughters. The parallel lines on Figure 4.1 suggest that the effects are very similar, and this is confirmed by the

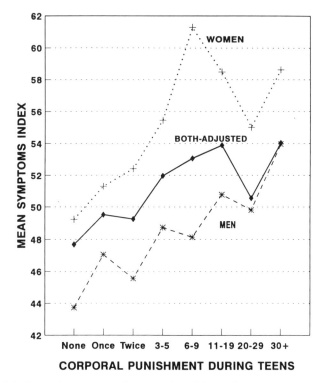

Figure 4.1. Depressive symptoms by corporal punishment by parents.

third row of Table 4.2, which indicates that there is not a significant interaction between gender of the child and corporal punishment. Finally, it is important to note that the significant effect of corporal punishment occurs despite controlling for possible confounding with the five other variables – SES, gender of the child, husband-to-wife violence, excessive drinking, and witnessing violence between parents. Table 4.2 shows that four of these variables are significantly related to depression. Thus, it is remarkable that corporal punishment per se accounts for any of the variance in depression after subtracting out their effect.

Gender of parent differences

Perhaps there is something unique about the effect of a mother hitting a teenage son or daughter. According to the presumed traditional pattern of gender roles, that should be the father's job. If so, "physical discipline" by fathers might not have the same adverse consequences. To test this, the analyses were replicated separately for corporal punishment by mothers and by fathers. The results were very similar to those shown in Table 4.2 and Figure 4.1.

Corporal punishment and suicidal thoughts

The relation of corporal punishment to suicidal ideation was examined because of its practical and theoretical importance. The theoretical issues are illustrated by Freud's observation (cited earlier) that suicide is "murderous impulses against others re-directed upon himself." Suicidal ideation was measured by asking how often the respondent "Thought about taking your own life" during the preceding 12 months.

The results of testing the hypothesis that corporal punishment is associated with an increased probability of suicidal thoughts are given in Table 4.3 and Figure 4.2. The findings are in some ways similar and in other ways different from the relation of corporal punishment to the Depressive Symptoms Index. They are similar in that with increasing amounts of corporal punishment, both depressive symptoms and thinking about suicide increase. In addition, replications testing the hypothesis separately for corporal punishment by mother and by father produced results that are very similar to those for depression. However, there are also important differences between the findings on depression and those on suicidal ideation. The main difference is that depression tends to increase with even one instance of corporal punishment in adolescence, whereas the plot lines for suicidal ideation in Figure 4.2 tend toward an exponential relationship. That is, little or no increases in suicidal thoughts occur until the two highest categories of corporal punishment are reached. Then the frequency of thinking about suicide jumps sharply. Perhaps this is because suicide is such an extreme step that it may take a high frequency of corporal punishment to do something as extreme as thinking about killing oneself.

Table 4.3. *Suicidal thoughts by corporal punishment, analysis of covariance*

| Source of variance | df | Corporal punishment by | | | |
| | | Mother | | Father | |
		F	$p<$	F	$p<$
Main effects					
Corporal punishment	6	6.81	.001	4.84	.001
Gender of respondent	1	2.86	.091	6.06	.014
Interaction effect					
Corporal punishment by gender	6	1.49	.178	0.34	.918
Covariates					
Socioeconomic status	1	0.67	.415	0.85	.357
Husband-to-wife violence	1	122.45	.001	112.62	.001
Heavy drinking	1	0.03	.862	0.46	.498
Violence between respondent's parents	1	31.48	.001	34.72	.001

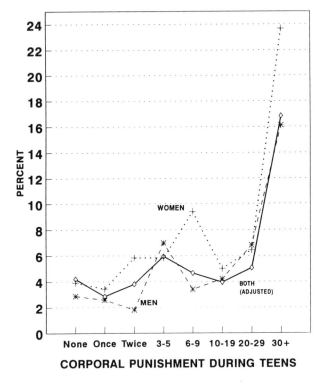

Figure 4.2. Thought about suicide by corporal punishment by parents.

Logistic regression analyses

The hypotheses were retested using logistic regression (logit) for several reasons. The most general reason is to examine the robustness of the findings across a different statistical analysis method. A more specific reason is that suicidal ideation was measured as a dichotomy, and unlike analysis of covariance, logit is intended for use with a categorical dependent variable. In addition, by categorizing the subjects into those who had depression scores at the 90th percentile or higher, one can use logit to test the hypothesis that corporal punishment tends to increase not only the average depression index score, but also the probability of being more severely depressed.

Figure 4.3 shows that the more corporal punishment experienced as a teenager, the greater the probability of being at or above the 90th percentile on the Depressive Symptoms Index (see Table 4.4 for regression coefficients). The separate plot lines in Figure 4.3 also show that the relationship holds regardless of whether the respondent experienced husband-to-wife violence in the previous 12 months (upper line) or did not (lower line); but in the latter case, the slope is considerably

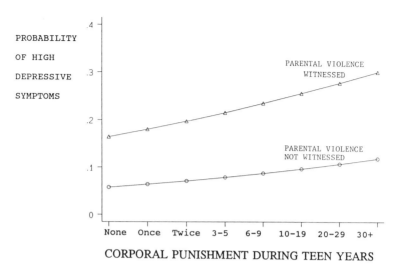

Figure 4.3. Probability of high depressive symptoms by corporal punishment during teen years.

Table 4.4. *Logistic regression analyses of depression and suicidal ideation on corporal punishment and five other variables*

Independent variable	Odds ratio	SE	t	p<
Depression[a]				
Corporal punishment	1.116	0.030	4.088	.001
Gender (1 = female)	1.869	0.227	5.145	.001
Socioeconomic status	0.978	0.003	−7.493	.001
Husband-to-wife violence	3.077	0.384	8.999	.001
Heavy drinking	1.295	0.240	1.394	.082
Violence between parents	1.233	0.181	1.429	.077
Suicidal ideation[b]				
Corporal punishment	1.118	0.040	3.120	.001
Gender (1 = female)	1.358	0.214	1.946	.003
Socioeconomic status	1.002	0.004	0.489	.310
Husband-to-wife violence	3.825	0.605	8.476	.001
Heavy drinking	1.251	0.300	0.934	.176
Violence between parents	1.745	0.314	3.096	.001

[a] Chi-square = 221.18, $n = 4,524$, $p < .001$.
[b] Chi-square = 117.33, $n = 4,534$, $p < .001$.

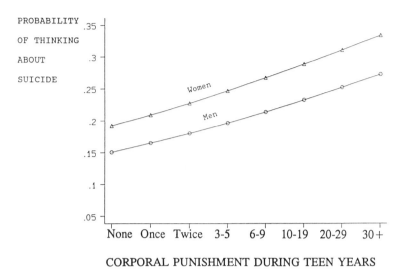

Figure 4.4. Probability of thinking about suicide by corporal punishment during teen years.

smaller. Figure 4.4 shows that the more corporal punishment experienced as a teenager, the greater the probability of thinking about suicide, and that this applies about equally to women and men.

Discussion and conclusions

This research tested the idea that the psychological damage to children that results from being physically attacked by a parent is not restricted to the extreme forms of violence known as physical "abuse" but also applies to the ordinary and legal corporal punishment of children.

About half the respondents in this nationally representative sample recalled having been hit by their parents when they were adolescents. This prevalence rate, which is consistent with the findings of other studies, is important because it indicates the degree to which physical violence is used in the socialization of U.S. children and also because it indicates that the relationship found between corporal punishment and depression cannot be attributed to a small minority of cases that fall outside the realm of ordinary corporal punishment. Confidence in the findings is further strengthened by the following. First, the relationship of corporal punishment to depressive symptoms and suicidal thoughts is net of a number of variables known to be related to depression and suicidal thoughts. Regardless of whether there was marital violence, and for men as well as women, for both low- and high-SES persons, for those who did and did not have a drinking problem, and for those who witnessed violence between their parents and those who did not, the more corporal punishment they experienced as a teen, the higher the Depressive Symptoms Index and the greater the occurrence of thoughts about committing suicide.

This is not to say that gender, SES, marital violence, and witnessing violence as a child are unrelated to depression. Far from it. The results of this study show that women have a significantly higher level of depressive symptoms than do men (which is consistent with numerous other studies), that low-SES respondents have more depressive symptoms (which is also consistent with many previous studies), and that being in a violent marriage is strongly associated with a high average number of depressive symptoms (Stets & Straus, 1990), as is witnessing violence between one's parents (Straus, 1992). This significant net effect means that after subtracting out the overlap of corporal punishment with these variables, corporal punishment by itself remains related to depression and suicidal ideation. It remains possible, of course, that uncontrolled factors account for the relationships obtained between corporal punishment and depression and suicidal ideation.

Second, there is no significant interaction of corporal punishment with gender of the child. Thus, corporal punishment tends to produce essentially the same increase in depressive symptoms for men and women.

Third, separate analyses were done for corporal punishment administered by fathers and mothers. The results of the two analyses are very similar. Thus, corporal punishment increases the probability of depression, regardless of whether it is administered by the child's mother or father.

Fourth, all the analyses were replicated using two other measures of marital violence – violence by the wife, and total couple violence. The results of controlling for these two variables produced findings that are essentially the same as those shown in Figures 4.1 and 4.2 and in Tables 4.2 and 4.3. Fifth, the analyses were also replicated using logistic regression, with results that led to identical conclusions.

Methodological problems

An important methodological problem arises because no data were available that would have permitted excluding from the sample those whose parents engaged not only in ordinary corporal punishment, but also in more severe acts of violence, that is, physical abuse. This confounding of ordinary corporal punishment with abuse is particularly likely for respondents who experienced frequent corporal punishment and might account for the relationships reported. While this confounding might have produced the finding that corporal punishment is related to depression and suicidal thoughts, research reported elsewhere (Straus, 1994) makes that possibility less likely. That research avoided the confounding of corporal punishment and physical abuse because it was possible to remove from the sample all children who were physically abused. In addition, it minimized the selective recall problem because it used data for the current year as reported by the parents. With these two sources of artifactual findings removed, the results still showed that the more corporal punishment is experienced, the higher the probability of the child having high levels of physical aggression, delinquency, and interpersonal problems with other children.

A second methodological problem stems from the fact that this study, like a previously reported study of corporal punishment and crime (Straus, 1991), is based on cross-sectional data. The findings in the previous paper suggest that the use of corporal punishment to correct a child's misbehavior in the long run has the opposite effect because it is associated with an *increased* probability of subsequent aggression and crime. However, the causal direction of the findings is ambiguous. Rather than corporal punishment causing the child to become aggressive or delinquent, it could be the other way around. Parents typically spank a child *because* he or she hit another child or hits them. Thus, it is just as plausible to say that the child's aggression or other misbehavior caused the spanking as it is to argue that spanking teaches aggression. The problem of which is cause and which is effect may be less serious in the present case because the hypothesized outcome (depression and thinking about suicide) is probably something for which parents do not usually hit a child. Nevertheless a longitudinal or experimental study is needed to deal with the question of causal direction.

Neurobiological processes

Another approach to investigating the processes linking corporal punishment and depression is suggested by research on the neurobiology of depression. At a recent conference on affective disorders there was wide agreement that depression is a heterogeneous disorder that may be caused by many things, but probably involves a final biological process of enduring structural and chemical changes in the brain:

One fact that could play a role in such long term changes is stress. Both animals and people who experience chronic stress respond by secreting glucocorticosteroids known as the "stress hormones." . . . this is the most robust biological concomitant of depression – showing in up to 50% of cases, especially severe ones. (Holden, 1991, p. 1451)

Several other *permanent* changes in brain functioning were reported as occurring in both animals and humans who experience continuing stress.

For children, one such continuing stress may be corporal punishment. It often begins in infancy and is particularly frequent for toddlers, many of whom are hit almost daily, and a third of whom are hit almost once a week (Straus, 1994). As reported earlier in this chapter, corporal punishment continues into the teen years for about half of all U.S. children. The changes in brain structure and functioning associated with the stress of having been physically assaulted for 13 or more years might explain the link between corporal punishment and depression reported in this chapter. It would be relatively easy to test this theory because it does not necessarily require either experimental or longitudinal data. It can be done by obtaining information on the chronicity of corporal punishment – readily provided by parents – and the level of "stress hormones" produced by children subjected to varying levels of corporal punishment.

The longitudinal, experimental, and neurobiological studies of corporal punishment suggested earlier are urgently needed because close to 100% of U.S. children experience corporal punishment (Straus, 1994; Wauchope & Straus, 1990) and because of the seriousness of the harmful effects that might be caused by corporal punishment. If longitudinal or experimental replications of the present findings confirm that corporal punishment is a risk factor for depression and suicide – or if neurobiological studies find that the more frequent the use of corporal punishment, the greater the level of brain functions associated with depression – it would have far-reaching implications for the "primary prevention" of mental illness.

NOTES

This chapter is part of a research program on corporal punishment at the Family Research Laboratory, University of New Hampshire, Durham, NH 03824. A program description and publications list will be sent on request. It is a pleasure to express appreciation to the members of the Family Research Laboratory Seminar for valuable comments and suggestions. The work has been supported by grants from several organizations, including the National Institute of Mental Health (grants R01MH40027 and T32MH15161), National Science Foundation (grant SES8520232), and the University of New Hampshire.

1 There is no standard definition of corporal punishment or physical punishment. In this chapter *corporal punishment* is defined as the use of physical force with the intention of causing a child to experience pain but not injury, for purposes of correction or control of the child's behavior. The most frequent forms are spanking, slapping, grabbing, or shoving a child "roughly" (i.e., with more force than is needed to move the child), and hitting with certain traditionally acceptable objects such as a hairbrush, belt, or paddle. However, the operationalization of corporal punishment in this paper (see "Methods" section) excludes hitting with an object on the grounds that it poses a significant risk of causing an injury that needs medical treatment and therefore crosses the line from corporal punishment to physical abuse. This operationalization therefore differs from the laws of every state in the United States, which give parents the right to hit a child with an object provided no serious injury results. It also differs from traditional cultural norms that sanction the use of objects such as hairbrushes, belts, and paddles. Excluding hitting with objects can also be justified on the basis of the gradual reduction in the frequency and severity of corporal punishment in U.S. society, which has led many people to regard hitting with such objects as physical abuse rather than corporal punishment.

Similar ambiguity applies to *spanking*. To some it means slapping a child repeatedly on the buttocks, traditionally the bare buttocks. But for most contemporary Americans, I believe it means any slapping or hitting, probably the most frequent form of which is to slap a child's hand for touching something. I will use the terms *corporal punishment, physical punishment, hitting,* and *spanking* as synonyms.

2 Greven (1991) argues that Freud could not bring himself to acknowledge the legitimate experiential basis for the fantasies of being beaten because he himself was a product of physical punishment and had internalized its values. He makes a similar argument to explain why contemporary psychiatrists and psychologists have not explored the effects of physical punishment.

3 A more detailed analysis of prevalence rates in Straus and Donnelly (1993) focused on consistency between parents in hitting adolescents. Of teenage sons who were victims of

corporal punishment, in just over half (52%) of the cases, they are hit by both parents. If it was only one parent who hit, sons were about equally likely to be hit by the mother (23%) as the father (25%). Of teenage daughters, 41% of those who experienced corporal punishment were hit by both parents. If they were hit by just one of the parents, it was twice as likely to be the mother (39%) than the father (20%).

4 These prevalence rates are for the total sample. However, because of missing data on one or more of the six independent variables, the sample used to examine the hypothesized relationship between corporal punishment and depression was reduced from 5,700 cases to 5,069 for corporal punishment by the mother and to 4,745 for corporal punishment by the father. Although those Ns are still very large, the loss of 11 and 17% of the cases, respectively, can bias the sample. The comparison of the prevalence rate for the reduced sample with the rates in Table 4.1 shows that all are within 3 percentage points.

REFERENCES

Aldrich, J. H., & Nelson, F. D. (1984). *Linear probability, logit and probit models*. Newberry Park, CA: Sage.

Carson, B. A. (1987, July). *Content analysis of childrearing manuals' advice about spanking*. Paper presented at the Third National Family Violence Research Conference, University of New Hampshire, Durham, NH.

Charney, E., & Weissman, M. M. (1988). Epidemiology of depressive and manic syndromes. In A. Georgotas & R. Cancro (Eds.), *Depression and mania* (pp. 26–52). New York: Elsevier.

Dohrenwend, B. P., Levav, I., Shrout, P. E., Schwartz, S., Naven, G., Link, B. G., Skodol, A. E., & Stueve, A. (1992). Socioeconomic status and psychiatric disorders: The causation-selection issue. *Science, 225,* 946–951.

Dohrenwend, B. S., Kranoff, L., Askenasy, A. R., & Dohrenwend, B. P. (1976). Exemplification of a method for scaling life events: The PERI life events scale. *Journal of Health and Social Behavior, 19,* 205–229.

Egeland, B., Sroufe, L. A., & Erickson, M. (1983). The developmental consequence of different patterns of maltreatment. *Child Abuse and Neglect, 7,* 459–469.

Elmer, E., & Gregg, G. (1967). Developmental characteristics of abused children. *Pediatrics, 69,* 596–602.

Greven, P. (1991). *Spare the child: The religious roots of physical punishment and the psychological impact of physical abuse*. New York: Knopf.

Hamilton, L. C. (1990). *Statistics with stata*. Pacific Grove, CA: Brooks/Cole.

Holden, C. (1991). Depression: The news isn't depressing. *Science, 254,* 1450–1452.

Jacobson, N. S., & Revenstorf, D. (1988). Statistics for assessing the clinical significance of psychotherapy techniques: Issues, problems and new developments. *Behavioral Assessment, 10,* 133–145.

Kaufman Kantor, G., & Straus, M. A. (1987). The drunken bum theory of wife beating. *Social Problems, 34,* 213–230.

McCord, J. (1988). Parental aggressiveness and physical punishment in long-term perspective. In G. T. Hotaling, D. Finkelhor, J. T. Kirkpatrick, & M. A. Straus (Eds.), *Family abuse and its consequences*. Newbury Park, CA: Sage.

Moore, D. W., & Straus, M. A. (1987). *Violence of parents towards their children, New Hampshire, 1987*. Report submitted to the New Hampshire Task Force on Child Abuse and Neglect. Durham: Family Research Laboratory, University of New Hampshire.

Newmann, J. P. (1984). Sex differences in symptoms of depression: Clinical disorder or normal distress. *Journal of Health and Social Behavior, 25,* 136–159.

Sears, R. R., Maccoby, E. E., & Levin, H. (1957). *Patterns of child rearing*. Evanston, IL: Row, Peterson.

Stets, J. E., & Straus, M. A. (1990). Gender differences in reporting marital violence and its medical and psychological consequences. In M. A. Straus & R. J. Gelles (Eds.), *Physical violence in American families: Risk factors and adaptations to violence in 8,145 families*. New Brunswick, NJ: Transaction Publishers.

Straus, M. A. (1979). Measuring intrafamily conflict and violence: The conflict tactics (CT) scales. *Journal of Marriage and the Family, 41,* 75–88.

Straus, M. A. (1983). Corporal punishment, child abuse, and wife-beating: What do they have in common? In D. Finkelhor, R. J. Gelles, G. T. Hotaling, & M. A. Straus (Eds.), *The dark side of families: Current family violence research* (pp. 213–234). Beverly Hills, CA: Sage.

Straus, M. A. (1990). The conflict tactics scales and its critics: An evaluation and new data on validity and reliability. In M. A. Straus & R. J. Gelles (Eds.), *Physical violence in American families: Risk factors and adaptations to violence in 8,145 families*. New Brunswick, NJ: Transaction Publishers.

Straus, M. A. (1991). Discipline and deviance: Physical punishment of children and violence and other crime in adulthood. *Social Problems, 38*(2), 101–123.

Straus, M. A. (1992). Children as witness to marital violence: A risk factor for life long problems among a nationally representative sample of American men and women. *Report of the 23rd Ross roundtable on children and violence*. Columbus, OH: Ross Laboratories.

Straus, M. A. (1994). *Beating the devil out of them: Corporal punishment in American families*. Lexington, MA: Lexington Books.

Straus, M. A., & Donnelly, D. A. (1993). Corporal Punishment of Teen Age Children in the United States. *Youth and Society, 24,* 419–442.

Straus, M. A., & Gelles, R. J. (1986). Societal change and change in family violence from 1975 to 1985 as revealed by two national surveys. *Journal of Marriage and the Family, 48,* 465–480.

Straus, M. A., & Gelles, R. J. (1990). *Physical violence in American families: Risk factors and adaptations to violence in 8,145 families*. New Brunswick, NJ: Transaction.

Vissing, Y. M., Straus, M. A., Gelles, R. J., & Harrop, J. W. (1991). Verbal aggression by parents and psychosocial problems of children. *Child Abuse and Neglect, 15,* 223–238.

Wauchope, B., & Straus, M. A. (1990). Physical punishment and physical abuse of American children: Incidence rates by age, gender, and occupational class. In M. A. Straus & R. J. Gelles (Eds.), *Physical violence in American families: Risk factors and adaptions to violence in 8,145 Families* (pp. 133–147). New Brunswick, NJ: Transaction.

Widom, C. S. (1989). The cycle of violence. *Science, 244*(4901), 160–166.

Wolfe, D. A. (1987). *Child abuse: Implications for child development and psychopathology: Vol. 10, Developmental and clinical psychology and psychiatry*. Newbury Park, CA: Sage.

II   Family socialization practices and antisocial behavior

5   Coercion as a basis for early age of onset for arrest

GERALD R. PATTERSON

At different developmental stages, antisocial behavior may be learned in very different ways and in very different settings. It is hypothesized that young antisocial children are most likely to acquire antisocial behaviors in the home (Patterson, Reid, & Dishion, 1992). In that setting, the most likely causal mechanism involves contingent use of aversive stimuli in escape-conditioning sequences. On the other hand, it is assumed that those who wait until adolescence to become antisocial are trained by members of the deviant peer group in settings where adult supervision is at a minimum. For them, the causal mechanisms are thought to be modeling, positive reinforcement, and avoidant conditioning rather than escape conditioning. Presumably, the early training in the home leads to early police arrest and chronic offending, whereas training in the peer group during mid-adolescence leads to late arrest but not to chronicity (Patterson, Capaldi, & Bank, 1991).

The present report is focused primarily on the early-onset path to chronic delinquent offending. There is a succession of problems to be considered. First, how is it that one family member reinforces another for being coercive? Much of this unlikely training is supposed to involve the exchange of aversive stimuli and escape-conditioning sequences. What is the evidence for such a process in family interaction? The vast bulk of family interaction, even when it involves aversive stimuli, seems relatively trivial in nature. How can the progression from trivial to high-amplitude coercive behaviors (physical assault) be explained? How does the progression move from coercive behaviors to antisocial behaviors? What is the evidence for the generalization from home to school? How well can we predict from this early training in the home and school to first police arrest and chronic juvenile offending? Each of these questions is considered in turn in this chapter.

Coercion mechanism

Some background assumptions

Very early in the study of coercion mechanisms, several tactical decisions were made. First, learning was differentiated from performance. A child may *learn* a great deal about delinquency or antisocial behavior, but seldom, if ever, *perform* delinquent or antisocial acts. In our society, children learn many forms of antisocial behavior from TV, other family members, and peers. A theory must explain why one child performs these acts at a higher rate than another (Patterson, 1982). The coercion model describes a performance theory for antisocial behavior designed to answer specific questions about what determines the frequency of performed antisocial behaviors. Second, all models that test various aspects of the theory are evaluated in terms of variance accounted for in criterion measures of antisocial behavior. Typically, all of the concepts are assessed by multiple indicators. This means that the theory must define the means for measuring both the determinants and the criterion variables.

Skinner (1969) and others have taken the position that contingencies provided by the social environment may play an important role in determining deviant behavior. Unfortunately, he never articulated the means for testing the deterministic role of reinforcing events as they occur in a natural setting. Like all major theories of human behavior, this theory was essentially based on findings from laboratory analogue studies. The findings strongly suggested that reinforcing events in the social environment *could* account for most of the variance in measures of individual differences in aggressivity. This argument, like other analogue theories about social cognition or imitation, remains unconvincing until it is tested in the real world of social interaction. The present report describes a series of bridging studies designed to reduce the gap between what might serve as determinants for aggression and what works in the real world. How do we transform an analogue model into one that can be tested in natural settings?

The contingencies at issue are embedded in the warp and woof of everyday social interaction. These banal beginnings seem out of place for a process that eventually leads to the high drama of delinquent behavior, chronicity, and violence. In a very real sense, the events that make up the initial process constitute a small fraction (less than 15%) of thousands of social acts and reactions that occur on a daily basis. Because of the limitations in our capacity to process incoming information, most of these events and their correlated antecedents and outcomes slip by unnoticed (Patterson, Reid, & Dishion, 1992). These unattended exchanges, however, determine a substantial part of familial coercive behavior. As a result, the story line provided by each member has little if anything to do with the contingencies that actually shape and maintain these behaviors. It is not that they are deeply buried in a cistern of repressed thoughts and acts; they simply were never placed in long-term memory in the first place. In more ways than we think, we are creatures of the immediate moment.

Escape conditioning

The term *coercion* applies only when aversive events are used contingent on the behavior of another person. For example, a dentist's behavior is aversive, but it is not contingent directly on any of the patient's specific ongoing social behavior. How does one decide whether an event is contingent or not? Events are said to be contingent if, given the occurrence of *A*, there is a significant increase in the likelihood that *B* will follow within the next few seconds (Patterson, 1982). For example, given that a sister teases (*A*), the likelihood is .30 that her brother will respond in kind (*B*). To put that figure into perspective, we need information about the likelihood of *B* given all other possible antecedents (i.e., if the base rate for *B* is only .05, then we might conclude that *A* is really functional in producing *B*). We believe that much of social interaction is made up of tiny two- or three-step probabilistic dances of this kind.

How do we decide which events are aversive and which are not? An early behavior coding system we used listed as many as 14 forms of aversive behavior (e.g., disapprove, argue, whine, yell, tease, hit). Reid (1978) summarizes the definitions for the code categories as well as the extensive series of studies on reactivity to observer presence and the effects of training on reliability. In one series of studies, parents were instructed to behave more positively than they normally did. The findings showed that neither normal nor clinical samples were able to *fake good*. Patterson (1982) reviewed a number of studies that showed high levels of agreement across social agents in their ratings of the aversive qualities for many categories of observed behaviors. Observation data also showed that, generally, the more aversive the event, the less frequent its occurrence and the greater its effect as a suppressant for ongoing prosocial behavior (Patterson & Cobb, 1971).

Mother–problem child dyads experienced a conflict about once every 6 minutes, as compared with once every 12 minutes for normal dyads (Snyder, Edwards, McGraw, Kilgore, & Holton, 1993). In the discussion that follows, it will become apparent that the rates are even higher than this for clinical samples. Earlier clinical studies showed that parents were involved in about 86% of all aversive exchanges involving the problem child (Patterson, 1984). Siblings were also involved in 59% of the aversive interactions with the problem child, which implies that it is commonplace for more than two people to be swept into family conflicts.

Step 1: The intrusion. A recent study of a clinical sample showed that 31% of mothers' behaviors were coded as aversive (Patterson, Reid, & Dishion, 1992). This is one aversive event about every 3 minutes. If the contributions of one or two siblings are taken into account, a problem child in these families must learn to cope with an aversive intrusion by family members an average of once every minute or two. In highly aversive families, coercive behaviors are often an effective means for terminating the aversive intrusions by other family members. In one study, about one-third of the problem child's coercive behaviors were in reaction to aversive intrusions (Patterson, 1982). Typically, the intrusions are minor ones. For example, a mother is simply scolding a child for not doing his homework. She is perhaps also demanding that he sit down right now and do it. One of the characteristics of mothers of problem children is that they tend to give vague commands and express a good deal of irritation while doing so (Snyder & Huntley, 1990).

Parents are also noncontingent in their support of prosocial skill development, so the problem-child-to-be also lacks many of the essential social survival skills. The lack of prosocial skills literally forces the mother to issue very high rates of parental commands. In an important sense, the irritable, scolding termagant is the product of parents' own noncontingent behavior.

Step 2. When the mother scolds about homework, the child may counterattack by arguing, yelling, whining, or claiming that she is always picking on him or her. Most likely, the child lies and claims that he or she has no homework to do. Observation data for a clinical sample showed that for the second step in the coercion dance, the likelihood of a negative reaction to the mother's aversive intrusion was .25 (two or three times higher than for normal samples) (Patterson, Reid, & Dishion, 1992). The child's aversive reaction (punishment) to the mother may in turn lead to several different outcomes. In the short run, the effect may be to suppress or sidetrack her command to do homework; in the long run, the effect of the punishment could teach her that she should just not bring the homework issue up. This kind of punishment by the problem child teaches many mothers to stop trying, particularly if they are pain-avoidant types.

Step 3. The next step in the sequence is crucial. If the mother is mollified by the child's argument, she stops scolding. In effect, the child wins. The short-term outcome is that no homework is completed that evening. The long-term outcome is that there is an increase in the likelihood that during future confrontations concerning homework, the child will select the same coercive behavior as a means of escaping an aversive situation.

As pointed out by our colleague Eleanor Maccoby, counterattacks were about equally functional in the homes of both clinical and normal samples (Patterson, 1982). For boys from either sample, a counterattack "worked" about 40% of the time. If counterattacks work equally well, then what explains the difference between normal and clinical samples? The answer requires an intraindividual perspective that simultaneously takes into account the relative utility of both prosocial reactions and coercive counterattacks. For example, Snyder and Patterson (1993) showed that in normal families, when presented with an aversive intrusion by mothers, the relative payoffs for the child were much higher for prosocial reactions such as the use of humor than they were for coercive behaviors. In problem-child families, it was the reverse. Within the family, the relative payoffs for coercive counterattacks were higher than those for prosocial reactions. Incidentally, the interesting implication from these same findings is that it is easier to head off an aversive intrusion in normal families than it is in deviant families.

Step 4. There is one additional outcome of conflict episodes that is of more than a little clinical interest. Our observation studies showed that as soon as the mother backed off, the problem child often terminated the counterattack immediately. This would occur even when the child's counterattacks (crying, anger, or whining) were obviously highly emotional. The emotional tap would be magically turned off within seconds when it became apparent that the child had "won."

In terms of escape conditioning, the long-term effect of this four-step dance (intrude aversively, counterattack, immediately back off, terminate counterattack) is to increase the likelihood that in the future the mother will submit; therefore, giving in works.

Escape conditioning in the real world. A series of tightly controlled studies showed that three-step sequences of mother intrudes aversively – child counterattacks – mother terminates aversion could be manipulated to produce significant increases in either deviant or prosocial behaviors (Patterson, 1982). What was interesting about these studies was that dramatic changes occurred in only a few trials. This was in marked contrast to the minuscule changes brought about by mothers' use of social reinforcers (i.e., many reinforcers for small changes).

These analogue studies showed that three-step pain-escape sequences could serve as determinants in a highly controlled laboratory setting. There are also laboratory analogue studies showing that imitation (Bandura, 1973) or social cognitions (Dodge, 1980) could be determinants for children's aggressivity. But in the present context, how does one identify a contingency in ongoing social interaction as a reinforcer? As discussed earlier, how much of the variance in children's coercive behavior is accounted for by information about three-step escape sequences (technically, negative reinforcement or escape conditioning)? Procedures for addressing these two questions were essentially developed in natural settings by a single individual and for that reason might very well be labeled the *Snyder procedures.*

First, are there *reinforcing arrangements* embedded in family interaction that have a significant effect on future response probabilities? Snyder and Patterson (1986) described a procedure for testing this. It begins with examination of a three-step sequence: mother behaves – child reacts – mother provides consequence. To start the analyses, an investigator must have some a priori means for classifying those maternal reactions that might function as positive reinforcers (e.g., talk, attend, laugh, approve) or as aversives in escape-conditioning arrangements. Presumably a reinforcer at Time 1 will alter the probability for a response occurring at Time 2.

Next, the investigator must have some way of determining when future probabilities have been altered. An episode is identified when the mother provides what is thought to be a "positive reinforcer" for a specific child behavior. Snyder determined empirically that following such an episode, a suitable waiting period to overcome thematic effects was about 30 seconds. If reinforcement occurred, then the next time the controlling stimulus (e.g., the mother's behavior at Time 1 as an antecedent) is presented it should be accompanied by a significant increase in the likelihood of the child's reacting in the same way he or she did at Time 1. Consequences, classified a priori as punishers, should have just the opposite effect. Intensive observation data for mother–child dyads showed that both positive and negative consequences embedded in ongoing mother–child interactions significantly altered future response probabilities (Snyder & Patterson, 1986). Systematic application of this type of Snyder procedure would tell us a great deal about which reinforcers and punishers occurring in the real world effectively control which sets of child behaviors.

How much of the variance in children's individual differences in antisocial behavior can be accounted for by escape conditioning (negative reinforcement)? How much, if any, is accounted for by positive reinforcement? The problem of applying the reinforcement metaphor to the real world has always been that there is no linear relationship between amount of reinforcement and strength of response. Herrnstein (1961) offered a brilliant solution to the problem: the matching law. He showed that in highly controlled laboratory settings, the relative rate of response to two or more keys closely matched the relative payoffs for reacting to the keys.

The matching law says something very important about how the effects of reinforcers as they occur in the real world should be studied. It stipulates that the study must proceed first on an intraindividual basis. In a given situation, the individual eventually adjusts his or her entire response repertoire to the payoffs being provided. The coercion model adds to this the idea that each individual sensitively shops for and selects the settings and the individuals within those settings that maximize the immediate payoffs.

Snyder and Patterson (1993) described a set of procedures for testing the matching law hypothesis in natural settings. For each dyad, intensive observation data for 10 child behaviors were collected in the home. Mothers' reactions were also coded for each response. Given a conflict situation (mother aversive–child aversive), the likelihood of a positive outcome (mother backs off) was calculated for each of the child's 10 behaviors. A matching correlation was estimated for each child separately. Does the rank order for mothers' payoffs match the rank order of what the child was most likely to do? The answer was an emphatic yes. The median intradyad correlations were .65 for the normal sample and .81 for the clinical sample. In each family, given an aversive intrusion by the mother, what the child was most likely to do sensitively matched the mother's payoff. Mothers in normal dyads were more likely to pay off highly skilled prosocial behavior. In the clinical dyads, mothers were most likely to pay off negative verbal and other forms of coercive behavior.

Even though the matching law analyses are at the intraindividual level, building a performance theory requires an explanation at the interindividual level. Snyder and Patterson (1993) provided a simple bridging solution for this problem. The likelihood a child will respond to mothers' aversive behavior with a counterattack summarizes the key information at the intraindividual level. The missing information concerns the frequency with which the controlling stimuli occur (e.g., mothers' aversive behaviors) in the child's real world. If we now introduce the information about the density of the aversive stimuli found in family interaction, then the product of these two terms predicts individual differences in performance. One variable describes the likelihood of a child reacting coercively given that the other is aversive; the second variable describes the density of aversive intrusions by other family members. When this was done, the equation accounted for 76% of the variance in the child's observed rate of coercive behavior.

Although the preliminary studies are promising, the Ns were very small. The Snyder studies were designed to be illustrative rather than confirmatory. We need dozens of studies of this kind before we can arrive at a solid conclusion about how effective escape- and avoidant-conditioning sequences are in accounting for individual differences in child coerciveness in the home. The preliminary studies indicate, however, that the concept of reinforcement is more than just a promising metaphor.

Structural dances

There is a surprising degree of orderliness to marital interactions (Gottman & Roy, 1990). Patterson (1979) reviewed data from several family interaction studies showing that simply knowing what the immediately prior behavior of the other family member was provided a basis of accounting for 30 to 50% of the variance in the child's next response. This high order of predictability is close to what had previously been found for social interaction among primates (Altmann, 1965). Each event in the social interaction stream tends to be correlated with the prior events and often is correlated with the next four or five events, as shown in sequential lag analyses (Patterson, 1982).

Many of the sequential links are overlearned, particularly those events associated with conflicts. Presumably, once interactional units have been overlearned they require very little cognitive processing. Leventhal and Schere (1987; cited in Smith & Lazarus, 1990) distinguished between conceptual and schematic processes as being qualitatively different. In the present context, well-practiced conflict exchanges among family members are thought to be examples of automatic or schematic processes that form small islands of increased predictability in ongoing family interactions.

Among family members in at-risk samples, the average duration of verbal negative exchanges was 65 seconds for one sample and 74 seconds for another (Patterson, Reid, & Dishion, 1992). These dances are engaged in by two and sometimes three family members simultaneously; each is responding on a more or less reflexive level.

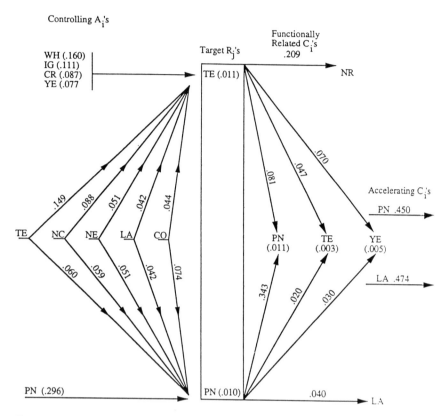

Figure 5.1. Functionally defined response class social aggression (from Patterson, Reid, & Dishion, 1992). The figures in parentheses are base rate values. The figures not in parentheses are conditional probabilities. Abbreviations: CO, command; CR, cry; IG, ignore; LA, laugh; NC, noncomply; NG, negativism; NR, no response; PN, physical negativism; TE, tease; WH, whine; YE, yell.

We shall see in a later section that it is these extended coercive exchanges of almost reflexive reactions that create a setting in which escalations in amplitude are very likely to occur.

Family observation data showed that each form of coercive behavior had a network of controlling stimuli (i.e., behaviors by other family members that would reliably produce the behavior) (Patterson & Cobb, 1971, 1973; Snyder, 1977). The connections were of course probabilistic in nature. What was particularly interesting about these connections was that some of them seemed to share the networks of controlling stimuli. For example, in Figure 5.1 are shown 10 behaviors of male siblings that reliably produced either hitting or teasing reactions from the target boys. There were 5 sibling behaviors that reliably evoked both hitting and teasing.

Any one of these shared sibling behaviors produced a 4- to 7-fold increase in the likelihood of a hitting response. They were also associated with a 4- to 14-fold increase in the likelihood of a teasing reaction. In a very real sense, hitting and teasing are functionally related; they are equivalent means for coping with male sibling intrusions.

There is a second sense in which hitting and teasing are functionally related. Analyses of family interaction sequences showed that the two responses are, in turn, correlated with three shared consequences also provided by male siblings. The dance now has three steps. Each step is correlated with the next step in the sequence. Also notice that if the sibling hits or laughs as a consequence, then the dance is likely to continue. This last step is important. It provides a reliable base for predicting lengthy episodes; these are the episodes that are associated with escalations in intensity.

Escalation

The web of probabilistic relations among interacting family members shows that some social interactions are structured. The vast bulk of the interactions, however, have only trivial implications (if any) for a theory about family conflict. Even those behaviors categorized as aversive seem relatively trivial in nature. Under what conditions does the process move from trivial to more severe acts?

It was hypothesized that, under certain circumstances, increasing the amplitude of coercive behavior was functional. Reid was the first to demonstrate that frequency of aversive events was the key determinant for escalators in child-abusive families (Reid, Patterson, & Loeber, 1981). In one sample of abusive mothers, the correlation between frequency and observed hitting was .87 (Lorber, Felton, & Reid, 1984) (i.e., frequency correlates with amplitude). As the duration of the conflict episode increased, so did the risk for hitting (Reid et al., 1981). Interestingly enough, duration of an episode also seems to relate to the number of people involved in the conflict. Vuchinich, Emery, and Cassidy (1988) showed that in families of normal adolescents, the average number of moves in a conflict was 3.7, but if another family member intervened the duration increased to 11.2 moves.

Studies of fighting mice, barroom brawls, and home observation data showed that trained coercers seemed to escalate conflicts more quickly than did their opponents (Patterson, 1982). For example, mice reinforced for repeated attacks eventually learned to escalate to high-amplitude aggression during the initial stages of an attack. It remained for investigators working with handicapped children in classroom-type settings to demonstrate that the driving mechanism for this kind of training was indeed escape conditioning (Carr, Newsom, & Binkoff, 1980). Their beautifully controlled single-subject designs showed that for some children a demanding task served as a powerful aversive stimulus. Escape from the demanding situation could be used to strengthen either prosocial or aggressive behavior. When one subject's aggressive behaviors produced escape from the aversive setting, the number of aggressive acts increased to 1,625 acts per session. Subsequent extinction trials again reduced the frequency to near zero levels.

If moderate levels of aggressive behaviors did not produce escape, the child escalated to higher amplitude aggressive behaviors directed against self and against others (Carr, 1988). These studies and the more recent work by Horner and Day (1991) provide strong support for the general relation between escape conditioning and deviant behavior, as well as for the escalation hypothesis.

Snyder et al. (1993) conducted extensive observations of mothers and their problem and nonproblem children. As expected, they found that problem dyads engaged in higher frequencies of conflict and that the episodes were significantly longer. Given a conflict, the problem dyads were more likely to escalate in intensity (.45) than were the nonproblem dyads (.34). In the two samples, escalation and deescalation seemed to serve two very different purposes. Normal dyads were more likely to end the conflict following deescalation (.62) than were problem dyads (.34). Clinical dyads were more likely to terminate a conflict following escalation than following deescalation (e.g., in clinical dyads, escalation worked better). In either sample, if conflict ended with an escalation, then the subsequent conflict was more likely to start at a higher level.

Self-control

When childhood traits are adequately measured, the measures are generalizable across settings and across time (Patterson, Duncan, Reid, & Bank, 1993). For example, in the study by Wright (1983) the across-setting correlations for aggressive behaviors in children were in the .60 range. From the perspective of the coercion model, the antisocial child actively selects individuals and settings within both the school and the home that tend to maximize the payoffs for coercive and antisocial behaviors. Alternatively, those with a cognitive persuasion would argue that this level of generalizability across settings is the expression of some internalized form of self-control (e.g., moral knowledge, identification with cultural norms, or ability to delay gratification and resist temptation) (Shaffer & Brody, 1981). How could these competence models be compared?

The model presented in Figure 5.2 assumes a latent construct assessed by three different indicators that describes what is meant by the child's self-control at two points in time. Notice that the measure of self-control avoids the tautologic error of assuming that antisocial behavior is itself evidence for a lack of self-control (Feldman & Weinberger, 1991). Two indicators might serve to define self-control. The analogue measure of moral development by Kohlberg, Ricks, and Snarey (1984) is widely accepted, as are the laboratory measures of delay of gratification (Mischel, 1968). From a self-control perspective, the key hypothesis to be tested is that *changes* in self-control covary with changes in the latent construct (teacher and peer ratings) assessing antisocial behavior. To date, such a simple and straightforward test of the contribution of self-control measures has not been made. Most investiga-

Age 7   Age 10

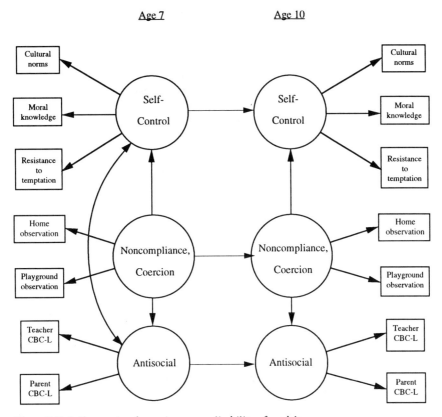

Figure 5.2. Self-control and coercion: generalizability of models.

tors have been satisfied with demonstrating a correlation between self-control measures and antisocial measures at one point in time.

The alternative coercion model is built around an observation-based measure of noncompliance/coercion assessed in the home and in the school. It is assumed that changes over time in noncompliance/coercion will covary with changes in adult ratings of antisocial behavior. The author assumes that, for children, the measure of self-control would add little to measures of coercion in accounting for change in antisocial behavior.

If preschool children are not reasonably compliant, they will also have low self-control on tests of moral knowledge or tests of delay of gratification. If they do not comply to these rules when the adult is present, then they certainly will not comply when the adult is absent. The hypothesis that observed compliance should covary with measures of self-control has been shown in a number of studies. For example, Kochanska (1991) showed that observed toddler compliance to the mother's requests correlated .34 with moral orientation assessed when the child was 8 to 10 years of age. For the subsample of families with ineffective parenting skills, the comparable correlation was .47.

From a behavioral perspective, the second variable required to understand behaviors often subsumed under the rubric of self-control pertains to the child's selection of social environments that match his or her repertoire. As the shopping hypothesis was outlined by Patterson, Reid, and Dishion (1992), individuals who are somewhat antisocial choose others who are similarly inclined. Highly conforming individuals identify a reference group of peers who share similar values about conforming to society's standards. The peer group provides the reinforcement that maintains the conforming behaviors. The noncompliant-coercive child is very likely to select, and be selected by, deviant members of the peer group. Studies of the interaction of deviant peer dyads have shown a sensitive matching of relative rates for rule-breaking talk to relative payoffs for this kind of talk. Furthermore, the amount of rule-breaking talk has correlated significantly with later police arrest (Dishion, French, & Patterson, in press).

From coerciveness to early police arrest

It is hypothesized that boys trained by family members to be antisocial are at risk for early police arrest. It is also hypothesized that boys who are arrested before age 14 are at severe risk for chronic offending during adolescence and for violent offending (Patterson et al., 1991; Patterson, DeBaryshe, & Ramsey, 1989). Presumably, there are striking differences between youths arrested before and after age 14 (Patterson & Yoerger, 1993a). The two groups have not only different histories leading to arrests, but also different outcomes. It is hypothesized that late-onset boys will be at significantly less risk for both chronic and violent offending. Data from the longitudinal Oregon Youth Study (OYS) are used to test the differential outcomes hypothesis.

Parenting practices and antisocial behavior

In our early clinical studies, observations in homes made it clear that parents needed to do two things: strengthen prosocial skills and at the same time weaken coercive child behavior by using effective but nonphysical discipline techniques such as time out or chores (Forgatch & Patterson, 1989). Threatening and scolding did little to interfere with the rich schedules of (negative) reinforcement available for coercive behaviors in distressed families. Presumably, effective discipline would weaken the child's tendency to select coercive responses as a means for coping with aversive experiences. Because of parental failure to be contingent, these families produce children who are both socially unskilled and extremely coercive.

Multiple indicators were used to define the latent constructs for parental discipline and monitoring practices, as well as for child antisocial behavior (Patterson,

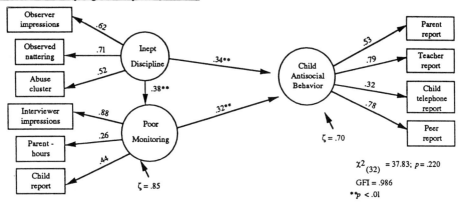

Model A. OYS boys aged 9-10 years (N = 201)

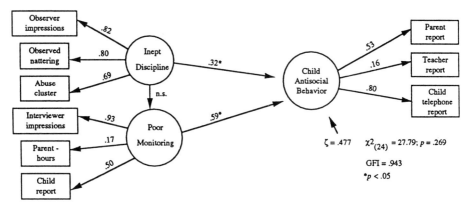

Model B. Boys of divorced parents 9-12 years (N = 96)

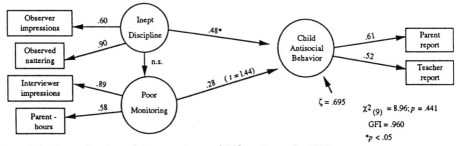

Model C: Clinical sample of boys and girls aged 5-12 (N = 71)

Figure 5.3. Two replications of the parenting model (from Forgatch, 1991).

1982). The assumption was that the use of multiple indicators partially overcomes the problems of bias inherent in social science measures; the effect is also to increase the generalizability of the resulting model (Bank & Patterson, 1992). The first parenting model was based on a sample of at-risk youths. As shown in Figure 5.3, there was an acceptable fit between the data set and the a priori clinical model. After partialing out the joint contribution of monitoring, the path coefficient of .34 showed that disrupted parental discipline covaried significantly with high rates of antisocial behavior for these Grade 4 boys. Together, the two measures of parenting practices accounted for 30% of the variance in the measures of child behavior. Forgatch (1991) replicated the basic parenting model for two at-risk samples. The models accounted for 30 and 52% of the variance in the criterion measures in these two samples. Metzler and Dishion (1992) collected data for three samples of normal adolescents ($N = 131$, 98, 643) and used adolescent and parent report data to define the constructs in a coercion model. The models accounted for 40 to 50% of the variance against a wide spectrum of criterion measures such as drug and alcohol use, sexual abuse, academic failure, and antisocial behavior. The findings strongly suggest that the parenting model is a robust one.

Correlations do not, of course, establish causality. Forgatch (1991) made a strong

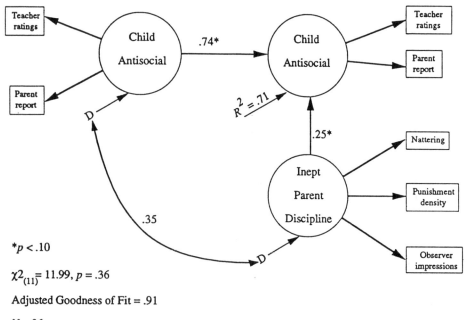

*p < .10

$\chi^2_{(11)} = 11.99$, $p = .36$

Adjusted Goodness of Fit = .91

$N = 86$

Figure 5.4. Experimental test for causal status of discipline practices (from Dishion, Patterson, & Kavanagh, 1992).

case for the necessity of subjecting parenting practices to experimental tests to determine their status as determinants for child antisocial behavior. In the first complete test, Dishion, Patterson, and Kavanagh (1992) randomly assigned 119 boys and girls, ages 10 through 14, to four intervention conditions. Two of the intervention procedures involved training parents in more effective discipline procedures following the general procedures for parent training therapy outlined by Forgatch and Patterson (1989) and by Patterson and Forgatch (1987). Teachers' ratings of antisocial behavior showed that reductions in these behaviors were significantly greater for families involved in parent training than for families involved in two other forms of intervention. Furthermore, as shown in Figure 5.4, the magnitude of the changes in antisocial behavior covaried with measures of effective discipline at termination. Two additional studies of this type are now under way. The critical test of the coercion model will involve experiments based on samples of toddlers. These studies will answer the question of how the process starts.

Coercion to antisocial acts

As problem children become increasingly coercive, parents' lack of skill is further exacerbated. Vuchinich, Teachman, and Crosby (1991) used OYS longitudinal data to demonstrate the bidirectional relation between parental discipline and child antisocial behavior. As problem children progress, they gain control of more and more household processes. For example, parents become increasingly hesitant to pressure children to tell them where they are going or what they are doing. The parents know that even if they had the information, they would be unlikely to win in a discipline confrontation involving any of these issues.

Having defeated the parents, children are free to explore the delights of a variety of avoidance arrangements (e.g., avoid boredom by skipping school, avoid work by stealing, avoid negative sanctions by lying). They are also free to explore the positive reinforcement produced by the "rush" that follows successful shoplifting or burglary. They may be out on the streets unsupervised 4 or 5 years earlier than other members of the peer group. On the street, they will find groups of older antisocial youths who can provide support and direct training for new forms of antisocial behavior.

It is hypothesized that there is a progression from high-rate, trivial forms of coercion to lower rate, more extreme forms (Patterson, 1982). It is assumed that the higher the frequency of coercive behaviors, the more likely the child is to move on to practice such antisocial acts as stealing, fire setting, truancy, physical assault, and the like. If problem behaviors are arranged from most to least frequent, the sequence corresponds to a progression from trivial to severe. It is assumed that the sequence is transitive (e.g., all youths who steal are fighters, but not all fighters are stealers). To make the sequence in Figure 5.5 as conservative as possible, the coercion data for the Grade 4 boys were based entirely on parental report, whereas the shift to extremes was based entirely on teacher report. In keeping with the

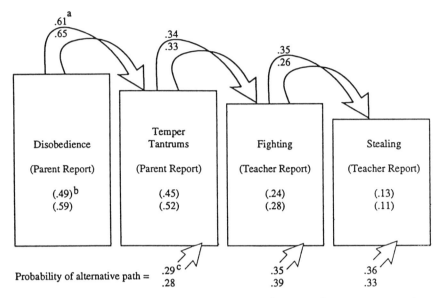

Figure 5.5. The progression from coercive to antisocial behaviors (from Patterson, Reid, & Dishion, 1992). The value marked with a superscript a is the proportion of boys in Cohort I who disobey and have temper tantrums. That marked with a b is the base rate of occurrence for the target behavior for Cohorts I (upper values) and II (lower level). That marked with a c is the proportion of boys not fitting the hypothesized progression for Cohorts I (upper values) and II (lower values).

transitivity idea, it can be seen that about two-thirds of the stealers were also described by teachers as fighters. Similarly, about two-thirds of the fighters had been previously identified by parents as having frequent temper tantrums. Notice also that at any particular point in the sequence, there is only a moderate risk for moving on to the next, more extreme step.

Guttman (1944) made the brilliant assumption that if such a progression is found, it reflects an underlying cause that applies to each event in turn. In the present instance, we assume that children who fight and steal come from families that provide rich contingencies for all the deviant behaviors in the sequence (i.e., the underlying process is escape and avoidant conditioning).

The problem with the progression example is that it is built on data collected very late in development (Grade 4). Presumably, the progression develops much earlier. Patterson and Duncan (1993) used mothers' ratings for a sample of normal preschool boys to identify a coercion progression as early as 24 months of age (i.e., noncompliance − temper tantrums − physical attack). In keeping with the present formulation, the mother-identified coercion progression during preschool significantly predicted both Grade 2 teacher ratings of fighting and a general score for oppositional defiant disorder. The findings support the assumed orderly relation between early forms of coercion and later development of antisocial acts.

Generalization to the school

The studies reviewed by Patterson, Reid, and Dishion (1992) showed that, given adequate measures, there were strong correlations across settings in antisocial behavior. For example, Ramsey, Patterson, and Walker (1990) used multiple indicators to define antisocial behaviors occurring in the home for Grade 4 boys. A year later they used a different set of indicators to define antisocial behavior occurring in schools. The path coefficient for the relationships across settings and time was .72. The effects of training in the home generalize to what happens in the school, and the effect of the generalization is disastrous.

Presumably, by Grade 3 most antisocial children have experienced two massive social failures, both of which are direct results of the coercive-antisocial pattern of behavior. Patterson and Yoerger (1993a) reviewed modeling studies showing a direct path from antisocial behavior to rejection by normal peers and academic failure. In both cases, the core noncompliance and coercive interpersonal style lead to predictable reactions from the social environment. It is assumed that both failures will function as feedback loops to keep the adolescent in the crime process.

The effect of context

It is assumed that the impact of context on child adjustment is mediated through its effect on parenting practices (Patterson, Reid, & Dishion, 1992). For example, the effect of increasing stress, divorce, illness, depression, or unemployment on child adjustment will be negligible unless these contextual variables disrupt parental discipline or monitoring practices. This mediating effect has been demonstrated in longitudinal designs (Elder, Downey, & Cross, 1986) as well as in cross-sectional designs (Laub & Sampson, 1988). Larzelere and Patterson (1990) used a structural equation model with OYS longitudinal data to demonstrate that the impact of social disadvantage on delinquent behavior was mediated by a latent construct measuring parenting practices.

Change in form

Extremely antisocial children form the initial core of the deviant peer group. According to Moffitt (1993), by early adolescence antisocial boys' explorations in antisocial attitudes, sexuality, substance use, and crime become increasingly valued by large numbers of adolescents. Findings from the Coie, Terry, and Zakriski (1992) study strongly support Moffitt's hypothesis about the central role played by "trained" antisocial boys in deviant peer groups. For example, their data from preadolescent normal samples showed that in some schools these early members of the deviant peer group were viewed as leaders, as less unhappy, and as socially preferred.

It is assumed that the final transformation of coercive and antisocial acts learned in the home takes place out on the street, in the company of other antisocial youths (Stoolmiller, 1990). As shown by Dishion and Patterson (1993), the combination of antisocial behavior, rejection by peers, and disrupted monitoring contributes significantly to the child's drift to deviant peers. Some of their analyses were based on actual observations of the social interactions of deviant dyads. The data showed that both members matched their relative rate of rule-breaking talk to the relative rate of reinforcement for that behavior. Under unsupervised conditions, the mutual training might include the specific skills involved in shoplifting, drug use, breaking and entering, and assault. Patterson (1993) demonstrated that intraindividual growth in two new forms (substance use and truancy) of antisocial behavior covaried over time. Increasing street time and increasing involvement with deviant peers significantly accounted for the growth in the new forms. For most current theories of delinquency, including the coercion model, the members of the deviant peer group are the proximal agents of change that directly transform childhood behaviors to delinquent acts.

Prediction of first arrest

The child's score for the composite measure of antisocial traits is analogous to an estimate of the overall frequency of coercive-antisocial acts that occur across settings. In keeping with this idea, composite scores were constructed for observed frequency and for ratings by parents, teachers, and peers. As expected, the correlation between the two composites was quite high (.56) (Bank & Patterson, 1992). Also, both composites were significantly related to future delinquent acts. A high trait score means a high frequency of antisocial acts. Assuming police arrest is a fortuitous affair, the more antisocial the boy, the greater the likelihood that he will be arrested first.

As noted earlier, the more antisocial the boy, the more likely he is to disrupt parental efforts to supervise and control. Consequently, the extremely antisocial youth is more likely to begin a street career at an earlier age. In effect, the extremely antisocial boy is probably at twice the risk for early arrest. He starts sooner on the street *and,* when there, performs antisocial acts at the highest frequency.

The evidence for the relation between the antisocial trait score and early onset for police arrest is exemplified in the data shown in Table 5.1 (Patterson, Crosby, & Vuchinich, 1992). Some at-risk boys were arrested as young as 6 and 7 years of age, and the crimes they committed were serious (e.g., burglary, theft). The arrest peak for the at-risk group was between ages 13 and 14.

Of the 53 boys arrested before age 14, only 6 scored below the median on the antisocial trait score. This is a very low false-negative error indeed. If, for preven-

Table 5.1. *First arrest as a function of age: early-onset group*

Age	Number arrested	
	At risk[a]	Not at risk
6	2	0
7	2	0
8	1	0
9	4	1
10	5	0
11	5	0
12	12	1
13	16	4
Total	47	6

[a] Score above median on composite antisocial score measured at Grade 4.

tion purposes, we used the trait score to identify those at risk for early start, then the prevention treatment would be misplaced for about 52% of the boys (false positives). An additional 17 of the antisocial boys were arrested prior to age 18. Given these late arrivals, the problem of misplaced treatment is considerably attenuated (false-positive error of 36%).

In their review of seven studies predicting delinquency on the basis of earlier aggression for boys, Stouthamer-Loeber and Loeber (1989) found that the relative improvement over chance (RIOC) score ranged from 16.4 to 54.4%, with a mean of 32.9%. In the present data set, the RIOC for predicting early onset was considerably better, 77.4%. As shown in the section that follows, early onset is related to chronicity, but late onset is not. Therefore, it makes more sense to predict early onset than to predict delinquency in general (i.e., early and late onset are really qualitatively different). For example, if our longitudinal data for the OYS were used to predict all delinquency (early and late), the RIOC would be 31.3%, a figure very close to that obtained in the review by Stouthamer-Loeber and Loeber.

Patterson, Crosby, and Vuchinich (1992) showed that measures of parental discipline practices collected at Grade 4 contributed significantly to increased risk for first police arrest during the ensuing 5 years. As predicted, when composite parenting practices and childhood antisocial trait scores were entered simultaneously, the contribution of parenting practices was nonsignificant and the composite measures of the trait and of social disadvantage accounted for most of the variance in the distribution of hazard rates.

Chronicity and violence. The earlier formulations (Patterson et al., 1989; Patterson et al., 1991) predicted that early-onset boys would be at significantly greater risk for chronic offending than would late-onset youth. An estimate of the correlation between age of onset and chronic offending for the OYS was .74 ($p < .05$) (Patterson & Yoerger, 1993a). Based on the OYS follow-up data currently available through age 17, the conditional likelihood of three or more police arrests given a first arrest before age 14 was .769.

It is hypothesized that the progression from trivial to severe applies to delinquent behavior in a manner analogous to the previously discussed findings for coercive and antisocial acts. In both instances it would be assumed that frequency of delinquent acts would correlate significantly with risk for committing violent acts (i.e., all violent offenders are frequent offenders, but the reverse is not necessarily true). To test this, Capaldi, Patterson, and Dishion (1993) examined the data from the OYS. Given three or more arrests during adolescence, the likelihood was .55 that at least one of the arrests would be for a violent crime. Almost every violent offender was a chronic offender. The analogous likelihood for Farrington's (1991) analyses of adult offenders was .49. In both instances, frequency is strongly related to violence. It may be that there are several paths to violence, but these findings suggest that for adolescent offenders frequency of performance defined the path for 16 out of 17 cases.

Blumstein, Cohen, Roth, and Visher (1986) reviewed findings from three longitudinal studies of juvenile offenders and showed that given four or more juvenile arrests, the likelihoods of adult offending were .92, .89, and .68. It seems, then, that high levels of childhood antisocial behavior are significantly related to early onset of offending. Early onset in turn is intimately related to a triad of outcomes: chronic offending, violent offending, and adult offending.

Implications

The general pattern of findings is consistent with the tradition established by Glueck and Glueck (1950, 1959, 1968). From this viewpoint, family process variables play a key role in determining delinquent behavior. A recent reanalysis of the Gluecks' data by Sampson and Laub (1993) offers strong support for this general perspective, including the idea that the effect of context on child adjustment is mediated through parenting practices. The coercion model we have based on OYS data makes three additional contributions to this early heritage.

Like many other models, the coercion model emphasizes the differential implication of early- and late-onset categories for chronic offending. In the present report, better than 76% of the boys who are arrested prior to age 14 were at risk for chronic offending. This is a startling figure. Although the findings from the OYS are not yet complete enough to give a firm estimate for chronicity for late-onset boys, even our most conservative estimates are that the risk for chronic offending is at least three times greater for the early-onset boys than for the late-onset boys (Patterson &

Yoerger, 1993b). As already noted, understanding the antecedents for early onset seems to be the key to understanding the interrelated triad of negative outcomes that includes chronic offending, violence, and adult offending. Presumably, the main contribution of the coercion model lies in its emphasis on the relation of the childhood antisocial behavior to early onset and in delineating the determinants for the early forms of the antisocial behavior.

The second contribution of the coercion model was to specify a priori that the histories for early and late onset would be significantly different (Patterson et al., 1989; Patterson et al., 1991). If they *are* qualitatively different, then they should be studied as separate entities. The data cited showed that early and late onset have very different implications for chronic offending and, presumably, for violence and adult offending. To what extent can the two forms of delinquent behavior be differentiated by family process and contextual variables? Capaldi and Patterson (1994) addressed those questions by using the longitudinal data from the OYS. They identified a single function that differentiated early from late onset. The structure coefficients showed that high scores on early-onset function would be characterized in order of their loadings by disrupted discipline, one or both parents unemployed, many family transitions (divorce, etc.), social disadvantage, and antisocial parents. Familial and contextual variables significantly differentiate early-from late-onset adolescents.

The histories for both early and late onset include training by members of the deviant peer group as the final arbiters for delinquent behavior. This is very much in keeping with the position of Elliott, Huizinga, and Ageton (1985). If a boy who entered this training mechanism in childhood was antisocial, then he will be arrested early. If he entered the deviant peer group late, or was less antisocial and only marginally skilled, then he will not be arrested until after age 14 (Patterson & Yoerger, 1993b). The preliminary analyses suggest that for the early-onset group it may be the interaction term (trait times date of peer involvement) that significantly differentiates them from the late-onset group.

The third contribution of the coercion model has been to detail the part of the process that is set in motion by ineffective parenting practices. Why do ineffective discipline and monitoring seem to produce antisocial behavior? The child could be simply imitating the explosive discipline practices of his or her parents. Ineffective parenting practices could contribute to a disrupted attachment, so the child never internalizes a set of appropriate controls; the child's behavior reflects a set of cognitive or temperamental deficits present at birth. There are many possibilities that could fit such a pattern of correlations. The past two decades of observation and laboratory studies have helped us begin to build a reasonable case for the underlying causal mechanism involving faulty contingencies.

Even at this early juncture, the findings suggest that no simplistic equation using one or two variables could adequately predict delinquency. In fact, that is not even the right question. What needs to be done first is to predict who will start first. Mixing early and late starters into a single class of delinquency is analogous to combining aardvarks with auks to form a class of words. White, Moffitt, Earls, Robins, and Silva (1990) reached a similar conclusion based on their review of delinquency prediction studies. As they noted, it is the heterogeneous nature of delinquency that seems to thwart efforts to make accurate predictions. The present analysis is a partial investigation into the nature of this heterogeneity and emphasizes the general utility of a focus on early onset.

NOTE

I gratefully acknowledge the contribution of Grant MH 37940 from the Center for Studies of Antisocial and Violent Behavior, NIMH, U.S. PHS (in collecting and processing the longitudinal data sets for the OYS), the support from MH 46690 from the Prevention Research Branch, NIMH, U.S. PHS, and MH 38318 from the Mood, Anxiety, and Personality Disorders Branch, NIMH, U.S. PHS. The general ideas emerged from discussions with a number of colleagues, including Lew Bank, Tom Dishion, Marion Forgatch, John Reid, Mike Stoolmiller, and Karen Yoerger.

REFERENCES

Altmann, S. (1965). Sociobiology of the rhesus monkey: II. Stochastics of social communication. *Journal of Theoretical Biology, 8,* 490–522.

Bandura, A. (1973). *Aggression: A social learning analysis.* Englewood Cliffs, NJ: Prentice-Hall.

Bank, L., & Patterson, G. R. (1992). Use of structural equation models in combining data from different levels of assessment. In J. C. Rosen & P. McReynolds (Eds.), *Advances in psychological assessment* (Vol. 8, pp. 41–74). New York: Plenum.

Blumstein, A., Cohen, J., Roth, J. A., & Visher, C. A. (Eds.). (1986). *Criminal careers and career criminals* (Vols. 1 and 2). Washington, DC: National Academy Press.

Capaldi, D. M., & Patterson, G. R. (1994). Interrelated influences of contextual factors on antisocial behavior in childhood and adolescence for males. In D. Fowles, P. Sutker, & S. H. Goodman (Eds.), *Progress in experimental personality and psychopathology research* (pp. 165–198). New York: Springer.

Capaldi, D. M., Patterson, G. R., & Dishion, T. J. (1993, March). *The violent adolescent male: Specialist or generalist?* Paper presented at the meeting of the Society for Research in Child Development, New Orleans.

Carr, E. G. (1988). Functional equivalence as a means of response generalization. In R. H. Horner, G. Dunlap, & R. L. Koegel (Eds.), *Generalization and maintenance: Life-style changes in applied settings* (pp. 221–241). Baltimore: Paul H. Brookes.

Carr, E. G., Newsom, C. D., & Binkoff, J. A. (1980). Escape as a factor in the aggressive behavior of two retarded children. *Journal of Applied Behavior Analysis, 13,* 101–117.

Coie, J. D., Terry, R., & Zakriski, A. (1992, April). *Early adolescent social influences on delinquent behavior.* Paper presented at the meeting of the Society for Life History Research, Philadelphia, PA.

Dishion, T. J., French, D., & Patterson G. R. (in press). The development and ecology of antisocial behavior. In D. Cicchetti & D. Cohen (Eds.), *Manual of developmental psychopathology.* Cambridge University Press.

Dishion, T. J., & Patterson, G. R. (1993). Antisocial behavior: Using a multiple gating strategy. In M. I. Singer, L. T. Singer, & T. M. Anglin (Eds.), *Handbook for screening adolescents at psychosocial risk* (pp. 375–399). New York: Lexington Books.

Dishion, T. J., Patterson, G. R., & Kavanagh K. (1992). An experimental test of the coercion model: Linking theory, measurement, and intervention. In J. McCord & R. Tremblay (Eds.), *Preventing antisocial behavior: interventions from birth through adolescence* (pp. 253–282). New York: Guilford.

Dodge, K. A. (1980). Social cognition and children's aggressive behavior. *Child Development, 51,* 162–170.

Elder, G. H., Downey, G., & Cross, C. E. (1986). Family ties and life chances: Hard times and hard choices in women's lives since the 1930s. In N. Datan, A. L. Green, & H. W. Reese (Eds.), *Life span developmental psychology: Intergenerational relations* (pp. 151–183). Hillsdale, NJ: Erlbaum.

Elliott, D. S., Huizinga, D., & Ageton, S. S. (1985). *Explaining delinquency and drug use.* Beverly Hills, CA: Sage.

Farrington, D. P. (1991). Childhood aggression and adult violence: Early precursors and later-life outcomes. In D. J. Pepler & K. H. Rubin (Eds.), *The development and treatment of childhood aggression* (pp. 5–29). Hillsdale, NJ: Erlbaum.

Feldman, S. S., & Weinberger, D. A. (1991). *Boys' self-restraint as a mediator of family influences and adolescent misconduct: A longitudinal study.* Unpublished manuscript.

Forgatch, M. S. (1991). The clinical science vortex: A developing theory of antisocial behavior. In D. Pepler & K. H. Rubin (Eds.), *The development and treatment of childhood aggression* (pp. 291–315). Hillsdale, NJ: Erlbaum.

Forgatch, M. S. & Patterson, G. R. (1989). *Parents and adolescents living together: Vol. 2. Family problem solving.* Eugene, OR: Castalia.

Glueck, S., & Glueck, E. (1950). *Unraveling juvenile delinquency.* Cambridge, MA: Harvard University Press.

Glueck, S., & Glueck, E. (1959). *Predicting delinquency and crime.* Cambridge, MA: Harvard University Press.

Glueck, S., & Glueck, E. (1968). *Delinquents and nondelinquents in perspective.* Cambridge, MA: Harvard University Press.

Gottman, J. M., & Roy, A. K. (1990). *Sequential analysis: A guide for behavioral researchers.* Cambridge University Press.

Guttman, L. A. (1944). A basis for scaling qualitative data. *American Sociological Review, 9,* 139–150.

Herrnstein, R. J. (1961). Relative and absolute strength of response as a function of frequency of reinforcement. *Journal of Experimental Analysis of Behavior, 4,* 267–272.

Horner, R. H., & Day, H. M. (1991). The effects of response efficiency on functionally equivalent competing behaviors. *Journal of Applied Behavior Analysis, 24,* 719–732.

Kochanska, G. (1991, April). *Child compliance and noncompliance in the origins of conscience.* Paper presented at the annual conference of the Society for Research in Child Development, Seattle, WA.

Kohlberg, L., Ricks, D., & Snarey J. (1984). Childhood development as a predictor of adaptation in adulthood. *Genetic Psychology Monographs, 110,* 94–162.

Larzelere, R. E., & Patterson, G. R. (1990). Parental management: Mediator of the effect of socioeconomic status on early delinquency. *Criminology, 28,* 301–324.

Laub, J. H., & Sampson, R. J. (1988). Unraveling families and delinquency: A reanalysis of the Gluecks' data. *Criminology, 26,* 355–380.

Leventhal, H., & Schere, K. R. (1987). The relationship of emotion to cognition: A functional approach to a semantic controversy. *Cognition and Emotion, 1,* 3–28.

Lorber, R., Felton, D. K., & Reid, J. B. (1984). A social learning approach to the reduction of coercive processes in child abusive families: A molecular analysis. *Advances in Behavior Research and Therapy, 6,* 29–45.

Metzler, C. W., & Dishion, T. J. (1992, November). *A model of the development of youthful problem behaviors.* Paper presented at the 18th annual conference of the Association for Behavior Analysis.

Mischel, W. (1968). *Personality and assessment.* New York: Wiley.

Moffitt, T. E. (1993). Adolescence-limited and life-course-persistent antisocial behavior: A developmental taxonomy. *Psychological Review, 100*(4), 674–701.

Patterson, G. R. (1979). Treatment for children with conduct problems: A review of outcome studies. In S. Feshbach & A. Fraczek (Eds.), *Aggression and behavior change: Biological and social process* (pp. 83–132). New York: Praeger.

Patterson, G. R. (1982). *A social learning approach: Vol. 3. Coercive family process.* Eugene, OR: Castalia.

Patterson, G. R. (1984). Siblings: Fellow travelers in a coercive system. In R. J. Blanchard & D. C. Blanchard (Eds.), *Advances in the study of aggression* (Vol. 1, pp. 173–215). New York: Academic.

Patterson, G. R. (1993). Orderly change in a stable world: The antisocial trait as a chimera. *Journal of Consulting and Clinical Psychology, 61,* 911–919.

Patterson, G. R., Capaldi, D. M., & Bank, L. (1991). An early starter model for predicting delinquency. In D. J. Pepler & K. H. Rubin (Eds.), *The development and treatment of childhood aggression* (pp. 139–168). Hillsdale, NJ: Erlbaum.

Patterson, G. R., & Cobb, J. A. (1971). A dyadic analysis of "aggressive" behaviors. In J. P. Hill (Ed.), *Minnesota Symposia on Child Psychology* (Vol. 5, pp. 72–129). Minneapolis: University of Minnesota Press.

Patterson, G. R., & Cobb, J. A. (1973). Stimulus control for classes of noxious behaviors. In J. F. Knutson (Ed.), *The control of aggression: Implications from basic research* (pp. 145–199). Chicago: Aldine.

Patterson, G. R., Crosby, L., & Vuchinich, S. (1992). Predicting risk for early police arrest. *Journal of Quantitative Criminology, 8,* 335–355.

Patterson, G. R., DeBaryshe, B. D., & Ramsey, E. (1989). A developmental perspective on antisocial behavior. *American Psychologist, 44,* 329–335.

Patterson, G. R., & Duncan, T. (1993). *Coercive progression for normal toddlers.* Unpublished manuscript.

Patterson, G. R., Duncan, T. E., Reid, J. B., & Bank, L. (1993). *Systematic maternal errors in predicting sons' future arrests.* Unpublished manuscript.

Patterson, G. R., & Forgatch, M. S. (1987). *Parents and adolescents living together: Part 1. The basics.* Eugene, OR: Castalia.

Patterson, G. R., Reid, J. B., & Dishion, T. J. (1992). *A social learning approach: Vol. 4. Antisocial boys.* Eugene, OR: Castalia.

Patterson, G. R., & Yoerger, K. (1993a). Development models for delinquent behavior. In S. Hodgins (Ed.), *Mental disorder and crime* (pp. 140–172). Newbury Park, CA: Sage.

Patterson, G. R., & Yoerger, K. (1993b). *Early and late onset for arrest.* Unpublished manuscript.

Ramsey, E., Patterson, G. R., & Walker, H. M. (1990). Generalization of the antisocial trait from home to school settings. *Journal of Applied Developmental Psychology, 11,* 209–223.

Reid, J. B. (Ed.). (1978). *A social learning approach to family intervention: Vol. 2. Observation in home settings.* Eugene, OR: Castalia.

Reid, J. B., Patterson, G. R., & Loeber, R. (1981). The abused child: Victim, instigator, or innocent bystander? In D. Bernstein (Ed.), *Response structure and organization* (pp. 47–68). Lincoln: University of Nebraska Press.

Sampson, R. J., & Laub J. H. J. (1993). *Crime in the making: Pathways and turning points through life.* Cambridge, MA: Harvard University Press.

Shaffer, D. R., & Brody, G. H. (1981). Parental and peer influences on moral development.

In R. W. Henderson (Ed.), *Parent–child interaction: Theory, research, and prospects* (pp. 83–124). New York: Academic.

Skinner, B. F. (1969). *Contingencies of reinforcement.* New York: Appleton-Century-Crofts.

Smith, C. A., & Lazarus, R. S. (1990). Emotion and adaptation. In L. A. Pervin (Ed.), *Handbook of personality: Theory and research* (pp. 609–637). New York: Guilford.

Snyder, J. J. (1977). A reinforcement analysis of interaction in problem and nonproblem families. *Journal of Abnormal Psychology, 86,* 528–535.

Snyder, J. J., Edwards, P., McGraw, K., Kilgore, H., & Holton, A. (1993). *Escalation and reinforcement in family conflict: Developmental origins of physical aggression.* Unpublished manuscript.

Snyder, J. J., & Huntley, D. (1990). Troubled families and troubled youth: The development of antisocial behavior and depression in children. In P. E. Leone (Ed.), *Understanding troubled and troubling youth* (pp. 194–225). Newbury Park, CA: Sage.

Snyder, J. J., & Patterson, G. R. (1986). The effects of consequences on patterns of social interaction: A quasi-experimental approach to reinforcement in natural interaction. *Child Development, 57,* 1257–1268.

Snyder, J. J., & Patterson, G. R. (1993). *The covariation between relative rate of occurrence and relative rate of pay offs for children's coercive behaviors.* Unpublished manuscript.

Stoolmiller, M. (1990). *Latent growth model analysis of the relation between antisocial behavior and wandering.* Unpublished doctoral dissertation, University of Oregon, Eugene.

Stouthamer-Loeber, M., & Loeber, R. (1989). The use of prediction data in understanding delinquency. In L. A. Bond & B. E. Compas (Eds.), *Primary prevention and promotion in the schools* (pp. 179–202). Newbury Park, CA: Sage.

Vuchinich, S., Emery, R. E., & Cassidy, J. (1988). Family members as third parties in dyadic family conflict: Strategies, alliances, and outcomes. *Child Development, 59,* 1293–1302.

Vuchinich, S., Teachman, J., & Crosby, L. (1991). Families and hazard rates that change over time: Some methodological issues in analyzing transitions. *Journal of Marriage and the Family, 53,* 898–912.

White, J., Moffitt, T. E., Earls, F., Robins, L. N., & Silva, P. A. (1990). How early can we tell? Preschool predictors of boys' conduct disorder and delinquency. *Criminology, 28,* 507–533.

Wright, J. C. (1983). *The structure and perception of behavioral consistency.* Unpublished doctoral dissertation, Stanford University, Stanford, CA.

6 Disentangling mother–child effects in the development of antisocial behavior

DENISE B. KANDEL AND PING WU

Introduction

Consistent relationships have been observed between the quality of parenting and the level of children's functioning. Positive parenting is related to fewer problematic behaviors and higher psychosocial development of children (Hoffman, 1983; Maccoby & Martin, 1983; Rohner, 1986; Steinberg, Elmen, & Mounts, 1989; Steinberg, Mounts, Lamborn, & Dornbusch, 1991), while parental rejection, harsh discipline, and lack of monitoring are related to increased child conduct problems (Loeber & Stouthamer-Loeber, 1986; MacEwen & Barling, 1991; Patterson, 1986; Patterson, Reid, & Dishion, 1992; Patterson & Stouthamer-Loeber, 1984; Rutter & Garmezy, 1983).

Most studies have assumed that children's behaviors are shaped by parents (Baldwin & Skinner, 1989; DiLalla, Mitchell, Arthur, & Pogliocca, 1988; Dornbusch, Ritter, Leiderman, Roberts, & Fraleigh, 1987; Hoffman, 1975; Johnson & Pandina, 1991; Miller, McCoy, Olson, & Wallace, 1986; Steinberg, Elmen, & Mounts, 1989; Steinberg et al., 1991). Bell (1968, 1977; Bell & Chapman, 1986) was one of the first developmental psychologists to challenge the traditional unidirectional model with evidence that children also influenced their parents' behavior toward them. He proposed that parents and children respond in terms of each person's tolerance of the other, setting up a system of reciprocal control. In particular, since children respond differently to different disciplinary techniques, parents try those techniques that seem to work best with their own child.

As is being increasingly recognized, the relationship between parent and child is dynamic, with each individual modifying the behavior of the other (Bell & Chapman, 1986; Lytton, 1990; Patterson, Reid, & Dishion, 1992). Parental influences on children are paralleled by children's effects on parents. The child's temperament, behaviors, and other characteristics, such as age, sex, and even attractive-

106

ness (Anderson, Lytton, & Romney, 1986; Bell, 1968; Bronstein, 1984; Clarke-Stewart, 1973; Clifford, 1959; Dion, 1974; Dix, Rubel, & Zambarano, 1989; Grusec & Kuczynski, 1980; McNally, Eisenberg, & Harris, 1991; Mulhern & Passman, 1981; Rheingold, 1969; Roberts, Block, & Block, 1984; Yarrow, Waxler, & Scott, 1971), determine to some extent the parent's reaction to and handling of the child. It is assumed that overactive and aggressive behavior on the part of the child induces parental punishment and hostility toward the child (Brunk & Henggeler, 1984; Buss, 1981; Stevens-Long, 1973). Responsive child behavior, on the other hand, leads to positive and supportive adult behaviors (Bugental, Caporael, & Shennum, 1980; Cantor & Gelfand, 1977). In a recent review of the transactional nature of parent–child interactions and conduct disorders in boys, Lytton (1990) suggests that child influence may be particularly strong, and even preeminent, for conduct disorders, while parental influence may be stronger for behaviors other than conduct disorders. Patterson's coercion model (1982; Patterson, Reid, & Dishion, 1992) is the most systematic theoretical exposition of the reciprocal process underlying the relationship between parental discipline and child coercion. In a series of elegant clinical, longitudinal epidemiological, and experimental studies, Patterson and his colleagues have laid the foundation for an understanding of the dynamic processes underlying the development of antisocial behavior in children.

Most studies are cross-sectional (Baldwin & Skinner, 1989; DiLalla et al., 1988; Miller et al., 1986; Steinberg et al., 1991), whereas longitudinal data are required to disentangle the reciprocal effects of child and parent on each other (Bell & Harper, 1977). Such data rarely have been presented (Mink & Nihara, 1986; Patterson, Reid, & Dishion, 1992).

In this chapter, we rely on panel data obtained at two points in time over a 6-year interval to examine the dynamic relationships between maternal parenting and child behavior and to determine the direction of influence between parent and child. Although we were especially interested in the relationship between parenting – particularly parental discipline – and antisocial child behavior, we broadened our inquiry to examine positive child behaviors and positive dimensions of parenting so as to place the issue of the relationships between parenting and child behavior in a broader and more comprehensive context. Our goal is to ascertain whether the direction and type of effects vary depending on the nature of parenting and of child behavior. We examine three maternal parenting dimensions and four child behaviors. The parenting dimensions include one negative dimension, punitive discipline, and two positive ones, closeness and supervision. The child behaviors include two negative behaviors, aggression and control problems, and two positive behaviors, positive relations with the parent and being rated as well adjusted. As background to the dynamic analyses, we first examine maternal parenting and child behaviors at two different periods in the child's life, childhood and early adolescence, to determine age-related changes in parenting styles and child behaviors. We then examine the dynamic relationships between parenting and the child's behavior. To what degree does parenting have an impact on the child's behavior and to what degree does the child's behavior have an impact on parenting?

Methods

Sample

The analyses are based on a longitudinal subsample of 208 mothers of children 9 years old and older who were interviewed twice over a 6-year interval, and a subset of 191 dyads of these mothers and their children. The mothers are the focal members of a longitudinal cohort that we have been following for 19 years since age 15 or 16.[1]

Adult respondents were first contacted in 1971 and reinterviewed in 1980, 1984, and 1990. In 1990, personal interviews were also conducted with the oldest child 9 and over living in the household. The 1,160 adults reinterviewed in 1990 represent 72% of the original target adolescents enrolled in the sample schools. Of the 625 women in the cohort, 223 (36%) had a child 9 or older in 1990. The 208 women, who reported on the same child both in the 1984 and 1990 surveys, are included in the major analyses reported in this chapter. Of the 208 children, 191 (92%) were also personally interviewed in 1990. (The sample sizes vary slightly from table to table because of missing cases.)

The analyses reported in this chapter are based on data collected in 1984 and 1990. The mothers were on the average aged 28.8 years (SD $= 0.8$) in 1984. The children ranged in age from 3 to 11 years (*M* age $= 7.4$ years, SD $= 2.4$) in 1984 and 9 to 17 years (*M* age $= 13.0$ years, SD $= 2.4$) in 1990.

Procedures

Data were obtained through structured personal household interviews, which took on the average 1½ hours to complete. In 1984, questions on parenting styles and child behaviors were asked of those who were parents. When there was no eligible natural child, parents were asked about stepchildren, if living in the household. (Only one mother in this analytical sample reported on a stepchild.) The same questions were repeated in 1990. Parents were asked about the same child across the two waves of data collection, although in some instances a different child was reported on.

In 1990, the assessments of parenting and child functioning were more extensive than those obtained in 1984. For the longitudinal analyses spanning the 6-year interval, identical measures of parenting and child behavior are used.

The children's responses are excluded from these major analyses because the child self-reported data are available only at the most recent wave of data collection, and for statistical considerations, the longitudinal analyses needed to be based on identical measures. However, we also report a set of limited analyses based on a subset of 191 mothers who were interviewed at both points in time and whose child also participated in the study at the second interview.

Maternal reported measures

Demographics. Respondents were asked their age and highest educational level completed, as well as the child's birth date.

Parenting. Three parenting measures cover positive as well as negative dimensions of parenting. The negative dimension is represented by punitive discipline and the positive dimension by closeness to the child and supervision, the latter a component of monitoring. The scales are modified from ones developed by Furstenberg (Furstenberg, Morgan, & Allison, 1986) and Simcha-Fagan (Simcha-Fagan & Schwartz, 1986). The parenting measures each include two to five items (Kandel, 1990). Punitive discipline measures harsh control techniques used by the parent. Closeness taps the parents' feelings of warmth toward the child. Supervision taps the parent's knowledge of the child's whereabouts.[2] The scale reliabilities, as measured by alpha, range from .32 for closeness and .55 for punitive discipline to .80 for supervision.

Child behavior. The four measures of child behavior – aggression, control problems, positive relations with parent, and well-adjustedness – were taken from Schaefer and Edgerton (1977) and Furstenberg (Furstenberg, Morgan, & Allison, 1986; Zill, 1983). The scales include three to six items each, with reliabilities ranging from .51 (well adjusted) to .79 (control problems). The aggression scale includes items such as "teases" or "bullies others."[3] Control problems tap mainly disobedience and negativism. Well-adjustedness includes being "very enthusiastic" and "happy." Positive relations describe the child's efforts to please his or her mother. The two scales within each positive and negative dimension have a relatively high correlation (.5 and .6) with each other and more modest correlations with scales across each dimension (see Table 6.A1 in the Appendix).

In addition, an eight-item aggression scale was constructed from identical symptom scales administered to parent and child [the Achenbach Child Behavior Checklist (CBCL) for parents and the Youth Self-Report (YSR) for children] to match the Furstenberg six-item aggression scale administered only to mothers.[4]

Child-reported measures

As we discuss later, a limitation of the major analyses is that the measures are based on data from a single informant. Limited additional analyses were carried out, which made use of data from mother–child dyads at the second interview. The same three parenting scales that had been administered to mothers were available for the children. Only the eight-item aggression subscale from the YSR was available to measure the children self-reported behaviors.[5]

Results

Parenting and children's behaviors at different ages

As background to the analysis of the dynamic relationships between parenting style and child behavior, we examined three processes as a function of the child's age: (1) the nature of maternal parenting, (2) the nature of the child's adjustment, as reported by mothers, and (3) the extent of the relationships between maternal parenting and the child's functioning. We examined these processes at two different points in the child's life, separated by 6 years. Reflecting the mean ages of the children, we refer to these two periods as childhood and early adolescence.

Child age and nature of parenting

As children grow up, parents engage in less active parenting (Table 6.1). The means on each parenting scale are consistently lower at the second point in time than they had been 6 years earlier.

Child age and functioning

Correlatively, as children become older, mothers are less likely to report in positive terms about the child. There are no changes with respect to control problems, and

Table 6.1. *Means and standard deviations of maternal parenting scales and maternal reports of child behaviors in childhood and early adolescence (N ≥ 190)*

	Childhood ages 3–11		Early adolescence ages 9–17	
	M	SD	M	SD
Maternal parenting				
Punitive discipline	2.1	0.39	1.9***	0.43
Closeness	3.7	0.44	3.6**	0.42
Supervision[a]	3.8	0.43	3.7*	0.50
Child behaviors				
Aggression	1.8	0.57	1.7*	0.55
Control problems	2.5	0.69	2.4†	0.71
Positive relations	3.4	0.47	3.2***	0.58
Well adjusted	3.7	0.44	3.5***	0.47

Note: Differences between childhood and adolescence: †$p < .10$; *$p < .05$; **$p < .01$; ***$p < .001$.
[a]$N = 157$. Questions asked only for children aged 6 and older.

Table 6.2. *Correlations between maternal parenting and the child's behaviors[a] at 6-year intervals, from childhood to early adolescence*

	Punitive discipline		Closeness		Supervision[b]	
	Age 3–11	Age 9–17	Age 3–11	Age 9–17	Age 3–11	Age 9–17
Aggression	.30***	.33***	−.14*	−.36***	−.14†	−.28***
Control problems	.18*	.39**	−.20**	−.46***	−.01	−.31***
Positive relations	−.07	−.20**	.35***	.47***	.19*	.31***
Well adjusted	−.02	−.26***	.24***	.49***	.26***	.31***
Total $N \geq$	198	198	198	198	148	198

[a] Maternal reports.
[b] Questions asked only for children 6 and older at Time 1.
†$p < .10$; *$p < .05$; **$p < .01$; ***$p < .001$.

smaller changes for aggression than for the positive dimensions of positive relations and being well adjusted (Table 6.1).

For both parenting and child behaviors, the changes over time tend to be generally larger among the older children, that is, those who were 7 or older at the first interview than among the younger ones (3–6) (data not presented).

Child age and the relationship between parenting and child functioning

The overall directions of the relationships between quality of maternal parenting and child functioning are as expected (Table 6.2). Children's negative behaviors are positively related to maternal punitive discipline and negatively related to maternal closeness and supervision. Correlatively, children's positive behaviors are negatively related to maternal punitive discipline and positively related to maternal closeness and supervision. The respective patterns of correlations are mirror images of each other.

Comparison of the correlations at the two different points in time also suggests that with the exception of the correlation between maternal punitive discipline and child aggression, the relationships between parenting and children's behavior become stronger from childhood to early adolescence.

Reciprocal relationships between quality of parenting and child behavior

Correlations at one point in time confound two processes: the impact of the parent on the child and that of the child on the parent. To examine the dynamic relationships between maternal parenting and child behavior and ascertain the extent to which each person influences the other, path analysis was carried out on the longitudinal data from the two surveys. This method allows one to determine

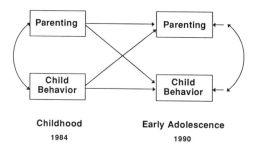

Figure 6.1. Cross-lag model: parenting and child behavior.

the relative strength of the effect of each variable measured at an earlier point in time on the other measured at the latter point, controlling for all other exogenous variables in the model. The models were estimated through LISREL VII (Jöreskog & Sörbom, 1989).

The general form of the model is displayed in Figure 6.1. Both the child's age and parental education were controlled for. We estimated 12 models, one for each of the four child behaviors in relation to the three parenting measures (Table 6.3). With the exception of the child's rating as well adjusted, the model explains a greater amount of variance in the children's behaviors than in quality of parenting.

The parameters of greatest interest with respect to the direction of the interpersonal effects are the standardized path coefficients between parenting and child behavior across time. The results suggest that different dynamic processes characterize different dimensions of parenting and different aspects of child behavior.

Patterns of relationships

Maternal harsh discipline appears to be more a determinant of the child's behavior than a response to it. Three of the four paths from harsh discipline to child functioning are statistically significant (or border on significance), whereas only one path, that of child control problems, affects harsh maternal discipline.

By contrast, level of maternal supervision appears to be completely a response to the child's behaviors. Supervision increases in response to positive behaviors on the part of the child, while supervision decreases when the child misbehaves.

Of the three parenting measures, maternal closeness most evidences a reciprocal feedback process between parent and child, both when the child behaves negatively and when the child behaves positively. The impact of maternal closeness on the child appears to be stronger for positive than for negative child behaviors, while the impact of the child on maternal closeness appears to be stronger for negative than for positive forms of child behaviors. Controlling for initial levels of positive parenting and child aggression, aggressive children appear to lead to lowered maternal monitoring and emotional withdrawal of mother from child.

Table 6.3. *Coefficients from cross-lag path models of the relationships between parenting and child behaviors*[a]

			Standardized path coefficients								
					From childhood to early adolescence			R^2		
Parenting	Child behaviors	Parent–child correlations in childhood	Parenting to behavior	Behavior to parenting	Parenting	Child behavior	Parent–child correlated residual errors in early adolescence	Parent	Child	N
Punitive	Aggression	.29***	.12†	.10	.41***	.50***	.17**	.23	.30	204
	Control problems	.16*	.15*	.21**	.40***	.53***	.16**	.25	.34	190
	Positive relations	−.06	−.08	−.07	.43***	.55***	−.14**	.22	.37	190
	Well adjusted	−.01	−.18**	−.04	.44***	.34***	−.19***	.22	.21	204
Closeness	Aggression	−.13†	−.02	−.15*	.41***	.54***	−.24***	.27	.29	204
	Control problems	−.18*	−.14*	−.20**	.39***	.53***	−.26***	.29	.33	190
	Positive relations	.33***	.15*	.18**	.37***	.51***	.19***	.28	.38	190
	Well-adjusted	.24***	.22***	.10	.40***	.30***	.28***	.26	.22	204
Supervision	Aggression	−.13	.02	−.23**	.08	.59***	−.14*	.16	.35	154
	Control problems	−.04	.02	−.14†	.07	.57***	−.25***	.13	.33	144
	Positive relations	.17*	.01	.22**	.04	.55***	.07	.16	.36	144
	Well adjusted	.25***	−.02	.22**	.05	.35***	.16*	.15	.16	154

[a]Based on maternal reports. Child's age and mother's education are controlled for in the models.
†$p < .10$; *$p < .05$; **$p < .01$; ***$p < .001$.

Thus, with respect to the child's antisocial behavior, the processes underlying control problems are somewhat more complex than those observed for aggression. For aggression, only one cross-lag path is significant with respect to each parenting dimension. Given an ongoing process, maternal harsh discipline increases the child's aggression. However, the path from the child's aggression to the mother's harsh discipline does not reach statistical significance. An opposite process characterizes supervision and closeness. The significant and negative relationship is from the child's behavior to parenting. Both cross-lag paths between maternal parenting and the child's control problems are statistically significant for two of the three dimensions of parenting. Punitive discipline exacerbates the child's control problems; closeness reduces them. In turn, the child's control problems increase maternal punitiveness and decrease maternal positive feelings toward the child.

A methodological note

A limitation of the analyses is that both parenting and children's behaviors are assessed on the basis of maternal reports. When the data are from a single informant, the model estimates confound structural effects and shared method variance. A person's characteristics, such as mood, cognitions, or social context, will influence not only reports of one's own behavior but reports of others' as well (see e.g., Reid, Kavanagh, & Baldwin, 1987; Patterson, Reid, & Dishion, 1992). As noted by Patterson, Reid, and Dishion (1992), longitudinal data may not necessarily alleviate the problem of shared method variance, since quality of affect has a high degree of stability over time (e.g., Watson & Clark, 1984). However, the biases in maternal reports may not be quite as problematic in the present study as in Watson and Clark (1984), since the interval between waves of data collection was 5 to 6 years long, rather than 2 years. Independent reports from mothers and children were available for the second wave of data but were not used in the longitudinal analyses because of the statistical advantage of having identical measures over time. In the absence of identical measures, changes in coefficients may reflect changes in method as well as in behaviors. To assess the potential impact of measures based on a single informant on our results, selected models were rerun such that at the second time point latent constructs, based on identical manifest indicators obtained from mother and child, replaced the measures based on single maternal reports. Latent constructs for maternal parenting could be constructed for each of the three parenting dimensions, and a single latent construct could be constructed for child aggression. The correlations between parent and child reports are .42 for punitive discipline, .30 for parental closeness, .24 for supervision, and .37 for child aggression (all significant at the .001 level). A path model could be run for each of the three parenting measures in relation to the child's aggression, in which single-informant measures were included for Time 1 and multiple informants' latent constructs were included for Time 2. The results of these three models are presented in Table 6.4. For ease of comparison, we reproduce the parallel coefficients based

Table 6.4. *Coefficients from cross-lag path models of the relationships between parenting and child aggression from models with and without children's reports in early adolescence*[a]

| | | Standardized path coefficients | | | From childhood to early adolescence | | Parent–child correlated residual errors in early adolescence | R² | | N |
		Parent–child correlations in childhood	Parenting to behavior	Behavior to parenting	Parenting	Child behavior		Parent	Child	
Parenting	Child behaviors									
Punitive[b]	Aggression	.32***	.23**	.14†	.51***	.48***	.18*	.36	.37	180
Punitive[c]	Aggression	.29***	.12†	.10	.41***	.50***	.17**	.23	.30	204
Closeness[b]	Aggression	-.16*	-.08	-.17†	.38***	.51***	-.19*	.43	.29	180
Closeness[c]	Aggression	-.13†	-.02	-.15*	.41***	.54***	-.24***	.27	.29	204
Supervision[b]	Aggression	-.10	-.10	-.36**	.10	.67***	-.40**	.40	.49	134
Supervision[c]	Aggression	-.13	.02	-.23**	.08	.59***	-.14*	.16	.35	154

[a] Child's age and mother's education are controlled for in the models.
[b] Coefficients are based on maternal reports in childhood and maternal and child reports in early adolescence.
[c] Coefficients are based on maternal reports (from Table 6.4).
†p < .10; *p < .05; **p < .01; ***p < .001.

on maternal reports from Table 6.3. The coefficients from the two sets of models are very similar. The relative size of the respective paths supports the conclusion, based on the earlier models, that the path from harsh parental discipline to child aggression is stronger than the path from child aggression to harsh parenting. There is a negative path from child aggression to parental supervision. These results confirm the usefulness of results based exclusively on maternal reports.

A hypothetical dynamic process underlying parenting and children's behaviors

Children's antisocial behavior

A dynamic developmental process underlying the relationships between quality of parenting and child behaviors can be generated from constructing a synthetic three-wave cohort on the basis of the empirical results of the two-wave models presented in Table 6.3 (see Figure 6.2).

Punitive, coercive behavior on the part of the mother leads to aggressive behavior on the part of the child (Figure 6.2). In turn, aggression in the child leads to withdrawal by mothers, reduced efforts at controlling the child, and a lowering in the quality of positive parenting that reduces negative behaviors in the child. Given initial levels of problematic behaviors and quality of parenting, harsh discipline leads to an exacerbation of the child's conduct problems, while close positive parenting leads to a reduction in these problems (Figure 6.2). Correlatively, the

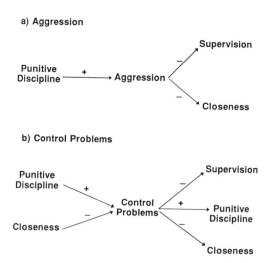

Figure 6.2. Assumed dynamic developmental process for children's antisocial behavior.

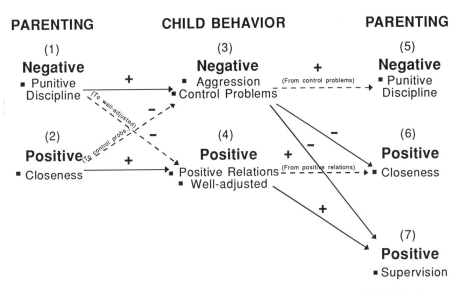

Figure 6.3. Assumed dynamic developmental process between parenting and child behavior. Solid arrows indicate that the significant paths are found in different models. Dashed arrows indicate that the significant paths are found only in selected models.

child's control problems lead to increasingly harsh discipline and lower levels of felt closeness and supervision on the part of the parent.

Children's negative and positive behaviors

The model of the dynamic developmental process underlying the relationships between quality of parenting and child behaviors can be broadened to reflect the complexity of family functioning. The positive behaviors can be introduced in the model simultaneously with the negative behaviors. The integrated model, based on Table 6.3, is displayed in Figure 6.3. The solid lines indicate that the significant paths are observed consistently across models for each relevant maternal and child measure, the dashed lines that the significant paths are observed only in selected models.

The dynamic nature of parent–child interactions is highlighted by the model. Specific parenting practices lead to greater subsequent manifestation of children's behaviors along the specific positive (or negative) dimension represented by the quality of parenting. This effect is stronger than the effect on the opposite type of behavior. Negative parenting has stronger effects on negative than on positive child behaviors, while positive parenting, as indexed by closeness between parent and child, has greater consequences for the child's positive than negative behaviors. In turn, children's behaviors affect the quality of parenting, especially its positive dimensions.

As regards the child's negative functioning, given an ongoing process, the mother's harsh discipline leads to an exacerbation of the child's aggression and control problems, while a close mother–child relationship reduces the child's control problems but has no impact on aggression. Correlatively, controlling for initial levels of problematic behaviors and negative parenting, the child's control problems lead to increasingly harsh maternal discipline. Furthermore, children who are aggressive and undercontrolled contribute to increasingly lower levels of positive parenting, namely, emotional withdrawal of the mother from the child and a lowering of maternal attempts at supervising the child.

In turn, the child's positive behaviors lead to a closer relationship between mother and child, especially to greater supervision of the child by the mother. By contrast, punitive discipline has a negative impact on the child's positive behaviors, although the path reaches significance only for the rating of the child as being well adjusted. Child positive behaviors have no effect on levels of maternal punitive discipline.

Discussion

Not only does this study confirm relationships between specific positive and negative parenting practices and specific child behaviors described by other investigators, but most importantly, it provides some understanding of the dynamic processes underlying relationships observed at one point in time.

Although active maternal parenting decreases as children become older, the strength of the relationships between parenting style and child behaviors increases with age. The influences of mother and child on each other increase from childhood to adolescence, at least on the outcomes measured in this study.

Our findings strongly support the existence of reciprocal relationships and influences between mothers and children. The type and degree of influences, however, depend on the specific behaviors of parent and child. Negative maternal parenting leads to more negative and fewer positive behaviors on the part of the child, while positive maternal parenting leads to more positive and fewer negative behaviors. Negative child behaviors influence both positive and negative dimensions of maternal parenting, while positive child behaviors influence only positive dimensions. Negative child behaviors appear to have a greater impact than positive behaviors on the quality of maternal parenting.

Because of the power differential between parent and child, any parental socialization attempt, whether positive or negative, can be interpreted as a form of coercion over the child, one form being more subtle than the other. However, negative maternal parenting has a somewhat greater impact in reinforcing negative behaviors in the child than positive maternal parenting has in decreasing such behaviors. Correlatively, negative child behaviors evoke a range of maternal responses, al-

Table 6.A1. *Zero-order correlations among variables in path models* (N ≥ 198)[a]

	Childhood									Early adolescence					
	Child's age	Mother's education	Punitive discipline	Close-ness	Super-vision	Aggres-sion	Control problems	Positive relations	Well adjusted	Punitive discipline	Close-ness	Super-vision	Aggres-sion	Control problems	Positive relations
Childhood															
Mother's education	−.29***														
Punitive discipline	.04	−.01													
Closeness	−.22**	−.02	−.16*												
Supervision	−.02	.17*	.08	.06											
Aggression	.02	−.09	.30***	−.14*	−.14†										
Control problems	−.07	.01	.18*	−.20**	−.01	.46***									
Positive relations	−.17*	.01	−.07	.35***	.19*	−.23***	−.28***								
Well adjusted	−.15*	.05	−.02	.24***	.26***	−.26***	−.19**	.48***							
Early adolescence															
Punitive discipline	−.13†	.11	.44***	−.20**	.12	.21**	.29***	−.07	−.03						
Closeness	−.23***	−.09	−.17*	.46***	−.07	−.19**	−.26***	.35***	.22**	−.32***					
Supervision	−.38***	.00	−.17*	.31***	.08	−.17*	−.08	.22**	.25***	−.15*	.34***				
Aggression	.07	−.03	.26***	−.10	−.05	.54***	.26***	−.16*	−.25***	.33***	−.36***	−.28***			
Control problems	−.04	.06	.25***	−.24***	.00	.42***	.56***	−.27***	−.24***	.39***	−.46***	−.31***	.54***		
Positive relations	−.26***	.09	−.13†	.36***	.10	−.14†	−.25***	.58***	.23***	−.20**	.47***	.31***	−.28***	−.28***	
Well adjusted	−.24***	−.02	−.19**	.33***	.05	−.22***	−.32***	.51***	.37***	−.26***	.49***	.31***	−.32***	−.36***	.62***

[a]Missing cases reduce the original size of the sample (N = 208). Since questions about supervision were asked only for children 6 and older at T1, correlations between Time 1 Supervision and other variables are based on N = 157. Parenting scales measure maternal behavior.

†p ≤ .10; *p ≤ .05; **p ≤ .01; ***p ≤ .001.

though lowering of positive maternal reinforcement is a more prominent response than escalation of negative reinforcement. Undercontrolled and aggressive children experience simultaneously over time increasingly harsher discipline administered by their mothers as well as reduced closeness and decreased maternal supervision. Thus, children who manifest behavioral problems suffer over time from an increase in the risk factors and a decrease in the protective factors created by quality parenting. Such children seem to elicit increasingly harsh maternal treatment and increasingly reduced maternal warmth and supervision.

Rather than conceiving of socialization exclusively as the expression of the greater power of parents over their children, a more accurate perspective should acknowledge the active contribution of children in shaping the behaviors of their parents, a contribution whose importance varies depending on the type of behavior and the dimension of parenting.

Appendix

Zero-order correlations among all variables included in the major analyses (models in Table 6.3) are presented in Table 6.A1.

NOTES

Work on this research has been partially supported by research grants DA03196, DA04866, and DA02867 (D. Kandel, principal investigator) and a research scientist award DA00081 to D. Kandel from the National Institute on Drug Abuse. Partial support for computer costs was provided by Mental Health Clinical Research Center Grant MH30906 from the NIMH to the New York State Psychiatric Institute. The research assistance of Christine Schaffran is gratefully acknowledged.
 1 The total cohort of men and women constitutes a representative sample of former adolescents enrolled in Grades 10 and 11 in New York State public schools in 1971–72, who were selected from a stratified sample of 18 high schools throughout New York State (Kandel, Single, & Kessler, 1976). The target population for the adult follow-up was drawn from the enrollment list of half the homerooms from Grades 10 and 11 and included students who were absent from school at the time of the initial study. The inclusion of these former absentees assures the representativeness of the sample and the inclusion of the most deviant youths (Kandel, Raveis, & Kandel, 1984).
 2 The following items are included in the maternal parenting scales, with frequency of occurrence scored on a 4-point scale ranging from 1 to 4: *Punitive discipline* (five items) (alpha = .55) – send child to room; make fun of child; spank or slap; yell at child; take away privileges (1 = never or almost never to 4 = very often). *Closeness* (two items) (alpha = .32) – how close do you feel to child? (1 = not at all to 4 = extremely); act cold or unfriendly (1 = very often to 4 = never or almost never). *Supervision* (two items) (alpha = .80) – know where child is; know who child is with (1 = never or almost never to 4 = very often).
 3 The following items are included in each child behavior scale, with frequency of manifestation of the behavior scored on a 4-point scale ranging from 1, not at all like my child, to 4, very much like my child: *Furstenberg's high aggression* (six items) (alpha = .72) – teases, picks on, bullies; cannot concentrate; cheats or tells lies; destroys belongings; acts too young for age; cannot sit still. *Schaefer's control problems* (five items) (alpha = .79) – keeps

after me for things after I say no; gives me a hard time; is hard to get along with; doesn't take no for an answer; seldom obeys. *Schaefer's positive relations* (five items) (alpha = .76) – works hard to please me; asks to do things for me; is anxious to please me; does things to cheer me up; tries to be helpful. *Furstenberg's well-adjustedness* (three items) (alpha = .51) – very enthusiastic; usually happy mood; polite.

4 Items were selected from the Achenbach Child Behavior Checklist to duplicate the six-item aggression scale (see note 3) (alpha = .72) – teases a lot; is cruel, bullies, is mean to others; cannot concentrate or pay attention for long; lies or cheats; destroys his or her own things; destroys things belonging to his or her family or other children; acts too young for his or her age; cannot sit still or is restless or hyperactive. The items are scored (0 = not true, 1 = somewhat or sometimes true, 2 = very true or often true).

5 The reliabilities of the scales among the children were very similar to those observed among mothers: .50 for punitive discipline, .37 for closeness, and .71 for supervision. The reliability for the Achenbach aggression subscale was .65.

REFERENCES

Anderson, K. E., Lytton, H., & Romney D. M. (1986). Mothers' interactions with normal and conduct-disordered boys: Who affects whom? *Developmental Psychology, 22,* 604–609.

Baldwin, D. V., & Skinner, M. L. (1989). Structural model for antisocial behavior: Generalization to single-mother families. *Developmental Psychology, 25,* 45–50.

Bell, R. Q. (1968). A reinterpretation of the direction of effects in studies of socialization. *Psychological Review, 75,* 81–95.

Bell, R. Q. (1977). Socialization findings re-examined. In R. Q. Bell & L. V. Harper (Eds.), *Child effects on adults* (pp. 53–84). Hillsdale, NJ: Erlbaum.

Bell, R. Q., & Chapman, M. (1986). Child effects in studies using experimental or brief longitudinal approaches to socialization. *Developmental Psychology, 22,* 595–603.

Bell, R. Q., & Harper, L. V. (1977). *Child effects on adults.* Hillsdale, NJ: Erlbaum.

Bronstein, P. (1984). Differences in mothers' and fathers' behaviors toward children: A cross-cultural comparison. *Developmental Psychology, 20,* 995–1003.

Brunk, M. A., & Henggeler, S. Q. (1984). Child influences on adult controls: An experimental investigation. *Developmental Psychology, 20,* 1074–1081.

Bugental, D. B., Caporael, L., & Shennum, W. A. (1980). Experimentally-produced child controllability: Effects on the potency of adult communication patterns. *Child Development, 51,* 520–528.

Buss, D. M. (1981). Predicting parent–child interactions from children's activity level. *Developmental Psychology, 17,* 59–69.

Cantor, N. L., & Gelfand, D. M. (1977). Effects of responsiveness and sex of children on adult's behavior. *Child Development, 48,* 232–238.

Clarke-Stewart, K. A. (1973). Interactions between mothers and their children: Characteristics and consequences. *Monographs of the Society for Research in Child Development, 38*(6–7, Serial No. 153).

Clifford, E. (1959). Discipline in the home: A controlled observational study of parental practices. *Journal of Genetic Psychology, 95,* 45–82.

DiLalla, L. F., Mitchell, C. M., Arthur, M. W., & Pagliocca, P. M. (1988). Aggression and delinquency: Family and environmental factors. *Journal of Youth and Adolescence, 17,* 233–246.

Dion, K. (1974). Children's physical attractiveness and sex as determinants of adult punitiveness. *Developmental Psychology, 10,* 772–778.

Dix, T., Rubel, D. N., & Zambarano, R. J. (1989). Mother's implicit theories of discipline:

Child effects, parent effects, and the attribution process. *Child Development, 60,* 1373–1391.

Dornbusch, S. M., Ritter, P. L., Leiderman, P. H., Roberts, D. F., & Fraleigh, M. J. (1987). The relation of parenting style to adolescent performance. *Child Development, 58,* 1244–1257.

Furstenberg, F. S., Morgan, S. P., & Allison, P. D. (1986). Paternal participation and children's well-being after marital disruption. Unpublished manuscript.

Grusec, J. E., & Kuczynski, L. (1980). Direction of effect on socialization: A comparison of the parent's versus the child's behavior as determinants of disciplinary techniques. *Developmental Psychology, 16,* 1–9.

Hoffman, M. L. (1975). Moral internalization, parental power, and the nature of the parent–child interaction. *Developmental Psychology, 11,* 228–239.

Hoffman, M. L. (1983). Empathy, guilt and social cognition. In W. F. Overton (Ed.), *The relationship between social and cognitive development* (pp. 1–51). Hillsdale, NJ: Erlbaum.

Johnson, V., & Pandina, R. J. (1991). Effects of the family environment on adolescent substance use, delinquency, and coping styles. *American Journal of Drug and Alcohol Abuse, 17,* 77–88.

Jöreskog, K. G., & Sörbom, D. (1989). *LISREL 7 user's reference guide.* Mooresville, IN: Scientific Software.

Kandel, D. B. (1990). Parenting styles, drug use and children's adjustment in families of young adults. *Journal of Marriage and the Family, 52,* 183–196.

Kandel, D. B., Raveis, V. H., & Kandel, P. (1984). Continuity in discontinuities: Adjustment in young adulthood of former school absentees and school dropouts. *Youth and Society, 13,* 325–352.

Kandel, D. B., Single, E., & Kessler, R. (1976). The epidemiology of drug use among New York State high school students: Distribution, trends, and change in rates of use. *American Journal of Public Health, 66,* 43–53.

Loeber, R., & Stouthamer-Loeber, M. (1986). Family factors as correlates and predictors of juvenile conduct problems and delinquency. In M. Tonry & N. Morris (Eds.), *Crime and Jusi ice: An Annual Review of Research* (Vol. 7, pp. 29–149). Chicago: University of Chicago Press.

Lytton, H. (1990). Child and parent effects in boys conduct disorder: A reinterpretation. *Developmental Psychology, 26,* 683–697.

Maccoby, E. E., & Martin, J. A. 1983. Socialization in the context of the family: Parent–child interaction. In E. M. Hetherington (Ed.), *Handbook of child psychology: Vol. 4. Socialization, personality, and social development* (pp. 1–101). New York: Wiley.

MacEwen, K. E., & Barling, J. (1991). Effects of maternal employment experiences on children's behavior via mood, cognitive difficulties, and parenting behavior. *Journal of Marriage and the Family, 53,* 635–644.

McNally, S., Eisenberg, N., & Harris, J. D. (1991). Consistency and change in maternal child-rearing practices and values: A longitudinal study. *Child Development, 62,* 190–198.

Miller, B. C., McCoy, J. K., Olson, T. D., & Wallace, C. M. (1986). Parental discipline and control attempts in relation to adolescent sexual attitudes and behavior. *Journal of Marriage and the Family, 48,* 503–512.

Mink, I. T., & Nihira, K. (1986). Family life-styles and child behaviors: A study of direction of effects. *Developmental Psychology, 22,* 610–616.

Mulhern, R. K., Jr., & Passman, R. H. (1981). Parental discipline as affected by the sex of the parent, the sex of the child, and the child's apparent responsiveness to discipline. *Developmental Psychology, 17,* 604–613.

Patterson, G. R. 1982. *Coercive family process: A social learning approach* (Vol. 3). Eugene, OR: Castalia.

Patterson, G. R. (1986). Maternal rejection: Determinant or product for deviant child behavior? In W. W. Hartup & Z. Rubin (Eds.), *Relationships and development* (pp. 73–94). Hillsdale, NJ: Erlbaum.

Patterson, G. R., Reid, J. B., & Dishion, T. J. (1992). *Antisocial boys*. Eugene, OR: Castalia.

Patterson, G. R., & Stouthamer-Loeber M. (1984). The correlation of family management practices and delinquency. *Child Development, 55,* 1299–1307.

Reid, J. B., Kavanagh, K., & Baldwin, D. V. (1987). Abusive parents' perceptions of child problem behaviors: An example of parental bias. *Journal of Abnormal Child Psychology, 15,* 457–466.

Rheingold, H. L. (1969). The social and socializing infant. In D. A. Goslin (Ed.), *Handbook of socialization theory and research* (pp. 779–790). Chicago: Rand McNally.

Roberts, G. C., Block, J. H., & Block, J. (1984). Continuity and change in parents' child-rearing practices. *Child Development, 55,* 586–597.

Rohner, R. P. (1986). *The warmth dimension: Foundations of parental acceptance-rejection theory.* Beverly Hills, CA: Sage.

Rutter, M., & Garmezy, N. (1983). Developmental psychopathology. In E. M. Hetherington (Ed.), *Handbook of child psychology* (Vol. 4, pp. 775–912). New York: Wiley.

Schaefer, E. S., & Edgerton, M. (1977). Parent's report of child behavior toward the parent inventory. Unpublished manuscript.

Simcha-Fagan, O., & Schwartz, J. E. (1986). Neighborhood and delinquency: An assessment of contextual effects. *Criminology, 24,* 667–703.

Steinberg, L., Elmen, J. D., & Mounts, N. S. (1989). Authoritative parenting, psychosocial maturity, and academic success among adolescents. *Child Development, 60,* 1424–1436.

Steinberg, L., Mounts, N. S., Lamborn, S. D., & Dornbusch, S. M. (1991). Authoritative parenting and adolescent adjustment across varied ecological niches. *Journal of Research on Adolescence, 1,* 19–36.

Stevens-Long, J. (1973). The effect of behavioral context on some aspects of adult disciplinary practice and affect. *Child Development, 44,* 476–484.

Watson, D., & Clark, L. A. (1984). Negative affectivity: The disposition to experience aversive emotional states. *Psychological Bulletin, 96,* 465–490.

Yarrow, M. R., Waxler, C. Z., & Scott, P. M. (1971). Child effects on behavior. *Developmental Psychology, 5,* 300–311.

Zill, N. (1983). *Happy, healthy, and insecure: A portrait of middle childhood in America.* Garden City, NY: Doubleday.

7 Family and child factors in stability and change in children's aggressiveness in elementary school

JOHN E. BATES, GREGORY S. PETTIT,
AND KENNETH A. DODGE

Parents of acting-out children tend to use coercive discipline tactics more frequently than do parents of well-behaved children, whether the parenting is assessed concurrent with or antecedent to child adjustment (Campbell, 1990; Hetherington & Martin, 1986; Patterson, 1982). Coercive discipline is central to most models of child adjustment. However, empirically, parent–child interaction indexes in previous studies have accounted for only moderate portions of the variance in child outcomes, especially when used as longitudinal predictors. One implication of this finding is that models need to include additional predictor measures. Many researchers, influenced by general systems models, are now assessing various other possible predictors, including positive parenting in addition to coercion, marital quality, socioeconomic stress, child temperament, and child intelligence.

For the present chapter, however, the focus is more on a different implication of the limited variance in adjustment outcomes accounted for by parental coerciveness: in addition to inadequate definition of the predictor, there could also be inadequate definition of the outcome. Clinical accounts of the complexities of individuals' adjustment histories and modern systems theory suggest the need for more richly described criterion variables, including a multidimensional, multisource definition of adjustment, as well as a dynamic, cross-time definition. To build useful dynamic models, we must try to improve models of developmental stability versus change.

This chapter considers the role of parental harshness in child aggressiveness in kindergarten and first grade, and at the same time considers a wide variety of possible factors in the stability versus change of aggressiveness, such as child tendencies toward fearfulness or family stress. Robins and Rutter (1990) suggested that identifying distinctive characteristics in cases of discontinuity would be useful in designing preventive interventions and therapies (also see Anthony & Cohler, 1987). Our more immediate objective, however, is a richer description of the natural history of important individual differences.

Predicting stability versus change in adjustment

This study is one of a number of recent investigations of stability versus change in aggressive behavioral adjustment. A number of change factors in externalizing-type disorders have been found in past studies. One kind of finding concerns the presence or absence of family risk factors. For example, Campbell, March, Pierce, Ewing, and Szumowski (1991) found that preschoolers' externalizing symptoms at a 1-year follow-up, even after controlling for initial level of symptoms, were greater in families in which mothers had originally described themselves as relatively depressed than in families in which mothers had not. This pattern held even though the mothers' depression did not correlate significantly with the initial level of child symptoms. A different kind of finding shows the value of looking at a fuller adjustment history in forecasting adaptation in the next developmental stage. Sroufe, Egeland, and Kreutzer (1990) predicted the elementary school adjustment of high-risk children all of whom were poorly adjusted in preschool but who differed in infancy-toddlerhood adjustment. Those children whose poor preschool adjustment had been preceded by normal development in the first few years of life adapted to elementary school considerably better than children who had been poorly adjusted in infancy-toddlerhood as well.

One could also ask whether the prediction of change in a socially relevant adjustment outcome is improved by adding to the initial assessment a wider range of facets of adjustment. Loeber, Farrington, Stouthamer-Loeber, and VanKammen (1992) followed a large number of children for 3 years. They found that increased delinquency was forecast by variables such as poor motivation for school and aggressive conduct problems, and decreased delinquency by better school motivation and less aggressiveness. A further predictor of change in adjustment is change in the environment. Patterson (1993) reported that when boys increased their level of antisocial behavior, the change was associated with increased amounts of time wandering the streets unsupervised and acquiring more deviant peers.

Another kind of predictor concerns personal strengths that may compensate for adverse rearing circumstances. For example, Masten (1989) found that among children who were exposed to high levels of family stress, those who had higher IQs showed less classroom disruptiveness than those who had lower IQs. There was no IQ-related difference in disruptiveness among those for whom stress was low. In Werner and Smith's (1982) study, children who were exposed to risk factors, but who did not develop adjustment problems, tended to have offsetting strengths, such as dispositions to be active and sociable.

Characteristics such as activity level and sociability could reflect temperament, that is, traits that are argued to be present from early in life, with some degree of stability, and to correspond to neural structures and processes that are, in theory at least, specifiable (Bates, 1989; Gray, 1991; Zuckerman, 1991). Of special interest are early appearing anxiety tendencies, which have been found several times to be stable predictors of analogous, internalizing aspects of adjustment (Bates, 1989,

1990; Caspi, Henry, McGee, Moffitt, & Silva, 1992), but whose role in the externalizing aspects of adjustment is not clear. Pianta and Caldwell (1990) found that a number of variables predicted the extent to which children's teacher-rated externalizing problems in first grade exceeded the levels predicted by the corresponding index in kindergarten. Both boys and girls who were seen as higher in internalizing problems in kindergarten and lower in verbal ability tended to be higher in externalizing in first grade than would have been predicted by kindergarten externalizing alone. In contrast to the Pianta and Caldwell findings with internalizing, however, Tremblay (1992) has reviewed several previous findings in which high anxiety predicted reduced risk of antisocial behavior. Pulkkinen (1992) has reported a similar negative correlation between both boys' and girls' anxiety ratings at age 8 and externalizing behavior problems at age 14, as well as with their problem drinking in early adulthood.

These studies of correlates of stability versus change in adjustment generally focus on linear models of change. In essence, linear models improve predictive validity by expanding the battery of predictors. A frequently suggested, though seldom seen alternative is to use nonlinear, interactive models. These models seek to specify the conditions under which a predictor variable operates in qualitatively different ways, as in the Mastan (1989) study mentioned previously. Given the limited amount of variance accounted for in linear models and the increasingly complex theoretical accounts of development, there are reasons for exploring nonlinear models (Rutter, 1982), despite the fact that one should not expect that they would often perform better than additive models (see Bates, 1989; Wiggins, 1973).

Tremblay (1992) provides an interesting example of nonlinear findings relevant to the present consideration of how anxiety tendencies are involved in the origins of externalizing disorders. Starting with a general three-dimensional theoretical model of personality, Tremblay classified a large sample of boys according to the interaction, or profile, of three personality dimensions rated in kindergarten. He then systematically explored the implications of various kindergarten profiles for adjustment at ages 10 to 12. The dimensions of hyperactive novelty-seeking and prosocial/cooperative (also referred to as reward dependence) rated in kindergarten had main effects (in the intuitive directions) on self-reported delinquency as well as teacher reports of fighting measured at age 10 to 12 and averaged across ages. However, the third dimension, harm avoidance (worries, fears novelty, cries easily – all variables related to the general construct of anxiety) related to the outcomes only via interactions with the other two personality dimensions, and differently for the different outcome measures. For example, among boys who had been rated high active and low prosocial, those who had also been rated low in harm avoidance/anxiety reported for themselves high delinquency about three times as often as those who had been rated high in harm avoidance/anxiety. The effect was opposite for the other outcome measure: kindergarten boys who were rated high active, low prosocial, and low anxiety were later classified about two-thirds as often into the teacher-rated group rated high in fighting than were boys rated high active, low prosocial, but high anxiety.

One of the goals of this study was to consider the predictive role of early parenting variables. We considered whether parenting variables predict later adjustment even when initial adjustment is controlled, as did Campbell et al. (1991). This study considered a 1-year span, with parenting assessed just prior to kindergarten and school adjustment assessed in kindergarten and first grade. If initial parent–child relationship measures predict first-grade aggression independent of the kindergarten to first-grade continuity in child aggressiveness, this might suggest that individual differences in aggression have different properties at the two points in development. For example, it could be speculated that early parental coerciveness has a "sleeper effect" on aggressiveness: variations in parental discipline might become more closely linked with aggressive adjustment as children move further into the school culture and there is less margin for deviance. It need not be assumed that it is the early parenting itself that affects child adjustment at school; the effect very well could be due to continued parental qualities along with a change in the child's reaction to parenting style or in the school's reaction to the child's aggressiveness. On the other hand, if parenting does predict initial aggression and does not predict later aggression after controlling for the effects of initial aggressiveness, it would suggest that the processes linking parenting to child aggressiveness are the same in kindergarten and first grade. The study is one of very few that has examined family factors in relation to changes in levels of child aggressiveness.

A further goal of the study was to advance descriptions of the role played by children's individual differences as contributors to adjustment and stability of adjustment. It has been widely believed in the field for the past 20 years or so that child temperament, especially difficult temperament (Bates, 1980; Thomas, Chess, & Birch, 1968), has been shown to antecede childhood behavior problems. However, in actuality it is only in the past 10 years that empirical confirmations of that hypothesis have begun to appear (Bates, 1989), and as yet there are relatively few studies of the topic. More specific findings on what temperament variables correlate with what adjustment outcome dimensions are even more recent (Bates, 1989, 1990; Caspi et al., 1992). So far, it appears that early fearful, inhibited, or anxious tendencies assessed via temperament measures predict most clearly later anxiety-type problems, whereas early resistance to parental control of activity or novelty seeking most clearly predict later acting-out traits, such as aggressiveness and excessive stimulation seeking. What has been even less well studied in children's development, however, is how the traits underlying excessive fear and excessive approach or dominance might interact with one another (with notable exceptions such as Lahey & Loeber, 1991; Tremblay, 1992; also see Zuckerman, 1991).

The Child Development Project

We conducted a study at three different sites – Nashville and Knoxville, Tennessee, and Bloomington, Indiana. Parents were recruited for the study as they enrolled their children for kindergarten, with a total of 589 children assessed initially. We tried to recruit families from the full range of socioeconomic status (SES); in fact,

26% of families were in the lowest two Hollingshead classes (Hollingshead, 1979) and 16% were in the highest class. We also tried to include both African-American and European-American families (Asian-Americans were not frequently present in our population); 17% were African-American. Boys constituted 52% of the sample. Gender ratios did not vary from site to site in the sample, but rates for other demographic and family ecological characteristics varied, as was expected, across sites. The most notable differences were that the Nashville sample was (1) highest in African-Americans, with 42% versus 11% in Knoxville and 3% in Bloomington, (2) lowest in SES scores (34.1 vs. 43.1 for Knoxville and 41.6 for Bloomington, with nearly identical SDs – average, 13.5), and (3) highest in single-parent families (44% vs. 35% for Knoxville and 28% for Bloomington). The number of first graders assessed was 555.

We collected a wide range of measures of the child and family, especially ones related to child aggressiveness and its hypothesized origins, which were the primary focus of the study. Not every variable was obtained on every child, with data lost for all the usual reasons, including a few parents who failed to complete one measure or another, a few teachers who failed to complete questionnaires, and a few classrooms where not enough pupils were given parental permission for sociometric assessments (we required that at least 70% of the class give ratings so we would have confidence in the generalizability). The missing data resulted in smaller ns for multivariate analyses.

This chapter focuses on aggression in the school. Aggression at home is an important variable, too, and individual differences in it are to a large extent independent of aggression at school, judging from the minimal overlap between parent and teacher ratings in a nonclinical sample (Achenbach & Edelbrock, 1986). However, we did consider whether externalizing problems perceived by the parents augmented the prediction of aggressiveness perceived by teachers in the first grade after considering kindergarten aggressiveness.

Measures of aggressiveness at school

One key measure of child aggressiveness was the Achenbach Teacher Report Form aggression composite (Achenbach & Edelbrock, 1986). The second and third measures were the reactive and proactive aggression scores from the Teacher Checklist (Coie & Dodge, 1988). The three teacher indexes were moderately highly correlated with one another and for some purposes were combined into one composite. The final aggressiveness indexes, derived from sociometric interviews (Coie, Dodge, & Cappotelli, 1982), measure the number of peer nominations for the roles of *fights, mean,* and *gets mad,* each standardized within the child's class. These three indexes also formed a composite for some analyses. Assessments were done during the winter or spring in both kindergarten and first grade, and parallel scores were computed for each year. Internal consistencies of composites formed by adding Z-score indexes of the scales were all quite satisfactory, whether the composites were three-item composites of either teacher scales or peer aggressiveness items or the composite of all six teacher and peer items, and whether kindergarten or first grade is considered. The alphas ranged from .83 to .87.

Predictor measures

For our evaluation of the linear effects of coercive parenting on the kindergarten and first-grade outcomes, we considered measures derived from assessments conducted in the summer before kindergarten or, for the approximately 20% of families who waited until the start of the school year to enroll their children, procedures done in the first few months of kindergarten. A detailed developmental history interview assessed discipline style, stress, and child care arrangements. In the same home visit, we also assessed (1) parents' social-cognitive problem solving via responses to hypothetical vignettes about child misbehavior, (2) family violence patterns via the Conflict Tactics Scale (Straus, 1979), and (3) explicit family values concerning aggression. To define family coerciveness for the first of our analyses, we used a composite measure of harsh discipline practices derived from mother reports and interviewer ratings during the developmental history interview. We also used a set of measures based on home observations of a selected subset of 165 of the families, chosen to represent high, medium, and low child aggressiveness as scored by both parents (where available) on the aggression scale of the Child Behavior Checklist (CBCL; Achenbach & Edelbrock, 1983). The two 2-hour observations were conducted at times when all family members were likely to be at home, typically around dinnertime. Observers used a narrative method previously shown to detect different overall levels of family adaptation (Pettit & Bates, 1989, 1990). After the observations, observers completed a detailed set of rating scales on family process, and the narrative records were segmented and coded by independent coders. Control, teaching, social contact, and reflective listening events were coded, as were complex, higher order events including coercion, intrusiveness, and several kinds of positive parenting.

In searching for correlates of change, we considered 33 descriptors of the family and child. The characteristics were assessed by the maternal interview and pre-kindergarten and pre–first-grade questionnaires, by structured prekindergarten tests of social information processing, and by teacher questionnaires and peer sociometrics during kindergarten. The predictor measures will be further described in conjunction with the findings. Reliability and validity of the measures in the study have been adequate to good in terms of interobserver agreement, mother–father convergence, internal consistency of composites, and convergence between measures and relevant criterion indexes. Details may be found in previous articles on the Child Development Project (Bates et al., in press; Dodge, Bates, & Pettit, 1990; Dodge, Pettit, & Bates, 1994; Strassberg, Dodge, Bates, & Pettit, 1992; Weiss, Dodge, Bates, & Pettit, 1992).

Family process antecedents to aggressiveness

Consistent with the theme of the present volume, we addressed questions about coercive family process in the development of aggressiveness. Our main focus was on a model involving coercion as measured by parent reports of harsh, potentially harmful discipline. A LISREL model (see Figure 7.1) showed that coercive family process predicted aggressiveness in kindergarten to a modest degree, and aggressiveness in kindergarten strongly predicted aggressiveness in first grade, but that family coercion did not significantly predict aggressiveness in first grade once kindergarten aggressiveness was controlled. Note that when simple bivariate correlations were considered, the correlation between the family process index and first-grade aggression was significant ($r = .21$, $p < .01$). For validational purposes, we also considered for the home observation subsample a model in which coercive family process was defined by a second-order measure of observer impressionistic rating composites, indexing the mother's positive, affectionate, and teaching actions and lack of coercive control, along with a composite of event codes indexing angry, coercive conflict, and the interview measure of harsh or potentially harmful discipline practices. The results of a LISREL analysis were virtually identical to those for the full sample model using only parental report measures.

Though analyses on the full sample probably provide the best estimate of population effects, one might also evaluate reliability of an effect by subdividing the sample. Because our sample was large, we considered the full sample, coercion–aggression model in the three separate sites of the study. A nested comparison of

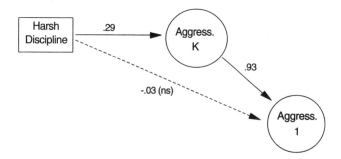

Figure 7.1. Coercion, defined by the single indicator composite of maternal interview report of harsh discipline before kindergarten (see Appendix for definition), predicting aggressiveness, defined by 6 indicators, including teacher ratings of aggression on the Teacher Report Form (TRF) and Teacher Checklist (TCL) and peer nominations in kindergarten and first grade. Loadings at Time 1/Time 2, respectively, were .69/.74 for TRF aggression, .60/.62 for TCL reactive aggression, .54/.41 for TCL proactive aggression, .64/.77 for peer fights, .72/.72 for being mean, and .74/.78 for gets mad. LISREL model allowed all 9 possible Time 1 to Time 2 teacher residual correlations to be estimated, accounting for teacher halo effects. In addition, 12 other residual correlations were estimated as indicated by the LISREL modification index ($N = 438$).

the three sites was not possible, so we repeated analyses for each site. The results were similar in the different sites, and each resembled the full sample result.

In summary, coercive discipline predicted aggressiveness in the first grade in a bivariate model, but the prediction can be explained more parsimoniously by the continuation of child aggressiveness and, we would assume, by continuity of family characteristics. There is no evidence for delayed effects of family process, at least as the constructs are defined here.

Correlates of change

As seen in the preceding model, individual differences in our latent measure of aggressiveness were highly stable from kindergarten to first grade, despite the fact that the child was rated in two distinct settings. The simple correlation between the kindergarten and first-grade composites of teacher and peer ratings of aggressiveness was .65. The correlation between the two latent, six-indicator constructs, which controlled for source of data and associated errors of measurement, was .93, as seen in Figure 7.1. (This finding applies to both girls and boys, according to a nonsignificant sex effect in nested LISREL models of the kindergarten to first-grade path coefficient.) Such high stability suggests there is relatively little variance or instability to explain. Nevertheless, since our sample was a large one, we expected that there would be enough cases showing notable change that there would be a reasonable chance of detecting some differences in changers versus nonchangers.

We examined the linear correlates of change on the aggressiveness variable, defined as first-grade aggressiveness minus kindergarten aggressiveness, with 33 different predictor variables. The predictors (listed in the Appendix) were selected as plausible correlates of change, many of them being conceptually similar to indexes found to correlate with change in recent studies in the literature. Theory and measurement limitations would not permit confident hypotheses about the correlates of change. However, the literature did support four general expectations.

1. Child internalizing behavior problems will be associated with change in aggressive behavior. The first item on our analysis plan was to consider the role of internalizing tendencies as a predictor of change in externalizing. On the basis of our reading of the temperament literature, we expected that levels of internalizing behavior problems would relate to change in aggressiveness. An anxious, socially withdrawn child might experience teacher and peer consequences for aggression differently than would a child who is low in internalizing. The expectation was supported by findings on the kindergarten teacher's index of internalizing. We analyzed via LISREL the degree to which aggressiveness in first grade was a function of internalizing in kindergarten. To a very modest but significant degree (path coefficient $= -.10$, $p < .05$), children who had been seen as reducing their aggression from kindergarten to first grade had been rated relatively high on internalizing problems in kindergarten (on the Achenbach Teacher Report Form items in common for both boys and girls), and children who got more aggressive were rated low

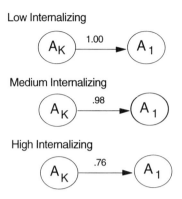

Low Internalizing

A_K ——1.00——▶ A_1

Medium Internalizing

A_K ——.98——▶ A_1

High Internalizing

A_K ——.76——▶ A_1

Figure 7.2. Stability of latent construct of aggressiveness from kindergarten to first grade within levels of internalizing. LISREL model allowed residuals for teacher measures to correlate across time, as well as 12 other residuals as indicated by the modification index. Path coefficient for high-internalizing group is significantly ($p < .05$) smaller than coefficients for low- and medium-internalizing groups ($N = 441$).

in internalizing. This finding converges with several other longitudinal ones described by Tremblay (1992), but not with those reported by Pianta and Caldwell (1990) and concurrent results reported by Achenbach and Edelbrock (1986). It should be noted, however, that our negative correlation involves an index of aggressiveness that includes peer perceptions rather than just teacher perceptions. The correlation between indexes of only the teacher perceptions of internalizing in kindergarten and externalizing in first grade was positive. Internalizing as perceived by the mother before either kindergarten or first grade did not predict the change score. The findings just reported were of linear relations between internalizing in kindergarten and the linear change in aggressiveness from kindergarten to first grade.

We next considered whether kindergarten internalizing might serve to moderate, in a nonlinear, interactive way, the stability of aggressiveness. We modeled this using LISREL, by dividing the sample into thirds on the basis of the kindergarten teachers' internalizing scores and comparing the links between the latent aggressiveness scores across the different subsamples. As shown in Figure 7.2, the correlation between aggressiveness in kindergarten and first grade was significantly lower ($p < .05$) in the high-internalizing group than in the low- and medium-internalizing groups, which were not significantly different from each other. These findings suggest that even though there is still considerable continuity of individual differences in aggressiveness in the high-internalizing group, there may be some high-internalizing children with high aggressiveness in kindergarten who become less aggressive by first grade or some with low aggressiveness who become more aggressive. We prefer the former interpretation to the latter because of the negative path between kindergarten internalizing and first-grade aggressiveness (controlling for kindergarten aggressiveness) in the whole sample.[1] Apparently this kind of process does not appear to operate universally, since the continuity of individual differences in aggressiveness was still moderately strong in the high-internalizing group.

2. Family stress will produce change in adjustment. *Stress,* defined as the sum of stressful events reported by the parents in the year prior to the start of kindergarten and in the year prior to the start of first grade, might have increased among the children whose behavior problems at school worsened, and decreased among those whose behavior improved. In fact, there was not a significant correlation between the aggression change score and the family stress over the year ending just before first grade. There was also not a significant correlation between the aggression change score and the change in level of family stress from before kindergarten to before first grade.

3. Initial child characteristics will predict changes in adjustment at school. We tentatively expected that children whose school behavior worsened would have started out with more negative and fewer positive traits, and the reverse for those who became less aggressive. One set of traits was assessed by parents' reports before kindergarten, including internalizing and externalizing behavior problems, and retrospective ratings assessing temperament traits of difficultness, inadaptability, and resistance to control. A second set of child traits were assessed by structured tests of a limited range of social-information-processing tendencies. A third set of traits were nonpathology variables assessed at school in kindergarten, including being liked by peers (either as rated by teachers or peers) and academic performance. According to the data, however, our expectation was incorrect. There were no significant correlations in the direction we had expected.

4. Parental discipline and aggression values will predict changes in adjustment. We expected that parents of children whose aggressiveness decreased would have espoused and demonstrated less coercive discipline, despite initial levels of child aggressiveness, and that the reverse would hold for parents of increasingly aggressive children. Again, our expectation was incorrect. Across all the different indexes, including observation, interview report, solutions to hypothetical child discipline problems, the Conflict Tactics Scale, and the aggressive family culture questionnaire, the expected pattern was not seen.

For the sake of considering possible nonlinear patterns of relationship with change versus continuity, we further examined mean scores on all of the candidate moderator variables for the group who changed from the bottom third of kindergarten aggression scores to the top third ($n = 16$) and those who changed in the opposite way ($n = 17$) in relation to each other and to the continuously low-, medium-, or high-aggression groups and the moderately changing groups (e.g., changing from low to medium aggression). The overall pattern − with no prediction of the change by this set of variables − was not changed by this inspection of data.

Conclusions

Coercive discipline practices were significantly associated to a modest degree with the level of child aggressiveness in the kindergarten class, and this in turn had a very high association with the level of aggressiveness shown in the first-grade class. We searched for but did not find any evidence that first-grade aggressiveness has any direct roots in prekindergarten coercive family process beyond the kindergarten–first-grade continuity in aggressiveness. It is conceivable that there could be aspects of the early family experience whose implications would appear some time after kindergarten, but we did not find such an effect.

Considering our effort to predict change in aggressiveness over one year of development, the study had limited success. The operational construct of aggressiveness, combining teacher and peer ratings, showed very high stability. In retrospect, although there were a few pertinent findings in the literature (e.g., Campbell et al., 1991; Pianta & Caldwell, 1990), we should not have expected many variables to correlate with change, since there was so little of it as we measured it.

Nevertheless, one important variable that did predict change was internalizing in kindergarten. To a slight but statistically significant degree, the higher the internalizing score in kindergarten, the less aggressiveness in first grade. Moreover, among highly internalizing children there was a significantly lower degree of stability of aggressiveness. We interpret these findings to reflect a process in which the traits underlying internalizing problems facilitate, in at least a few children, learning to inhibit aggression as the result of aversive conditioning. Punishment of aggression would occur at school and perhaps at home as well.

Conclusions about child internalizing must be restricted to such tendencies as shown at school; the maternal perceptions on the CBCL internalizing problems factor (before kindergarten or before first grade) and on the retrospective temperament scale of unadaptability to novelty (assessed before kindergarten) were not predictive of change in aggressiveness at school. These noneffects could suggest the importance of school versus family context for assessing the internalizing traits relevant to change in aggressiveness. They could also be related to the fact that internalizing traits tend to be relatively unstable, so the lack of effect could be due to the fact that parents reported on internalizing traits several months before the teachers did so.

Further efforts to model stability and change will be made as the children of the study are followed into adolescence. It should become increasingly possible to observe change, assuming that even the limited discontinuity present from kindergarten to first grade will compound every year. We will continue to search for the initial conditions that predict which children will be continually aggressive, late starters in aggressiveness (Patterson, 1992), and early dropouts from the aggressiveness trajectory. We will be especially interested not only in the initial adjustment and temperament profiles of the children, but also in the many possible changes in the families, including divorces, economic and other stressors, and even direct, focal efforts by family members to reduce child behavior problems. We will continue to search for linear and, where feasible, configural patterns of prediction. Ultimately, we hope this effort toward a better description of children's developmental trajectories will contribute to basic, scientific understanding of development and to the efficacy of early screening and the prevention of aggressive behavior disorders.

Appendix: Measures used as predictors of change

   I. Family characteristics (based on prekindergarten mother interview and questionnaire measures)
     A. Discipline practices, attitudes, and family conflict
       1. Harsh discipline: composed of 12 informational report and interviewer-rating items
         a. Frequency and methods of spanking
         b. Overall restrictiveness of discipline
         c. Likelihood of physical harm being experienced by child
       2. Hypothetical discipline problem solving: Concerns and Constraints Questionnaire
         a. Degree of concern about minor misbehavior
         b. Use of reasoning techniques
         c. Use of power-assertive techniques
       3. Aggression values: Culture Questionnaire
         a. Approve of some child aggression toward peers
         b. Approve of child watching TV violence
         c. Aggression and competition in family
       4. Conflict practices: Straus's Conflict Tactics Scale
         a. Parents use competent tactics with child
         b. Parents use aggressive tactics with child
         c. Parents use competent tactics with each other
         d. Parents use aggressive tactics with each other
     B. Family stress
       1. Stressful events from age 4 years to prekindergarten: interview
       2. Stressful events from prekindergarten to pre–first grade: Changes and Adjustments Questionnaire
       3. Stress difference: Z score of 2 minus Z score of 1
  II. Child characteristics
     A. In the family (based on mother interview and questionnaires)
       1. Behavior problems: Achenbach CBCL
         a. Externalizing prekindergarten
         b. Internalizing prekindergarten
         c. Externalizing pre–first grade
         d. Internalizing pre–first grade

2. Retrospectively rated infant temperament: Retrospective Infant Characteristics Questionnaire
   a. Difficult and demanding
   b. Unadaptable to novelty
   c. Resistant to control
3. Amount of time in nonparental care: reported in mother interview summarized from birth to kindergarten age

B. Hypothetical peer problem solving: social-information-processing characteristics (based on video/cartoon/story vignettes)
   1. Aggressive solutions
   2. Novel solutions
   3. Competent solutions
   4. Ineffectual solutions
   5. Accurate attributions for hostile or benign stories
   6. Hostile attributions for ambiguous stories

C. In kindergarten
   1. Teacher ratings
      a. Internalizing: Achenbach Teacher Report Form, cross-gender items
      b. Academic performance: questionnaire
      c. Peers liking: Teacher Checklist
   2. Peer sociometrics
      a. Positive: nominations for like most, good entry, doesn't get mad, gets along well with teacher, plus overall rating as playmate
      b. Disliking: nominations for like least

NOTES

The study was supported by NIMH Grant 42498. The authors are grateful to the families who participated in the study and to the many members of the research team. They are especially grateful to Dr. Denny Marvinney, Dr. Steve McFadyen-Ketchum, and Dr. Rick Viken for their help in data analysis.

1. Explorations of correlations between teacher ratings of internalizing in kindergarten and child aggressiveness in first grade within the three levels of internalizing revealed an interesting pattern, despite the somewhat more limited distributions on internalizing scores within each group. In the low- and medium-internalizing groups, the more internalizing the child in kindergarten, the more aggressive the child was in first grade ($r = .25$, .16, respectively, $p < .01$, .05). In the high-internalizing group, however, the correlation was negative and nonsignificant ($r = -.08$). We also analyzed to see whether the social withdrawal and anxiety components of internalizing might have differential linkages with aggression. It appears that the positive links between kindergarten internalizing and first-grade aggressiveness were largely due to the social withdrawal component of internalizing, which was correlated positively with first-grade aggressiveness in each group ($r = .31$, .24, .10; $p < .01$, .01, n.s., for the low-, medium-, and high-internalizing groups, respectively), while the anxiety scale was correlated negatively in each group ($r = -.06$, $-.22$, $-.22$; n.s., $p < .01$, .01, respectively).

REFERENCES

Achenbach, T. M., & Edelbrock, C. (1983). *Manual for the Child Behavior Checklist and Revised Child Behavior Profile.* Burlington: University of Vermont, Department of Psychiatry.

Achenbach, T. M., & Edelbrock, C. (1986). *Manual for the Teacher's Report Form and teacher version of the Child Behavior Profile.* Burlington: University of Vermont, Department of Psychiatry.

Anthony, E. J., & Cohler, B. J. (Eds.). (1987). *The invulnerable child.* New York: Guilford.

Bates, J. E. (1980). The concept of difficult temperament. *Merrill-Palmer Quarterly, 26,* 299–319.

Bates, J. E. (1989). Applications of temperament concepts. In G. A. Kohnstamm, J. E. Bates, & M. K. Rothbart (Eds.), *Temperament in childhood* (pp. 321–355). Chichester: Wiley.

Bates, J. E. (1990). Conceptual and empirical linkages between temperament and behavior problems: A commentary on the Sanson, Prior, and Kyrios study. *Merrill-Palmer Quarterly, 36,* 193–199.

Bates, J. E., Marvinney, D., Kelly, T., Dodge, K. A., Bennett, D. S., & Pettit, G. S. (in press). Child care history and kindergarten adjustment. *Developmental Psychology.*

Campbell, S. B. (1990). *Behavior problems in preschool children.* New York: Guilford.

Campbell, S. B., March, C. L., Pierce, E. W., Ewing, L. J., & Szumowski, E. K. (1991). Hard-to-manage preschool boys: Family context and the stability of externalizing behavior. *Journal of Abnormal Child Psychology, 19,* 301–318.

Caspi, A., Henry, B., McGee, R. O., Moffitt, T. E., & Silva, P. A. (1992). *Temperamental origins of child and adolescent behavior problems: From age 3 to age 15.* Unpublished manuscript. University of Wisconsin, Madison.

Coie, J. D., & Dodge, K. A. (1988). Multiple sources of data on social behavior and social status in the school: A cross-age comparison. *Child Development, 59,* 815–829.

Coie, J. D., Dodge, K. A., & Coppotelli, H. (1982). Dimensions and types of social status: A cross-age perspective. *Developmental Psychology, 18,* 557–570.

Dodge, K. A., Bates, J. E., & Pettit, G. S. (1990). Mechanisms in the cycle of violence. *Science, 250,* 1678–1683.

Dodge, K. A., Pettit, G. S., & Bates, J. E. (1994). Socialization mediators of the relation between socioeconomic status and child conduct problems. *Child Development, 65,* 649–665.

Gray, J. A. (1991). The neuropsychology of temperament. In J. Strelau & A. Angleitner (Eds.), *Explorations in temperament: International perspectives on theory and measurement* (pp. 105–128). New York: Plenum.

Hetherington, E. M., & Martin, B. (1986). Family factors and psychopathology in children. In H. C. Quay & J. S. Werry (Eds.), *Psychopathological disorders of childhood* (3rd ed., pp. 332–390). New York: Wiley.

Hollingshead, A. A. (1979). *Four-factor index of social status.* Unpublished manuscript. Yale University, New Haven, CT.

Lahey, B. B., & Loeber, R. (1991, June). *A preliminary developmental-psychobiological model of conduct disorder.* Paper presented at the meeting of the Society for Research in Child and Adolescent Psychopathology, Zandvoort, the Netherlands.

Loeber, R., Farrington, D. P., Stouthamer-Loeber, M., & VanKammen, W. B. (1992, May). *Predictors of disruptive behavior: Longitudinal findings from the Pittsburgh Youth Study.* Paper presented at the meeting of Society for Life History Research, Philadelphia.

Masten, A. S. (1989). Resilience in development: Implications of the study of successful adaptation for developmental psychopathology. In D. Cicchetti (Ed.), *The emergence of a discipline: Rochester Symposium on Developmental Psychopathology* (Vol 1., pp. 261–294). Hillsdale, NJ: Erlbaum.

Patterson, G. R. (1982). *Coercive family process.* Eugene, OR: Castalia.

Patterson, G. R. (1993). Orderly change in a stable world: The antisocial trait as a chimera. *Journal of Consulting and Clinical Psychology, 61,* 911–919.

Pettit, G. S., & Bates, J. E. (1989). Family interaction patterns and children's behavior problems from infancy to age 4 years: Validation of a new method of naturalistic observation. *Developmental Psychology, 25,* 413–420.

Pettit, G. S., & Bates, J. E. (1990). Describing family interaction patterns in early childhood: A "social events" perspective. *Journal of Applied Developmental Psychology, 11,* 395–418.

Pianta, R. C., & Caldwell, C. B. (1990). Stability of externalizing symptoms from kindergarten to first grade and factors related to instability. *Development and Psychopathology, 2,* 247–258.

Pulkkinen, L. (1992, December). *From coping strategies to life styles: A longitudinal study.* Colloquium at Indiana University, Bloomington.

Robins, L. N., & Rutter, M. (Eds.). (1990). *Straight and devious pathways from childhood to adulthood.* Cambridge University Press.

Rutter, M. (1982). Statistical and personal interactions: Facets and perspectives. In D. Magnusson & V. L. Allen (Eds.), *Human development: An interactionist perspective* (pp. 295–317). New York: Academic.

Sroufe, L. A., Egeland, B., & Kreutzer, T. (1990). The fate of early experience following developmental change: Longitudinal approaches to individual adaptation. *Child Development, 61,* 1363–1373.

Strassberg, Z., Dodge, K. A., Bates, J. E., & Pettit, G. S. (1992). The longitudinal relation between parental conflict strategies and children's socioeconomic standing in kindergarten. *Merrill-Palmer Quarterly, 38,* 447–493.

Straus, M. A. (1979). Measuring intrafamily conflict and violence: The Conflict Tactics Scale. *Journal of Marriage and the Family, 41,* 75–88.

Thomas, A., Chess, S., & Birch, H. G. (1968). *Temperament and behavior disorders in children.* New York: New York University Press/London: University of London Press.

Tremblay, R. (1992). The prediction of delinquent behavior from childhood behavior: Personality theory revisited. In J. McCord (Ed.), *Advances in criminological theory:* Vol. 3, *Facts, frameworks and forecasts* (pp. 193–230). New Brunswick, NJ: Transactions Publications.

Weiss, B., Dodge, K., Bates, J. E., & Pettit, G. S. (1992). Some consequences of early harsh discipline: Child aggression and a maladaptive social information processing style. *Child Development, 63,* 1321–1335.

Werner, E. E., & Smith, R. S. (1982). *Vulnerable but invincible: A study of resilient children.* New York: McGraw-Hill.

Wiggins, J. S. (1973). *Personality and prediction: Principles of personality assessment.* Reading, MA: Addison-Wesley.

Zuckerman, M. (1991). *Psychobiology of personality.* Cambridge University Press.

8 Kindergarten behavioral patterns, parental practices, and early adolescent antisocial behavior

RICHARD E. TREMBLAY

I will readily concede that the difficulty of inculcating in children a sweet and cheerful obedience arises partly from their nature. There are trying children, just as there are trying dogs that howl and make themselves disagreeable for no discoverable reason but their inherent "cussedness." There are, I doubt not, conscientious painstaking mothers who have been baffled by having to manage what appears to be the utterly unmanageable. Yet I think that we ought to be very slow to pronounce any child unmanageable.

J. Sully (1895, p. 290)

Harsh, inconsistent, and erratic discipline, lack of supervision, parental rejection, disharmony, separations, or absence, parental modeling, family history of antisocial behavior, and disturbances of parent–child attachment have repeatedly arisen in the literature as important predictors of aggressive and antisocial behavior (e.g., Eron, Huesmann, & Zelli, 1991; Farrington & Hawkins, 1991; Loeber & Dishion, 1983; McCord, 1979; Widom, 1989). In their review of this literature, Loeber and Stouthamer-Loeber (1986) proposed four paradigms of family processes and antisocial or criminal behaviors: (1) the neglect paradigm, examining parental involvement with their children and parental supervision; (2) the conflict paradigm, stressing parental disciplinary practices and rejection of children; (3) the deviant behaviors and attitudes paradigm, focusing on parental criminality and deviant attitudes; and (4) the disruption paradigm, refering to marital conflict and parental absence. From all the evidence for the linkage between family processes and antisocial behavior in children, the first two paradigms particularly stand out: lack of parental control, supervision, or monitoring, and poor disciplinary practices. Interestingly, Sully (1895) had reached similar conclusions from "aspects of children's minds which happen to have come under my notice" (p. v):

What is beyond doubt is that the slovenly discipline – if indeed discipline it is to be called – which consists in alternations of gusking fondness with almost savage severity, or fits of government and restraint interpolated between long periods of neglect and laisser faire, is precisely what develops the rebellious and low-resisting propensities. (p. 291)

The studies on which the conclusions reached by Loeber & Stouthamer-Loeber (1986) stand were focused on adolescents, or at best preadolescents, whose behavior was already antisocial. With such samples, when the children's preceding behavior is not taken into account, one is left wondering to what extent parenting practices were driven by the children's deviant behavior. Even though it has been clearly shown that children's behavior and characteristics do have an impact on adults' behavior toward them (Bell & Chapman, 1986), child effects on caretakers are still not well integrated in our theories of socialization and our data analyses. Lytton (1990) revived this debate with reference to antisocial behavior. He concluded from a review of different areas of research that children have biological predispositions to conduct disorders that interact with environmental factors. There is certainly no evidence that children are born with an antisocial orientation, but there is evidence that some children are easier to socialize than others (Maccoby, 1986; Maccoby & Jacklin, 1980).

Some time ago Eysenck (1964; Eysenck & Gudjonsson, 1989) suggested that extraverted children need parents who have better control over them than do introverted children. His reasoning was that because extraverts have lower physiological arousability, they are less easy to condition; they will thus be less easily socialized. On the other hand, because introverts have higher physiological arousability, they are easier to condition and will thus be easier to socialize. From this reasoning it was predicted that extraverts would be more at risk of antisocial disorders, while introverts would be more at risk of dysthymic disorders (Eysenck, 1967). A number of studies have indeed shown that extraversion in children and adolescents is concurrently associated with, and predicts, antisocial behavior (for a review, see Eysenck & Gudjonsson, 1989). Raine & Venables (1981) made one of the few attempts to test the conditionability hypothesis by studying the conditionability of both individuals and the environment in which they were conditioned. They hypothesized that children who are easy to condition would become antisocial in environments with antisocial values. The results of their study confirmed this hypothesis, although their measure of environments (social class) that foster prosocial or antisocial behavior was far from ideal; but the important point here is that we clearly need to take into account both individual and environmental differences if we are to better understand the socialization process.

For this study, Gray's (1970, 1981, 1982) behavior model was used to measure kindergarten children's personality dimensions and to test Eysenck's hypothesis that extroverted children need more parental control than do introverted children to prevent them from becoming antisocial. Gray suggested that extraversion was a product of two orthogonal dimensions labeled impulsivity and anxiety (see Figure 8.1) that correspond to two biological systems, the behavioral activation system (BAS) (impulsivity) and the behavioral inhibition system (BIS) (anxiety). Gray agrees with Eysenck that introverts (high anxiety–low impulsivity) are more suscep-

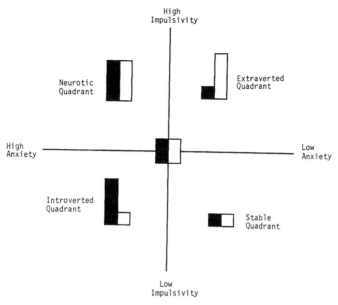

Figure 8.1. Personality dimensions and susceptibility to reward (open blocks) and punishment (solid blocks) (adapted from Gray, 1992).

tible to punishment than are extraverts (low anxiety–high impulsivity), but he suggests that the latter are more susceptible to rewards than the former. Thus, socialization practices that rely mainly on punishment would be more effective with introverts, while those that rely mainly on reward would be more effective with extraverts. Parents would thus need to be sensitive to their child's behavioral pattern to choose the appropriate socialization practices.

From a different but complementary perspective, Bell (1979) has proposed a control system theory for parents' socialization practices. He suggested that adequate parents will adjust their behavior to the child's behavior. For example, if children are overactive parents will intervene to reduce the activity level, but they will stimulate children if they are underactive. Others have also concluded that the most effective parenting approach is an authoritative one based on controlling and responsive parenting behavior (Maccoby & Martin, 1983). Thus, one would expect that an adequate mix of rewards and punishment would be given by parents who are in control of the socialization process.

Four hypotheses can be extracted from the preceding theoretical considerations concerning children's behavioral patterns, parenting, and delinquent outcome. First, it can be hypothesized from personality theories (Eysenck, 1967; Gray, 1982) and the study of children's effects on parents (Bell & Chapman, 1986) that kindergarten boys' impulsivity and anxiety will have an impact on mothers' controlling and punitive behavior. We hypothesized that boys' high impulsivity and low anxiety should lead parents to be more controlling and more punitive, while low impulsivity and high anxiety should have the reverse impact on parents. The second hypothesis concerns the link between behavioral patterns in kindergarten and early adolescent delinquent behavior: as suggested by Eysenck (1967) and Gray (1982), impulsive-not-anxious boys (extraverts) should be more at risk of antisocial behavior than not-impulsive-anxious boys (introverts). The third hypothesis concerns the effect of parental punitiveness on later antisocial behavior: as suggested by Gray (1982), impulsive-not-anxious boys (extraverts) would profit less from punitive parents than would not-impulsive-anxious boys (introverts), with reference to later antisocial behavior. Finally, the fourth hypothesis concerns the effect of mothers' controlling behavior on later antisocial behavior of their sons: as suggested by Bell (1979) as well as Maccoby and Martin (1983), boys who have controlling parents should be less at risk of later antisocial behavior, independently of the boys' behavioral patterns.

Method

In 1984 teachers were asked to rate the behavior of every male kindergarten child in areas of Montréal with lower socioeconomic status. A total of 1,034 culturally homogeneous boys (Caucasian, French-speaking, nonimmigrant families) were thus rated with the Social Behavior Questionnaire (SBQ) (Tremblay et al., 1991) on different dimensions, including *anxiety* (worried, fearful, cries easily; alpha = .72) and *impulsivity* (squirmy, fidgety, restless; alpha = .89). It should be noted that the impulsivity and anxiety dimensions did not include any antisocial behaviors. (Studies of antisocial behavior often include such behavior in the predictors. While such studies measure the stability of antisocial behavior, they do not examine the predictive value of personality for antisocial behavior.) Four years later, when the boys were age 10, both mothers and boys answered questionnaires meant to assess parental behavior. Mother's *controlling attitude* was assessed with 16 items from the Emotional Climate for Children Questionnaire (Falender & Mehrabian, 1980). Eight items measured controlling attitudes, such as I don't tolerate temper tantrums, it is important to have a fixed bedtime, parents should not back down. Eight other items measured laissez-faire attitudes, such as I feel my child knows what is best for him, I don't like to place a lot of rules on my child, my child should not have special manners for adults. Boys responded to a questionnaire (LeBlanc, 1990) that included 5 questions on each boy's perception of how frequently his parents used different *types of punishment* (They forbid you to do something you like to do, they scold you, they say you have hurt them, they hit you, they call you names; alpha = .61). Finally, 6 and 7 years after kindergarten when they were ages 12 and 13, the boys responded to a *self-reported delinquency* questionnaire (delinquent acts in the past 12 months) that included 11 items covering stealing (steal from school, steal from store, steal from home, keep object worth

$10, steal bicycle, sell stolen goods, keep object worth between $10 and $100, steal objects worth more than $100, break and enter, enter without paying, trespass; alpha = .80), 3 items covering drug use (drink alcohol, get drunk, take drugs; alpha = .66), 6 items covering vandalism (destroy school material, destroy other material, vandalize at school, destroy objects at home, vandalize car, set fires; alpha = .63), and 7 items covering aggression (strong-arm, gang fights, use weapon in a fight, fist fight, beat up someone, carry a weapon, throw objects at persons; alpha = .76). A total score for the 27 items was also computed to obtain a total delinquency score (alpha = .88). The mean score from ages 12 and 13 years for each scale was used to increase the stability of the dependent measure. Complete data from 86% of the subjects were available when mothers' reports of control were used, and 92% of the subjects when boys' reports of punishment were used.

Analyses of variance and logistic regressions were performed to test the hypotheses. For each analysis, anxiety (high–low) and impulsivity (high–low) were used to categorize boys' personality. To categorize parenting, mother control (high–low) and boys' report of parental punishment (high–low) were used. The high–low classification for each variable was created by splitting the subjects at the median.

Results

Whether kindergarten teachers' ratings of boys' impulsivity and anxiety predicted mothers' self-report of child control and boys' report of parental punitiveness at age 10 was first examined. Results are presented in Table 8.1. It can be seen that, as predicted, the percentage of low-controlling mothers at age 10 increased with kindergarten boys' decrease in impulsivity and increase in anxiety. The extraverted boys who had the highest impulsivity score and the lowest anxiety score had a majority of mothers (57%) who expressed the importance of controlling their child's behavior, while introverted boys (low impulsivity, high anxiety) had a majority of mothers (60%) who expressed the importance of having low control over their child. A logistic regression analysis indicated significant main effects for boys' impulsivity (beta = .20; $p < .005$) and anxiety (beta = −.14; $p < .05$) in predicting mothers' high or low control (goodness-of-fit χ^2 (859) = 862.00; $p = .46$). There were no significant interaction effects between impulsivity and anxiety.

Results for the total punitiveness score reported by the boys at age 10 (Table 8.1) did not confirm the hypothesis that parents of impulsive or low-anxiety boys would be more punitive. The logistic regression analysis using kindergarten teachers' ratings of impulsivity and anxiety to predict high or low punitiveness reported by the boys did not reveal any significant main effects or interactions.

Because the total punitiveness score was constructed from five items that referred to different techniques of punishment, three of these techniques were examined to see if different patterns of association could be observed. Mothers' report of control was also included as an independent variable to verify if it predicted different types of sons' report of parental punitiveness. Results for physical punishment are re-

Table 8.1. *Boys' kindergarten personality and parenting at age 10*

Personality	Mother control			Parental punitiveness		
	N	Low (%)	High (%)	N	Low (%)	High (%)
Extraverts (Imp +, anx −)	209	43	57	226	54	46
Neurotics (Imp +, anx +)	173	50	50	185	45	55
Stables (Imp −, anx −)	280	53	47	301	55	45
Introverts (Imp −, anx +)	200	60	40	209	52	48

ported in Table 8.2. It can be observed that within each personality category, more boys with mothers who reported preferring high control reported having never been physically punished. A logistic regression analysis confirmed that high–low mother control significantly discriminated those who reported ever being physically punished from those who reported never being physically punished (beta = .27, $p = .0002$). A logistic regression also confirmed a three-way interaction for mother control, son impulsivity, and anxiety, when boys who reported often being physically punished were compared with the others (beta = − .25; $p = .04$). It can be seen from Table 8.2 that more extraverts (high impulsivity, low anxiety) and introverts (low impulsivity, high anxiety) with high-controlling mothers, compared with those with low-controlling mothers, reported frequent physical punishment, while the reverse was observed for neurotics (high impulsivity, high anxiety) and stables (low impulsivity, low anxiety). The difference between high- and low-controlling mothers was largest for extraverts.

Table 8.3 describes the results for parental punishment by forbidding the child to do an activity he likes. It can be seen again that more boys with low-controlling mothers reported never being punished by being forbidden to do an activity they liked. The logistic regression confirmed that high–low mother control significantly discriminated the boys who reported never being punished in this way (beta = .15; $p = .04$). Interestingly, impulsivity also discriminated these boys (beta = .20; $p = .04$). As can be seen from Table 8.3, only 12.2 to 13.7% of the boys who were low impulsive (stables and introverts) in kindergarten reported often being forbidden to do an activity they liked, while close to 20% of the high impulsives (except for the extraverts with low-controlling mothers) reported being often punished in such a way. A similar analysis was performed for a love-oriented discipline technique (the item asked how frequently parents punished the child by saying that the child's behavior had hurt them), but no significant effects were observed.

Table 8.2. *Percentage of boys who report parental physical punishment at age 10, by category of mothers' report of control, and boys' personality in kindergarten*

Personality	Mother control	Punished		
		Never	Sometimes	Often
Extraverts	High			
(Imp +, anx −)	(*n* = 118)	35.6	50.8	13.6
	Low			
	(*n* = 90)	42.2	52.2	5.6
Neurotics	High			
(Imp +, anx +)	(*n* = 86)	24.4	65.1	10.5
	Low			
	(*n* = 85)	42.4	45.9	11.8
Stables	High			
(Imp −, anx −)	(*n* = 130)	25.4	69.2	5.4
	Low			
	(*n* = 148)	43.2	48.0	8.8
Introverts	High			
(Imp −, anx +)	(*n* = 78)	32.1	59.0	9.0
	Low			
	(*n* = 117)	38.5	55.6	6.0

Whether mothers' reports of parental control and kindergarten child behavior predicted age 12 to 13 antisocial behavior was then examined. Results of the MANOVA analysis are reported in Table 8.4. It can be observed that there were main effects of impulsive and anxious kindergarten behavior for self-reported stealing, aggression, vandalism, and drug use at ages 12 to 13. These results confirm the second hypothesis that kindergarten boys who are impulsive and not anxious (extraverts) are more at risk of later delinquency than those who are not impulsive and anxious (introverts). No main effects were observed for mothers' control, thus invalidating the fourth hypothesis that mother control at age 10 has an independent effect in predicting future delinquent behavior. However, significant three-way interactions (univariate) were observed between boys' impulsivity, anxiety, and mothers' control, for the antisocial behaviors of stealing, aggression, and vandalism. Identical results were obtained with the ANOVA analysis for total delinquency as the dependent variable.

Figure 8.2 represents the three-way interaction for the prediction of total delinquency at ages 12 to 13. It can be observed that there were two trends for the difference in delinquency between boys with mothers who preferred low or high control. The stable and neurotic boys with low-controlling mothers tended to report more frequent delinquent behavior. However, this difference was not statistically significant. On the other hand, the extraverted and introverted boys with low-

Table 8.3. *Percentage of boys who report parental punishment by being forbidden to do an activity they like at age 10, by category of mother report of control and boys' personality in kindergarten*

Personality	Mother control	Punished		
		Never	Sometimes	Often
Extraverts	High	32.5	47.9	19.7
(Imp +, anx −)	(n = 117)			
	Low	37.8	50.0	12.2
	(n = 90)			
Neurotics	High	15.1	64.0	20.9
(Imp +, anx +)	(n = 86)			
	Low	37.2	44.2	18.6
	(n = 86)			
Stables	High	30.5	55.7	13.7
(Imp −, anx −)	(n = 131)			
	Low	31.1	56.8	12.2
	(n = 148)			
Introverts	High	30.4	57.0	12.7
(Imp −, anx +)	(n = 79)			
	Low	34.2	53.0	12.8
	(n = 117)			

controlling mothers tended to report less frequent delinquent behavior. In this case, t tests within subgroups indicated a significant difference in total self-reported delinquency between introverts with low- and high-controlling mothers (t (198) = 2.77; $p < .008$).[1] It should be noted, however, that although the introverts with high-controlling mothers reported more delinquent behavior than those with low-controlling mothers, their level of total reported delinquency was still lower than all of the six other groups.

The same MANOVA and ANOVA procedures were used with boys' reported parental punitiveness (total score) at age 10 replacing mother control as the independent variable. The main effects for impulsivity and anxiety were obviously observed, but no main effects or interaction effects were observed for parental punitiveness. Because different results had been observed for the different punitive techniques, each was used separately with anxiety and impulsivity to see if results would be different from those obtained from the total punitiveness score. For each of those analyses, the punishment variable was divided into three levels: never punished, sometimes punished, often punished. Significant punishment effects were observed for being forbidden to do an activity boys liked and physical punishment, but not for the parents' reference to having been hurt. Boys who were often forbidden to do an activity they liked or were physically punished had significantly

Table 8.4. *Kindergarten personality, mother control, and antisocial behavior at ages 12 to 13*

Kindergarten, personality	Age 10, mother control	Age 12 to 13 antisocial behavior				
		Stealing	Aggression	Vandalism	Drugs	Total
Extraverts (Imp+, anx−)	High (n = 119)	12.8	9.4	6.8	3.9	32.9
	Low (n = 90)	12.5	9.2	6.6	3.9	32.2
Neurotics (Imp+, anx+)	High (n = 86)	12.1	8.6	6.5	3.6	30.8
	Low (n = 87)	12.4	8.9	6.7	3.7	31.7
Stables (Imp−, anx−)	High (n = 131)	12.3	8.6	6.5	3.7	31.1
	Low (n = 149)	12.5	8.6	6.5	3.7	31.3
Introverts (Imp−, anx+)	High (n = 80)	12.2	8.3	6.5	3.7	30.7
	Low (n = 120)	11.6	7.9	6.3	3.5	29.3
Univariate F	Impulsivity	4.7**	24.5***	8.5**	3.3*	14.2***
	Anxiety	10.2***	14.3***	4.2**	7.4**	13.6***
	Control	0.3	0.1	1.1	0.3	0.4
	Imp. × Anx. × Cntr.	5.3**	3.0*	3.9**	2.3	5.2**

$*p \leq .10$; $**p \leq .05$; $***p \leq .001$.

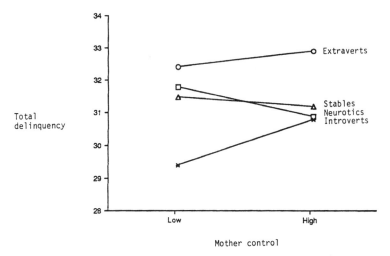

Figure 8.2. Representation of the three-way interaction effect between kindergarten impulsivity, anxiety, and maternal control (when boys were age 10) on age 12 to 13 total delinquency.

higher total delinquency scores than those who were never or sometimes punished in that way, $F(2, 907) = 4.43$, $p = .01$, and $F(2, 904) = 3.43$, $p = .03$, respectively. Those who reported being often forbidden to do an activity they liked also reported stealing more often, $F(2, 907) = 5.69$, $p = .003$, and more fighting, $F(2, 907) = 4.30$, $p = .01$, *while those who reported being often physically punished also reported more stealing*, $F(2, 904) = 4.44$, $p = .01$, and more vandalism, $F(2, 904) = 4.31$, $p = .01$. No significant interaction effects were observed between the punishment techniques reported at age 10 and the kindergarten personality dimensions (impulsivity and anxiety) with reference to later delinquent behavior.

Discussion

The major aim of this study was to examine, with a longitudinal data set, the hypothesis that parental control and punitiveness at age 10 would add to the value of kindergarten behavior to predict delinquency in early adolescence. Because the subjects were chosen from schools in areas with lower socioeconomic status, socioeconomic effects shown in previous studies (Raine & Venables, 1981) were to a large extent controlled.

   The extent to which boys' kindergarten behavior could explain mothers' later report of a controlling attitude and boys' report of parental punitiveness was first examined. Results confirmed that kindergarten boys' impulsiveness and anxiety, two classic personality dimensions (Eysenck, 1967; Gray, 1982), predicted mothers' report of a controlling tendency 4 years later. The more boys were impulsive and the less they were anxious, the more their mothers were controlling. If mothers' controlling attitude had been the "cause" of the boys' behavior, one would have expected to observe that high-controlling mothers had introverted sons, while low-controlling mothers would have had extraverted sons (see Maccoby & Martin, 1983, for a review of this issue). Our results fit the child effect paradigm (Bell, 1979), that is, mothers with extraverted sons should react in a controlling way to reduce the intensity of their sons' behavior, while mothers with introverted sons should react by stimulation to increase the intensity of their behavior; they also fit Eysenck's (1964; Eysenck & Gudjonsson, 1989) suggestion that because extraverts have lower physiological arousability, they are less easy to condition, and will thus need parents who will exert more control.

The same analysis using a total score from boys' report of parental punitiveness as the dependent variable did not indicate any kindergarten personality effects. An attempt was made to see if the inclusion of mothers' reported control would help predict boys' report of parental punitiveness, and if there were differences between types of punishment. Results from these analyses showed that mothers who reported a preference for high control of child's behavior had boys who tended to report more punitive behavior from their parents. This was true for use of physical punishment and limiting the boys' activity, but not for a love-oriented discipline technique (reference to the parents' feelings). Boys' report of being restricted from doing activities they liked was associated with high-impulsive behavior in kindergarten. This result could be explained by the fact that parents of impulsive boys naturally tend to put limits on the range of their activity when they misbehave or by the fact that impulsive boys will be more sensitive to limits that are put on their behavior and thus be more conscious of these forms of punishment. The boys who reported being often physically punished were found most often in the impulsives, but within this group very few impulsive, not anxious boys (extraverts) who had low-controlling mothers reported being often physically punished.

Thus, the first set of analyses of the link between kindergarten personality and parental behavior at age 10 indicated that mothers' reports of controlling behavior were predicted from impulsive and anxious behavior in kindergarten, while boys' reports of different forms of power-assertive parental punitiveness at age 10 were associated with both kindergarten personality and concurrent mothers' reports of control. Impulsive boys in kindergarten were especially likely at age 10 to have mothers who would report a preference for high control of their children, and to report that their own parents frequently resorted to power-assertive punitiveness. The extraverted boys with low-controlling mothers were the exception. Fewer reported that their parents used power-assertive techniques. It would be useful to study why this group differentiates itself.

The analysis of the link between behavior patterns in kindergarten and antisocial behavior in adolescence confirmed Eysenck's (1964, 1967) hypothesis that extraverts would be more at risk of delinquency than would introverts. Although a few other longitudinal studies starting from childhood had previously confirmed this hypothesis (e.g., Farrington, 1986; Pulkkinen, 1982), no study, to our knowledge, had yet shown significant predictions from personality measured as early as kindergarten.

The results did not confirm the hypothesis (based on Gray, 1982) that extraverts would profit less than introverts from punitive parents. This hypothesis was tested using boys' reports of parental punitiveness when they were aged 10. It could be argued that parents' reports of punitiveness would have been a more adequate measure. However, one can also argue that the extent to which parental punitiveness has an impact on a child must be reflected in what the child perceives. Thus, children's perceptions of punitiveness could be better predictors than parental perceptions, or even external observer perceptions. It is possible that the instruments we have used to obtain the boys' perceptions is inadequate. The questions refer to parents' behavior rather than separate mothers' and fathers' behaviors. We have shown elsewhere that differentiating mothers' and fathers' behaviors toward disruptive boys better predicts later antisocial behavior than aggregating mothers' and fathers' behavior (Tremblay et al., 1993).

The results also did not confirm our fourth hypothesis that mothers' controlling behavior would prevent antisocial behavior for each of the four personality categories we had assessed (introverts, extraverts, neurotics, and stables). We, however, observed an interesting differential impact of mothers' controlling behavior on boys' antisocial behavior with reference to the four personality categories. The level of mothers' control (high or low) did not have a significant impact on boys' antisocial behavior for the neurotic and stable groups, while it did for the introverts, and showed a trend in the same direction for the extraverts.

Table 8.1 and Figure 8.1 can be used to understand these results. The trend of the results from Table 8.1 appears to mirror Gray's hypothesis concerning the susceptibility to rewards and punishment depicted in Figure 8.1. In Table 8.1, more mothers of extraverted boys (depicted in Figure 8.1 as less susceptible to punishment and more to rewards) report using high control, while fewer mothers of introverted boys (depicted in Figure 8.1 as more susceptible to punishment) report using high control. The results for neurotics and stable boys, who are hypothesized by Gray to be equally susceptible to rewards and punishment (Figure 8.1), albeit at different levels, indicate that half the mothers tend to favor high control, while the other half tend to favor low control. It would appear that the more a boy is driven by the reward system (behavioral activating system, BAS) in comparison with the punishment system (behavioral inhibiting system, BIS), the more the mother will be compelled to resort to controlling strategies. The exact reverse appears likely when a boy is driven more by the BIS than the BAS. However, when both systems are in equilibrium, whatever their intensity, mothers may resort to either high- or low-controlling-parenting behavior. From this perspective, mothers' levels of controlling behavior appears to be an effect based on the child in the case of extraverts and introverts, while it may be more an expression of the mothers' individual tendencies in the case of neurotics and stables. This hypothesis could be tested by including mothers' personalities in the analysis (see, e.g., Bugenthal & Shennum, 1984). Unfortunately this information was not available for this study.

With reference to the delinquency outcome, mothers' controlling attitudes would thus need to be interpreted differently for the four personality categories. In the case of neurotics and stables, a mother's controlling behavior would be determined more by her personality than by the son's personality, and would not have a significant impact on the son's future antisocial behavior. In the case of extraverts and introverts, the level of a mother's control would be determined more by the son's than the mother's personality, and would be associated with later antisocial behavior.

However, extraverts and introverts with high-controlling mothers were observed to be more delinquent. To understand why this link is positively related to delinquency for both extraverts and introverts, we need once again to resort to the parent–child effect paradigm. We have seen that extraverts tend to have mothers who prefer high control, while introverts tend to have mothers who prefer low control. It can be hypothesized that the trend for high-control mothers to have more delinquent boys, within the extraverted sample, is the reflection of a child effect; that is, mothers' high control and sons' frequent delinquency are both effects of high-externalizing behavior (high impulsivity and low anxiety). On the other hand, the trend for high-control mothers to have more delinquent sons in the introverts could be a maternal effect. Because introverts are presumably more sensitive to punishment than any of the three other personality groups, they may be those who are more susceptible to react negatively to what would appear as unnecessary control. However, it should be recalled that although the introverts with high-controlling mothers report more delinquent behavior than those with low-controlling mothers, they still report less delinquent behavior than all the other groups.

This study is one of the few attempts to take into account both children's personalities and parental behavior in explaining boys' antisocial behavior. Data were also collected longitudinally (from age 6 to 13), and from different sources (teachers, mothers, boys), thus preventing artificially produced colinearity. The results are interesting, but they are still limited by the correlational nature of longitudinal studies. We need experimental studies that will enable us to test if changes in parental behavior will have differential impacts on children with different personalities. These studies can be made in laboratory experiments, but preventive intervention studies are good models for such experiments (see, e.g., Farrington, 1992). However, prevention studies should be devised in such a way that they will test complex person–environment interaction effects.

NOTES

This research was supported by grants from Canada's NWGP and SSHRC funding agencies, and Quebec's CQRS and FCAR funding agencies. The author is grateful to Hélène Beauchesne, Lucille David, and Lyse Desmarais-Gervais for coordinating the data collection and data management, Hélène Boileau and Maria Rosa for data analyses, Minh Trinh for the documentation, and Francine Plourde for typing the manuscript. Pierre Charlebois, Claude Gagnon, and Serge Larivée contributed to the planning of this study.

1. Similar significant differences were observed for the stealing, vandalism, and drug-use subscales.

REFERENCES

Bell, R. Q., & Chapman, M. (1986). Child effects in studies using experimental or brief longitudinal approaches to socialization. *Developmental Psychology, 22,* 595–603.

Bell, R. Q. (1979). Parent, child, and reciprocal influences. *American Psychologist, 34*(10), 821–826.

Bugental, D. E., & Shennum, W. A. (1984). "Difficult" children as elicitors and targets of adult communication patterns: An attributional-behavioral transactional analysis. *Monograph of the Society for Research in Child Development, 49*(Serial No. 1205, 1).

Eron, L. D., Huesmann, L. R., & Zelli, A. (1991). The role of parental variables in the learning of aggression. In D. J. Pepler & K. H. Rubin (Eds.), *The development and treatment of childhood aggression* (pp. 169–188). Hillsdale, NJ: Erlbaum.

Eysenck, H. J. (1964). *Crime and personality.* London: Routledge & Kegan Paul.

Eysenck, H. J. (1967). *The biological basis of personality.* Springfield, IL: Thomas.

Eysenck, H. J., & Gudjonsson, G. H. (1989). *The causes and cures of criminality.* New York: Plenum.

Falender, C. A., & Mehrabian, A. (1980). The emotional climate for children as inferred from parental attitudes: A preliminary validation of three scales. *Educational and Psychological Measurement, 40,* 1033–1042.

Farrington, D. P. (1986). Stepping stones to adult criminal careers. In D. Olweus, J. Block, & M. Radke-Yarrow (Eds.), *Development of antisocial and prosocial behavior* (pp. 359–384). New York: Academic.

Farrington, D. P. (1992). The need for longitudinal experimental research on offending and antisocial behavior. In J. McCord & R. E. Tremblay (Eds.), *Preventing antisocial behavior: Interventions from birth through adolescence* (pp. 353–376). New York: Guilford.

Farrington, D. P., & Hawkins, J. D. (1991). Predicting participation, early onset and later persistence in officially recorded offending. *Criminal Behaviour and Mental Health, 1,* 1–33.

Gray, J. A. (1970). The psychophysiological basis of introversion–extraversion. *Behavioral Research and Therapy, 8,* 249–266.

Gray, J. A. (1981). A critique of Eysenck's theory of personality. In H. J. Eysenck (Ed.), *A model for personality* (pp. 246–276). New York: Springer.

Gray, J. A. (1982). *The neuropsychology of anxiety.* New York: Oxford University Press.

LeBlanc, M. (1990). *Manuel sur les mesures de l'adaptation sociale et personnelle pour les adolescents québécois (MASPAQ).* Montréal: Université de Montréal, Groupe de Recherche sur l'Inadaptation Psychosociale chez l'Enfant.

Loeber, R., & Dishion, T. J. (1983). Early predictors of male delinquency: A review. *Psychological Bulletin, 94,* 68–99.

Loeber, R., & Stouthamer-Loeber, M. (1986). Family factors as correlates and predictors of juvenile conduct problems and delinquency. In M. Tonry & N. Morris (Eds.), *Crime and justice: An annual review of research* (pp. 29–149). Chicago: University of Chicago Press.

Lytton, H. (1990). Child and parent effects in boys' conduct disorder: A reinterpretation. *Developmental Psychology, 26,* 683–697.

Maccoby, E. E. (1986). Social groupings in childhood: Their relationships to prosocial and antisocial behavior in boys and girls. In D. Olweus, J. Block, & M. Radke-Yarrow (Eds.), *Development of antisocial and prosocial behavior: Research theories, and issues*. New York: Academic.

Maccoby, E. E., & Jacklin, C. N. (1980). Sex differences in aggression: A rejoinder and reprise. *Child Development, 51,* 964–980.

Maccoby, E. E., & Martin, J. A. (1983). Socialization in the context of the family: Parent–child interaction. In P. H. Mussen (Ed.), *Handbook of Child Psychology* (pp. 1–101). Toronto: Wiley.

McCord, J. (1979). Some child-rearing antecedents of criminal behavior in adult men. *Journal of Personality and Social Psychology, 37,* 1477–1486.

Pulkkinen, L. (1982). Self-control and continuity from childhood to late adolescence. In P. B. Baltes & O. G. Brim (Eds.), *Life-span development and behavior* (Vol. 4, pp. 63–105). New York: Academic.

Raine, A., & Venables, P. (1981). Classical conditioning and socialization: A biosocial interaction. *Personality and Individual Differences, 2*(4), 273–283.

Sully, J. (1895). *Studies of childhood.* London: Longmans, Green.

Tremblay, R. E., Gagnon, C., Vitaro, F., Dobkin, P., Banville, P., & Boileau, H. (1993). *Fathers' and mothers' behavioral dimorphism with disruptive kindergarten boys predicts conduct disorder at puberty.* Unpublished manuscript.

Tremblay, R. E., Loeber, R., Gagnon, C., Charlebois, P., Larivée, S., & LeBlanc, M. (1991). Disruptive boys with stable and unstable high fighting behavior patterns during junior elementary school. *Journal of Abnormal Child Psychology, 19,* 285–300.

Widom, C. S. (1989). The cycle of violence. *Science, 16*(244), 160–166.

9 The reciprocal influence of punishment and child behavior disorder

PATRICIA COHEN AND JUDITH S. BROOK

The association between punishment and conduct problems has been the subject of numerous investigations over the past two decades (Farrington, 1978; Hawkins, Catalano, & Miller, 1992; Holmes & Robins, 1988; McCord, 1979; Tremblay et al., 1991). That punishment is related to conduct problems is now beyond question. Hawkins, Catalano, and Miller (1992) have reviewed findings from several cross-sectional and prospective studies showing a relationship between punishment and conduct problems. Intervention studies have also indicated that children benefit from appropriate parental discipline (Hawkins, Catalano, Jones, & Fine, 1987; Patterson, 1982; Tremblay et al., 1991; Wahler & Dumas, 1987). Despite the fact that studies have varied with regard to assessment of punishment and conduct problems and in sample composition, the findings converge in the conclusion that youngsters who are exposed to punishment have higher rates of delinquency.

What accounts for the linkages between punishment and conduct problems? The effect may be causal in that parental punishment converts preexisting tendencies into later delinquency. According to this hypothesis, conduct problems and antisocial behavior are, in part, consequences of inadequate discipline. This could come about in several different ways. Several notable theorists (e.g., Hirschi, 1969) concur that difficulties in rearing interfere with the development of attachments that would insulate the adolescent from conduct problems. Another mechanism for a causal effect of punishment is through the modeling of coercive and aggressive behavior that (inadvertently) teaches children the very behavior it is designed to suppress. Support for the causal model can be found in the longitudinal studies of several investigators (Cohen & Brook, 1987; Farrington, 1978; Holmes & Robins, 1988; Johnson, 1979; McCord, 1979, 1988, 1991; Zucker, 1976).

An alternative explanation for the association between punishment and conduct problems is that the causal effect is in the opposite direction. The underlying hypothesis of this model is that individuals who exhibit conduct problems evoke

154

harsher discipline. In this perspective adolescents are exposed to power assertive techniques of discipline because of the burdens they place on those with whom they interact. It has been shown that mothers who encounter misbehaving children (not their own) will tend to react with the same kinds of power-assertive techniques shown by the children's real mothers. Another posited mechanism is that parental rejection tends to promote misbehavior in some children, which is then handled maladaptively by the parent. Support for this model can be found in Wahler and Dumas (1987), who note that children may behave in an aversive manner so as to gain their parents' attention, despite the fact that the attention is negative.

It is possible, of course, that the relationship between punishment and negative behavior is not causal at all but rather represents the fact that each is correlated with other influences. Adolescents with conduct problems may, for instance, have fewer social skills, making it more difficult for them to maintain appropriate interactions with their parents. Furthermore there may be other confounders, such as age, gender, socioeconomic status, or parental problems such as mental illness, sociopathy, or conflict.

Even should we find evidence of causal effects, it is likely that we will find the relationship between punishment and behavior problems over the span of childhood to be reciprocal. According to the reciprocal model, punishment is related to conduct problems in the child, which in turn is related to further ineffective parental discipline. The reciprocal model is dynamic in nature and requires consideration of the likelihood that these effects may not be constant across the years from early childhood through late adolescence. In relevant work, Patterson, DeBaryshe, and Ramsey (1989) noted that children's behaviors at one stage predict reactions from the social environment of the child at the next stage. This then results in further reactions from the child and further alterations in the reactions from the social environment. Patterson and colleagues have noted that this "action–reaction" sequence puts the antisocial child at greater risk for later criminal behavior.

The purpose of this article is to test these models of the linkage between discipline and conduct problems. We build on the research of others, but our approach differs in several ways. First, the current sample size is larger and more representative of the general population than is typical of previous studies. Second, our study includes data on youngsters from preschool years. Third, we attempt to assess the magnitude of the impact of punishment on both a diagnostic measure of conduct disorder and on scaled measures of behavior problems.

We examine potential differences between boys and girls in the linkages between parental punishment and child behavior. We hypothesize that the pathways may differ depending on whether the youngster is in early or later adolescence (Steinberg, 1987). Adolescence consists of a number of substages that reflect not only physical changes, but psychological and behavioral ones as well. Developmental changes in the adolescent also generate changes in the parent–child relationship. Parental monitoring continues to diminish during adolescence as children assume more responsibility for the regulation of their own behavior (White, Pandina, & LaGrange, 1987). Therefore, one might assume that punishment has a greater negative effect on younger than on older adolescents.

Sample

The study children were originally sampled in 1975 (T1) when they were ages 1 to 10. At that time two upstate New York counties were studied to determine the relationship of child and family problems to area-based social indicators (Kogan, Smith, & Jenkins, 1977). We randomly sampled 976 families with age-eligible children from 100 randomly sampled neighborhoods in the two counties. A follow-up was undertaken in 1983 (T2) to identify early risks for childhood psychopathology. Seventy-five percent of the original sample was located and reinterviewed. Families living in urban poverty areas were slightly more likely not to be located at the time of the follow-up. In both the original and follow-up interviews, 50% of the children were girls. The age distribution of the original sample was roughly 100 children at each age between 1 and 10 years. Because families with younger children were somewhat more likely to be lost to follow-up, 48% of the children who had been ages 1 to 5 were available for the follow-up assessments. Maternal education ranged from sixth grade to doctoral degree, with a median at high school graduate. Sixteen percent of the sample was living in a single-parent household at follow-up. African-Americans constituted 5% of the sample at follow-up and 8% of the area population as a whole. Thirty-two percent of the sample lived in rural areas or in small towns at the time of the follow-up.

A second follow-up series of interviews completed in 1985–86 (T3) included 96% of those seen in the first follow-up, as well as about half of those who were located but with whom we were not able to schedule interviews in 1983. Demographic characteristics were essentially the same in both follow-up samples. Participating families resided in more than 30 different states.

In each family, interviews were carried out with one parent, usually the mother, and, for the follow-up interviews, the study child. Mothers and children were interviewed simultaneously but separately in their homes by two trained interviewers.

Measures

Psychiatric diagnoses including conduct disorder were assessed by structured diagnostic interviews of mother and youth using the Diagnostic Interview Schedule for Children (DISC) (Costello, Edelbrock, Dulcan, & Kalas, 1984), as modified and supplemented by our group. Responses from maternal and youth interviews were combined by computer algorithms described elsewhere (Cohen, Velez, Kohn, Schwab-Stone, & Johnson, 1987) to produce DSM-III-R diagnoses at three levels – mild, moderate, and severe. Despite the orientation of the original DISC toward the DSM-III system, we were able to employ information gathered in the other

Table 9.1. *Measure of power-assertive punishment*

During the last month when [study child] did something he/she should not do, or didn't do something he/she should do, which of these methods have you used to correct his/her behavior?

Score consists of a count of number of methods.

Did you scold _____?
Did you spank or slap _____?
Did you scream at _____?
Did you make _____ stay in his/her room?
Did you take away a privilege or something _____ likes?
Did you threaten to punish _____ whether you followed through or not?
Did you remove _____ from what he/she was doing?

---

sections of the interviews to supplement the DISC where demands of the revised diagnostic system had changed. Evidence of the validity of these diagnoses is provided elsewhere (Cohen, Johnson, Lewis, & Brook 1990; Cohen, Johnson, Struening, & Brook, 1989; Cohen, O'Connor, Lewis, & Malachowski, 1987; Cohen, Velez, Brook, & Smith, 1989; Velez, Johnson, & Cohen, 1989). Behavior problems in early childhood were assessed by a series of questions devised by the original investigators (Kogan et al., 1977) with internal consistency reliabilities of .46 for 1-year-olds, .75 for 2- to 4-year-olds, and .81 for 5- to 10-year-olds.

Our measure of punishment was first obtained in the interviews of mothers when the children were ages 1 to 10 (see Table 9.1). Mothers indicated which of a series of power-assertive techniques of controlling or disciplining the child they had employed during the previous month. This measure had an internal consistency reliability of .50 for mothers of 1-year-olds, .44 for mothers of 2- to 4-year-olds, and .62 for mothers of 5- to 10-year-olds. During the follow-up assessments, measures of punishment were obtained from both parent and child with an internal consistency reliability of .76.

We also treated early childhood punishment as a dichotomy in some analyses by selecting the 25th percentile on the basis of an examination of the item-response curve for later conduct disorder. This variable enabled us to compute both odds ratios and the fraction of conduct disorder cases potentially attributable to punishment. In this measure we defined 75% of the children as having been exposed to risky levels of punishment. This cut-off discriminates not only very extreme or abusive behavior but also levels of punishment that are well within the norm of appropriate parenting as defined in our society.

Other measures used in these analyses included socioeconomic status (SES), combining maternal and paternal education, occupational status of father, and family income. Maternal sociopathy was documented from maternal reports of problems with drugs, alcohol, or the police; maternal psychopathology was documented from maternal reports of having or having sought help for an emotional problem. Parental conflict was measured by a subscale of the Locke-Wallace measure (Locke & Wallace, 1959). Maternal rejection was measured by a series of questions regarding maternal dissatisfaction with the child's looks, manners, friends, behavior, and achievement (original to this study). Mother–child closeness was a measure that combined subscales of maternal affection, support, and mother–child communication as reported in child and mother interviews (adapted from Schaefer, 1965, and Avgar, Bronfenbrenner, & Henderson, 1977). Maternal tolerance of deviance was adapted from a measure devised for youth (Jessor, Graves, Hanson, & Jessor, 1968).

Analytic methods

We employed logistic regression analyses to assess the odds of diagnosable levels of behavior problems in children whose parents used punishment as compared with those who were less inclined to do so. Another perspective on the magnitude of this potential is given by the attributable risk, an estimate of the proportion of cases of conduct disorder that may be attributed to the effects of a risk factor (parental punishment).

Findings

In the first analyses dichotomized measures were used to demonstrate the relationship of punishment to seriously problematic outcomes and to show the attributable risk of conduct disorder associated with punitive disciplinary measures. As can be seen in Table 9.2, children were more than twice as likely to show conduct disorder 8 years later if they were among the more punished group, and more than 3 times as likely to have conduct disorder 10 years later when they were ages 12 to 20.

The attributable risk is the proportion of all cases of conduct disorder that may be

Table 9.2. *Prevalence of conduct disorder in adolescence among those punished and not punished at ages 1 to 10*

Adolescent conduct disorder	Early childhood punishment	
	No	Yes
8 years later	($n = 192$)	($n = 529$)
%	6.0	12.5
n	11	65
10 years later	($n = 192$)	($n = 531$)
%	3.0	11.1
n	5	56

due to parental punishment. Calculation of this value is determined by combining information on the rates of disorder in the exposed and unexposed populations with the prevalence of the risk factor (Kahn & Sempos, 1989, pp. 72–83). The attributable risk was fully 45% for the cases of conduct disorder at T2 and 67% for the cases of conduct disorder at T3. According to these estimates, if all parents treated their children the way the least punishing quarter of the families did we might expect to have half as many cases of conduct disorder 8 years later and only one-third as many cases 10 years later.

These projections assume that the entire relationship between these variables is due to the causal effect of punishment on conduct disorder. However, in fact, early discipline may be correlated with a number of other risks that may confound the relationship with conduct disorder. These relationships were systematically explored.

Punishment methods were more frequently used on the younger children in early to middle childhood, a progression that continued in adolescence. There was no difference in punishment of sons (72%) and daughters (74%). SES only slightly differentiated mothers who used more of these techniques from those using fewer, with 76% of those at or below median SES using punishment compared with 69% of those with higher SES ($p < .05$). However, the presence of early behavior problems as reported by mothers was strongly related to contemporary punishment, with more problems among those children who were more punished. In fact only one child of those identified as having behavior problems was not in the more punished group. We considered three kinds of problems in the mothers to be potential confounders, namely, sociopathy (problems with drinking, drugs, or the police), parental conflict, and psychopathology. Neither maternal sociopathy nor parental conflict was related to levels of punishment. However, maternal psychopathology was related to higher levels of punishment, a finding consistent with studies of depressed mothers.

How do these same variables relate to conduct disorder 8 and 10 years later? SES was only marginally related to conduct disorder in this sample. However, early behavior problems were a powerful predictor of later conduct disorder, with such children three or more times as likely to show disorder. There were also associations between age and gender and later conduct disorder, with boys at much higher risk than girls. When we examined the relationship of parental problems with adolescent conduct disorder we found significant relationships with maternal sociopathy and with parental conflict, but no relationship with maternal psychopathology.

Considering these bivariate relationships together, we found that the most potent common relationship was with early behavior problems. Maternal sociopathy, parental conflict, and maternal psychopathology were each related to either punishment or conduct disorder, but not both. Therefore, these variables cannot account for the relationship between punishment and conduct disorder. However, the child-initiated model is a plausible alternative explanation of the relationship between punishment and conduct disorder. To check for these alternative hypotheses we

Table 9.3. *Conduct disorder at ages 10 to 18 associated with early punishment* (N = 721)

	Odds ratio	Confidence limits
Odds ratio punished/not punished	2.13	1.09–4.14
Removing children with early behavior problems	2.26	1.13–4.51
Partialing effects of age, gender, social class, and family covariates	2.14	1.05–4.36
Partialing age, gender, SES, and early problems	2.02	.99–4.15

conducted a series of logistic regression analyses in which we controlled for each of these alternative hypotheses (Table 9.3).

In the first analysis we examined conduct disorder at the first follow-up. As can be seen, when we removed the effect of early behavior problems by excluding children manifesting these problems the odds ratio was not decreased. When we included age, sex, SES, and the three parental problems, again the odds were only somewhat lower and were still significantly elevated.

These same analyses were repeated using the second follow-up (Table 9.4). Here the relationships were consistently larger, and the effect of removing the influence of the covariates was to enhance the magnitude of the odds ratio. Replication of these analyses for boys and girls separately produced virtually identical odds ratios. The interaction between punishment and gender was not significant.

Thus, it is reasonable to conclude that there exists a causal role for early discipline and that it is a powerful effect. However, these analyses do not rule out the effects of child behavior on parenting. Therefore, we used these longitudinal data to produce estimates of the ongoing reciprocal effects of child behavior and discipline on each other. For these analyses we turned to the more powerful measurement inherent in the scaled dimensions of our constructs.

Reciprocal causation between two variables may be estimated, even with cross-sectional data, provided that it is possible to identify other variables that are theoretically and empirically causally related to each of the two variables but not to both (Goldberger & Duncan, 1973). We had anticipated that we would be able to find such appropriate "instruments" for child problem behavior and for punishment by the parent. However, we were unable to find T1 correlates of either variable that were not related to the other variable as well, and these analyses could not be done. We therefore turned to cross-lagged analyses to produce alternative estimates of the directionality of these influences. These analyses were carried out for the sample as a whole and also separately for the younger and older members of the cohort.

For the sample as a whole the cycle of coercion was very apparent in the

Table 9.4. *Conduct disorder at ages 12 to 20 associated with early punishment* (N = 723)

	Odds ratio	Confidence limits
Odds ratio punished/not punished	4.08	1.61–10.37
Removing children with early behavior problems	4.05	1.59–10.31
Partialing effects of age, gender, social class, and family covariates	3.55	1.38–9.14
Partialing effects of age, gender, SES, and early problems	3.33	1.29–8.63
Girls only, partialing all effects	3.34	0.74–15.08
Boys only, partialing all effects	3.35	0.98–11.42

movement from early and middle childhood to adolescence with effects of conduct disorder on subsequent punishment as well as effects of punishment on changes in conduct disorder (see Figure 9.1). However, there was no evidence of an increase in punishment as a reaction to conduct disorder in adolescence. There was an increase in the stability of both parent and child behaviors over time (but note also the shorter interval from T2 to T3 as compared with the T1 to T2 interval).

In the younger children the evidence of the cycle of coercion in the period from early childhood (under age 6) to late childhood (9 to 13) was stronger. In the period from late childhood (9 to 13) to early adolescence (12 to 16) the effect of conduct disorder on punishment dropped out, whereas the effect of punishment on conduct disorder remained.

For older children, even in the transition from middle childhood (ages 6 to 10) to middle adolescence (ages 14 to 18) the lagged effects were not significant. Their behaviors were somewhat more stable than those in the younger sample. Nor were there significant effects from middle adolescence to late adolescence in either direction, although both parent and child behaviors were quite stable.

These analyses, of course, need elaboration. In accord with our theoretical review of the literature, we examined four other propositions, as follows:

1. The lack of mother–child closeness or attachment accounts for the effect of punishment.
2. Punishment operates specifically in the vulnerable (those with early behavior problems) to produce unique or larger effects on subsequent mother–child closeness and child conduct problems.
3. Maternal rejection of the child is the underlying cause of the effect of punishment.
4. Punishment is reflective of maternal attitude toward deviance, which is a confounder of the relationship.

To test these propositions we included each of these variables in the longitudinal equations. Findings on these analyses indicated the following:

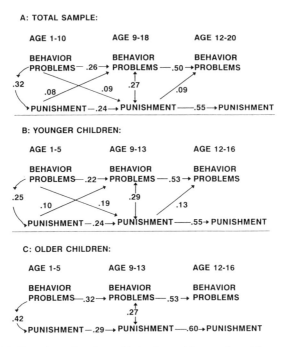

Figure 9.1. Cross-lagged analyses of behavior problems and punishment.

1. The effects of punishment of child conduct problems were not attributable to a lack of mother–child closeness, although such a lack was an independent predictor of behavior problems. The relationship between punishment and conduct problems was unchanged.
2. Punishment did indeed interact with early conduct problems. The effects of punishment on future behavior problems were greatest in those children who were contemporaneously showing behavior problems. However, even among those with few such problems punishment was a risk for future problems.
3. Maternal rejection was also related to behavior problems but did not account for or change substantially the effect of punishment.
4. Maternal tolerance of deviance was higher in the mothers of children with behavior problems. Again, this relationship did not alter estimated effects of punishment practices.

We therefore conclude that the causal effect of punishment on conduct disorder is real. Although the frequency of use of coercive methods is undoubtedly substantially influenced by the operant behavior of the child during early childhood, on the whole, the magnitude of the estimates and the fact that the influence begins so early in life lead us to conclude that the predominant influence is from punishment to conduct problems. Once begun, punishment has a more potent negative effect on the temperamentally vulnerable. On the evidence presented here, parental punishment practices take on a stability during later childhood and adolescence that is uninfluenced by the level of the child's problem behavior. However, they continue to have a negative influence on the child's behavior.

We did not find significant gender differences in the influence of punishment on conduct disorder. In contrast, Nye (1958) assumed that there were gender differences in the influence of parental control on delinquency. Parental control, however, involves monitoring that is likely to be more vigilant for daughters than for sons. In a related vein, Hagan, Simpson, and Gillis (1987) reasoned that since parental control is greater for females than for males, it is likely to have a greater effect on female delinquency. Our data, however, suggest that effects of punishment may be quite comparable for boys and girls.

REFERENCES

Avgar, A., Bronfenbrenner, U., & Henderson, C. R., Jr. (1977). Socialization practices of parents, teachers, and peers in Israel: Kibbutz, moshav, and city. *Child Development, 48,* 1219–1227.

Cohen, P., & Brook, J. S. (1987). Family factors related to the persistence of psychopathology in childhood and adolescence. *Psychiatry, 50*(4), 332–345.

Cohen, P., Johnson, J., Lewis, S. A., & Brook, J. S. (1990). Single parenthood and employment: Double jeopardy? In J. Eckenrode & S. Gore (Eds.), *Transmitting stress between work and family* (pp. 117–132). New York: Plenum.

Cohen, P., Johnson, J., Struening, E. L., & Brook, J. S. (1989). Family mobility as a risk factor for psychopathology in childhood. In B. Cooper & T. Helgason (Eds.), *Epidemiology and the prevention of mental disorders* (pp. 145–155). London: Routledge.

Cohen, P., O'Connor, P., Lewis, S., & Malachowski, B. (1987). A comparison of the agreement between DISC and K-SADS-PP interviews of an epidemiological sample of children. *Journal of the American Academy of Child Psychiatry, 26,* 662–667.

Cohen, P., Velez, C. N., Brook, J. S., & Smith, J. (1989). Mechanisms of the relationship between perinatal problems, early childhood illness, and psychopathology in late childhood and adolescence. *Child Development, 60,* 701–709.

Cohen, P., Velez, C. N., Kohn, M., Schwab-Stone, M., & Johnson, J. (1987) Child psychiatric diagnosis by computer algorithm: Theoretical issues and empirical tests. *Journal of the American Academy of Child and Adolescent Psychiatry, 26,* 631–638.

Costello, A. J., Edelbrock, C. S., Dulcan, M. K., & Kalas, R. (1984). *Testing of the NIMH Diagnostic Interview Schedule for Children (DISC) in a clinical population* (Contract No. DB-81-0027). Final report to the Center for Epidemiological Studies, National Institute for Mental Health, University of Pittsburgh.

Farrington, D. P. (1978). The family backgrounds of aggressive youths. In L. A. Hersov & M. Berger (Eds.), *Aggression and antisocial behavior in childhood and adolescence* (pp. 73–93). Oxford: Pergamon Press.

Goldberger, A. S., & Duncan, O. D. (1973). *Structural equation models in the social sciences.* New York: Seminar Press.

Hagan, J., Simpson, J., & Gillis, A. R. (1987). Class in the household: A power-control theory of gender and delinquency. *American Journal of Sociology, 92,* 788–816.

Hawkins, J. D., Catalano, R. F., Jones, G., & Fine, D. N. (1987). Delinquency prevention through parent training: Results and issues from work in progress. In J. Q. Wilson & G. C. Loury (Eds.), *From children to citizens: Families, schools, and delinquency prevention* (Vol. 3, pp. 186–204). New York: Springer-Verlag.

Hawkins, J. D., Catalano, R. F., & Miller, J. Y. (1992). Risk and protective factors for alcohol and other drug problems in adolescence and early adulthood: Implications for substance abuse prevention. *Psychological Bulletin, 112,* 64–105.

Hirschi, T. (1969). *Causes of delinquency.* Berkeley: University of California Press.

Holmes, S. J., & Robins, L. N. (1988). The role of parental disciplinary practices in the development of depression and alcoholism. *Psychiatry, 51,* 24–35.

Jessor, R., Graves, T. D., Hanson, R. C., & Jessor, S. L. (1968). *Society, personality, and deviant behavior: A study of a tri-ethnic community.* New York: Holt, Rinehart, & Winston.

Johnson, R. (1979). *Juvenile delinquency and its origins.* Cambridge University Press.

Kahn, H. A., & Sempos, C. T. (1989) *Statistical methods in epidemiology.* New York: Oxford University Press.

Kogan, L. S., Smith, J., & Jenkins, S. (1977). Ecological validity of indicator data as predictors of survey findings. *Journal of Social Service Research, 1,* 117–132.

Locke, H. S., & Wallace, K. M. (1959). Short marital adjustment and prediction tests: Their reliability and validity. *Marriage and Family Living, 21,* 251–255.

McCord, J. (1979). Some child-rearing antecedents of criminal behavior in adult men. *Journal of Personality and Social Psychology, 37,* 1477–1486.

McCord, J. (1988). Parental behavior in the cycle of aggression. *Psychiatry, 51,* 14–23.

McCord, J. (1991). Family relationships, juvenile delinquency, and adult criminality. *Criminology, 29*(3), 397–417.

Nye, F. I. (1958). *Family relationships and delinquent behavior.* New York: Wiley.

Patterson, G. R. (1982). *A social learning approach: Vol. 3. Coercive family process.* Eugene, OR: Castalia.

Patterson, G. R., DeBaryshe, B. D., & Ramsey, E. (1989). A developmental perspective on antisocial behavior. *American Psychologist, 44*(2), 329–335.

Schaefer, E. S. (1965). Children's report of parental behavior: An inventory. *Child Development, 36,* 413–424.

Steinberg, L. (1987). Familial factors in delinquency: A developmental perspective. *Journal of Adolescent Research, 2,* 255–268.

Tremblay, R. E., McCord, J., Boileau, H., Charlebois, P., Gagnon, C., LeBlanc, M., & Larivee, S. (1991). Can disruptive boys be helped to become competent? *Psychiatry, 54,* 148–161.

Velez, C. N., Johnson, J., & Cohen, P. (1989). Longitudinal analyses of selected risk factors for childhood psychopathology. *Journal of the American Academy of Child and Adolescent Psychiatry, 28,* 861–864.

Wahler, R. G., & Dumas, J. E. (1987). Family factors in childhood psychology: Toward a coercion–neglect model. In T. Jacob (Ed.), *Family interaction and psychopathology: Theories, methods, and findings* (pp. 581–627). New York: Plenum.

White, H. R., Pandina, R. J., & LaGrange, R. L. (1987). Longitudinal predictors of serious substance use and delinquency. *Criminology, 25,* 715–740.

Zucker, R. A. (1976). Parental influences on the drinking patterns of their children. In M. Greenblatt & M. A. Schuckit (Eds.), *Alcoholism problems in women and children.* New York: Grune & Stratton.

10 The development of coercive family processes: the interaction between aversive toddler behavior and parenting factors

KATE KEENAN AND DANIEL S. SHAW

Introduction

The purpose of the study reported here was to identify developmental precursors of coercive parent–child interaction and child externalizing behavior by examining child and parental behavior, and the interaction of the two during a period critical to the child's socialization process, ages 1 to 2. Although much research has been conducted on the maintenance of coercive family processes and its relation to child externalizing behavior, few investigators have examined the precursors of coercive processes in the early parent–child relationship. Several consistent findings in the development of externalizing behavior in children have served to highlight the importance of the early parent–child relationship. First, aggressive and disruptive behavior are already stable behavioral patterns in school-age children, especially for boys (Cummings, Iannotti, & Zahn-Waxler, 1989; Huessman, Eron, Lefkowitz, & Walder, 1984; Olweus, 1979). Second, family management practices are related to the development of both prosocial and antisocial behavior in children (Block, Block, & Morrison, 1981; Londerville & Main, 1981; Loeber & Stouthamer-Loeber, 1986; Martin, 1981; McCord, 1979; Patterson, 1982; Patterson, Capaldi, & Bank, 1991). Therefore, factors involved in the initiation of coercive family processes and child externalizing behavior may be first evident in the toddler period, when parents and children begin to engage in struggles for the first time.

Although little is known about the stability of aggression in preschool children, among school-age children and adolescents stability of aggression has been well established. Loeber (1982) presented evidence for the contribution of four factors to the stability of antisocial and delinquent child behavior: density, occurrence in more than one setting, variety of behavior, and early age of onset. The last factor, early age of onset, was particularly useful in predicting the chronicity, rate, and seriousness of later antisocial behavior. Olweus (1979) presented stability coeffi-

165

cients generated from a meta-analysis of 16 studies on the aggressive behavior of boys and concluded that stability of aggression was comparable to that of intelligence, and that the determination of stability rested within individual reaction tendencies and motivation. Thus, from the early school years to adolescence, and even adulthood, stability of aggression is moderate to high, particularly for boys. In addition, early onset of externalizing behavior problems is highly predictive of later antisocial behavior.

There is some evidence that the reported high stability of aggression in school-age children can be replicated in the preschool period. For example, in a sample of 43 middle-class children (22 boys and 21 girls), Cummings et al. (1989) found moderate to high correlations on aggression scores from ages 2 to 5 ($r = .47$ to .76). Observers' global ratings at age 2 were also predictive of later aggressive behavior. In one of the few studies on children from a low-socioeconomic background, Rose, Rose, and Feldman (1989) demonstrated stability of externalizing behavior problems from age 2 to 5 ($r = .53$ to .73) using two standardized versions of the Achenbach Child Behavior Checklist (Achenbach, Edelbrock, & Howell, 1987). Thus, within the first 2 years of life, behavioral aggression emerges and has the capacity to become a stable feature from preschool into adolescence. The question remains, however, which factors serve to increase the likelihood of continued aggression from preschool to school age?

Child-rearing practices and the quality of the parent–child relationship have also been found to be implicated in the development and maintenance of externalizing behaviors at school age and adolescence. In two reviews by Loeber and colleagues, harsh, inconsistent discipline practices and lack of parental involvement and supervision were demonstrated to be consistently strong predictors of current and later antisocial behavior (Loeber & Dishion, 1983; Loeber & Stouthamer-Loeber, 1986). The latter of these two factors has been conceptualized by researchers of normal socialization as a lack of maternal responsiveness (Crockenberg, 1981; Egeland & Farber 1984; Isabella & Belsky, 1991; Shaw & Bell, 1993; Sroufe, 1983). A lack of responsiveness and sensitivity to an infant/toddler may provide a link to the later observed neglect and uninvolvement that is related to school-age children's externalizing behavior problems.

Finally, Patterson (1982) has identified a pattern of coercive interaction between parents and children that is higher in families of antisocial children than in non–clinically referred families. The two aforementioned components – negative child behavior and poor parenting skills – appear salient for the development of the coercive cycle. For example, child aversive behavior such as noncompliance, aggression, or hyperactivity met with inconsistent discipline may result in the parent negatively reinforcing aversive child behavior. The coercive interaction serves to escalate both child and parent negative behaviors. This pattern of negative child behavior and parental reinforcement has been identified in middle-class families of school-age children and adolescents with disruptive behavior problems, and has been the primary focus of intervention efforts (Kazdin, 1987).

Most researchers examining factors related to the development of coercive family processes and child externalizing behavior have extended their assessment window only to early school age. Although most children who are clinically referred for disruptive behavior are school age, such a truncated assessment window may impede the identification of some etiological factors. Thus, there is a need to examine earlier junctures in the parent–child relationship, junctures that, when explored, may reveal factors involved in the initiation of coercive family processes and child externalizing behavior. It is the purpose of this study to extend the assessment window to infancy and the toddler period, a time during which the foundation for negative parent–child interaction may be set. During this period, aggressive behavior emerges, reaches a peak, and declines in normal development (Martin, Larzelere, & Amberson, 1986; Szegal, 1985). At the same time, the socialization process begins and both parent and child struggle with limit setting for the first time.

Additionally, because the aim of this study is to map out developmental processes toward coercive interactions, an interactionist perspective is applied, one that conceptualizes the development of externalizing behavior problems as an *ongoing,* reciprocal process between the child and his or her caretaking environment (Sameroff, 1990). For example, using Patterson's (1982) model of coercive family interactions, Martin (1981) provided evidence for a reciprocal, interactional model in the development of problem child behavior, encompassing both mother and child contributions, as well as the interaction between the two. Using a well-educated middle-class sample, maternal responsiveness, infant demandingness, and the interaction of these two variables at 10 months of age were identified as strong predictors of later child noncompliance at 22 months and coercive child behavior at 42 months. Relations were significant only for boys.

The present study attempted to extend both Patterson's and Martin's interactional principles to the identification of precursors of coercive parent–child interaction among a sample of high-risk infants/toddlers. Further, since this study is driven from a developmental framework, sex differences in the prevalence, stability, and correlates of aggression were also examined. One hallmark of the toddler period is the child's new encounter with parental restrictions. There is some evidence that parental discipline strategies are different for boys and girls (Zahn-Waxler, 1992). Thus, in the development of coercive processes and child externalizing behavior, sex differences in aggressive behavior and differential effects of parenting styles may be linked to differences in boys' and girls' manifestation of later externalizing behavior.

Method

Subjects

Subjects were 89 mother–child dyads (52 male and 37 female children) recruited from the Women, Infants, and Children (WIC) Nutritional Supplement Program of Allegheny County, Pennsylvania, as part of a larger longitudinal study of child development. Mothers of infants 6 to 11 months of age were recruited in the clinic waiting room by the one of the principal investigators of the project. Mothers were informed that the investigators aimed to study child development and mother–child interaction patterns, and that they would be paid $15.00 for each lab visit and an additional $10.00 for transportation costs. Upon agreeing to participate, informed consent was obtained and the first lab visit was scheduled to coincide within 2 weeks of the child's first birthday. Mothers were contacted 2 weeks before the assessment by mail and 1 week before by phone to confirm the appointment. Of the 129 women who agreed to take part in the study, 102 (79.0%) participated in the first laboratory assessment at 12 months. Of these, 89 (87.0%) participated in the 12-, 18-, and 24-month assessments. No significant differences were found between the 89 mothers who participated in all three lab assessments compared with those participating in only the first, on demographic characteristics or on depressive symptomatology. Mothers who participated in all three lab assessments rated themselves as having a more aggressive personality than mothers who did not complete all three lab assessments. Demographic information on the sample is presented in Table 10.1.

Table 10.1. *Demographic characteristics* (N = 89)

Race of child		*Sex of child*	
Caucasian	52	Male	52
African-American	31	Female	37
Mixed	6		
		Marital status	
Family income (per year)		Single	37
<$6,000	33	Married	28
<$12,000	27	Living together	15
<$18,000	16	Separated/divorced	9
<$24,000	8		
<$30,000	2	*Maternal education*	
>$30,000	3	Junior high	1
		Partial high school	16
Maternal age		High school/ GED	47
16–19	11	Partial college	23
20–23	26	College degree	2
24–27	24		
28–31	16		
over 30	12		
Maternal occupation			
Unemployed	65		
Menial service	1		
Un-/semiskilled	5		
Skilled/clerical	12		
Semiprofessional	5		
Professional	1		

Table 10.2. *Protocol for laboratory assessments*

	Time (min)
12-month	
Free play – mother, child, and mother's examiner	15
No-toys situation – mother and child	3
High-chair task – mother and child	3
Problem-solving tasks – mother and child	12
Break	10
Ainsworth Strange Situation Test	21
Free play – mother's examiner reenters	3
18-month	
Free play – mother, child, and mother's examiner	15
Cleanup – mother and child	5
No-toys situation – mother and child	3
Problem-solving tasks – mother and child	12
Break	10
Ainsworth Strange Situation Test	21
Free play – mother's examiner reenters	5
24-month	
Free play – mother, child, and mother's examiner	15
Get-to tasks – mother and child	6
Cleanup – mother and child	5
Problem-solving tasks – mother and child	12
No-toys situation – mother and child	3
Martin Disinhibition Task (animal sounds) – mother and child	2
Break	10
Ainsworth Strange Situation Test	21
Free play – mother's examiner reenters	3

Procedures

Videotaped lab assessments were conducted at ages 12, 18, and 24 months, and a home visit was conducted at 15 months. Two laboratories were used, one for the 12- and 24-month assessments, and one for the 18-month assessment, both equipped with a one-way mirror through which the assessment was videotaped. Upon entering the lab, the mother was informed that once her child was comfortable, she should set him or her down in front of the toys on the floor and have a seat with the examiner to complete questionnaires. Unless otherwise specified, mothers were instructed to attend to their children as they normally would throughout the assessment.

Each lab assessment lasted approximately 90 minutes and consisted of seven different components (Table 10.2). The first component was a free play situation lasting 15 minutes, followed by a cleanup task, a situation with no toys in the room (Martin, 1981), and three mother–child problem-solving tasks (based on the work of Matas, Arend, & Sroufe, 1978). After a 10-minute break, the lab visit continued with an assessment of mother–child attachment, as measured by the Strange Situation Test (Ainsworth & Wittig, 1969). The final component of the lab assessment began when the examiner returned to the room and continued to work on the questionnaires with the mother for 5 minutes Table 10.2 lists the sequence and timing of each of the lab components.

The order of tasks varied slightly across the three lab visits, so that the no-toys situation occurred after the cleanup task at the 18-month assessment, and after problem-solving tasks at the 24-month assessment. Additionally, the 12-month assessment included a high-chair task, and the 24-month assessment included a set of mother–child interaction tasks and a disinhibition task (Table 10.2).

Self-report measures

Three self-report inventories were administered to mothers at the 18-month lab visit to assess possible correlates of childhood behavior problems. These included the aggression factor from the Personality Research Form, the Beck Depression Inventory, and a demographic questionnaire.

Personality Research Form (PRF) (Jackson, 1989). The 16-item aggression factor of the PRF was administered to mothers at the 18-month assessment. Mothers respond to items such as, "Sometimes I feel like smashing things" and "I seldom feel like hitting anyone" (reverse scored), by indicating whether an item is generally true or false for themselves. For the purpose of this study, maternal aggressive personality was used as a predictor of child aggression based on previous research demonstrating an effect of an aggressive personality on maternal responsiveness (Egeland & Farber, 1984). Both internal consistency (.87) and test–retest reliability (.84) are high for the aggression factor (Jackson, 1989).

The Beck Depression Inventory (BDI) (Beck, Ward, Mendelon, Mock, & Erbaugh, 1961). The BDI is a widely used continuous measurement of depressive symptom-atology. The BDI was administered to mothers when the children were 12, 18, and 24 months old. Split-half reliability has been reported to range from .86 to .93 (Beck & Beamesderfer, 1974; Reynolds & Gould, 1981). The BDI was developed to assess current affect, and consequently uses an ascertainment window of 2 weeks. For the purpose of this study, instructions for completing the inventory were revised so as to cover the mother's general affect over the past 6 months so as to assess the existence of a depressive trait. The BDI was included as a predictor of child aggression, based on research demonstrating a relation between maternal depression and negative reinforcement of child aggression (Zahn-Waxler, Iannotti, Cummings, & Denham, 1990).

Demographic questionnaire. This inventory was completed at all laboratory assess-ments and included questions regarding the occupational status of mother and partner, monthly family income, the size of the house (number of rooms), the number of people living in the house, and a history of child care. For the purpose of the present study, a history of police contact for anyone living in the home was used as a predictor of child aggression, based on results from previous studies demonstrating a relation between parental criminality and child externalizing problems (Mednick, Gabrielli, & Hutchings, 1987; Robins, West, & Herjanic, 1975).

Behavioral codes

In this study, maternal responsiveness and child aggression were coded from videotapes and used as predictor variables of later child aggression.

Maternal responsiveness. When the infant was 12 months old, mother and infant were observed in a high-chair task designed to evaluate maternal responsiveness (Martin, 1981). In the situation, the infant is placed in a high chair facing away from the mother with nothing to do for 3 minutes, while the mother completes a questionnaire. Mother is instructed to complete the questionnaire but also to attend to her infant in whatever way she deems appropriate. The one restriction is that the infant cannot be removed from the high chair. Behavioral frequencies are coded and scores are derived for the following variables: (1) maternal behaviors – look at infant, smile, vocalize, and touch or hold infant; (2) infant behaviors – look at mother, smile, vocalize, touch mother, and fuss/cry. From these behaviors, using an intensity-matching model (i.e., time series analysis with weighted scores for specific maternal and infant behaviors), a contingent measure of maternal responsiveness was obtained (see Martin, 1981, for more detailed information on the formation of these and other factors). Reliabilities, based on percent agreement for each code, ranged from .84 (infant smile) to .96 (infant look) with a mean of .91.

Aggression. At 18 and 24 months, aggression was coded during the cleanup task, the situation with no toys in the room, and during specific segments of the Strange Situation Test: when the stranger initially plays with the child, the first separation, the second separation, the reunion with the stranger, and during the free play situation at the end of the assessment. The total coding time was 23 minutes. These segments were thought to provide ecological validity, that is, taking toys away from children and leaving children with other caretakers are situations that routinely occur in most children's lives. Thus, behaviors exhibited under these circumstances are thought to be similar to those exhibited in the child's daily environment.

During the cleanup task the mother was instructed to have the child put all the toys in a basket. She was permitted to say anything she wished to her child, but was not allowed to clean up the toys herself. After 5 minutes the mother was signaled with a knock to clean up any remaining toys, place the basket outside the lab, and close the door. The no-toys situation began as soon as the basket was placed outside the door. In this task the child had no toys to play with for 3 minutes while the mother was instructed to work on two questionnaires and attend to her child as she normally would (see Martin, 1981). The Strange Situation Test was administered in the standard format (see Ainsworth & Wittig, 1969), and the free play situation consisted of unstructured child play while the mother and examiner completed the remaining questionnaires.

The behavioral codes for aggression were developed by the authors, based on previous investigations of disruptive behavior in the preschool period. The five codes for aggressive behavior were coded simultaneously during the four lab components of the 18- and 24-month assessments. The first four codes assessed aggression directed at the mother or at the examiners (including both the mother's examiner and the "stranger"). These codes included throwing toys at mother, throwing toys at the examiner, hitting or kicking mother, and hitting or kicking the examiner. The fifth code assessed aggression directed at the toys or objects in the room (e.g., hammering the mirror, pounding or stepping on toys, kicking the door). In addition to coding specific aggressive behaviors, the coders provided a summary rating to characterize the behavior of the child throughout the assessment. This 4-point scale – (1) unaggressive, (2) mildly aggressive, (3) moderately aggressive, or (4) severely aggressive – was adapted from Cummings and colleagues (1989) and modified to enhance compatibility with other classification systems.

Maternal response to aggression. Maternal response to child aggression was coded by independent observers but was contingent on the coding of the child's aggressive behavior. Thus, maternal response was assessed following child aggressive behaviors that were identified first by the child aggression coding team. Five codes were used to assess the nature and intensity of the mother's response: verbal prohibition, physical restriction, nonverbal prohibition, verbal nonprohibition, and a 2-second interval of no response. Because of the low frequency of some of the codes, all verbal and physical responses were combined into one code.

Undergraduate psychology majors who were blind to the study hypotheses comprised the two coding teams (one team for each behavioral assessment: maternal responsiveness and child aggression). The teams were trained for 4 to 6 months, during which they attended weekly meetings and completed homework assignments of coding tapes. All raters were supervised by the principal investigator, and reliability checks were conducted randomly on 10% of the tapes coded by each rater. Interrater reliabilities, based on percent agreement for each code, were at or above 85%.

Data reduction

Aggression was analyzed as both a molecular, continuous measure of frequency of aggressive acts and as a molar, categorical variable based on the ratings of none, mild, moderate, and severe. The mean global rating at both 18 and 24 months was mild (a rating of 2). Overall, the mean frequency of aggression was low, but the variability was wide (range = 0 to 151 and 0 to 99 at 18 and 24 months, respectively).

Results

Results will be presented in four stages: (1) stability of aggression from 18 to 24 months, (2) sex differences in the frequency of aggression, (3) correlates of aggression for boys and girls, and (4) precursors to coercive parent–child interaction and child externalizing behavior.

Stability of aggression from 18 to 24 months

To test the relation between aggression at 18 and 24 months, Pearson correlation coefficients were calculated between 18 and 24 months for both the summed frequency and global ratings of aggressive codes. Results are presented in Table 10.3 for the total sample, and separately for boys and girls. For the total sample, both the total summed aggression and global rating at 18 months were significantly correlated with the global rating at 24 months ($r = .23$, $p < .05$, and $r = .30$, $p < .01$, respectively). For boys, a significant relation was found between 18-month summed and 24-month global ratings of aggression ($r = .23$, $p < .05$). The global ratings for girls from 18 to 24 months were moderately stable and significant ($r = .35$, $p < .05$) (see Table 10.3).

Chi-square analyses were used as a further comparison between boys and girls on the stability of the global ratings of aggression. The chi-square analysis was significant for girls (df = 4, $\chi^2(4) = 12.9$, $p < .05$) but not for boys (df = 9, $\chi^2(9) = 13.7$, ns). However, a large part of girls' stability of aggression was accounted for by those who were rated unaggressive at both 18 and 24 months; 72.7% of the girls rated as unaggressive at 18 months were again rated as unaggressive at 24 months, while 45% of the mildly aggressive girls and 33.3% of the girls rated as moderately aggressive demonstrated stability.

Differences in the stability of aggression between boys and girls were examined

Table 10.3. *Stability of aggression from 18 to 24 months for boys and girls*

	Total (N = 89)	Boys (N = 52)	Girls (N = 37)
Summed aggression from 18 to 24 months	.10	.10	.01
Summed aggression at 18 to global rating at 24 months	.23*	.23*	.13
Global rating at 18 to summed aggression at 24 months	.08	−.01	.21
Global rating from 18 to 24 months	.30**	.22†	.35*

Note: Pearson correlation coefficients: †$p < .10$; *$p < .05$; **$p < .01$.

by comparing the magnitude of difference between Pearson correlation coefficients for males and females using Fisher Z tests; no significant differences were found.

Sex differences in the frequency of aggression

A repeated measures MANOVA, with the global and summed aggression scores at 18 and 24 months as the dependent variables and gender serving as a covariate, was used to examine differences in the base rates of aggression between boys and girls. The results revealed no significant differences in the frequency of aggression for boys and girls at 18 and 24 months. There was a slight but nonsignificant increase in aggression for girls from 18 to 24 months. Post hoc univariate tests showed that both object-related and summed aggression scores were higher for boys than for girls. These differences, however, need to be interpreted cautiously since the repeated measures MANOVA was not significant.

Correlates of aggression for boys and girls

Pearson correlation coefficients were conducted to test relations between (1) maternal aggressive personality, (2) maternal depression, (3) maternal responsiveness (using the Martin high-chair task), (4) maternal response to aggression, (5) familial criminality and the following measures of aggression: 18-month summed and global aggression, and 24-month summed and global aggression. Because maternal response to aggression (18 months) was examined by computing the percentage of mother's lack of response to child aggression, only those children exhibiting at least one incident of aggression at 18 months were included in this analysis ($n = 64$). Results are presented for boys and girls separately in Table 10.4. Correlations are not presented between maternal response to aggression and 18-month summed and global aggression because of the interdependence between them.

For boys, no significant correlates of aggression were found at 18 months. At 24 months, however, both 12-month maternal unresponsiveness and familial criminality were related to boys' summed and global aggression ratings (Table 10.4). Results for girls were disparate from those of boys. First, 18-month summed aggression was significantly related to familial criminality and marginally correlated with maternal aggressive personality. In addition, 12-month maternal depression was significantly related to girls' 18-month global aggression, and a trend was noted for the relation between 18-month maternal depression and girls' aggression. At 24 months, however, there was a significant negative relation between maternal depression and girls' global ratings of aggression (see Table 10.4).

Precursors to coercive parent–child interaction and child externalizing behavior problems

Finally, based on the results from the correlational analyses, and the work of Martin (1981), hierarchical multiple regression procedures were conducted to develop a

Table 10.4. *Correlates of aggression at 18 and 24 months for boys and girls*

| | Boys | | | | Girls | | | |
| | 18 months | | 24 months | | 18 months | | 24 months | |
	Summed	Global	Summed	Global	Summed	Global	Summed	Global
Maternal responsiveness (12 months)	.02	.04	−.30*	−.31*	−.13	.14	−.10	.04
Maternal depression (12 months)	.13	.04	−.02	.13	.17	.31*	.09	−.15
Maternal aggressive personality (18 months)	.13	.15	−.02	.14	.24†	.12	−.06	−.05
Maternal depression (18 months)	−.12	−.06	.00	.17	.25†	.27†	−.07	−.34*
Familial criminality (18 months)	.09	−.08	.37**	.31*	.31*	.17	.03	.08
Maternal response to aggression (18 months)	na	na	.08	.19	na	na	.32†	.03
Global agression (24 months)	.23*	.22†	na	na	.13	.35*	na	na

Note: Pearson correlation coefficients: †$p < .10$; *$p < .05$; **$p < .01$; na, not applicable.

model of coercive parent–child interaction and its relation to later child aggression. Regressions were computed for boys and girls separately. Relations among maternal demographic variables and global aggression scores at 24 months were computed first, but no significant relations were found. Results will be presented first for boys.

Given the strength of relations with boys' 24-month aggression, global aggression at 18 months and 12-month maternal responsiveness were chosen as independent variables for the analysis. Additionally, an interaction term between 18-month global aggression and 12-month maternal responsiveness was created, based on Martin's research indicating a significant interaction between maternal unresponsiveness and aversive infant behavior predicting later externalizing child behavior above and beyond that of each variable's independent influence. Results are presented in Table 10.5. Though both 12-month maternal responsiveness and 18-month global aggression accounted for some of the variance in predicting 24-month

Table 10.5. *Prediction of age 2 aggression for boys and girls: hierarchical multiple regression*

Independent variable	Multiple R	R^2	R^2 change	F	Sig. F change
Boys' global aggression at 24 months					
Global aggression					
(18 months)	.31	.10	.10	2.57	.12
Maternal responsiveness					
(12 months)	.44	.19	.10	2.76	.08
Aggression × responsiveness					
interaction	.62	.38	.19	4.52	.02
Girls' global aggression at 24 months					
Global aggression					
(18 months)	.35	.13	.13	4.74	.04
Maternal depressive symp-					
tomatology (18 months)	.57	.32	.19	7.68	.002

global aggression ratings, the regression equation attained statistical significance only when their interaction term was entered. At 24 months, 18-month aggression, 12-month maternal responsiveness, and their interaction term accounted for 38% of the variance in global aggression ratings. That is, high levels of aggression and low levels of maternal responsiveness were significantly associated with later child aggression.

Results for girls were quite different (Table 10.5). In predicting girls' global ratings of aggression, maternal depressive symptomatology contributed unique variance, which when entered after the 18-month global rating, resulted in a multiple R of .57, accounting for 32% of the variance. However, maternal depressive symptomatology was *negatively* related to later aggression. An interaction between maternal depression and girls' 18-month aggression was computed and tested, but was found to be nonsignificant.

Discussion

Previous research has demonstrated that externalizing behavior problems in school-age children and adolescents, and coercive parent–child interaction are linked to ineffective parenting practices. A separate body of work has shown that aggressive behavior is highly stable from early childhood to adolescence. Despite this, few efforts have been made to trace the early developmental antecedents of coercive parent–child interaction and child externalizing behavior problems. The results from the present study provide preliminary evidence for the identification of these precursors beginning in infancy. Both child and parent behaviors, and the interaction of the two, proved to be significant predictors of age 2 aggression for boys. For girls, both child and maternal factors (i.e., maternal depression) were significantly related to later aggression, but the interaction of the two was not.

As with school-age children, moderate stability of aggression from 18 to 24 months was found for toddlers from low-income families. There were few differences in frequency and stability of aggression between boys and girls. Both sexes engaged in more object-related aggression than interpersonal aggression. In terms of the prediction of aggression at 18 and 24 months, although familial criminality was significantly related to both boys' (24-month) and girls' (18-month) aggression, only maternal depression continued to demonstrate a significant relation with child aggression for girls only. However, over time, the strength of maternal depression as a predictor of girls' aggression changed; maternal depressive symptomatology measured at 12 and 18 months was positively related to girls' aggression at 18 months, then negatively related to girls' aggression at 24 months. The negative correlation may be indicative of a transformation of behavior problems in girls, from externalizing to internalizing. For example, as girls become cognitively capable of perspective taking and empathy, they may begin to identify with their mothers' affective state. Follow-up data are needed to demonstrate whether the change in the influence of maternal depression on girls' aggressive behavior reflects such a transformation in the development of behavior problems.

The results for boys regarding the prediction of aggression at age 2 are in agreement with the findings of Martin (1981) and Patterson and colleagues' proposed early starter model of coercion (1991). In Martin's study of well-educated, middle-class mothers and their 10- to 42-month-old infants, noncompliance at 22 months was accounted for by the independent influences of maternal unresponsiveness, infant demandingness, and their interaction term. At 42 months, 10-month maternal and infant characteristics were still predictive of child coercive behavior and maternal behavior, more so than that of infants; the effect of the interaction term was no longer significant. In the present study of low-income mothers and their infants the same pattern emerged. At 24 months, both maternal responsiveness and infant behavior (in the form of previous aggression) were predictive of aggression, and their interaction term accounted for significant variance above and beyond that contributed by the individual variables.

Patterson and colleagues (1991) have hypothesized that coercive cycles of interaction emerge in early childhood because of hyperactivity or any other condition that produces irritability, to which the parent responds aversively but ineffectively. In the present study, regarding boys, the combination of early aversive child behavior and inadequate responsiveness to infant behavior was related to aggression at age 2. It is unclear whether the parent's early lack of responsiveness was a function of earlier unrewarding interactions with a difficult infant, or if the infant's aggression at 18 months was a response to the mother's lack of attentiveness to earlier less aversive infant cues. It may take initial extreme behavior on the part of one participant (e.g., high levels of aversive infant behavior) or moderate levels of both behaviors to produce high rates of later coercive interactions.

In this study, parent–child coercion was not measured directly. However, our findings, in conjunction with those of Martin (1981), suggest that precursors to parent–child coercion can be identified in the toddler period. For example, in both Martin's and this study, the interaction of maternal unresponsiveness and disruptive child behavior predicted later disruptive child behavior. According to Patterson and colleagues (1991), early child disruptive behavior should promote later ineffective parenting practices and high levels of parent–child coercive interaction.

As in Martin's study, the results for girls are less conclusive. Although both child and parental factors appear important in developing a pathway to later child aggression, in the present study no interaction between the two was found to be significant. It is possible that a more clearly defined model would be revealed for internalizing rather than externalizing problems. For example, the foundations for a coercive cycle between teachers and dependent girls has been documented by Fagot (1984). In a study of toddlers in a preschool classroom, stability of girls' dependency problems was related to positive teacher responses such as joining the girls' play.

In sum, the results from the present study indicate that, for some children, precursors to the development of coercive interaction exist in the toddler period. Future research is needed to refine the model presented in this paper for the development of early coercive interaction and problem behaviors, as well as to understand the effects of sex differences and socialization practices on the changing manifestations of such behavior.

NOTE

This study was supported by grants to Daniel Shaw and Joan Vondra from the following organizations within the University of Pittsburgh: the Mental Health Clinical Research Center for Affective Disorders, the Office of Child Development, the School of Education in conjunction with the Buhl Foundation, and the Faculty of Arts and Sciences. Requests for reprints should be sent to Shaw at the Department of Psychology, Clinical Psychology Center, 604 OEH, 4015 O'Hara Street, University of Pittsburgh, Pittsburgh, PA, 15260. Portions of this paper were presented at the Conference for Life History Research, Philadelphia, PA (May 1992).

REFERENCES

Achenbach, T. M., Edelbrock, C., & Howell, C. (1987). Empirically-based assessment of the behavioral/emotional problems of 2–3 year old children. *Journal of Abnormal Child Psychology*, 15(4), 629–650.

Ainsworth, M. D. S., & Wittig, B. A. (1969). Attachment and the exploratory behavior of one-year olds in a strange situation. In B. M. Foss (Ed.), *Determinants of infant behavior* (Vol. 4, pp. 113–136). London: Methuen.

Beck, A. T., & Beamesderfer, A. (1974). Assessment of depression: The Depression Inventory. In P. Pichot (Ed.), *Psychological measurement in psychopharmacology: Modern problems in pharmacopsychiatry* (Vol. 7; pp. 151–169). Basel: Kanger.

Beck, A. T., Ward, C. H., Mendelon, M., Mock, J. E., & Erbaugh, J. K. (1961). An inventory for measuring depression. *Archives of General Psychiatry, 4,* 561–571.

Block, J. H., Block, J., & Morrison, A. (1981). Parental agreement–disagreement on child-rearing orientations and gender related personality correlates in children. *Child Development, 52,* 965–974.

Crockenberg, S. B. (1981). Infant irritability, mother responsiveness, and social support influences on the security of infant–mother attachment. *Child Development, 52,* 857–865.

Cummings, E. M., Iannotti, R. J., & Zahn-Waxler, C. (1989). Aggression between peers in early childhood: Individual continuity and developmental change. *Child Development, 69,* 887–895.

Egeland, B., & Farber, E. A. (1984). Infant–mother attachment: Factors related to its development and changes over time. *Child Development, 55,* 753–771.

Fagot, B. I. (1984). The consequences of problem behavior in toddler children. *Journal of Abnormal Child Psychology, 12*(3), 385–396.

Huessman, L. R., Eron, L. E., Lefkowitz, M. M., & Walder, L. O. (1984). Stability of aggression over time and generation. *Developmental Psychology, 20*(6), 1120–1134.

Isabella, R. A., & Belsky, J. (1991). Interactional synchrony and the origins of infant–mother attachment: A replication study. *Child Development, 62,* 373–384.

Jackson, D. H. (1989). *Personality Research Form Manual* (3rd ed.). New York: Research Psychologists Press.

Kazdin, A. E. (1987). Treatment of antisocial behavior in children: Current status and future directions. *Psychological Bulletin, 102*(2), 187–203.

Loeber, R. (1982). The stability of antisocial and delinquent child behavior: A review. *Child Development, 53,* 1431–1446.

Loeber, R., & Dishion, T. (1983). Early predictors of male delinquency: A review. *Psychological Bulletin, 94*(1), 68–99.

Loeber, R., & Stouthamer-Loeber, M. (1986). Family factors as correlates and predictors of juvenile conduct problems and delinquency. In M. Tonry, and N. Morris (Eds.), *Crime and Justice* (pp. 29–149). Chicago: University of Chicago Press.

Londerville, S., & Main, M. (1981). Security of attachment, compliance, and maternal training methods in the second year of life. *Developmental Psychology, 17,* 289–299.

Martin, J. (1981). A longitudinal study of the consequence of early mother–infant interaction: A microanalytic approach. *Monographs for the Society for Research in Child Development, 46*(3).

Martin, J. A., Larzelere, R. E., & Amberson, T. G. (1986, May). Developmental changes in behavior problems during the toddler years. Paper presented at the convention of the Western Psychological Association, Seattle, WA.

Matas, L., Arend, R., & Sroufe, L. A. (1978). Continuity of adaptation in the second year: The relationship between attachment and later competence. *Child Development, 49,* 547–556.

McCord, J. (1979). Some child-rearing antecedents of criminal behavior in adult men. *Journal of Personality and Social Psychology, 37*(9), 1477–1486.

Mednick, S. A., Gabrielli, W. F., & Hutchings, B. (1987). Genetic factors in the etiology of criminal behavior. In S. A. Mednick, T. E. Moffitt, and S. A. Stack (Eds.), *The causes of crime* (pp. 74–91). Cambridge University Press.

Olweus, D. (1979). Stability of aggressive patterns in males: A review. *Psychological Bulletin, 86,* 852–875.

Patterson, G. R. (1982). *Coercive family process.* Eugene, OR: Castalia.

Patterson, G. R., Capaldi, D., & Bank, L. (1991). An early starter model for predicting delinquency. In D. Pepler and K. H. Rubin (Eds.), *The development and treatment of childhood aggression* (pp. 139–168). Hillsdale, NJ: Erlbaum.

Reynolds, W. M., & Gould, J. W. (1981). A psychometric investigation of the standard and short form Beck Depression Inventory. *Journal of Consulting and Clinical Psychology, 49,* 306–307.

Robins, L. N., West, P. A., & Herjanic, B. L. (1975). Arrests and delinquency in two generations: A study of black urban families and their children. *Journal of Child Psychology and Psychiatry, 16,* 125–140.

Rose, S. L., Rose, S. A., & Feldman, J. F. (1989). Stability of behavior problems in very young children. *Development and Psychopathology, 1,* 5–19.

Sameroff, A. J. (1990, June). *Prevention of developmental psychopathology using the transactional model: Perspectives on host, risk agent, and environment interactions.* Paper presented at the Conference on the Present Status and Future Needs of Research on Prevention of Mental Disorders, Washington, DC.

Shaw, D. S., & Bell, R. Q. (1993). Developmental theories of parental contributors to antisocial behavior. *Journal of Abnormal Child Psychology, 21,* 493–517.

Sroufe, L. A. (1983). Infant–caregiver attachment and patterns of adaptation in preschool. In M. Perlmutter (Ed.), *Development and policy concerning children with special needs: Minnesota Symposium on Child Psychology* (Vol. 16, pp. 41–83). Hillsdale, NJ: Erlbaum.

Szegal, B. (1985). Stages in the development of aggressive behavior in early childhood. *Aggressive Behavior, 11,* 315–321.

Zahn-Waxler, C. (1992, November). *Gender issues in conduct disorder.* Paper presented at the NIMH Conference on Developmental Perspectives on Conduct Disorder, Washington, DC.

Zahn-Waxler, C., Iannotti, R. J., Cummings, E. M., & Denham, S. (1990). Antecedents of problem behaviors in children of depressed mothers. *Development and Psychopathology, 2,* 271–291.

III   Aggression and coercion in the schools

11 The impact of peer relationships on aggression in childhood: inhibition through coercion or promotion through peer support

MICHEL BOIVIN AND FRANK VITARO

According to Patterson, Reid, and Dishion (1992), aversive interactional patterns within the family provide for the early training of young boys' aggression and antisocial behavior. The coercive family process refers to a pattern of reciprocal exchanges in which poor family management practices such as inconsistent and ineffective parental responses are coupled with the child's persistent aversive behavior. The typical pattern is one of escalation and negative reinforcements. The coercion process usually starts with an exchange of often trivial, innocuous responses between a parent and a child. It quickly degenerates as the two actors are prompted to accentuate the punitive aspect of their behavior so as to control or coerce the other. When one actor gives in (usually the parent), this cyclical pattern is terminated by the removal of the aversive stimuli (i.e., the child's aversive behavior), thus negatively reinforcing such behaviors. Hence, by this coercive process the child is likely to learn quickly to become the initiator and the victim of aggressive behavior while training his or her parents to use highly punitive strategies. Coercive family processes may originate from a combination of factors such as a difficult child, the lack of parental competence, and an exposure to environmental stressors, but the crucial point is that they are exacerbated by a process of negative reciprocal exchange and bolstered by intermittent negative reinforcements.

There are reasons to believe that aggression learned in the coercive family system (between ages 4 and 9) will be generalized to the peer system and will lead to difficulties in peer relationships. For instance, Bierman and Smoot (1991) have shown that punitive and ineffective discipline in the home is related to child conduct problems at school and poor peer relations. The relation between aggression and peer rejection is also well established (Asher & Coie, 1990; Coie, Belding, & Underwood, 1988) and there is evidence showing that aggression leads to peer rejection (Coie & Kupersmidt, 1983; Dodge, 1983). Furthermore, according to Dodge's work (Dodge, Pettit, McClaskey, & Brown, 1986), peer-rejected aggressive children exhibit social-information-processing deficits and biases likely to hamper their integration within the peer group. These deficits and biases are manifested in children's inability to attend to and decode relevant social cues and in their over-attribution of hostile intents to others in ambiguous situations. Dodge also showed that these deficiencies can be traced back to early aversive family experiences such as exposure to physical harm (Dodge, Bates, & Pettit, 1990). It is likely that the child's experience within the coercive family also deprives the child from learning social skills that are essential to establish mutually satisfying peer relationships (Patterson et al., 1992).

Yet despite these deficiencies, there is also evidence indicating that aggressive children are not totally isolated from the peer group and are often part of a peer cluster even though they might be rejected by a substantial proportion of children in that group (Boivin, Coté, & Dion, 1991). This finding is consistent with other studies indicating that aggressive children tend to affiliate with others who share similar behavior patterns with respect to aggression (Cairns, Cairns, Neckerman, Gest, & Gariépy, 1988). This kind of affiliation would perhaps be likely to reinforce positive attitudes toward aggression and, eventually, to generate occasions for delinquent and antisocial acts (Cairns & Cairns, 1992).

It is not clear whether these deviant peer clusters are a by-product of peer rejection or simply the result of a proactive selection process based on common goals, needs, values, and behavior (Cairns & Cairns, 1991). We also know very little about the peer cluster dynamics supporting or inhibiting the expression of aggression through in-group or out-group coercive patterns.

For those reasons, it appears important to distinguish aggressive children who are part of a peer cluster from those who are not involved in a peer cluster. To the extent that these clusters involve converging aggression related behavior, norms, and values, they could support the expression of aggression and even offer protection from out-group coercion attempts. If this is true, out-group coercion attempts would be more likely to affect those aggressive children who are not involved in a peer cluster.

The general purpose of the study reported here was to examine the role of peer relationships in modulating aggression among middle elementary school aggressive boys (third, fourth, and fifth graders). In a first set of analyses, two groups of aggressive boys (those who were involved in a peer cluster vs. those who were not) were compared with respect to psychological discomfort, the quality of the peer experiences, and aggression over a 1-year period. More specifically, it was hypothesized that the uninvolved aggressive boys would be more likely to be perceived as sensitive/isolated, to experience social anxiety, to have a negative peer status, and to be victimized by their peers than aggressive boys who are involved in a peer network. Given the aversive nature of this experience (and perhaps also the lack of peer support), they would also be more likely to reduce their aggression over time.

Subsequently, in a second set of analyses, we examined the potential impact of being involved with other aggressive children with respect to aggression. It was hypothesized that aggressive boys would be involved with more aggressive peers than their nonaggressive counterparts. We also wanted to evaluate whether the aggression trajectory of these boys was related to the aggression profile of the boys' associates.

Method

Subjects

The children were met in the spring semester of 1989 (T1) and then 1 year later, in the spring of 1990 (T2), as part of an ongoing longitudinal study. Children's participation in the study required written parental authorization. The participation rate for each year was over 95%. Following this, a total of 1,271 third-, fourth-, and fifth-grade children (631 girls and 640 boys) attending 10 different elementary schools (55 classes) in Quebec City were evaluated in 1989. One year later, 1,192 fourth-, fifth-, and sixth-grade children (598 girls and 594 boys) from the same schools were assessed (51 classes). Although both boys and girls were included in the data, only 451 boys for whom the aggression score (peer assessed) was available at both years were considered in the present study. Three factors explained attrition: (1) three teachers did not agree to participate in the study at T2; (2) some boys were absent from school when the data collection took place at T2; and (3) some of the boys' families moved to other neighborhoods. Each year, the classes were balanced with respect to gender. The composition of each class was stable through-out the academic year, and children had been in the same classroom at least 8 months before the study assessments. These French-Canadian boys came from a variety of socioeconomic environments, and their mean age was 115 months in the spring of 1989. They were individually interviewed and completed questionnaires in the class setting both years of the study.

Selection measures

Aggression. Peer perception of aggression was assessed using specific items of the aggression-disruption subscale of Revised Class Play (Masten, Morison, & Pellegrini, 1985), a peer assessment inventory. With the help of a picture roster representing all children in the class, the children had to choose two peers who best fit each behavioral descriptor. Instead of the more general subscales, specific items were considered because the former yield scores that are ambiguous, confounding peer assessment of behavior and peer acceptance (see Coie, Dodge, & Kupersmidt, 1990; Parkhurst & Asher, 1992; Rubin, Hymel, LeMare, & Rowden, 1989, for discussions of this point). Therefore, an aggression score (alpha = .89) was obtained by summing the peer nominations on items (2) gets into a lot of fights, (5) loses temper easily, (21) too bossy, and (29) picks on other kids. These scores were standardized within each class.

Peer clusters. The children were also individually interviewed to get a composite social map of the peer clusters in the classroom social structure following Cairns, Perrin, and Cairns's (1985) method. This procedure is typically based on children's free recall of affiliative networks and has shown its reliability among middle elementary school children (Boivin & Coté, 1991). The child was asked to name "the children who often hang around together" and could identify as many children or groups as wished. Two matrices were calculated for each class, one each for the boys and the girls. Each cell in the matrix represented the frequency with which the respondents selectively associated each child with each of his or her peers. Each co-occurrence was noted for every child named in a network. The peer clusters and the affiliative relations among children within each cluster were identified according to a decision rule based on a minimum of 30% agreement (see Cairns et al., 1985). That is, all associations reaching 30% agreement or greater across respondents were retained to compose the picture of the social networks within the class. This procedure has proved to be as robust as more elaborate mathematical solutions (Cairns, Kindermann, & Gariépy, 1986). Further, this method of assessment has shown itself to be highly appropriate in the school context and requires only a limited number of respondents (10 to 20) to obtain a reliable picture.

Two aspects were considered with respect to the peer network: (1) being involved in a peer cluster or not for the first set of analyses and (2) the behavior profile of the peer group members involved with the subject for the second set of analyses (i.e., the mean aggression score of those associated with the target boy).

Selection procedures

Boys scoring above the 85th percentile at T1 were considered aggressive. This percentile coincides with having at least a standardized score of 1.25 or above on peer-assessed aggression. For the first set of analyses, 64 aggressive boys for whom the data were available both years of the study were considered. The aggressive status of these boys was also confirmed by teacher assessments on an aggression subscale of Rutter's Social Behaviour Questionnaire. This teacher subscale consisted of the addition of three items, each rated on a three-point scale. The items were (5) frequently fights with other children, (9) irritable, and (26) bullies other children, and the total score ranged from 0 to 6. The mean score was 2.43 for the peer-assessed aggressive boys and 0.54 for the nonaggressive boys, $t(427) = 11.30$, $p < .001$.

Of these 64 aggressive boys, 41 (64%) were involved in a peer cluster and 23 were uninvolved. There were 18 aggressive boys in third grade, 7 of whom were involved with peers (39%). In fourth grade, 22 of the 29 boys identified as aggressive (76%) were involved in a peer cluster. Finally, 12 of the 17 boys identified as aggressive in fifth grade (71%) were involved in a peer cluster. Among the 41 boys involved in a peer cluster, 6 were associated with only one child, 18 with two peers, 7 with three peers, 5 with four peers, and 5 with more than four. These two groups (i.e., aggressive-involved and aggressive-uninvolved) were compared on four measures at T1 and T2.

Other measures

Social preference. During the individual interview in which a picture nomination procedure was used, children were asked to select the three children with whom they would like the most (LM) to share three activities (play, invitation to a birthday party, sit next to in the bus on an excursion day) and the three children with whom they would least like (LL) to share the same activities. The LM and LL scores were obtained by summing up the choices each child received from all classmates on all three questions. These scores were standardized within each class. A social preference score (SP) was computed by the substraction of the LL from the LM score (Coie & Dodge, 1983) and then standardized within each class (alpha = .93).

Peer-assessed isolation/sensitiveness. Also using specific items on the Revised Class Play assessment, an isolation/sensitiveness score was obtained by summing up the peer nominations on items (3) rather play alone than with others, (11) feelings get hurt easily, (18) very shy, and (24) usually sad. Here again, items pertaining to peer acceptance were excluded. These scores were standardized within each class (alpha = .83).

Victimization by peers. The children also had to nominate peers on specific items of Perry, Kusel, and Perry's (1988) Modified Peer Nomination Inventory. A victimization score (alpha = .93) was computed by summing up the peer nominations received on items (3) kids make fun of him; (10) he gets called names by other kids; (22) he gets hit and pushed by other kids; (25) kids try to hurt his feelings. This score was standardized within each class. This peer nomination inventory was completed only by a portion of the sample for technical reasons. Therefore, the data at T1 and T2 were available only for 41 aggressive boys (27 involved in a peer network and 14 uninvolved).

Social anxiety. In the class setting, the children also completed Franke and Hymel's (1984) social anxiety scale, a six-item (5-point scale) self-report questionnaire assessing feelings of social anxiety in peer interactions. This scale has good internal consistency, test–retest reliability, and validity (Franke & Hymel, 1984; Hymel & Franke, 1985). In the present study, the internal consistency was also found to be adequate (alpha = .77). These scores were standardized within each class.

Results

In the first set of analyses, we were interested in comparing aggressive boys involved in a peer network (AI) and aggressive boys uninvolved in a peer network (AU) with

Table 11.1. *Means (standard deviations) of isolation/sensitiveness, social anxiety, social preference, and victimization by peers (Z scores) at T1 and T2 for aggressive boys involved and uninvolved with peers*

	T1		T2	
	Aggressive involved	Aggressive uninvolved	Aggressive involved	Aggressive uninvolved
Isolation/sensitiveness	−0.29 (0.54)	0.26 (0.87)	−0.49 (0.96)	−0.08 (1.51)
Social anxiety	−0.29 (0.90)	0.16 (1.32)	−0.22 (0.83)	0.16 (0.96)
Social preference	−0.39 (1.22)	−1.22 (0.90)	−0.56 (1.02)	−1.13 (1.07)
Victimization	0.21 (0.74)	1.52 (1.42)	0.22 (0.96)	1.25 (1.72)

respect to (1) psychological discomfort, as expressed by the peer perceptions of isolation/sensitiveness and the self-rated social anxiety, (2) the quality of the peer experiences as reflected by the social preference and peer victimization scores, and (3) peer-rated aggression. Further, we were also interested in examining the changes over time on these dimensions and how these changes related to peer network membership. The presence of age differences was also examined through three-way factorial designs (i.e., aggressive group, age, and time factors). Since no significant age-related differences (i.e., main effects or interactions) were revealed, only two-way ANOVAs (i.e., aggressive group and time factors) will be reported here for the purpose of clarity.

The mean scores at T1 and T2 of peer-assessed isolation/sensitiveness and self-rated social anxiety for the two groups are presented in Table 11.1. The scores on each dimension were submitted to a 2 (group) × 2 (time) repeated measure ANOVA.

On isolation/sensitiveness, the ANOVA revealed significant main differences with respect to group, $F(1, 62) = 4.58$, $p < .04$, and time, $F(1, 62) = 5.88$, $p < .02$, but not for a group by time interaction. Table 11.1 shows that the AU boys were perceived by peers as more isolated/sensitive than were AI boys. It also indicates that both groups were viewed as less isolated/sensitive 1 year later, although the two groups continued to differ. The ANOVA on self-rated social anxiety indicated a main effect for group, $F(1, 60) = 3.88$, $p < .05$, but not for time or for a group by time interaction. Table 11.1 indicates that the AU boys expressed higher levels of social anxiety at T1 and T2 than did the AI boys.

The mean scores of social preference and peer victimization for the two groups at both times are also presented in Table 11.1. These scores were submitted to the

Z scores

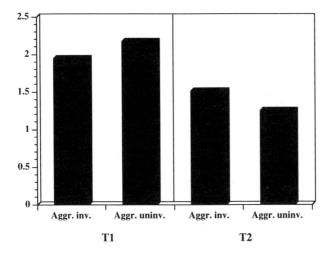

Figure 11.1. Aggression scores at T1 and T2 of aggressive boys involved and uninvolved with peers.

same type of repeated measure ANOVA. A significant group main effect was found for victimization, $F(1, 39) = 11.77$, $p < .001$, and social preference, $F(1, 62) = 7.50$, $p < .01$, but there was no time or group by time interaction effects. Table 11.1 indicates that, at T1 and T2, the peer status of AU boys was more negative and that they were more victimized by peers than were AI boys.

Figure 11.1 illustrates the mean scores of peer-rated aggression at T1 and at T2 for the two groups. The 2 (group) $\times$ 2 (time) repeated measure ANOVA revealed a significant main effect for time, $F(1, 62) = 27.58$, $p < .001$, and a marginally significant group by time interaction effect, $F(1, 62) = 3.70$, $p < .06$. A breakdown into simple main effects of the previous interaction showed a significant decrease from T1 to T2 in the AU group but not in the AI group. This pattern and the data presented in Figure 11.1 indicate that the peers perceived AU boys as less aggressive after 1 year (T1: $M = 2.17$, SD $= 0.62$; T2: $M = 1.25$, SD $= 1.26$), whereas the peer perception of AI boys' aggression did not change significantly (T1: $M = 1.94$, SD $= 0.49$; T2: $M = 1.51$, SD $= 1.12$).

To further examine the nature of the changes in aggression from T1 to T2, separate 2 (group) $\times$ 2 (time) repeated measure ANOVAs were performed for each item of the aggression scale: (2) gets into a lot of fights, (5) loses temper easily, (21) too bossy, and (29) picks on other kids. A significant time main effect was found on each of the four items, but a significant group by time interaction was revealed only for "gets into a lot of fights," $F(1. 62) = 6.82$, $p < .01$, and "loses temper easily," $F(1.62) = 4.43$, $p < .04$, and not for "too bossy" and "picks on other kids." Examination of simple main effects showed that only AU boys (T1: $M = 2.69$, $SD = 1.22$; T2: $M = 1.38$, $SD = 1.53$) and not AI boys (T1: $M = 2.29$, $SD = 1.26$; T2: $M = 1.84$, $SD = 1.60$) received significantly less nominations on "gets into a lot of fights" at T2 than at T1. The same pattern was found for "loses temper easily" over time, although AU boys (T1: $M = 2.33$, $SD = 1.14$; T2: $M = 1.33$, $SD = 1.32$) were already nominated more often on this item than were AI boys (T1: $M = 1.60$, $SD = 1.20$; T2: $M = 1.44$, $SD = 1.50$) at T1.

In summary, the general trend was for both AI and AU boys to be nominated less often on aggression items from T1 to T2, a pattern partly reflecting a regression to the mean artifact. However, the significant group by time interactions also indicated that AU boys reduced their aggression more than AI boys did and that these differential changes occurred on specific dimensions of aggression.

Associates' characteristics

In a second set of analyses, our attention turned to the associates' level of aggression. Associates were the peer group members involved with the target boy as defined by the Cairns et al. (1985) procedure described earlier. More specifically, we were interested in evaluating (1) whether aggressive boys were involved with more aggressive associates than were nonaggressive boys and (2) how this pattern changed over time in relation to the changes in aggression. Since the boys were often involved with more than one associate, an average aggression score across associates was computed.

First, we examined the associates' aggression scores at T1 and T2 for boys who were either aggressive or nonaggressive at T1. This type of analysis requires the selection of aggressive and nonaggressive boys who were associated (i.e., involved) with at least one peer at T1 and T2. Twenty-nine aggressive boys and 143 nonaggressive boys were associated with at least one peer at T1 and T2. Their associates' aggression scores are presented in Figure 11.2.

As in previous analyses, these scores were submitted to a 2 (group) $\times$ 2 (time) repeated measure ANOVA. This ANOVA revealed a significant main effect for group $F(1, 170) = 8.69$, $p < .04$, but no time effect or group by time interaction. At T1 and T2, aggressive boys (T1: $M = 0.77$, $SD = 1.74$; T2: $M = 0.63$, $SD = 0.70$) associated with more aggressive peers than their nonaggressive counterparts (T1: $M = 0.27$, $SD = 0.71$; $M = 0.33$, $SD = 0.70$).

Following up on this idea, aggressive and nonaggressive boys involved in a peer cluster (at T1 and T2) were subdivided further on the basis of their aggression profile at T1 and T2. Four subgroups were considered: aggressive boys who remained aggressive (A–A: $n = 20$; T1: $M = 2.16$, $SD = 0.59$; T2: $M = 2.28$, $SD = 0.64$); nonaggressive boys who became aggressive (NA–A: $n = 18$; T1:$M = 0.44$, $SD = 0.42$; T2: $M = 1.85$, $SD = .57$); aggressive boys who became nonaggressive (A–NA: $n = 9$; T1: $M = 1.75$, $SD = 0.36$; T2: $M = 0.46$, $SD = 0.43$);

Z scores

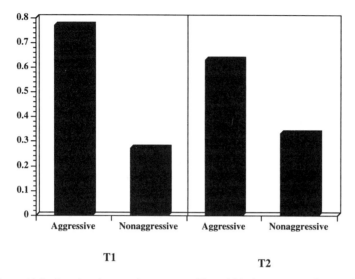

Figure 11.2. Associates' aggression scores at T1 and T2 for aggressive boys and nonaggressive boys.

nonaggressive boys who remained nonaggressive (NA–NA: $n = 125$; T1: $M = -0.10$, SD $= 0.45$; T2: $M = -0.03$, SD $= 0.48$).

The associates' aggression scores at T1 and T2 for these subgroups are presented in Table 11.2. These scores were submitted to a 4 (group) × 2 (time) repeated measure ANOVA. Three specific contrasts were performed, each aggressive subgroup (A–A, NA–A, A–NA) being compared to the NA–NA group. The analysis revealed only a significant group main effect for the contrast opposing the A–A group and the NA–NA group, $F(1, 168) = 12.71$, $p < .001$. The A–A boys' associates were more aggressive than the NA–NA associates at both times. The comparisons involving the NA–A and A–NA groups were not significant. There was no group by time interaction.

We also examined individual aggression scores at T1 and T2 for boys who were associated with aggressive or nonaggressive peers at T1. For that purpose, the boys were divided into two groups on the basis of their associates' aggression score at T1 (above or below .5 Z score). Seventy-one boys were categorized as being associated with more aggressive peers and 134 with less aggressive peers. The aggressive scores of these boys at T1 and T2 are presented in Figure 11.3. A 2 (group: aggressive vs. nonaggressive peer group) × 2 (time) ANOVA on the boys' aggression scores revealed a significant main effect for group, $F(1, 203) = 4.42$, $p < .04$, but no time effect or group by time interaction. The boys involved with more aggressive peers

Table 11.2. *Means (and standard deviations) of the associates' aggression scores at T1 and T2 as a function of the subjects' aggression trajectory from T1 to T2*

	Associates' aggression scores	
Subjects' aggression trajectory	T1	T2
Aggressive–aggressive	0.98	0.72
	(2.06)	(0.75)
Nonaggressive–aggressive	0.33	0.53
	(0.65)	(0.64)
Aggressive–nonaggressive	0.30	0.43
	(0.36)	(0.55)
Nonaggressive–nonaggressive	0.26	0.30
	(0.72)	(0.70)

at T1 (T1: $M = 0.62$, SD $= .99$; T2: $M = 0.69$, SD $= 1.06$) were more aggressive at T1 and T2 than were boys involved with less aggressive peers (T1: $M = 0.32$, SD $= .96$; T2: $M = 0.43$, SD $= 1.01$).

Finally, a similar analysis was performed considering this time the boys' aggression score in relation to their network's score at T1. The boys were categorized as either more aggressive than their peer network ($n = 99$) or less aggressive than their peer network ($n = 105$). The 2 (group) $\times$ 2 (time) ANOVA on the boys' aggression scores indicated a significant main effect for group, $F(1, 202) = 68.54$, $p < .001$, but more importantly, a significant group by time interaction, $F(1, 202) = 9.25$, $p < .003$. There was no time main effect. A breakdown into simple main effects indicated that boys who were more aggressive than their peer network at T1 did not change significantly their aggression score (T1: $M = 0.99$, SD $= 1.01$; T2: $M = 0.91$, SD $= 1.08$), whereas those who were less aggressive than their peer network became significantly more aggressive over time (T1: $M = -0.11$, SD $= 0.55$; T2: $M = 0.16$, SD $= 0.85$).

Discussion

The general aim of the study reported here was to examine the link between specific peer relationship dimensions and the course of aggression over time, as well as to document the peer influence process that might be involved. Overall the results suggest that the nature of the peer relationships may indeed play a role in the expression of aggression. For instance, aggressive boys who were uninvolved with peers were more likely to decrease their aggression over time than aggressive boys who were involved with peers.

With respect to the changes in aggression, it is interesting to note that the

Z scores

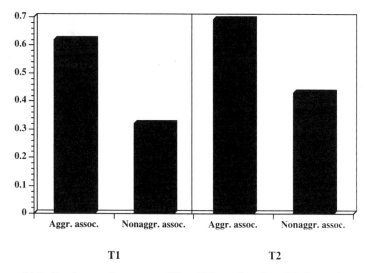

Figure 11.3. Boys' aggression scores at T1 and T2 as a function of their associates' aggression at T1.

reduction specific to AU boys was for behaviors such as "gets into a lot of fights" and "loses temper easily" but not on "too bossy" and "picks on other kids." To the extent that "loses temper easily" and "gets into a lot of fights" could be viewed as manifestations of reactive aggression, whereas the latter two ("too bossy" and "picks on other kids") are signs of proactive aggression (Dodge & Coie, 1987), this indicates that the observed reduction specific to AU boys could be restricted to reactive aggression (and not proactive aggression). The AU boys' higher scores at T1 on the "loses temper easily" item may reflect a lack of emotional control. In other words, it could be that these children are more likely to overreact in conflictual situations, a behavior that might draw negative responses by peers (i.e., victimization). It could also reflect a reputation brought about by the fact that these boys are more often subjected to aversive peer experiences.

The modulating process of peer relationships on aggression is probably multifaceted, and the presumed peer influence may involve different mechanisms depending on the position of the aggressive boy in the peer structure. For AU boys the peer influence could perhaps inhibit aggression through coercive means (i.e., victimization, rejection), whereas peer network membership could provide for the reinforcement of this behavioral tendency through in-group support.

As for inhibition, it is interesting to note that the two most striking between-group differences were for victimization and social preference. The peer experiences of the AU boys were very negative. More specifically, these boys were found to have a very negative peer status (i.e., social preference scores) and to be highly victimized by peers in contrast to their IA peers. The AU boys also showed signs of psychological discomfort as they were more socially anxious and viewed by their peers as more isolated/sensitive than their AU peers.

This pattern of results could very well reflect a coercive process by peers, the combination of aggression and uninvolvement with peers leading to a negative peer status and eliciting aversive behaviors from peers. These negative behaviors from peers would perhaps be manifested in response to the AU boys' emotional outbursts (i.e., AU boys scored higher than AI boys on "loses temper easily" at T1) but also because these boys would be perceived as socially vulnerable and safe targets. Given the aversive nature of their peer experiences, it is not surprising to find these boys more socially anxious. Moreover, their social anxiety and sensitiveness could explain why these negative experiences were followed by a reduction in reactive aggression despite continued victimization. Perhaps due to a lack of peer support, these aggressive boys were more vulnerable to peers' negative feedback and adjusted their aggressive behavior accordingly, in a sense complying to peer pressure.

In contrast, aggressive boys who were part of a peer cluster were found more likely to maintain their aggressive profile (mostly of a proactive type) from T1 to T2. They were also less victimized and rejected by peers. Further, they did not seem to experience much social anxiety nor were they perceived as isolated/sensitive by classmates. Perhaps support from members of their peer network makes it less likely that peers will retaliate with negative behaviors toward them. In fact, the victimization scores of these children were typically within the range of the classroom mean (see Table 11.1).

A support system for aggression would be particularly effective if the members of the network were themselves aggressive. As expected, the aggressive boys' associates were more aggressive than the nonaggressive boys' associates at T1 and at T2. This was especially true for boys who maintained their aggressive profile over time (i.e., the A–A group).

This pattern of results is consistent with other studies indicating that aggressive boys tend to affiliate with other aggressive boys (Cairns et al., 1988). It is also in line with the view that these peer affiliations may perpetuate, consolidate, or even promote aggression (Cairns & Cairns, 1992). Again, it is possible to speculate on the processes involved. Peer group membership could protect the boys from outgroup coercion attempts, containing the aversive consequences for behaving aggressively and thereby impeding the deterring effect of retaliatory responses. These affiliations could also provide the strategic alliances through which aggressive children might gain access to resources by coercive means, therefore learning that aggression pays. Finally, these relationship networks could also promote aggression-related norms and values, thus providing a cognitive framework supportive of these behavioral tendencies. Cairns and Cairns (1991) have recently argued that children's affiliations are strongly biased toward social synchrony, this bias being manifested most notably in the biselection of aggressive children as well as in the consolidation of aggressive norms within the peer group context. Other researchers have also stressed this tendency for individuals who associate to increase their behavioral similarity (Bukowski & Newcomb, 1994).

In sum, for a majority of aggressive boys who are part of a peer network, reinforcement contingencies, modeling, and use of coercive strategies within the network may explain the maintenance of aggressive behavior patterns. Coercive interactions between aggressive children and out-group peers is also plausible. These coercive interactions with outsiders may, in turn, be positively reinforced by peers in the network.

This study supports the relevance of distinguishing aggressive boys involved in a peer network from those who are not involved in a peer network, and emphasizes the need to study prospectively the developmental trajectories of these children. We also need to know more about the nature and functions of these affiliative relationships because they might have important implications for the treatment of unpopular, aggressive boys. Indeed, we should be concerned about the fact that affiliative relationships may serve to maintain aggressive behavior patterns when training aggressive, unpopular boys to be more socially skilled and accepted. Direct observations at the network level are needed to clarify the patterns and processes through which aggressive and nonaggressive children interact with the members of their respective networks. Given the correlational nature of the data presented here, we should be cautious in drawing any conclusions on the mechanisms involved. Therefore, these interpretations should be seen as speculations awaiting further empirical confirmations.

NOTE

This study was made possible by research grants from the Social Sciences and Humanities Research Council of Canada, the Conseil Québécois de la Recherche Sociale, the Fonds de Recherche en Santé du Québec, the FCAR Foundation, and the Richelieu Foundation. The authors wish to express their appreciation to the administration and the children of the Québec Catholic School Board, the Découvreurs School Board, the Montcalm School Board, and the Charlesbourg School Board for their participation in the study. Requests for reprints should be sent to the first author, Ecole de Psychologie, Pavillon F. A. Savard, Université Laval, Ste-Foy, Québec, Canada, G1K 7P4.

REFERENCES

Asher, S. R., & Coie, J. D. (1990). *Peer rejection in childhood.* Cambridge University Press.
Bierman, K. L., & Smoot, D. L. (1991). Linking family characteristics with poor peer relations: The mediating role of conduct problems. *Journal of Abnormal Child Psychology, 19,* 341–356.
Boivin, M., & Coté, L. (1991, April). *Peer network, peer status and aggression among middle elementary school children.* Poster presented at the Biennial Meeting of the Society for Research in Child Development, Seattle, WA.
Boivin, M., Coté, L., & Dion M. (1991, July). The self-perceptions and peer experiences of aggressive-rejected and withdrawn-rejected children. In S. Asher (Chair), *Self-perceptions among children with poor peer relations.* Symposium conducted at the 11th Biennial

Meetings of the International Society for the Study of Behavioral Development, Minneapolis, MN.

Bukowski, W. M., & Newcomb, A. F. (1994). [Interpersonal similarity in the development and stability of adolescent friendship relations.] Unpublished raw data.

Cairns, R. B., & Cairns, B. D. (1991). Social cognition and social networks: A developmental perspective. In D. J. Pepler & K. H. Rubin (Eds.), *The development and treatment of childhood aggression* (pp. 249–278). Hillsdale, NJ: Erlbaum.

Cairns, R. B., & Cairns, B. D. (1992). The sociogenesis of aggressive and antisocial behaviors. In J. McCord (Ed.), *Facts, frameworks, and forecasts: Advances in criminological theory* (Vol. 3, pp. 157–191). New Brunswick, NJ: Transaction Publications.

Cairns, R. B., Cairns, B. D., Neckerman, H. J., Gest, S. D., & Gariépy, J.-L. (1988). Social networks and aggressive behavior: Peer support or peer rejection? *Developmental Psychology, 25,* 320–330.

Cairns, R. B., Kindermann, T., & Gariépy, J.-L. (1986). *Cognitive sociometry: How to identify peer clusters through composite social maps.* Chapel Hill: University of North Carolina, Social Developmental Laboratory.

Cairns, R. B., Perrin, J. E., & Cairns, B. D. (1985). Social structure and social cognition in early adolescence: Affiliative patterns. *Journal of Early Adolescence, 5,* 339–355.

Coie, J. D., Belding, M., & Underwood, M. (1988). Aggression and peer rejection in childhood. In B. B. Lahey & A. Kazdin (Eds.), *Advances in clinical child psychology* (pp. 125–158). New York: Plenum.

Coie, J. D., & Dodge, K. A. (1983). Continuities and changes in children's social status: A five-year longitudinal study. *Merrill-Palmer Quarterly, 29,* 262–282.

Coie, J. D., Dodge, K. A., & Kupersmidt, J. (1990). Peer group behavior and social status. In S. R. Asher & J. D. Coie (Eds.), *Peer rejection in childhood* (pp. 17–59). Cambridge University Press.

Coie, J. D., & Kupersmidt, J. B. (1983). A behavioral analysis of emerging social status in boys' groups. *Child Development, 54,* 1400–1416.

Dodge, K. A. (1983). Behavioral antecedents of peer social status. *Child Development, 54,* 1386–1399.

Dodge, K. A., Bates, J. E., & Pettit, G. S. (1990). Mechanisms in the cycle of violence. *Science, 250,* 1678–1683.

Dodge, K. A., & Coie, J. D. (1987). Social-information-processing factors in reactive and proactive aggression in children's peer groups. *Journal of Personality and Social Psychology, 53,* 1146–1158.

Dodge, K. A., Pettit, G. S., McClaskey, C. L., & Brown, M. M. (1986). Social competence in children. *Monographs of the Society for Research in Child Development, 51*(2, Serial No. 213).

Franke, S., & Hymel, S. (1984, May). *Social anxiety in children: Development of self-report measures.* Paper presented at the Third Biennial Meeting of the University of Waterloo Conference on Child Development, Waterloo, Ontario.

Hymel, S., & Franke, S. (1985). Children's peer relations: Assessing self-perceptions. In B. Schneider, K. Rubin, & J. Ledingham (Eds.), *Peer relationships and social skills in childhood: Issues in assessment and training* (pp. 75–92). New York: Springer-Verlag.

Masten, A. S., Morison, P., & Pellegrini, D. S. (1985). A revised class play method of peer assessment. *Developmental Psychology, 21,* 523–533.

Parkhurst, J. T., & Asher, S. R. (1992). Peer rejection in middle school: Subgroup differences in behavior, loneliness, and interpersonal concerns. *Developmental Psychology, 28* (2), 231–241.

Patterson, G. R., Reid, J. B., & Dishion, T. J. (1992). *Antisocial boys.* Eugene, OR: Castalia.

Perry, G. D., Kusel, S. J., & Perry, L. L. (1988). Victims of peer aggression. *Developmental Psychology, 24,* 807–814.

Rubin, K. H., Hymel, S., LeMare, L. & Rowden, L. (1989). Children experiencing social difficulties: Sociometric neglect reconsidered. *Canadian Journal of Behavioral Sciences, 21,* 94–111.

12 Classroom seating and juvenile delinquency

PIERRE CHARLEBOIS, FRANKIE BERNÈCHE,
MARC LE BLANC, CLAUDE GAGNON,
AND SERGE LARIVÉE

Introduction

Early cognitive and affective experiences in elementary school affect later social competence and adaptation. Scholastic underachievement predicts a continuing cycle of problems such as school failure, poor self-esteem, attendance and disciplinary problems, school dropout, unemployment, and criminal activity (Butler, Marsh, Sheppard, & Sheppard, 1985; Cowen, Peterson, Babigian, Izzo, & Trost, 1973; Farrington, 1986; Loeber & Dishion, 1983). Initially, underachievement was attributed mainly to problems within the individual, but educators gradually began to consider how pupils' behavior was affected by the educational environment (Dowling, 1985; Rutter, Maughan, Mortimore, & Ouston, 1979). Teaching a group of children is a complex activity that involves numerous behavior management and learning management decisions. It is therefore quite understandable that the consequences of some decisions for individuals are not always recognized by teachers.

Research in the classroom has focused mainly on the identification of a univariate relationship between academic achievement and classroom behaviors (Feldhusen, Thurston, & Benning, 1970; Lambert, 1972; Spivack, Marcus, & Swift, 1986), peer status (Kupersmidt & Coie, 1990), and teachers' interaction styles (Brophy & Good, 1974; Cohen & Cohen, 1987). Although classroom environment is assumed to be a potent determinant of student outcome (Fraser, 1986; Keyser & Barling, 1981; Moos, 1980; Wright & Cowen, 1982), little attention has been given to the interdependence of student, behavior, and environment in the effectiveness of schools. Two important, though often neglected, ecological variables within the classroom environment are seating arrangements and the location of pupils.

Although many teachers consider the classroom layout relatively unimportant when compared with the student–teacher relationship (Sommer, 1977), it influ-

198

ences task performance and social interactions in the classroom. Studies by Rosenfield, Lambert, and Black (1985), Weinstein (1979), and Zifferblatt (1972) showed that elementary school students seated in circles engaged in significantly more on-task behaviors than those in rows and clusters and that cluster seating facilitated social interaction but impeded on-task behaviors during independent seat work. Unfortunately empirical studies of the effect of desk arrangements on classroom behavior have not controled for child characteristics, for instance, attention deficits or conduct disorder (see Ambramowitz & O'Leary, 1991, for a review). Because attention problems are frequently situation related, exposure to extraneous distractions and excessive stimulation resulting from seating arrangements could be considerably disadvantageous for children with low self-control.

An examination of the research literature on the effect of seating positions on behavior shows that studies were conducted mainly with high school and college students (Koneya, 1976; Weinstein, 1979). Generalization of these findings to younger populations is risky because high school students select their own seats, whereas elementary school children are generally assigned to a seating location by the teacher. According to MacPherson (1984), adolescents attributed meaning to their choice of seating location in the classroom. The front of the room was associated with attention to academic matters and dependence on the teachers. The rear was associated with reduced opportunities for attention to academic matters, freedom from teacher control, and freedom for student interaction. If we assume that students' beliefs are based on past experience, these findings are indicative of the importance of seating allocation in elementary school. Being assigned to an unfavorable location for long periods could have serious consequences on the child's academic and social development (Nijiokiktjien, 1988). More exploration is needed to advance knowledge on the interaction between students' characteristics and seating positions in the classroom.

Student and teacher behaviors, desk arrangement, and seating location represent interacting domains of the classroom environment. Although conceptual frameworks describing the interdependence of person behavior and environment in determining human psychological functioning have been available for a long time (Lewin's 1936 model was followed by Moos's in 1980 and Bandura's in 1986), research in the classroom was limited to the effect of specific domains on cognitive, affective, and social outcomes (MacAulay, 1990). The hypothesis that desk arrangements and seat allocation are related to teachers' expectations for academic performance was formulated by Getzel (1974), but to our knowledge it was never documented empirically. If task organization (norms for task accomplishment and procedural systems within which tasks are embedded) reflects teachers' expectations and goals for students' physical, mental, and social activities (Anderson, Stevens, Prawat, & Nickerson, 1988), the same hypothesis could be made concerning seat allocation by the teacher.

Select aspects of data collected in a longitudinal follow-up of a risk group offered the opportunity to study potential coercion resulting from decisions made by elementary school teachers. The present study explored the interactions between seat allocation, student behaviors, and teacher behaviors in elementary schools and their relationship to outcomes such as peer acceptance and self-reported delinquency.

Method

Data for the present study were collected as part of a 7-year longitudinal research project that began in the spring of 1984. French-Canadian boys attending kindergarten for the first time in 54 schools located in low-SES (socioeconomic status) districts of Montreal were selected for the study 1 year prior to their entry into elementary school. Various demographic characteristics were obtained from the mothers by female research assistants during telephone interviews. Families' SES was low, with parents averaging 10 years of schooling and maintaining a mean of 38 (out of a maximum score of 78) for occupational prestige (Blishen & McRoberts, 1976). Sixty-four percent of the families were intact, 27% were single-parent families, and 9% were blended families. They had an average of 2.1 children, and the mothers were, on average, 26.9 years old at the birth of their first child.

Subjects

Subjects for the longitudinal study observational group consisted of 32 disruptive boys who had a score of 8 or more on the "aggressiveness-hyperactivity" scale of the Behar Preschool Behavior Questionnaire (BPQR; Behar & Stringfield, 1974) (average for low-SES population of 313 boys; M of 3.0 and SD of 4.5. Boys' IQ (WISC-R) averaged 97.6, with an SD of 13.5. Seating locations were recorded twice prior to observation of teacher–child interactions (February and March) and once prior to the sociometric assessments (April) at ages 9 and 11. Seating locations and teacher–child interactions were also recorded for three control boys in each of the target boys' classrooms at ages 9 ($n = 96$) and 11 years ($n = 96$). All teachers ($n = 64$) were female. Self-reported delinquency was assessed for the 32 disruptive boys at age 12.

Assessment procedure

Selection of the risk group. The BPBQ was distributed to the kindergarten teachers at the end of the school year (May and June). Questionnaires were returned to our laboratory by mail when completed. The BPBQ has proved reliable in the assessment of behavioral problems in children. Test–retest assessment and interjudge agreement were used by Behar and Stringfield (1974) to verify the instrument's reliability. Kindergarten children were assessed twice within a 4-month interval by five teachers. Mean correlations were high for the aggressiveness score ($r = .93$) and the hyperactivity score ($r = .94$). These findings are consistent with those of

Zimmermann-Tansella, Minghetti, Tacconi, and Tansella (1978) for an Italian sample. Interjudge agreement assessed by Behar and Stringfield (1974) between seven teachers and seven assistants was high for the aggressiveness score ($r = .81$) and moderately high for the hyperactivity score ($r = .67$). The BPBQ has been widely used both in North America and Europe and has shown stability in factor structure across cultures, gender, ages, and SES (Tremblay, Desmarais-Gervais, Gagnon, & Charlebois, 1987). Rubin and Clark (1983) conducted a concurrent validity study in which all subjects were rated on the BPBQ and for SES, observed and recorded in a preschool setting for play behavior, and evaluated for the development of social-problem-solving skills. Results showed that children rated high on the BPBQ maladjustment scale were found to be less mature, more aggressive, less popular among their peers, and more likely to propose negative affect strategies in the social-problem-solving tasks.

Observations of teachers' and boys' behaviors. Observations were conducted during regular classroom activities on six different occasions (three each at ages 9 and 11) in February, March, and April (alternating morning and afternoon sessions) for a total of approximately 360 minutes for each classroom. Female observers received extensive training (approximately 120 hours) with practice tapes and direct observations. The interobserver agreement (number of agreements / number of agreements + number of disagreements × 100) before conducting observations in classrooms averaged 80%. Reliability checks were conducted weekly during data collection. The observer located the target child and three other boys seated in different rows than those of the target boy (one each in the front, middle, and back). She sat in the back of the classroom unobtrusively making sure she got a clear view of the children and teacher. The observation schedule was conducted as follows: observers focused alternatively on the target boy's interactions with the teacher for 5 minutes, then on the first control boy's interactions with the teacher for 5 minutes, and so on for the other two control boys. This observation schedule was repeated systematically after observers had rested for 5 minutes until the end of the period. A time-sampling method was used with 15-second frames, in which the initiator (adult or child), the boy's behavior, and the immediate response to this behavior by the other individual were recorded on a computerized event recorder (Holmes, 1982). Positive, negative, and neutral adult–child interactions were recorded in the classroom using the Family Process Code (Dishion et al., 1984). Four categories (directs, stimulates, silent, neglect) were added to the coding system to describe the learning management strategies used by the teachers (see Table 12.1). A neglect category was created to indicate a teachers' individual relationship with another child in the classroom at the moment the target child was observed. The category of teacher remaining silent was used to describe opportunities provided to children for self-regulation (Anderson et al., 1988). Two categories (task appropriate, task inappropriate) were also added to the coding system to describe the child's interest in the task (Dodge, Coie, & Brake, 1982). This study focused on the boys' disruptive

Table 12.1. *Categories and codes used in classroom observations*

Boys' disruptive behaviors	Teachers' behaviors
Negative verbalization	Negative verbalization
Negative vocalization	Negative vocalization
Negative nonverbal	Negative nonverbal
Verbal attack	Verbal attack
Refusal	Refusal
Noncompliance	Noncompliance
Tease	Tease
Task appropriate	Directs
Task inappropriate	Stimulates
	Silent
	Neglect

behaviors and involvement in learning activities. Behaviors such as refusal, noncompliance, negative verbalization, and negative vocalization were included in the definition of disruptive behaviors along with off-task behaviors (daydreaming, playing with objects, and excessive mobility) because they have the same effect on learning achievements. Such behaviors have frequently been associated with academic underachievement and later antisocial behavior (Spivack, Marcus, & Swift, 1986). Scores were computed for each behavioral category by dividing the total frequency of each category by total frequency for all categories. Separate reliability coefficients (Cronbach's alpha) computed for each behavior category at T2 and at T3 averaged .81 and .74 for the teachers' and the boys' observations, respectively.

Assessment of location in the classroom. Seating location of the target boy was noted by observers on a diagram representing the exact seating arrangement on six occasions (three each at ages 9 and 11). Given that 87.5% (56 out of 64) of the classroom seating arrangements were in rows and columns, location was coded according to the matrix presented in Figure 12.1. Eight classroom (12%) arrangements were clusters. Seating location in these classrooms was estimated according to the same matrix. Each cell in the matrix was coded according to its vertical and horizontal distance from the teacher's desk. The matrix was designed to represent the number of steps it would take the teacher to walk from her desk to a given seating location. Pupils with scores of 0 to 2 (approximately 10 steps or less) were considered to be sitting in the front of the classroom, pupils with scores of 3 or 4 (approximately 20 steps) were considered to be sitting in the middle, and pupils' scores of 5 or 6 (approximately 30 steps) were considered to be sitting in the back. The following criterion was used to determine the boys' most representative seating location over a 2-year period. If a boy was observed sitting in the same location for at least three

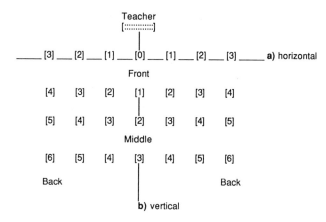

Figure 12.1. Seating location coding matrix.

occasions out of six, he was assigned to that category (front, middle, or back group). Eighty-four percent of the boys (27/32) were seated in the same location on at least four occasions, 9.3% of the boys (3/32) on three occasions. Two boys who were seated twice each in the front, middle, and back were arbitrarily assigned to the middle group. Interviews with teachers conducted before the first observation revealed that seating allocation was determined by the teacher in all 64 classes. No significant differences, $F(2, 31) = 1.9$, ns, were found for the number of pupils in the classrooms (front: $M = 21.2$, SD $= 6.5$; middle: $M = 23.4$, SD $= 6.4$; back: $M = 25.8$, SD $= 3.1$). It is noteworthy that 9 of 12 boys (75%) seated in the front and 6 of 11 boys (55%) seated in the back of the classroom had failed a grade by age 9, compared with 3 of 9 boys (33.3%) seated in the middle.

Assessment of popularity. Subjects were administered the Pupil Evaluation Inventory (PEI; Pekarik, Prinz, & Liebert, 1976) in the classroom at the end of each school year and were informed of the confidentiality of their response. Given a roster of the children in their class, they were asked to name three classmates "they liked most," who "seem to always understand what is going on," "start fights," "disturb the classroom the most," "laugh at others," "tell lies," "cheat," "make up stories," "say they can beat other kids," "are too shy to make friends," "are sad and don't want to play with the other kids," "are alone in a corner," and "have fewer friends." The assessment procedure was validated for a French-Canadian population (560 boys and 555 girls in first grade, 618 boys and 676 girls in fourth grade, and 882 boys and 818 girls in seventh grade) by Schwartzman, Ledingham, and Serbin (1985). The PEI has been widely used in North America and has proved reliable in determining acceptance by peers in the children's social groups (Kupersmidt & Coie, 1990). Popularity is rated on a standardized Z score, a high positive score indicating high popularity, a negative score, unpopularity. A mean popularity score was computed using the Z scores at ages 9 and 11.

Assessment of outcome. Self-reported delinquency was assessed at age 12. To prevent any labeling of the children as being in the high-risk group, at least four other boys were selected randomly in each classroom. All boys were excused from normal academic activities with the teachers' permission for approximately 1 hour while they completed the questionnaire. The boys were told that they had been randomly selected to answer questions that would help researchers get a better understanding of the development of boys during elementary school. Each subgroup of approximately five boys was accompanied by a female assistant to a secluded room chosen with the help of the school principal. Seating arrangement ensured confidentiality. Walkmans (audiotape recorders) and questionnaire forms were distributed to each boy once he was seated. The boys were told that they would hear each question on the questionnaire in the earphones and would be given 20 seconds to respond. They were assured that this questionnaire was strictly confidential and that the information would only be used for research purposes (numbers were used to identify the subjects). Help was offered by the assistant in case of technical problems or any difficulty in understanding the questions. The Self-Reported Delinquency Questionnaire (SRDQ) is composed of 24 items (see Table 12.2) whose answers are

Table 12.2. *Self-reported antisocial behaviors (in the last 12 months) assessed at age 12*

Fighting	*Vandalism*
Group fighting	Destroying equipment (sport, music,
Threatening to beat up or force other	etc.) at school
Using weapon in fight (stick, knife, gun, rocks)	Destroying something not yours
Fighting with fists	Breaking school windows, walls, etc.
Beating someone who did no wrong	Destroying objects not yours at home
Throwing rocks, bottles, etc. at others	Breaking parts of car (antennas,
Carrying an arm (chain, gun, knife, etc.)	tires, etc.)
	Setting a fire
Stealing	Trespassing
Stealing objects worth more than $10 from	
school	
Shoplifting	
Stealing object worth more than $100	
Entering without paying	
Stealing money at home	
Stealing object worth less than $10	
Stealing object worth $10 to $100	
Stealing a bicycle	
Buying, using, or selling stolen goods	
Burglary	

Source: SRDQ (Le Blanc, 1994).

dichotomized as to the presence or absence of the described act. The instrument was validated by LeBlanc (1994) in Montreal with a sample of male and female subjects from various socioeconomic areas ($N = 7,470$). Each scale had good reliability and excellent concurrent, discriminant, and predictive validity. The distribution on the criminal delinquency scale in this study population is almost identical to that observed by LeBlanc et al. (1990), with 20% of subjects reporting no delinquent acts, 30% reporting 1 to 2 acts, 28% reporting 3 to 6 acts, 15% reporting 7 to 11 acts, and 7% reporting 12 to 21 acts. Individuals who reported 3 or more delinquent acts at the onset of adolescence were classified in the high-delinquency group and those who reported 2 or fewer delinquent acts in the low-delinquency group.

Results

The relationships between seating location, boys' behaviors, and teachers' behaviors were assessed by two-way analyses of variance (seating location × behavior). As can be seen from Table 12.3, the analysis for the risk group showed a significant effect for boys' disruptive behaviors, $F(2, 32) = 6.2$, $p < .005$, a significant effect for teachers' neglect, $F(2, 32) = 3.4$, $p < .04$, and a significant effect for teachers' silence, $F(2, 32) = 9.5$, $p < .0006$. At-risk boys seated in the front and in the back were more disruptive than boys seated in the middle of the classroom. Teachers were more neglectful and more intrusive (less silent) toward the at-risk boys seated in the front and back. No significant effect was found for teachers' positive, aversive, directive, stimulative, and neutral behaviors. The analysis for the control group showed no significant effect for the boys' disruptive behaviors and no significant effect for teachers' positive, aversive, directive, stimulating, neutral, and neglectful behaviors. A significant effect was found for teachers' silence, $F(2, 196) = 4.4$, $p < .05$.

A comparison of the two groups showed that boys in the risk group were significantly more disruptive, $t(32) = 6.52$, $p < .001$; $M = 21.7$, $SD = 8.7$, than boys in the control group ($M = 10.6$, $SD = 4.2$). The differences found in teachers' behaviors of neglect and silence with the at-risk boys seated in different locations were also found with the control boys. They initiated less individual relationship with the student (neglect) and provided fewer opportunities to practice self-regulation (remaining silent) to children of both groups seated in the front and in the back of the classroom. These results seem to indicate that teachers established the same type of relationship with children seated in these specific positions, regardless of their disruptive behavior.

These findings suggest that the interdependence of person and behavior was the same for front and back seating locations. A post hoc analysis on items with significant differences in the risk group showed that the teachers' and boys' behaviors were similar in the front and back seating groups, and significantly different from the middle group (Scheffe procedure, ranges for the .05 level). Therefore, subjects seated in the front and back were regrouped in a category called extremity

Table 12.3. Means and analysis of variance for risk group's, control group's, and teachers' behaviors as a function of seating location in the classroom

	Risk group (N=32)							Control group (N=192)						
	Front		Middle		Back			Front		Middle		Back		
	M	SD	M	SD	M	SD	F value	M	SD	M	SD	M	SD	F value
Boys														
Disruptive	21.7	(7.1)	15.2	(6.9)	27.2	(8.4)	6.2***	9.1	(2.9)	10.3	(4.5)	12.5	(5.4)	1.7
Teachers														
Positive	1.1	(0.97)	1.1	(1.4)	1.1	(0.63)	0.0	0.8	(0.82)	0.45	(0.39)	0.44	(0.65)	0.0
Aversive	3.2	(1.7)	1.7	(1.3)	2.7	(1.9)	1.9	1.5	(0.87)	1.3	(0.43)	1.0	(0.31)	0.0
Directive	10.8	(4.2)	8.3	(1.1)	9.6	(3.6)	1.0	8.9	(4.1)	10.6	(5.4)	9.1	(5.7)	0.0
Stimulative	6.7	(3.2)	6.6	(3.5)	6.8	(3.6)	0.0	6.9	(6.6)	9.0	(4.1)	6.9	(7.0)	0.0
Neutral	27.5	(6.9)	33.0	(8.9)	31.2	(8.6)	1.2	26.2	(8.3)	25.8	(7.5)	30.0	(10.3)	0.0
Neglectful	34.8	(9.1)	23.6	(9.1)	32.6	(11.7)	3.4*	40.3	(13.9)	25.3	(11.7)	35.3	(17.4)	2.6
Silent	14.4	(5.0)	23.9	(5.9)	14.6	(5.5)	9.5****	14.6	(6.7)	25.1	(7.2)	16.1	(10.6)	4.4*

*$p<.05$; **$p<.01$; ***$p<.005$; ****$p<.0006$.

Table 12.4. *Mean, standard deviation, and analysis of variance for boys' behavior, teachers' behaviors, and outcome as a function of middle seating location versus seating in extremities*

	Extremities ($n = 23$)		Middle ($n = 9$)		
	M	SD	M	SD	t value
Boys					
Disruptive	24.2	8.1	15.2	6.9	3.1***
Teachers					
Silent/intrusive	14.5	5.1	23.9	5.9	4.5***
Neglectful	33.7	10.3	23.6	9.1	2.7**
Aversive	2.9	1.8	1.7	1.3	2.1*
Outcome					
Delinquency	4.3	3.3	1.9	2.3	2.3*
Popularity	−0.5	0.6	0.0	0.7	1.89

*$p < .05$; **$p < .01$; ***$p < .005$.

Table 12.5. *Standardized canonical discriminant function coefficients*

Boys' disruptive behaviors	.86
Teachers' silence/intrusion	.74
Teachers' neglect	.37
Boys' self-reported delinquency	.35
Boys' popularity	.30
Teachers' aversive behaviors	.19
Canonical correlation	.79
Eigenvalue	1.7

group. As can be seen in Table 12.4, comparisons of the extremity group with the middle group showed significant differences in the boys' disruptive behaviors, $t(32) = 3.1$, $p < .006$; in the teachers' silent/intrusive behaviors, $t(32) = 4.5$, $p < .001$; in teachers' neglect, $t(32) = 2.7$, $p < .01$; and in teachers' aversive behaviors, $t(32) = 2.1$, $p < .04$. The same trend was observed for outcome variables with a significant difference for self-reported delinquency $t(32) = 2.3$, $p < .05$, and a marginally significant difference for unpopularity $t(32) = 1.9$, $p < .06$. These results were confirmed by a discriminant function analysis. The standardized canonical discriminant function coefficients for each of these variables are presented in Table 12.5. The canonical correlation was .79 with an eigenvalue of 1.7, and 93.5% of the grouped cases were correctly classified in the extremity group or the middle group.

Discussion

Although the present findings should be interpreted with some caution due to the small number of subjects, they seem to indicate that the interdependence of boys' behaviors, teachers' behaviors, and seating allocation in the classroom is associated with unpopularity in the peer group and self-reported delinquency. The results raise some important issues concerning the coercive nature of decisions taken by the teachers.

Research on classroom effects has provided considerable evidence of a positive link between differential treatment practices in the classroom and student achievement (Wienstein et al., 1991). The present study has sought to demonstrate that seating allocation plays an important and often unrecognized role in such practices. Boys assigned to the front and to the back of the classroom had less individual interactions with the teacher (neglect), had fewer opportunities to practice self-regulation (teacher remaining silent), and were exposed to more aversive behaviors from the teacher than were boys assigned to seats in the middle of the classroom. While considering alternative interpretations for this differential treatment by teachers, we must keep in mind that seating location was determined by teachers in all the classrooms observed.

To demonstrate a significant contribution of seating location on the teacher–child relationship, the boys' disruptive behavior as the main effect had to be controlled. Results indicated that the boys' disruptive behavior was not a sufficient explanation for differential treatment by the teachers, because teachers' interactions with nondisruptive boys (control group) seated in the extremities of the classroom were very similar. This seems to indicate a relationship between the teachers' behaviors and the seating arrangement. Arrangements in rows and columns, for instance, limit the possibility of individual relationships with each student and generate situations of differential treatment. However, this did not explain why this type of classroom arrangement was preferred by teachers and why some children are assigned to the disadvantageous seating positions in that setting. Although the boys' disruptive behaviors cannot be completely eliminated as a cause for the differential treatment they received, the findings provoked us to search for other causes.

Two facts suggested that we turn to the literature on teacher expectations for possible explanations. First, most of the disruptive boys (84.5%) in the present study were seated in the same location at ages 9 and 11 years, in spite of a yearly change of classroom and teacher. This stability is impressive considering it extended over 3 years of schooling. Second, 65% of the boys who were seated in the extremities versus 33.3% of those in the middle group had failed grades at age 9.

Previous research has shown that prior student achievement is an important factor in teacher expectations (Good, 1981; Kerman, 1979) and that teachers behave in different ways toward students of whom they had high versus low expectations. Students who were expected to do less received fewer positive, nonverbal communications of warmth and personal regards from the teacher (Anderson et al., 1988; Proctor, 1984; Weinstein, 1989). Similar evidence of differential treatment for boys seated in the extremities of the classroom versus the middle was found in this study.

Though this similarity does not establish a direct causal relationship between seating allocation and teachers' expectations, it certainly constitutes a serious base for further investigation. Post hoc interviews with two experienced psychoeducators (counseling with more than 150 elementary school teachers in the school district where this study was conducted) revealed that some disruptive boys were assigned to front seating for more control and some to the back because teachers became exasperated with their behavior. These boys would tend to be shifted from one extremity of the classroom to the other more frequently than the other children. Considering the stability in seating location observed, the boys' low academic achievement, and their disruptive behavior, we speculate that information on these disruptive boys was communicated from one teacher to another, thus setting the stage for differential treatment.

Coercion resulting from differential treatment in the classroom is well documented. Repeated exposure to negative treatment shapes students' self-perceptions and decreases their opportunity to learn (Proctor, 1984; Weinstein et al., 1991). Findings from the present study contributed to this knowledge by drawing attention to the subtlety of the process. Teachers were not overtly different in their behavior with different children in the classroom. Their verbal communication (positive, directive, stimulative, neutral) with boys in the risk group was not significantly different from that with boys in the control group. Differential treatment with boys seated in the extremities of the classroom was expressed mostly by teacher neglect (less individual relationship) and by fewer opportunities to practice self-regulation (teacher remaining silent). Concerning this latter point, Anderson et al. (1988) argue that students' self-esteem is increased when they experience success stemming from self-regulation. Results from the present study show that although no significant group variances were found within the different verbal categories, teachers' total verbal communication with boys seated in the front and the back of the classroom was greater than teachers' silence. Considering that the boys selected for this study were hyperactive, aggressive, and distractible, a lack of opportunities to exercice self-control could be very damaging to their self-esteem (Martin, Welsh, McKay, & Bareuther, 1984; Zentall, 1985). A follow-up on these boys showed that those who were seated in the extremities of the classroom reported more delinquency at age 12 than did boys from the same risk group who were seated in the middle of the classroom. This appears to indicate that more opportunities for individual relationship with the teacher and opportunities for self-regulation effectively protected against school failure and juvenile delinquency for some of the at-risk boys.

Although the preceding comments may give the impression that seating location is the key element of a coercive class environment, this is not the case. As suggested by Bandura's (1986) concept of reciprocal determinism, it constitutes one component of the classroom organization that is interdependent with persons and behaviors in determining psychological functioning in this setting. We would hypothesize that seating positions do not have the same coercive potential for every child in the classroom. High achievers would be less stigmatized by a seating allocation in the front or the back of the classroom than would children with learning and/or behavior problems. The coercive effect is possibly a result of an interaction between the significance of seating allocation for the teacher and children's characteristics and behavior. Weinstein (1989) showed that children are aware (as early as the first grade) of teachers' expectations and that such cues could affect children's motivation. This type of coercion is considered to be subtle because decisions relative to classroom layout are considered relatively unimportant and innocuous by teachers (Sommer, 1977), and the negative consequences of such decisions are not noticeable in the short run. If further research could make more explicit the causal relationships between the persons, behaviors, and environment in the classroom, it could contribute greatly to our understanding of protective factors against school failure and delinquency.

NOTE

This study was funded by grants from Quebec Government's Funding Programs, C.Q.R.S., F.C.A.R., and Canada's C.R.S.H. We thank Lise Gervais-Desmarais and François Levert for data analysis; Lucille David, Louise Bineau, Suzanne Langelier, Suzanne Monday for data collection; Minh T. Trinh for documentation, and Line Arès for manuscript preparation.

REFERENCES

Ambramowitz, A. J., & O'Leary, S. G. (1991). Behavioral interventions for the classroom: Implications for students with ADHD, *School Psychology Review, 20,* 220–234.

Anderson, L. M., Stevens, D. D., Prawat, R. S., & Nickerson J. (1988). Classroom task environments and students' task-related beliefs. *Elementary School Journal, 88,* 281–295.

Bandura, A. (1986). *Social foundations of thought and action: A social cognitive theory.* Englewood Cliffs, NJ: Prentice-Hall.

Behar, L. B., & Stringfield, S. (1974). A behaviour rating scale for the preschool child. *Developmental Psychology, 10,* 601–610.

Blishen, B. R., & McRoberts, M. A. (1976). A revised socio-economic index for occupation in Canada. *Canadian Review of Sociology and Anthropology, 13,* 71–79.

Brophy, J. E., & Good, T. L. (1974). *Teacher–student relationships: Causes and consequences.* New York: Holt, Rinehart, & Winston.

Butler, S. R., Marsh, H. W., Sheppard, M. J., & Sheppard, J. L. (1985). Seven-year longitudinal study of early prediction of reading achievement. *Journal of Educational Psychology, 77,* 349–361.

Cohen, L., & Cohen, A. (1987). *Disruptive behaviour: A sourcebook for teachers.* London: Harper & Row.

Cowen, E. L., Peterson, A., Babigian, H., Izzo, L. D., & Trost, M. A. (1973). Long-term follow-up of early detected vulnerable children. *Journal of Consulting Clinical Psychology, 41,* 438–446.

Dishion, T., Gardner, K., Patterson, G. R., Reid, J. B., Spyrou, S., & Thibodeaux, S. (1984). The Family Process Code: A Multidimensional system for observing family interactions. Unpublished technical report, Eugene, OR: Social Learning Center.

Dodge, K. A., Coie, J. D., & Brake, N. P. (1982). Behavior patterns of socially rejected and neglected pre-adolescents: The roles of social approach and aggression. *Journal of Abnormal and Child Psychology, 10,* 389–410.

Dowling, E. (1985). Theoretical frame work: A joint systems approach to educational problems with children. In E. Dowling & E. Osborne (Eds.), *The family and the school: A joint systems approach to problems with children* (pp. 5–30). London: Routledge & Kegan Paul.

Farrington, D. P. (1986). Stepping stones to adult criminal careers. In D. Olweus, J. Block, & M. R. Radke-Yarrow. *Development of antisocial and prosocial behavior* (pp. 359–384). New York: Academic.

Feldhusen, N. D., Thurston, J. B., & Benning, J. J. (1970). Longitudinal analyses of classroom behavior and school achievement. *Journal of Experimental Education, 38,* 4–10.

Fraser, B. J. (1986). *Classroom Environment.* London: Croom Helm.

Getzel, J. W. (1974). Images of the classroom and visions of the learner. *School Review, 82,* 527–540.

Good, T. L. (1981). Teacher expectations and student perceptions: A decade of research. *Educational Leadership, 38,* 415–421.

Holmes, R. (1982). *OS-3 General mode manual.* Seattle, WA: Observational Systems.

Kerman, S. (1979). Teacher expectations and student achievement. *Phi Delta Kappan, 60,* 716–718.

Keyser, V., & Barling, J. (1981). Determinants of children's self-efficacy beliefs in an academic environment. *Cognitive Therapy and Research, 5,* 29–39.

Koneya, M. (1976). Location and interaction in row-and-column seating arrangements. *Environments and Behavior, 8,* 265–282.

Kupersmidt, J. B., & Coie, J. D. (1990). Preadolescent peer status, aggression and school adjustment as predictors of externalizing problems in adolescence. *Child Development, 61,* 1350–1362.

Lambert, N. M. (1972). Intellectual and non-intellectual predictors of high school status. *Journal of Educational Psychology, 6,* 247–259.

LeBlanc, M. (1994). *Manuel des mesures de l'adaptation sociale et personnelle pour les adolescents québécois.* Montreal: GRIP.

Lewin, K. (1936). *Principles of topological psychology.* New York: McGraw.

Loeber, R., & Dishion, T. J. (1983). Early predictors of male delinquency: A review. *Psychological Bulletin, 94,* 68–99.

MacAulay, D. J. (1990). Classroom environment: A literature review. *Educational Psychology, 10,* 239–253.

MacPherson, J. C. (1984). Environments and interaction in row and column classrooms. *Environment and Behavior, 16,* 481–502.

Martin, C. A., Welsh, R. J., McKay, S. E., & Bareuther, C. M. (1984). Hyperactivity (attention-deficit disorder). *Journal of Family Practice, 19,* 367–380.

Moos, R. H. (1980). *Evaluating educational environments: Procedures measures, findings and policy implications.* San Francisco: Jossey-Bass.

Nijiokiktjien, C. (1988). *Psychiatric behavioural neurology, Vol. 1, Clinical principle.* Amsterdam: Sugi.

Pekarik, E. G., Prinz, R. J., & Liebert, D. E. (1976). The Pupil Evaluation Inventory: A sociometric technique for assessing children's social behavior. *Journal of Abnormal Child Psychology, 4,* 83–97.

Proctor, C. P. (1984). Teacher expectations: A model for school improvement. *Elementary School Journal, 84,* 469–481.

Rosenfield, P., Lambert, N. M., & Black, A. (1985). Desk arrangement effects on pupils classroom behavior. *Journal of Educational Psychology, 77,* 101–108.

Rubin, K. H., & Clark, M. L. (1983). Preschool teachers' ratings of behavioral problems: Observational, sociometric, and social-cognitive correlates. *Journal of Abnormal Child Psychology, 11,* 273–286.

Rutter, M., Maughan, B., Mortimore, P., & Ouston, J. (1979). *Fifteen thousand hours: Secondary schools and their effects on children.* London: Open Book.

Schwartzman, A. E., Ledingham, J. E., Serbin, L. A. (1985). Identification of children at risk for adult schizophrenia: A longitudinal study. *International Review of Applied Psychology, 34,* 363–380.

Sommer, R. (1977). Classroom layout. *Theory into Practice, 16,* 174–175.

Spivack, G., Marcus, J., & Swift, M. (1986). Early classroom behaviors and later misconduct. *Developmental Psychology, 22,* 124–131.

Tremblay, R. E., Desmarais-Gervais, L., Gagnon, C., & Charlebois, P. (1987). The Preschool Behavior Questionnaire: Stability of its factor structure between cultures, sexes, ages, and socio-economic classes. *International Journal of Behavioral Development, 10,* 467–484.

Weinstein, R. S. (1979). The physical environment of the school: A review of the research. *Review of Educational Research, 49,* 577–610.

Weinstein, R. S. (1989). Perception of classroom processes and student motivation: Children's view of self-fulfilling prophecies. In R. E. Ames & C. Ames (Eds.), *Research on motivation in education* (Vol. 3, pp. 374–392). New York: Academic.

Weinstein, R. S., Soulé, C. R., Collins, R., Cone, J., Mehlhorn, M., & Simontocchi, K. (1991). Expectations and high school change: Teacher–researcher collaboration to prevent school failure. *American Journal of Community Psychology, 10,* 687–703.

Wright, S., & Cowen, E. L. (1982). Student perception of school environment and its relationship to mood, achievement, popularity and adjustment. *American Journal of Community Psychology, 10,* 687–703.

Zentall, S. S. (1985). Stimulus-control factors in search performance of hyperactive children. *Journal of Learning Disabilities, 18,* 480–485.

Zifferblatt, S. (1972). Architecture and human behavior: Toward an understanding of a functional relationship. *Educational Technology, 12,* 54–57.

Zimmermann-Tansella, C., Minghetti, S., Tacconi, A., & Tansella, M. (1978). The Children's Behaviour Questionnaire for completion by teachers in an Italian sample: Preliminary results. *Journal of Child Psychology and Psychiatry and Allied Disciplines, 19,* 167–173.

13 Social skills training and aggression in the peer group

DEBRA J. PEPLER, WENDY CRAIG,
AND WILLIAM L. ROBERTS

Longitudinal research indicates that aggressive children are at risk for continuing the coercive lifestyles that engendered their aggressive problems. Children who are aggressive at age 8 have a high probability of extending their aggressive behavior patterns into adulthood. Disruptive and bellicose children have a tendency to become adults who are at risk for marital conflict and child abuse, to engage in criminal behavior, and to become addicted to drugs and/or alcohol (e.g., Farrington, 1991; Huesmann, Eron, Lefkowitz, & Walder, 1984). Although aggressive behavior patterns are remarkably stable (Loeber, 1990; Olweus, 1979), they are expressed differently at various stages of development and are sensitive to different risk factors during those stages (Loeber, 1990). The interaction of individual characteristics with risk factors seems to determine the developmental path for aggressive children. In other words, children's behavioral, affective, and cognitive processes likely affect and are affected by parental and peer influences to direct the life course (Loeber, 1990). In this chapter, we focus on the role of peers in maintaining and exacerbating the developmental course of aggressive children. Peer influence is examined in the context of an intervention designed to interrupt the maladaptive trajectory of aggressive children by improving peer interactions.

Developmental course of aggressive children

Peer relations have been identified as a salient risk factor in the development of aggressive behavior problems. There is growing evidence that peer interaction plays multiple roles in social, cognitive, and moral development. In a review of research, Parker and Asher (1987) proposed a model to describe the contribution of peer relations to the development of antisocial behavior and maladjustment. This model identifies inadequate social skills as leading to low peer acceptance and deviant peer experiences. The intervention described in this chapter focuses on promoting children's social skills and improving their peer acceptance. The research measures and observations assess these two features of the model, as well as peer experiences in the naturalistic setting of the school playground.

Prior to entering the sphere of peer influences, children's socialization experiences within the family play a major role in developing aggressive behaviors (Patterson, 1986). Parents of aggressive children appear to fail in teaching compliance and appropriate social problem solving. Furthermore, according to Patterson (1982), these parents inadvertently reinforce the use of aversive and aggressive behaviors, which leads to coercive family interactions. Within the family context, aggressive children's formative experiences appear to be imbalanced in favor of learning antisocial, aggressive behaviors.

As they move beyond the family, aggressive children tend to transfer established patterns of noncompliance and antisocial behavior to peer and school contexts. For many aggressive children, interactions with teachers and peers become similarly coercive, and consequently, aggressive children are likely to experience both academic and peer relational problems (Patterson, 1986). Observations of aggressive children in peer interaction reveal a continuity with the coercive behavior patterns established at home. Aggressive children exhibit significantly more inappropriate play, insults, threats, hitting, and exclusion of peers than do average children (Dodge, 1986; Dodge, Coie, Pettit, & Price, 1990). They are less likely to engage in social conversation or to continue in group activities than are other children (Coie & Kupersmidt, 1983; Dodge, 1986). As in family interactions, there appears to be an imbalance in peer interactions, with many negative behaviors and few positive behaviors directed toward peers.

This pattern of behaviors tends to establish interactions and perceptions that are hostile in both directions. Aggressive children's negative behaviors are met with negative responses by peers (Dodge, 1986). For many aggressive children, these negative peer interactions lead to peer rejection. This developmental course from aggressive behavior to low peer acceptance has been demonstrated by the research of Dodge (1986) and Coie and Kupersmidt (1983). They introduced aggressive boys to a group of unfamiliar peers. The aggressive boys' behavior with peers was maladaptive, and within three sessions they had acquired a negative status within the new peer group (Coie & Kupersmidt, 1983). As a consequence of their unskilled social behavior, aggressive boys tended to be quickly rejected by unfamiliar peers.

Once children have established negative reputations and have been rejected by peers, a number of other behavioral and social-cognitive processes appear to support and elicit deviant behaviors. First, some deviant behaviors develop in response to peer rejection. Observations of aggressive boys indicate that they tend to increase inappropriate social behaviors and decrease social approaches to peers after acquiring a negative reputation (Coie & Kupersmidt, 1983; Dodge et al., 1990). Second, peer relations of aggressive children are characterized by reciprocally hostile perceptions and expectations between aggressive children and their peers. Aggressive children develop a bias toward interpreting peers' behaviors as hostile, and peers tend to perceive aggressive children as hostile and to blame them for negative behaviors (Dodge, 1980; Dodge & Frame, 1982; Hymel, Wagner, & Butler, 1990). This reciprocal hostile attributional bias likely supports hostile interactions between aggressive children and their peers. A cycle of behaviors and cognitions may be established that maintains and exacerbates negative interactions between rejected, aggressive children and their peers (Hymel et al., 1990).

Third, the trend for rejected children to associate less and less with popular and skilled members of the social group and more with other rejected children may support aggressive behavior patterns (Cairns & Cairns, 1991; Hartup, 1989; Snyder, Dishion, & Patterson, 1986). Aggressive children tend to associate with children who will accept them and who are like themselves in terms of behaviors, values, and goals (Hymel et al., 1990). Many aggressive children become members of the "out-group" rather than the "in-group," and their socialization experiences are further imbalanced in the direction of negative and coercive interactions. Limited opportunity for positive peer interactions may place rejected children at risk for continuing to learn and employ aggressive behaviors (Parker & Asher, 1987).

In considering the socialization experiences of aggressive children, it becomes apparent that a linear, unidirectional causal model is inadequate to capture the complexities of the process. There are several feedback loops that may exacerbate the situation for aggressive children. First, negative peer experiences impact on socialization efforts within the family. As aggressive children acquire increasingly deviant behavior patterns with peers, parents tend to experience more difficulty in controlling and monitoring their children's behaviors at home (Capaldi, 1992; Patterson, 1982, 1986). Second, aggressive children's increasingly deviant social behaviors in peer interactions may provide additional support to peers' negative perceptions and rejection of them. Finally, the isolation of many aggressive children and the formation of out-groups of deviant peers may further contribute to the development of antisocial behaviors (Cairns, Cairns, Neckerman, Gest, & Gariépy, 1988). These negative socialization processes within the peer group are postulated to set antisocial children on a path of alienation and further deviance.

In summary, theoretical models and empirical data suggest that aggressive children's dysfunctional behavioral, affective, and cognitive processes are initiated at home and transferred to the peer group, where they may be fostered, maintained, and exacerbated. While the models and data may represent the developmental path for a large proportion of aggressive children, it is important to recognize that there is considerable variability in the developmental trajectories of aggressive children. The development of antisocial behavior depends on the interaction of individual characteristics and exposure to risk factors at critical developmental periods (Loeber, 1990). There may also be factors that protect children from negative socialization experiences. Protective factors may reside within the child (e.g., leadership qualities, intelligence) or within his or her social system (e.g., a significant adult who supports the child in developing appropriate social skills and self-confidence) (Rutter, 1990). Given that aggressive children comprise a heterogeneous group, interventions need to be formulated with both a central tendency and an individual difference perspective (Loeber, 1990). A potential point of intervention in the developmental trajectory of aggressive and antisocial behavior is when children demonstrate poor social skills and begin to experience problems in peer relations.

Social skills training: interrupting the negative socialization process

Social skills training has been implemented to provide aggressive children with a foundation in the prosocial behaviors and social-cognitive skills in which they are deficient and that are necessary for successful peer interaction. School-based programs are ideal for this type of intervention because school is a primary context in which children interact with peers, providing a natural opportunity to assess and train their peer relational skills.

The research described in this chapter extended our work on social skills training with aggressive children (Pepler, King, & Byrd, 1991; Pepler, King, Craig, Byrd, & Bream, 1992). In our previous evaluations of the effectiveness of social skills training, teachers and parents generally perceived an improvement in the behavior problems and social skills of aggressive children; however, peer assessments failed to reflect a similar improvement (Pepler et al., 1992). The discrepancy between adult and peer perceptions of aggressive behaviors has led us to consider potential reasons for the lack of success in improving the peer reputations of aggressive children through social skills training.

There are two lines of reasoning to explain the discrepancy between adult and peer perceptions of aggressive children. The first possibility is that there was no change in the peer behaviors of children following social skill training, but there may have been a change in interactions with teachers and other adults, or teachers and parents who had participated in the program may have misperceived improvements. Conversely, there may have been an improvement in the behaviors of aggressive children toward peers after social skills training, but peers may have failed to recognize these improvements, perhaps because their expectations led them to continue interpreting the aggressive children's behavior as aggressive. Reputational processes and peer interactions may continue to elicit and support negative behaviors and perceptions. The research described in this chapter employed direct observations of peer interactions on the playground to investigate behavioral improvement with social skills training and the role of peers in ameliorating or exacerbating aggressive behavior problems.

Method

The Earlscourt Social Skills Group Programme (ESSGP) is a didactic, experiential program designed to improve the self-control and social skills of aggressive, noncompliant children between the ages of 6 and 12. This school-based program is offered to groups of seven children twice a week for 12 to 15 weeks. Eight basic skills are taught: problem solving, knowing your feelings, listening, following instructions, joining in, using self-control, responding to teasing, and keeping out of fights. Parent groups are offered to parents of children in the program to facilitate the children's learning of the skills and to help parents acquire new child management techniques. Other efforts are directed to the generalization of learned skills to the classroom and peer interactions. These include homework assignments, teacher involvement and contact, and the teaching of a skill to the child's entire class (see Pepler et al., 1991, for more details on the program).

Subjects

The present study comprised 41 aggressive children (30 boys and 11 girls) and 41 nonaggressive children matched on age, gender, and ethnicity. The children were in Grades 1 to 6 in two elementary schools within metropolitan Toronto. Their mean age was 9.7 years. The subjects were from low- to middle-income families and varied with respect to ethnicity (43% Caucasian, 25% African descent, 14% Asian descent, and 18% mixed or other ethnicity). The aggressive children participated in either a fall or spring social skills training program. The data for the fall and spring cohorts were combined for the analyses.

The children were nominated by their classroom teachers as aggressive or socially competent. Group assignment was validated by comparing the teacher-nominated aggressive children to a sample of teacher-nominated socially competent children on the Teacher Report Form of the Child Behavior Checklist (CBCL) and on peer nominations. Teachers rated the aggressive children as having behavior problems in the clinical range and significantly more behavior problems than did the nonaggressive children, $F(3, 37) = 24.1$, $p < .001$. There were also significant differences between the aggressive and nonaggressive groups on the peer reputation measure, $F(3, 69) = 21.6$, $p < .001$. Aggressive children were rated by same-sex peers as having a significantly less positive [$F(1, 71) = 10.85$, $p < .001$] and more aggressive reputation [$F(1, 71) = 55.28$, $p < .001$] than did nonaggressive children.

Instruments

The following instruments were administered to the aggressive children, their teachers, or classmates in the fall, winter, and/or spring. The fall and winter data comprised pre- and posttests for children in the fall social skills program, whereas the winter and spring data comprised pre- and posttests for children in the spring social skills training program.

Child measure. The Marsh Self-Description Questionnaire (Marsh, Smith, & Barnes, 1983) was administered to all aggressive and nonaggressive children. The questionnaire comprises eight subscales: physical abilities, physical appearance, relationships with peers, relationship with parents, reading, mathematics, school subjects, and total self-concept. The questionnaire was administered individually: children in primary grades (1 to 3) answered on a 3-point scale; children in junior grades (4 to 6) answered on a 5-point scale. Scores were standardized within grade level to account for the differences in scales.

Teacher measures. Teachers completed two measures for all aggressive and nonaggressive children in the study. First, they completed the Teacher Report Form of the Child Behavior Checklist (CBCL-TRF) (Achenbach & Edelbrock, 1986). This is a 118-item measure that assesses behavior problems on two broad dimensions: internalizing and externalizing. The externalizing scale taps aggressive, hyperactive, and delinquent behavior problems, whereas the internalizing scale assesses problems such as anxiety, withdrawal, and depression. The scales have been normed and standardized, providing indications of behavior problems in the clinical range (i.e., in the top 10% for age group and gender).

The teacher version of the Marsh Self-Description Questionnaire (Marsh et al., 1983) was completed by classroom teachers for all aggressive and nonaggressive children. On this measure, teachers indicate what they believe the child's self-concept is for the same eight domains on the child self-concept measure.

Peer measures. All classmates of children in the study completed two peer measures, which were administered individually to children in Grades 1 to 3 and were group administered to children in Grades 4 to 6. Peer reputations were rated with a measure adapted from the Revised Class Play assessment (Masten, Morison, & Pelligrini, 1985). Children were asked to pretend that they were directors in a play and choose a classmate who would best play each of the parts of someone who starts fights, disturbs others, gets angry easily, cooperates, is a leader, is good at sports, is funny, is unhappy, plays fair, is often left out, picks on other kids, has trouble making friends, and has many friends. Scores were standardized within class by gender. This measure yields three scores for sociability-leadership, aggressive-disruptive, and sensitive-isolated.

Classmates of children in the study also completed a sociometric status measure (Asher & Dodge, 1986). Students were asked to nominate three children in their class with whom they like to play during recess or lunchtime. In addition, they rated how much they liked to play with each of their classmates on a 5-point scale. Peer liking, disliking, social impact, and social preference scores were computed, as well as sociometric status categories; all scores were standardized within class by gender (see Coie & Dodge, 1988).

Observations of playground interactions

Children wore a remote microphone and were videotaped for two 10-minute periods during unstructured time on the playground at three points in time (fall, winter, and spring) corresponding to the questionnaire administration (see Pepler & Craig,

1994, for details of the observation technology and procedure). Videotapes were coded by research assistants blind to group membership. Coding was conducted in two stages: first for play states and a second time for a fine-grained analysis of behaviors. Coded states included unoccupied, solitary engaged, onlooker, parallel, together, cooperative play, and fantasy play. Behaviors coded included talk, verbal rejection, verbal attack, gossip, touch, rough and tumble play, and physical aggression. Each behavior was coded for affective valence on a 5-point scale from unrestrained positive to unrestrained negative. For example, an aggressive behavior could be coded with positive valence (when accompanied by laughter and positive affect) or with negative valence (when accompanied with angry facial gestures and harsh tone of voice). The social overtures and responses of peers to the target children were also coded. Kappa coefficients were calculated for the frequencies, durations, and sequences of states and events with a 5-second tolerance interval. Kappas were .76 for state coding and .69 for event coding.

Results

To compare the ratings and behaviors of aggressive and nonaggressive children and to assess the effectiveness of social skills training, we conducted 2 (group) × 2 (time: pre–post) multivariate analyses of variance for repeated measures. Means, standard deviations, and F values (group by time) for the outcome measures are reported in Table 13.1.

Self-concept: child rating. Children's responses on the self-description questionnaire indicated that both aggressive and nonaggressive children perceived themselves very positively at both pre- and posttraining times. There were no significant main effects or interactions.

Self-concept: teacher rating. When teachers were asked about children's self-concept, their ratings indicated that the aggressive children had lower self-esteem than did nonaggressive children, multivariate $F(7, 53) = 3.09$, $p = .008$. The group by time interaction was not significant, indicating no improvement in these teacher ratings following social skills training.

Teacher ratings of behavior problems. There was a significant group by time interaction for teachers' ratings of behavior problems, multivariate $F(3, 37) = 4.73$, $p = .007$. Ratings of aggressive children's behavior problems were significantly lower following social skills training, with fewer externalizing and total behavior problems. Ratings for the nonaggressive children indicated few behavior problems and remained stable over time.

Peer ratings. There was a significant main effect for group on the peer reputation measure with the aggressive group being rated as more aggressive and isolated and less sociable than the nonaggressive group, multivariate $F(3, 59) = 20.19$, $p < .001$.

Table 13.1. *Means and F values of outcome measures as a function of group and time*

Group measure	Aggressive		Nonaggressive		F^a	p
	Pretest	Posttest	Pretest	Posttest		
Self-concept[b]	0.1	−0.2	0.2	0.0	0.13	ns
(child rating)	(1.1)	(0.9)	(0.9)	1.0		
Self-concept	5.5	5.6	7.0	6.8	1.68	ns
(teacher rating)	(1.6)	(6.8)	(1.5)	(1.5)		
TRF Ext.[c]	64.9	58.1	43.8	44.1	14.5	.00
	(7.1)	(10.4)	(3.9)	(3.9)		
TRF Int.[c]	55.8	50.1	46.4	44.2	3.0	.09
	(7.0)	(6.4)	(5.2)	(2.6)		
TRF total[c]	63.3	55.9	41.7	40.9	11.0	.002
	(7.1)	(10.9)	(5.1)	(4.7)		
Peer sociable[b]	−0.8	−0.7	0.7	−0.7	0.3	ns
	(1.8)	(2.8)	(3.2)	(2.8)		
Peer aggressive	3.1	4.1	−1.4	−1.2	0.7	ns
	(3.9)	(4.4)	(1.3)	(1.6)		
Peer isolated	0.4	0.4	−0.6	−0.8	0.3	ns
	(2.0)	(1.8)	(0.9)	(1.0)		
Peer like	−0.2	0.0	0.0	0.3	0.0	ns
	(1.1)	(1.0)	(1.0)	(1.0)		
Peer dislike	0.6	0.2	−0.7	−0.6	5.9	.02
	(0.1)	(1.2)	(0.6)	(0.7)		
Peer preference	−0.5	−0.1	0.3	0.5	1.2	ns
	(1.1)	(1.2)	(0.8)	(0.8)		
Peer impact	0.3	0.2	−0.6	−0.3	3.7	.06
	(1.0)	(1.0)	(0.7)	(0.9)		

Note: Standard deviations are in parentheses.
[a] F values are for group by time interactions.
[b] Mean scores on the child self-concept and the peer ratings are expressed as standardized scores (i.e., Z scores).
[c] Higher scores on the externalizing, internalizing, and total scales indicate more behavior problems.

There was no significant main effect for time or group by time interaction, indicating that peer reputations for both the aggressive and nonaggressive children remained stable over time.

In contrast to peer reputation data, the peer sociometric classifications indicated improvement following social skills training (see Table 13.2 for the distributions of aggressive and nonaggressive children by sociometric classifications). Prior to social skills training, 37% of the aggressive children and 2% of the nonaggressive children were rejected according to peer ratings. Following social skills training, 12% of the aggressive children and 2% of the nonaggressive children were rejected. There was a significant difference in the proportions of rejected children in the aggressive

Table 13.2. *Distribution of aggressive and nonaggressive children in sociometric classifications before and after social skills training*

Group classification	Aggressive		Nonaggressive	
	Pretest	Posttest	Pretest	Posttest
Popular	4	6	11	7
Average	4	4	6	1
Controversial	4	6	0	0
Rejected	15	5	1	1
Neglected	3	3	7	6
Other	13	17	16	26

group before and after social skills training, $Z = 2.20$, $p < .05$. There was no difference in the proportions of nonaggressive children rejected at pre- and post-tests.

The peer liking, disliking, social impact, and social preference scores indicated a main effect for group, multivariate $F(4, 55) = 7.84$, $p < .001$. The aggressive children were more disliked, less preferred, and had higher social impact scores than did nonaggressive children. The univariate analysis indicated a significant group by time interaction for dislike scores. The aggressive children were rated by peers as less disliked following social skills training, suggesting an improvement in the quality of their peer relations. Peer ratings for the nonaggressive children remained relatively constant.

These self, teacher, and peer reports present conflicting results. Aggressive children reported positive self-perceptions, whereas teachers rated aggressive children as having poorer self-concepts than did nonaggressive children, with no improvement following social skills training. Teachers rated aggressive children's behavior problems in the clinical range prior to social skills training and significantly improved following training. Peer ratings of aggressiveness did not reflect an improvement following social skills training. Peer sociometric ratings, however, indicated improvement in two domains: fewer aggressive children were rejected by their classmates, and they were less disliked following social skills training. While peers did not perceive aggressive children's behavior problems as improved, their perceptions of the aggressive children were less negative following social skills training. To understand these discrepancies, we conducted naturalistic playground observations of the aggressive children before and after social skills training.

Observations of playground interactions

For the playground observations, children were observed an average of 20, 23, and 24 minutes in the fall, winter, and spring, respectively. Individual times ranged

Table 13.3. *Mean times spent in solitary activities and peer contexts as a proportion of total time observed (percent)*

Group play state	Aggressive		Nonaggressive	
	Pretest	Posttest	Pretest	Posttest
Solitary	0.09	0.09	0.12	0.10
	(0.15)	(0.09)	(0.16)	(0.10)
Peer	0.64	0.73	0.65	0.72
	(0.23)	(0.18)	(0.21)	(0.19)

Note: Solitary activities included the following states: unoccupied, solitary engaged, and onlooker. Peer activities included parallel play, together, together touching, cooperative play, and fantasy play. States were summed across targets (same- and opposite-sex peers and same- and mixed-sex peer groups). Proportions do not total 1.00 because some states ("uncodable") and some targets ("unknown," "staff") were not included in the analysis. Standard deviations are in parentheses.

from 5 to 59 minutes. There were 26, 49, and 46 children filmed on the playground in the three observations periods, respectively. State and behavioral data on playground interactions were analyzed to assess the effectiveness of social skills training on the peer interactions of aggressive children and to compare their behavior with that of nonaggressive peers.

States

Proportional times for states were summed to form two categories: solitary (unoccupied, solitary engaged, and onlooker) and with peer (parallel, together, together touching, cooperative play, and fantasy play). These two states were the dependent variables in a 2 (group) × 2 (pre–post) repeated measures multivariate analysis of variance with equal cell weights.

Across all conditions and groups, children spent significantly more time with peers than in solitary activities. Children spent a mean of 10% of their observed time in solitary activities (95% confidence interval = 7.8 to 12.3) compared with 68% in peer contexts (95% confidence interval = 64.8 to 72.2). As shown in Table 13.3, there were no significant differences between the aggressive and nonaggressive groups for either peer or solitary activities, multivariate $F(2, 57) = 0.57$, $p > .55$. Nor was there, contrary to our expectation, a significant time by group interaction, multivariate $F(2, 57) = 0.40$, $p > .65$.

Behaviors

In the analysis of behavior observed on the playground, two types of aggression were examined: verbal and physical (including all valence ratings). These were

Table 13.4. *Mean rates (per minute) of verbal and physical aggression initiated by child and received from peers*

Group behavior	Aggressive		Nonaggressive	
	Pretest	Posttest	Pretest	Posttest
Initiated behavior				
Verbal	0.05	0.06	0.01	0.03
aggression	(0.08)	(0.09)	(0.02)	(0.06)
Physical	0.11	0.13	0.09	0.10
aggression	(0.15)	(0.13)	(0.12)	(0.10)
Received behavior				
Verbal	0.10	0.02	0.01	0.02
aggression	(0.02)	(0.03)	(0.03)	(0.05)
Physical	0.09	0.06	0.09	0.12
aggression	(0.13)	(0.07)	(0.09)	(0.16)

Note: Standard deviations are in parentheses.

identified as initiated by the aggressive and nonaggressive target children or received by them. Rates (events per minute) for verbal and physical aggression were entered as dependent variables in a 2 (group) by 2 (pre–post) repeated measures multivariate analysis of variance with equal cell weights. The MANOVA for initiated behavior indicated that the aggressive children were generally more aggressive than the nonaggressive children, multivariate $F(2, 46) = 3.41$, $p < .05$ (see Table 13.4). This was accounted for primarily by a significant group difference in verbal aggression, univariate $F(1, 47) = 6.96$, $p < .02$; there was no difference between groups in the rate of physical aggression, univariate $F(1, 47) = 1.03$, $p > .30$.

Contrary to expectations, rates of aggression did not change following social skills training: neither the main effect for time nor the time by group interaction was significant, multivariate $F(2, 46) = 0.98$, $p > .35$, and $F(2, 46) = 0.11$, $p > .85$, respectively.

Despite a greater frequency of initiated verbal aggression, aggressive children were no more likely than nonaggressive children to be the targets of aggression by peers, multivariate $F(2, 46) = 0.69$, $p > .50$, a situation that was stable over time, multivariate $F(2, 46) = 0.16$, $p > .85$, for the main effect; for the time by group interaction, multivariate $F(2, 46) = 1.35$, $p > .25$.

Discussion

The purpose of this study was to evaluate the effectiveness of social skills training with aggressive children from multiple perspectives: self-ratings, teacher ratings, peer ratings, and naturalistic observations of playground interactions. While aggressive children themselves did not indicate that they were experiencing problems at any time, teacher and peer ratings indicated that the aggressive children in this study exhibited a wide range of behavior problems and had negative peer reputations prior to social skills training. Teachers' ratings of the children indicated a significant improvement in aggressive behavior problems following social skills training. Peer ratings of aggressiveness, however, did not reflect a similar improvement. On the other hand, a substantial proportion of the aggressive children were no longer rejected by peers, and they were rated as less disliked by peers following social skills training. Our analyses of playground interactions present a picture of relatively stable behavior patterns. With social skills training, there was no change in the duration of time that aggressive children spent in the company of others or in the rate of aggression by these children or directed to these children.

To some extent, the results of this research replicate those of our earlier evaluations of social skills training: teachers indicated that social skills training was effective, whereas peer ratings of aggressive behavior did not reflect an improvement in the behavior problems of aggressive children. Although behavioral improvements were not evident in observations of playground behavior, perhaps there was an improvement in the classroom, which formed the basis for teachers' ratings. The social skills training was adult directed and somewhat didactic; therefore, skills may have readily generalized to the classroom and interactions with teachers. On the other hand, teachers' ratings may reflect their hopes and aspirations that these disruptive children would change with the panacea of social skills training. We are currently analyzing classroom observations of the aggressive children to determine whether there were actual behavioral changes in the context in which teachers' judgments were based.

Peer assessments of aggressive behavior problems indicate no change following social skills training. These peer assessments correspond to the observed stability in playground behaviors. Peers may be in a better position than teachers to judge aggressive children's behavioral improvements in peer interactions. In general, teachers may be relatively unaware of the nature of playground interactions and, therefore, unable to make judgments about the quality of peer behaviors. This lack of awareness by teachers is suggested by a subsequent analysis of the playground tapes. We found that teachers intervened in only 3% of bullying episodes on the playground and only appeared in the camera frame during an additional 11% of the episodes (Craig & Pepler, 1994).

While classmates' perceptions of behavior problems revealed no improvement, their sociometric ratings of aggressive children were not as negative following social skills training. Aggressive children appear to have become more accepted by their peers following the interventions. This parallels the improvement in teacher ratings. Classmates may also have based their ratings on improvements in behavior problems within the classroom, as there were no changes in observed playground behaviors. Several questions remain regarding the nature of aggressive children's playground interactions and the role of peers. Why do aggressive children continue to initiate aggressive interactions, even after extensive social skills training? Are there processes within the peer group that maintain aggressive children's involvement in coercive interactions with peers? Do negative peer reputations, hostile attributional biases, and alienation processes underlie the stability of reciprocally hostile interactions between aggressive children and their peers?

In this study, the effectiveness of social skills training was assessed, in part, by naturalistic observations on the playground, where aggressive children were expected to demonstrate their newly acquired skills. The transfer of skills from formal training sessions to naturalistic interactions appears to be more difficult than anticipated. There were no improvements in the rates of aggressive behaviors following social skills training. On the other hand, aggressive children were not isolated: they spent as much time with peers as did nonaggressive children. The nature of peer interaction, however, may provide a clue to the difficulty of ameliorating aggressive behavior problems. Aggression appears to be somewhat normative on the playground, being exhibited by both groups within the present study. While aggressive children were observed to be more verbally aggressive than were their peers, they were not much more physically aggressive than children identified by teachers as socially competent. Aggressive children physically attacked others about once every 5 minutes, whereas nonaggressive children attacked others about once every 6 minutes. Aggressive and nonaggressive children were equally likely to initiate or be the recipients of physical aggression. Given the ambient levels of aggression on the playground, it may be difficult for aggressive children to employ their newly acquired social skills. Future research must examine the processes within the peer group that may be responsible for sustaining coercive interactions on the playground.

Peer relations have been identified as a critical risk factor in the developmental course of antisocial behavior (e.g., Patterson, DeBarsyshe, & Ramsey, 1989). It follows that interventions with aggressive children must take into account negative peer influences by directly involving peers who comprise part of the problem. Social skills training has been utilized as an intervention to interrupt the negative socialization processes within the peer group. The basic tenet of social skills training is that providing aggressive children with critical social and social-cognitive skills will enable them to experience successful interactions with peers. The data emerging from this study suggest that processes associated with peer interaction are complex and may contribute to the problems of aggressive children. Consequently, social skills training for aggressive children may be inadequate unless it encompasses the peer group. Other researchers have begun to document the difficulties that aggressive children experience at the hands of their peers. Peer interactions involving aggressive children are reciprocally coercive, similar to their interactions within the family (Patterson, 1982). For example, Huesmann, Eron, and Guerra (1992) describe aggressive children being victimized at the hands of their peers. Interventions therefore must reflect the bidirectional nature of the coercive interaction and address not only the problematic behavior patterns of aggressive children, but also the behaviors of peers that may instigate, maintain, and/or exacerbate the antisocial behaviors of aggressive children.

The results of this study substantiate the call for a multiple systems perspective within interventions for aggressive children (Kazdin, 1987). The targeted problems must be clearly specified and relevant to the context in which change is expected. In the present study, social skills training was limited to an adult-directed group experience with other aggressive children. The change in teacher perceptions suggests that the targeted skills and program delivery may have been appropriate for improving behaviors in an adult-directed context but not adequate to transfer to the playground context where peer interactions are dominant.

One approach to studying the life history of antisocial individuals is to intervene in their developmental trajectory by targeting a putative risk factor (Tremblay, this volume). With this intervention study, we have attempted to interrupt the well-documented continuity of antisocial behaviors over time by addressing the peer problems of aggressive children. The intervention appears to be effective in changing aggressive children's behavior within a classroom context, as reported by teachers. Social skills training also ameliorated negative peer perceptions of aggressive children; however, it did not seem to improve classmates' ratings of aggressiveness or observed aggressiveness on the playground. At this point, we are pursuing several analyses of the observational data to explore this dilemma. First, there may be individual differences in responsiveness to the program that are obscured by group data. We know that a number of children were no longer rejected by their peers at the end of social skills training. Perhaps the peer interactions of these children will reflect improvement following social skills training. Second, we are examining qualitative features of aggressive and nonaggressive children's peer interactions. For example, are the interactions of aggressive children marked by more hostility and anger? If we can differentiate the qualities of positive and negative peer relations, this will provide direction for future interventions of this nature. Finally, we are continuing to explore the methodology of remote observations as a unique means of entering the world of aggressive children and understanding the complexities of their peer interactions.

NOTE

The research described in this chapter was funded by the Ontario Mental Health Foundation. We would like to thank the clinicians, teachers, children, and parents who assisted us in evaluating the Earlscourt Social Skills Group Program. We are also indebted to Susan Koschmider, Paul O'Connell, and Kirsten Madsen for their endless hours of observational coding. Reprints can be requested from Debra Pepler, Department of Psychology, York University, 4700 Keele Street, North York, Ontario, Canada M3J 1P3.

REFERENCES

Achenbach, T. M., and Edelbrock, C. (1986). *Manual for the Teacher's Report Form and Teacher Version of the Child Behavior Profile.* Burlington: University of Vermont, Department of Psychiatry.

Asher, S. R., & Dodge, K. A. (1986). Identifying children who are rejected by their peers. *Developmental Psychology, 22,* 444–449.

Cairns, R. B., & Cairns, B. D. (1991). Social cognition and social networks: A developmental perspective. In D. Pepler & K. Rubin (Eds.), *The development and treatment of childhood aggression* (pp. 389–410). Hillsdale, NJ: Erlbaum.

Cairns, R. B., Cairns, B. D., Neckerman, H. J., Gest, S. D., & Gariépy, J.-L. (1988). Social networks and aggressive behavior: Peer support or peer rejection? *Developmental Psychology, 24,* 815–823.

Capaldi, D. M. (1992). Co-occurrence of conduct problems and depressive symptoms in early adolescent boys: II. A 2-year follow-up at Grade 8. *Development and Psychopathology, 4,* 125–144.

Coie, J. D., & Dodge, K. A. (1988). Multiple sources of data on social behavior and social status in the school: A cross-age comparison. *Child Development, 59,* 815–829.

Coie, J. D., & Kupersmidt, J. B. (1983). A behavioral analysis of emerging social status in boys' groups. *Child Development, 54,* 1400–1416.

Craig, W. M., & Pepler, D. J. (1994). Naturalistic observations of bullying and victimization in the school yard. Manuscript submitted for publication.

Dodge, K. A. (1980). Social cognition and children's aggressive behavior. *Child Development, 51,* 162–170.

Dodge, K. A. (1986). A social information processing model of social competence in children. In M. Perlmutter (Ed.), *Minnesota Symposia on Child Psychology* (pp. 77–125). Hillsdale, NJ: Erlbaum.

Dodge, K. A., Coie, J. D., Pettit, G. S., & Price, J. M. (1990). Peer status and aggression in boys' groups: Developmental and contextual analyses. *Child Development, 61,* 1289–1309.

Dodge, K. A., & Frame, C. L. (1982). Social cognitive biases and deficits in aggressive boys. *Child Development, 51,* 620–635.

Farrington, D. (1991). Childhood aggression and adult violence: Early precursors and later-life outcomes. In D. Pepler & K. Rubin (Eds.), *The development and treatment of childhood aggression* (pp. 411–448). Hillsdale, NJ: Erlbaum.

Hartup, W. W. (1989). Social relationships and their developmental significance. *American Psychologist, 44,* 120–126.

Huesmann, L. R., Eron, L. D., Lefkowitz, M. M., & Walder, L. O. (1984). The stability of aggression over time and generations. *Developmental Psychology, 20,* 1071–1078.

Huesmann, L. R., Eron, L. D., & Guerra, N. G. (1992, April). Victimization and aggression. Paper presented at the Society for Life History Research Meetings, Philadelphia.

Hymel, S., Wagner, E., and Butler, L. J. (1990). Reputational bias: View from the peer group. In S. R. Asher & J. D. Coie (Eds.), *Peer rejection in childhood.* Cambridge University Press.

Kazdin, A. E. (1987). Treatment of antisocial behavior in children: Current status and future directions. *Psychological Bulletin, 102,* 187–203.

Loeber, R. (1990). Development and risk factors of juvenile antisocial behavior and delinquency. *Clinical Psychology Review, 10,* 1–41.

Marsh, H. W., Smith, I. D., & Barnes, J. (1983). Multitrait-multimethod analyses of the Self-Description Questionnaire: Student–teacher agreement on multidimensional ratings of student self-concept. *American Educational Research Journal, 20,* 333–357.

Masten, A. S., Morison, P., and Pelligrini, D. S. (1985). A revised class play method of peer assessment. *Developmental Psychology, 21* (3), 523–533.

Olweus, D. (1979). Stability of aggressive reaction pattern in males: A review. *Psychological Bulletin, 86,* 852–872.

Parker, J. G., and Asher, S. R. (1987). Peer relations and later personal adjustment: Are low-accepted children at risk? *Psychological Bulletin, 102–103,* 357–389.

Patterson, G. R. (1982). *Coercive family process: A social learning approach,* Vol. 3. Eugene, OR: Castalia.

Patterson, G. R. (1986). Performance models for antisocial boys. *American Psychologist, 41* (4), 432–444.

Patterson, G. R., DeBarsyshe, B. D., & Ramsey, E. (1989). A developmental perspective on antisocial behavior. *American Psychologist, 44,* 329–335.

Pepler, D. J., & Craig, W. M. (1994). A peek behind the fence: Naturalistic observations of children using video cameras and remote microphones. Manuscript submitted for publication.

Pepler, D. J., King, G., & Byrd, W. (1991). A social-cognitively based social skills training program for aggressive children. In D. Pepler & K. Rubin (Eds.), *The development and treatment of childhood aggression* (pp. 411–448). Hillsdale, NJ: Erlbaum.

Pepler, D. J., King, G., Craig, W., Byrd, W., & Bream, L. (1992). Effectiveness of social skills training with aggressive children. Unpublished manuscript.

Rutter, M. (1990). Psychosocial resilience and protective mechanisms. In J. Rolf, A. Masten, D. Cicchetti, K. Nuechterlein, & S. Weintraub (Eds.), *Risk and protective factors in the development of psychopathology.* Cambridge University Press.

Snyder, J., Dishion, T. J., & Patterson, G. R. (1986). Determinants and consequences of associating with deviant peers during preadolescence and adolescence. *Journal of Early Adolescence, 6,* 29–43.

14   Early adolescent social influences on delinquent behavior

JOHN D. COIE, ROBERT TERRY, AUDREY ZAKRISKI,
AND JOHN LOCHMAN

The goal of this chapter is to examine the links between three constructs of potential predictive and clinical significance for the development of adolescent delinquent behavior: (1) early childhood aggressive behavior and poor peer relations, (2) the development of peer social networks in early adolescence, and (3) concurrent antisocial behavior and poor peer relations in early adolescence. Generally, these constructs have been investigated separately; however, for at least some children, they may be part of the same developmental process. Therefore, following a short review of the literature pertaining to each of these areas, we will present our own data in answer to the following questions suggested by this literature:

1. What is the general structure of peer networks in early adolescence? Are there developmental differences in the way these peer networks form?
2. Are there peer cliques that can be identified as consisting of individuals who are more likely to engage in deviant behavior? If so, what are the behavioral and social relational correlates that distinguish these cliques from more normative peer cliques?
3. What are the implications of early childhood antisocial behavior and poor peer relations for the development of adolescent delinquency in the context of the adolescent peer network environment? That is, does a greater likelihood of delinquency arise out of the formation of these deviant peer cliques, or is the deviant peer clique an epiphenomenon of both earlier childhood antisocial behavior and poor peer relations, which themselves are the precipitating factors in the development of adolescent delinquency?

A useful developmental framework for answering these questions has been suggested by Cairns and Cairns (1991). Their analysis suggests that only a multilevel approach to these questions is satisfactory because behavior results from a hierarchy of influences in which development generally is constrained. We intend to focus on three levels of constraining influences. The first is the general propensity of individuals, apart from higher order social influences, to engage in childhood aggressive

229

behavior and have difficulty relating to their peers. The second is the influence of the peer social network during early adolescence as it shapes and organizes the behavior of the individual. The structure of social relations among adolescents and the location of individuals within the peer network may have important behavioral consequences for both the individual and the peer system as a whole. Finally, there are cultural-ecological-economic factors that may transcend organizing efforts on the part of the individual and the immediate social group. It is our goal to identify which of these three levels of behavioral influences and constraints are most likely to precipitate the formation of adolescent delinquent behavior, by simultaneously modeling the dynamic nature of these three levels of the system. These issues will be taken up throughout the chapter as we address each of the questions, in turn.

The genesis of delinquent behavior

The causal roles of family and individual characteristics on the development of delinquent behavior have been well documented (Farrington & West, 1990; Patterson, DeBaryshe, & Ramsey, 1989). The significance of peer factors is less well established. Several investigators have demonstrated that deviant peer associations have a significant influence on adolescent delinquency (Cairns, Cairns, & Neckerman, 1989; Elliott, Huizinga, & Ageton, 1985; Patterson, Capaldi, & Bank, 1991). An alternative perspective is that association with deviant peers is merely a secondary outcome of the processes that produce delinquency.

These two diverging viewpoints share the belief that associating with deviant peers is quite common for delinquents. It has been well documented that children at risk for delinquency have poor social skills (Glueck & Glueck, 1950; Klein & Crawford, 1967), experience academic failure (Dishion, Loeber, Stouthammer-Loeber, & Patterson, 1983; Hawkins & Lishner, 1987), and are rejected by the peer group at large (Kupersmidt & Coie, 1990; Parker & Asher, 1987). Research suggests that because of these factors, rejected, aggressive children associate with other deviant peers (Dishion, Patterson, Stoolmiller, & Skinner, 1991; Snyder, Dishion, & Patterson, 1986).

The process and outcome of this association, however, is where disagreement emerges. Some suggest that deviant children associate with deviant peers just because they are similar or because they do not have any other options. This benign process of "association by default" is thought to have no impact on a child's inevitable involvement in delinquency, a process that was already set in motion by individual dispositions and family influences at a much earlier age (Hirschi, 1969). Hirschi first proposed this idea in his social control theory. He believed that weak bonds to conventional society were the causes of delinquency and that association with deviant peers was merely a secondary outcome of that process. His original theory did not see delinquents as particularly bonded to their delinquent peers and contained no causal role for these deviant peer associations. Subsequent modifications of this theory (Elliott et al., 1985) have suggested that in addition to the weak bonds with conventional society, delinquents do form bonds with deviant peers, and consequently these associations generate and reinforce delinquent behavior.

Those who argue for the role of deviant peer associations in the development of delinquency suggest an active process of association, which has been described by Patterson (Patterson, Littman, & Bricker, 1967; Patterson, Reid, & Dishion, 1992) as "shopping." According to this model, children at risk for delinquency come to associate together because they maximize social reinforcements for each other. Patterson argues that this reinforcement both sustains and accelerates an already existing developmental process toward delinquency. In an institutional setting, for example, delinquent peers have been shown to provide considerable positive reinforcement for both deviant behavior and punishment for socially conforming acts (Buehler, Patterson, & Furniss, 1966).

Several longitudinal studies provide support for the role of deviant peers in promoting adolescent delinquency. Patterson and colleagues (Patterson et al., 1991) have demonstrated the predictive contribution of deviant peer associations to adolescent antisocial behavior. In turn, Dishion (Dishion et al., 1991) demonstrated that childhood peer relations (social preference) and academic performance are important predictors of early adolescent deviant peer associations and continue to be viable predictors even when earlier deviant peer associations are a part of the prediction model.

Further support for the value of peer factors in predicting adolescent conduct problems comes from some of our own longitudinal research (Coie, Lochman, Terry, & Hyman, 1992). Third-grade peer rejection and aggressiveness each predicted a composite measure of externalizing problems in sixth grade, using outcome data combined from parent and teacher reports, as well as self-reports. Measures of deviant peer associations were not obtained for the two consecutive sixth-grade cohorts that were assessed in that study, so it was not possible to determine whether the deviant peer construct served as a partial mediator between the two childhood variables and adolescent problem behavior.

Moffitt (1993) has suggested that deviant peer associations may be related to the large portion of delinquency that occurs among adolescents who commit these offenses primarily during adolescence, but she argues that this may not be the case for those adolescents who have begun their antisocial careers at a much earlier age. The latter delinquents she refers to as the life-course-persistent group and believes them to be at early risk because of a combination of biological and family factors. They are the ones most likely to continue their antisocial behavior into adulthood, whereas the adolescence-limited group largely desist as they move from the adolescent peer culture into the world of jobs and marriage. As a group, the adolescence-limited group, or the late starters in Patterson's terms, are less likely to have childhood peer problems, and thus are more likely to belong to groups that would have a deviant influence on their behavior.

This distinction between two groups of adolescents who are likely to exhibit delinquent behavior is a useful one for thinking about the role of deviant peer associations and adolescent conduct problems. It leads to the hypothesis that deviant peer groups are much more important to time-limited delinquency and possibly related to less serious forms of criminal activity, generally. The early starters, Moffitt's life-course-persistent group, may be less likely to be central members of any peer group, and deviant peer associations may not be very much of a causal factor in their adolescent delinquency. These ideas throw open the possibility of several relations between childhood peer relations and aggression, adolescent delinquency, and peer social networks. A recent study by Farrington illustrates some of this complexity. Farrington's (1990) efforts to predict delinquency yielded six significant predictors; deviant peer association was not one of them. It was only when different patterns of delinquency were examined (Farrington & Hawkins, 1991) that deviant peer association became predictive – specifically, participation in delinquency but not early-onset or persistent delinquency.

Adolescent social networks

In the first study to be described, we investigated the social networks of sixth- and eighth-grade adolescents and the way that concurrent behavior and total-group peer social relations seem to be involved in the structure of such networks.

The eighth-grade sample for this study consisted of 578 children from four inner-city schools. The sample was predominantly African-American (90%), of lower middle to low socioeconomic status (SES) (65% eligibility for free and reduced-fee lunch program), and 51% female. The sixth-grade sample consisted of 635 children with approximately the same demographic characteristics.

We used a variant of the standard sociometric questionnaire to assess the peer group estimates of an individual's behavioral and social relational profile, as well as the structure of the peer social network. Using an unlimited nomination technique, adolescents were asked to nominate as many grademates in their school as "fit" various descriptions of sociometric likability and dislikability, behavioral traits (aggressiveness, leadership, shyness), and other social constructs (unhappy, trustworthy). The data were then optimally scaled using an item–response theory model because both theory and research suggest that modeling interindividual differences in perceptual biases when making choice judgments can drastically reduce construct measurement error (Cronbach, 1955; Terry, 1992).

To assess the peer social network, these same adolescents were asked to mark the names of peers that they hang out with, as well as the names of those peers who hang out with other kids who get into trouble (Dishion et al., 1991). To derive the number of peer cliques within each school, we used a q-type factor analysis with oblique rotation on a correlation matrix that indexed the extent to which each dyadic pair was consistently named as a pair that hangs out together (Terry, 1989). That is, a third person, when nominating who they hang out with, will as a consequence also nominate others who may hang out with each other through their association with the nominee. If a particular dyadic nomination pattern is consistent across all other individuals in the sample, then a perfect correlation between the dyadic partners is obtained, indicating that the dyadic partners do in fact hang out with each other in the consensus view of others in the sample.

This factor analytic technique placed multiple individuals in the same clique if their mutual dyadic partnerships were sufficiently correlated. The same factor analysis was used to determine the extent to which each member belongs to a clique through the reference structure loadings. The loadings of subjects on clique factors indicate the unique relationship that individuals have with other clique members, after partialing out that relationship due to overlapping degrees of membership in other cliques. A subject's loading on any given clique may be thought of as the extent to which he or she is a central member in that clique. These loadings provide a continuous index of "clique centrality" in contrast to Cairns, Cairns, Neckerman, Gest, and Gariépy's (1988) use of categories such as nuclear, secondary, and peripheral membership. Our continuous index maintains the fuzzy nature of clique categorization, recognizing that adolescents can belong to more than one peer clique with varying degrees of centrality (Terry, 1989). Given the sample size and the significance of individual loadings, a loading of $r = .25$ or above was considered sufficient to index categorical membership in a peer clique. All cliques were constrained to have at least three participating members to be defined as a clique, in accordance with standard social network theory (Cartwright & Harary, 1956).

To assess the degree of deviancy of peer cliques, we identified the extent to which each of the identified social cliques was composed of kids who get into trouble. This was achieved by taking the correlation between subjects' scores on "hangs around with kids who get into trouble" and their loadings on each clique (the index of central participancy in each clique). Deviant peer groups were designated as those with a statistically significant positive correlation. An individual's deviancy score was defined as the product of his or her degree of membership in a clique and the clique's deviancy index, summed across all cliques. Thus, the individual deviancy index models not only the degree of deviance of a particular clique, but the strength of an individual's centrality in such a group. This approach differs from the index used by both Elliot et al. (1985) and Dishion et al. (1991), which does not take into account the degree of clique participation by the individual and is based on the individual's reputation for hanging around with those who get into trouble, rather than on the agreement of that group's members that the individual is one of them.

Our data confirmed the existence of identifiable and separable peer cliques, ranging from the largest clique of 27 participating members to the smallest possible minimum clique size of 3. The schools, which averaged about 152 children in each grade level, had an average of 18 cliques per grade. These peer cliques had an average of 8 members; there were no systematic differences in clique size by either school or grade, after the population size was taken into account. Most of the adolescents were identified as being members of a clique; only 7% of the student body were isolates. With the exception of one school that had a greater percentage

Table 14.1. *Descriptive characteristics of peer networks by school and grade*

	School (grade)							
	A		D		G		T	
	(6)	(8)	(6)	(8)	(6)	(8)	(6)	(8)
Population size	127	128	230	173	149	121	129	156
Total number of peer cliques	19	15	27	21	19	8	19	17
Mean clique size	6.1	8.0	8.0	8.0	7.4	14.6	6.2	8.1
Max. clique size	10	19	16	20	14	27	9	17
Min. clique size	3	4	4	3	3	7	3	4
% Isolates	6.3	6.3	5.7	3.5	5.4	3.3	9.3	12.2
Total number of deviant peer cliques	4	3	6	2	2	2	2	4
% sample in deviant peer cliques	20.5	24.2	25.2	11.0	14.1	32.2	8.5	16.7

of isolates, there were no systematic grade or school differences in numbers of social isolates. This fits with Cairns and Cairns's (1991) suggestion that most adolescents are associated with some peer group. Table 14.1 contains more detailed information on the clique structure of the schools.

We next analyzed the extent to which some of these peer cliques could be considered as deviant. Across all the schools, about 18% of the peer cliques identified within each social network could be considered to be deviant because of the significant correlation between the *trouble* item and the peer clique loadings. These correlations ranged from $r = .82$, for one particularly deviant peer clique, to a low of $r = .12$ for one of the milder deviant peer cliques in one of the larger schools. To rule out the possibility that the extent of peer clique deviancy is a function merely of the size of the peer clique, we analyzed the correlation between clique size and the individual deviant peer index score within each peer group. The average correlation was $r = -.11$, which was not significant. Most importantly, the range of the correlations was from $r = .40$ in one school (indicating that larger peer cliques were more deviant) to $r = -.78$ in another (indicating that smaller peer cliques were more deviant). Thus, clique size had no apparent relation to deviancy.

Although our primary interest in these cliques was with deviancy, one theory about clique formation is the "birds of a feather" idea. To investigate the validity of

Table 14.2. *Intraclass correlations as an index of within-clique similarity on selected behavioral and social attributes by school and by grade*

Attribute	Grade		School			
	6	8	A	D	G	T
Aggression	.16	.35	.13	.38	.34	.19
Social preference	.14	.27	.19	.19	.28	.17
Social visibility	.18	.25	.18	.22	.23	.24
Deviant	.68	.68	.67	.72	.77	.56
Loner	.07	.07	.12	.07	.06	.04
Unhappy	.11	.09	.11	.07	.13	.09
Leadership	.12	.21	.16	.16	.22	.21

Note: All intraclass correlations are significant at the $p < .05$ level except for those pertaining to being a loner or unhappy.

this idea, we examined the extent to which adolescents in the same peer clique were described by their peers as having similar social characteristics. Intraclass correlations were computed that indexed the extent to which children of similar characteristics hung around together. Table 14.2 contains these correlations. In general, they suggest that adolescents within cliques are more similar to each other than to adolescents in other peer cliques on all behavioral and social indices other than being a loner or being unhappy. Interestingly, it was the characteristics of being considered deviant and aggressive that best fit this "birds of a feather" theory. Social preference and leadership were characteristics that did not fit the theory as well, and this makes sense when one considers that almost all groups have leaders, and popularity may be related to centrality of group membership. Our results suggest less within-cluster similarity than that found by Cairns et al. (1988). This discrepancy can be explained by the fact that the Cairns et al. (1988) study computed intraclass correlations for only the nuclear members of each social clique (about 33% of the total peer group). We included all participating, identifiable members of peer cliques in our computation of these correlations (93% of the total peer group). Because nuclear members of a peer group are likely to be more similar to each other than to secondary or peripheral members, this discrepancy is readily explained by the way the homophily theory was tested.

As Table 14.2 reflects, there were grade-level differences in this phenomenon of clique homogeneity. The sixth-grade cliques were less homogeneous than those identified in eighth grade. One reason for this may be that the sixth grade is a period of social transition for these adolescents since they have just moved from elementary school to middle school in this school system. As a result of 13 elementary schools merging into 4 middle schools, sixth graders are less likely to know each other, and cliques may be formed initially on the basis of class assignments. As they get to know each other better, these middle school students may gravitate to peer cliques on the basis of behavioral similarity (Newcomb, 1961; Schachter, 1959). A second explanation, which is at the heart of the theory that deviant peer associations lead to increased antisocial behavior, is that clique members actually become more similar in their behavior the longer they associate with each other.

Another explanation is that these group similarities are more apparent than real. In other words, adolescents acquire reputations based on the people with whom they associate. Group reputations may be established by the characteristics of the more central and visible members of a peer group and thus influence the social image of other members. It is likely that all three factors are, to some extent, codetermining influences on this process; however, given the cross-sectional nature of our data, it was not possible to test these ideas. We are currently collecting longitudinal data on the sixth-grade sample that will allow us to more fully address this question. The significance of differences in school social climate for deviant peer group influence was suggested in our data by the fact that two schools, D and G, had greater clique homogeneity on aggression than did the other two. Each of these schools had large cliques that were described as highly aggressive and deviant, whereas this was not the case in the other two schools. One clique in school D had a correlation between the "gets into trouble" item and individual clique loadings of $r = .82$, while in school G, a correlation of $r = .68$ was obtained. This indicates a very strong relation between centrality of clique membership and getting into trouble. These cliques had 19 and 24 members, respectively. In the other two schools, it was harder to identify major deviant gangs; instead, kids who get into trouble were distributed across more of the peer cliques in these other schools. The presence of large, aggressive, and delinquent gangs may make for a radically different climate of peer influence on deviant behavior across the two sets of schools.

The next question we addressed was whether deviant and nondeviant cliques differed on behavioral characteristics other than trouble making. Further analyses were undertaken to establish whether there were mean differences in behavior or social preference between deviant peer cliques and more normal peer cliques. Somewhat surprisingly, mean differences on other items suggested that members of deviant peer cliques were more socially preferred, $F(1, 1197) = 26.83$, $p < .01$, had greater social visibility, $F(1, 1197) = 125.783$, $p < .01$, were less unhappy, $F(1, 1197) = 13.05$, $p < .01$, and were seen as being leaders, $F(1, 1197) = 4.43$, $p < .04$. Not surprisingly, they also were seen as being more aggressive, $F(1, 1197) = 280.60$, $p < .01$. Table 14.3 contains the means for these contrasts. There were also developmental differences in the contrasts between deviant and nondeviant group members. In sixth grade, deviant group members were perceived as more unhappy and less aggressive than their eighth-grade counterparts.

Some of these behavioral differences between members of deviant and nondeviant cliques were qualified by statistical interactions involving schools. In the two schools described earlier as having large, homogeneously deviant gangs, the deviant

Table 14.3. *Mean behavioral and social profiles of deviant and nondeviant peer cliques*

Attribute	Deviant peer clique	Nondeviant peer clique
Social preference	0.34	− 0.07
Social visibility	0.65	− 0.15
Unhappiness	− 0.20	0.04
Leadership	0.11	− 0.02
Aggression	0.92	− 0.21

peer group members were more well liked by their peers than were deviant peer group members in the other two schools ($M = .47$ vs. $M = .13$). These are interesting findings and reflect the fact that deviant peer groups do not have the same social implications for all school settings. There are several plausible explanations for the strong connection between popularity and deviant gang membership in the two schools. One explanation is that the school culture is one in which aggression and delinquent activity is generally admired. A second explanation is that the very size and coherence of these large gangs makes it possible for strong mutual liking within the groups to be sufficient to make the overall social preference score appear to be high relative to the rest of the student body.

Pathways to delinquency

The goal of this second study was to test a developmental model of adolescent delinquency in the context of different competing levels of influence on the development of behavior. We analyzed longitudinal data on 151 girls and 133 boys from the third grade until approximately $1\frac{1}{2}$ years after they finished the eighth grade. Sociometric measures of peer status and aggressiveness were obtained in the third grade (see Coie, Dodge, & Coppotelli, 1982). When these children reached the eighth grade, they were again assessed on these same two constructs. Peer social network data were also collected along with the deviant peer indices described previously.

Delinquency data in the form of frequency of police contacts were obtained for each of these children throughout the longitudinal observation period. For the purposes of our analyses, the time frame during which these delinquent episodes took place was broken down into two periods: (1) just after third-grade sociometric assessment until just prior to the eighth-grade sociometric assessment; and (2) for the $1\frac{1}{2}$-year period just after this eighth-grade assessment. For our analyses, we defined *arrest* as the occurrence of a police contact during the specified time frame, rather than adjudication status, since it is common practice to release youthful offenders after arrest rather than to adjudicate.

During the $6\frac{1}{2}$ years of follow-up, 7.3% of the girls and 10.8% of the boys were

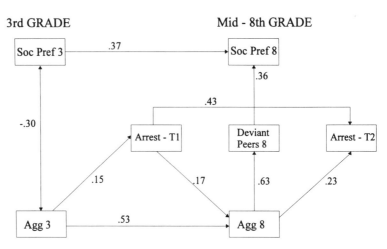

Figure 14.1. Structural model of the development of delinquency for males ($N = 133$). The variables are Soc Pref 3 = social preference in Grade 3; Soc Pref 8 = social preference in Grade 8; Arrest – T1 = arrest prior to Grade 8; Deviant Peers – 8 = deviant peers index; Arrest – T2 = arrest after Grade 8; Agg 3 = aggression in Grade 3; and Agg 8 = aggression in Grade 8.

involved in an incident serious enough to have been arrested by the police. To model longitudinally the development of delinquency, we used path-analytic techniques (Bollen, 1989) to depict simultaneously the influences of earlier social variables on adolescent delinquency and the influences of delinquency on the formation of peer social networks. Developmental models for boys and girls were tested separately.

Figure 14.1 contains the fitted model for boys. Standard goodness-of-fit indices reveal an acceptable fit to the data, which accounts for about 3% of the pre–eighth grade delinquency and about 30% of the subsequent delinquency. The model indicates that third-grade aggression status is significantly predictive of early adolescent delinquency, with early childhood social relations having no effect. Subsequent delinquency is more complicated, suggesting direct influences of both earlier delinquency and eighth-grade aggression status, as well as indirect effects of third-grade aggression status and early delinquency. These indirect effects can be seen to influence later delinquency primarily through the maintenance of aggressive behavior from third to eighth grade. Of greater interest for this chapter is the negligible apparent influence of associations with deviant peers on later delinquency and the fact that early delinquency has only an indirect connection to later involvement with deviant peers. It would seem that associating with deviant peers is an epiphenomenon of being aggressive. This suggests that behavioral similarities may lead to the formation of deviant peer cliques, rather than deviant peer cliques leading to increased antisocial behavior. Even more surprising is the fact that membership in deviant peer cliques had a positive direct effect on general social status in the total peer group (social preference scores). In the context of these inner city middle schools, aggression and membership in deviant peer groups appear to enhance social status, rather than jeopardize it. This is somewhat in contradiction to Patterson's "shopping hypothesis," which suggests that children at risk for delinquency associate with each other to maximize their social reinforcement. In our data, social reinforcement seems to accrue not only from the immediate deviant peer group members, but possibly from the *total peer group as a whole.*

It is also somewhat surprising that social preference, both early and late, appears to have no influence, whether direct or indirect, on subsequent delinquent behavior. This model suggests that social preference serves as a marker variable for the underlying individual dispositions toward aggressive behavior; similarly, subsequent association with like-minded peers also serves as a marker variable for antisocial tendencies.

Because of a concern that the use of our derived peer deviancy index may have constrained the data to fit this particular model, we fit the model using the same measure of deviant peer association used by Dishion and colleagues, namely, total nominations on the "hangs around with kids who get into trouble" item. The overall look and fit of the model did not change substantially when we made this substitution. The only change in the model was a stronger relation from aggression in eighth grade to the deviant peer association variable. This is to be expected since our deviant peer index was specifically devised to describe the extent of participation in a deviant clique, and a less substantial correlation with aggressiveness was obtained because we "softened" the reputational association between aggressiveness and associating with deviant peers by mapping it onto the subjects' actual positions in the peer network. Thus, the more peripheral the member, the less would be the effect of secondary association with the aggression status of more central members.

Figure 14.2 provides the fitted model for girls. Standard goodness-of-fit indices revealed an acceptable fit to the data. The model accounts for about 2% of the pre–eighth-grade delinquency and about 8% of the subsequent observed delinquency. In general, our model for girls is much less predictive of subsequent delinquency than that for boys, no doubt because of the lower rate of arrest for girls. There was only a direct effect of aggressiveness in eighth grade that predicts subsequent delinquency. Previous delinquent behavior had only an indirect effect on subsequent delinquency, though it had a direct effect on eighth-grade aggression. In contrast to the boys, for whom early aggression predicted delinquency, it was negative third-grade peer status that significantly predicted early delinquency. Girls' early delinquent behavior, in turn, predicted poorer peer relations in eighth grade. As with boys, association with deviant peers again was determined by aggressiveness, but unlike the boys, deviant peer associations were unrelated to eighth-grade peer status.

To summarize, for girls, it appears that negative peer status in early childhood is

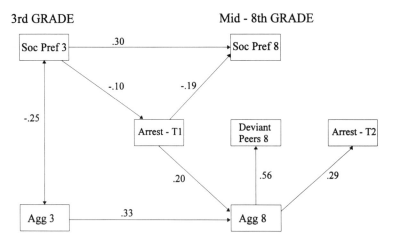

Figure 14.2. Structural model of the development of delinquency for females ($N = 151$). The variables are Soc Pref 3 = social preference in Grade 3; Soc Pref 8 = social preference in Grade 8; Arrest – T1 = arrest prior to Grade 8; Deviant Peers – 8 = deviant peers index; Arrest – T2 = arrest after Grade 8; Agg 3 = aggression in Grade 3; and Agg 8 = aggression in Grade 8.

likely to increase the likelihood of early delinquent behavior, which subsequently leads to further rejection and aggression. In turn, eighth-grade aggression is the primary influence on subsequent later delinquent behavior. Involvement in deviant peer groups seems to have little influence in the context of an individual's disposition for antisocial behavior.

Some cautions for this second study must be noted. As with any structural model, the risk of overfitting is always present (Cliff, 1983; MacCallum, Roznowski, & Necowitz, 1992). Another caution concerns the large number of models that can potentially be fit to these data (approximately 4^{21} models). It is a mistake to fit a single model to data and fail to investigate other substantively interesting and potentially viable models (Glymour, Scheines, Spirtes, & Kelly, 1987). Fortunately, because of the fairly large size of our data set compared with the size of our models, it is likely that our results will be fairly stable (see MacCallum et al., 1992).

The fact that social preference did not have any significant influence on police contact, either directly or indirectly, was surprising, given the findings of Dishion and colleagues (1991) and our own prediction data. One explanation for this failure may be found in a developmental phenomenon that is endemic to longitudinal studies such as this. Subjects change school systems or are retained in grade. Because of the nature of the social network data collection, for this study we were limited to that part of the sample who stayed in the school system and were not retained in grade. Unfortunately for this study, half of the subjects who were both aggressive and rejected in third grade, the group with the highest rate of middle school conduct problems (Coie et al., 1992), were retained in grade and were lost to these particular analyses. It is possible that the group whose delinquent careers would best fit the Patterson "shopping" model for deviant peer associations were not represented adequately in this study.

Conclusions

This chapter illustrates some of the complexity of attempting to trace the contributions of individual behavior, peer social network, and school context on early adolescent delinquency. The children of greatest interest do not all follow development paths that make it easy to track these influences. The presence of strong school context effects is hinted at in the data, but its impact could not be examined directly. While this is an important goal for future research, it is clear that it will be no small undertaking.

We have outlined a method for identifying adolescent peer cliques that is based on a consensus of the group members themselves, rather than on peer reputation. Using this method, it turns out that most adolescents in the predominantly inner-city, African-American middle school population have at least one primary membership in a peer clique; few true isolates were identified. Giordano's interviews with adolescents in similar peer contexts provide similar conclusions (Giordano & Cernkovich, 1991).

Within the adolescent peer social network itself, certain cliques stood out as containing a disproportionate share of adolescents who were aggressive or got into trouble. The contextual influence of school culture was evidenced by the fact that certain schools were more likely to contain large gangs of deviant adolescents while other schools did not.

In general, the peer cliques follow Cairns's concept of homophily, in that within-clique similarity of behavior and peer status was greater than across-clique similarity. Because of a developmental trend toward greater intergroup similarity with age, the possibility exists that a clique exercises its influence on members' behavior by peer pressure, modeling, and social reinforcement. It is also possible that alternative explanations such as greater self-selection into peer groups are possible. The fact that deviant peer association did not predict subsequent police contact but was itself predicted by aggressive behavior and indirectly by previous arrest, tends to support the latter explanation. Only longitudinal data could help differentiate among these alternatives.

One truly disturbing aspect of these findings is that deviant peer association leads to accepted peer status in eighth grade in these school contexts. The fact that peers do not perceive eighth-grade deviant peer group members as unhappy, in the way that their sixth-grade deviant peer group counterparts are, gives further reason for concern. Being deviant in later middle school is not associated with unhappiness. It is important to determine whether this is part of a general pattern of development that subsides in later adolescence and marks a temporary fascination with rebellious-ness and behavior that is unacceptable to adults, or whether this is a reflection of an increasing general acceptance of violence and antisocial activity in a population that has little perceived opportunity for becoming economically successful as adults.

In an earlier study (Coie et al., 1992), many of the males in the sample reported themselves to be involved frequently in aggressive activity. Thus, the concept of deviant peer association may not be the same as it would be in more middle-class peer contexts. Most peer cliques in this sample contained some kids who get into trouble, and as noted earlier, the proportion of cliques that would be considered deviant was quite high. Because of this high prevalence of aggression and conduct problems, generally, peer associations may have had less influence on delinquent outcomes for this sample. Instead, earlier police contact, along with personal aggressiveness, accounted for subsequent police contact in the male side of this peer culture. If this explanation is correct, it may suggest that there are features of our current models for explaining adolescent delinquency that do not fit what is happening in contemporary inner-city neighborhoods and schools. Violence may permeate these settings to such an extent that constructs like "deviant peers" have lost some of their meaning. That this is an age-related phenomenon and does not characterize all urban youth is reflected in the negative correlation, albeit moderate, between social preference and aggression at the third-grade level.

Although further replications are required before drawing too strong a conclusion from findings such as these, the results of this study suggest we should be cautious about our efforts to construct developmental models of delinquency and antisocial behavior that fail to include social contexts such as neighborhood and community setting. Much of our best longitudinal data has come from relatively stable commu-nities that do not reflect the levels of poverty that characterize our current urban underclass. Because of this, the models we develop from them may be quite misleading in describing the precise way that either biological or social processes influence antisocial behavior.

REFERENCES

Bollen, K. (1989), *Structural equations with latent variables*. New York: Wiley.
Buehler, R. E., Patterson, G. R., & Furniss, J. M. (1966). The reinforcement of behavior in institutional settings. *Behavior Research and Therapy, 4*, 157–167.
Cairns, R. B., & Cairns, B. D. (1991). Social cognition and social networks: A develop-mental perspective. In D. Pepler & K. Rubin (Eds.), *The development and treatment of childhood aggression* (pp. 249–278). Hillsdale, NJ: Erlbaum.
Cairns, R. B., Cairns, B. D., & Neckerman, H. J. (1989). Early school dropout: Configura-tions and determinants. *Child Development, 60*, 1437–1452.
Cairns, R. B., Cairns, B. D., Neckerman, H. J., Gest, S., & Gariépy, J.-L. (1988). Social networks and aggressive behavior: Peer support or peer rejection? *Developmental Psychology, 24*, 815–823.
Cartwright, D., and Harary, F. (1956). Structural balance: A generalization of Heider's theory. *Psychological Review, 63*, 277–292.

Cliff, N. (1983). Some cautions concerning the application of causal modeling methods. *Multivariate Behavioral Research, 18,* 115–126.

Coie, J. D., Dodge, K. A., & Coppotelli, H. (1982). Dimensions and types of social status: A cross-age perspective. *Developmental Psychology, 18,* 557–570.

Coie, J. D., Lochman, J., Terry, R., & Hyman, C. (1992). Predicting adolescent disorders from childhood aggression and peer relations. *Journal of Consulting and Clinical Psychology, 60,* 783–792.

Cronbach, L. J. (1955). Processes affecting scores on "understanding of others and assumed similarities." *Psychological Bulletin, 3,* 177–193.

Dishion, T. J., Loeber, R., Stouthamer-Loeber, M., & Patterson, G. R. (1983). Social skills deficits and male adolescent delinquency. *Journal of Abnormal Child Psychology, 12,* 37–54.

Dishion, T. J., Patterson, G. R., Stoolmiller, M., & Skinner, M. L. (1991). Family, school, and behavioral antecedents to early adolescent involvement with antisocial peers. *Developmental Psychology, 27,* 172–180.

Elliott, D. S., Huizinga, D., & Ageton, S. S. (1985). *Explaining delinquency and drug use.* Beverly Hills, CA: Sage.

Farrington, D. P. (1990). Implications of criminal career research for the prevention of offending. *Journal of Adolescence, 13,* 93–113.

Farrington, D. P., & Hawkins, J. D. (1991). Predicting participation, early onset and later persistence in officially recorded offending. *Criminal Behavior and Mental Health, 1,* 1–33.

Farrington, D. P., & West, D. J. (1990). The Cambridge study in delinquent development: A long-term follow-up of 411 London males. In H. J. Kerner & G. Kaiser (Eds.), *Criminality: Personality, behavior and life history.* New York: Springer Verlag.

Giordano, P. C., & Cernkovich, S. A. (1991). *A theory of black adolescent social relations.* Paper presented at the annual meeting of the American Sociological Association, Cincinnati, OH.

Glueck, S., & Glueck, E. (1950). *Unraveling juvenile delinquency.* Cambridge, MA: Harvard University Press.

Glymour, C., Scheines, R., Spirtes, P., & Kelly, K. (1987). *Discovering causal structure: Artificial intelligence, philosophy of science, and statistical modeling.* Orlando, FL: Academic.

Hawkins, J. D., & Lishner, D. M. (1987). Schooling and delinquency. In E. H. Johnson (Ed.), *Handbook on crime and delinquency prevention* (pp. 179–221). New York: Greenwood Press.

Hirshchi, T. (1969). *Causes of delinquency.* Berkeley: University of California Press.

Klein, M. W., & Crawford, L. Y. (1967). Groups, gangs, and cohesiveness. *Journal of Research in Crime and Delinquency, 4,* 63–75.

Kupersmidt, J. B., & Coie, J. D. (1990). Preadolescent peer status, aggression, and school adjustment as predictors of externalizing problems in adolescence. *Child Development, 61,* 1350–1362.

MacCallum, R. C., Roznowski, M., & Necowitz, L. B. (1992). Model modifications in covariance structure analysis: The problem of capitalization on chance. *Psychological Bulletin, 111,* 490–504.

Moffitt, T. E. (1993). Adolescence-limited and life-course-persistent antisocial behavior: A developmental taxonomy. *Psychological Review, 100,* 674–701.

Newcomb, T. M. (1961). *The acquaintance process.* New York: Holt, Rinehart, & Winston.

Parker, J. G., & Asher, S. R. (1987). Peer relations and later personal adjustment: Are low accepted children "at risk"? *Psychological Bulletin, 102,* 357–389.

Patterson, G. R., Capaldi, D., & Bank, L. (1991). An early starter model for predicting delinquency. In D. J. Pepler & K. H. Rubin (Eds.), *The development and treatment of childhood aggression.* Hillsdale, NJ: Erlbaum.

Patterson, G. R., DeBaryshe, B. D., & Ramsey, E. (1989). A developmental perspective on antisocial behavior. *American Psychologist, 44,* 329–335.

Patterson, G. R., Littman, R. A., & Bricker, W. (1967). Assertive behavior in children: A step toward a theory of aggression. *Monographs of the Society for Research in Child Development, 32* (5, Serial No. 113).

Patterson, G. R., Reid, J. B., & Dishion, T. J. (1992). *Antisocial boys.* Eugene, OR: Castelia.

Schachter, S. (1959). *The psychology of affiliation.* Stanford, CA: Stanford University Press.

Snyder, J. J., Dishion, T. J., & Patterson, G. R. (1986). Determinants and consequences of associating with deviant peers during preadolescence and adolescence. *Journal of Early Adolescence, 6,* 20–43.

Terry, R. (1989, April). *A psychometric approach to identifying social cliques.* Paper presented at the biennial meeting of the Society for Research in Child Development, Seattle, WA.

Terry, R. (1992). A probabilistic choice model of person perception: Implications for sociometric assessment. Unpublished manuscript, Duke University.

IV Deviance, crime, and discipline

15 The long-term effect of punitive discipline

JOHN H. LAUB AND ROBERT J. SAMPSON

The motivation for this chapter stems from our attempt to integrate three diverse areas of research. The first concerns families and delinquency. Over the past two decades, theorists, researchers, and policy makers have refocused attention on the role of the family in explaining delinquency (see, e.g., Farrington, 1987; Hirschi, 1969, 1983; Loeber & Stouthamer-Loeber, 1986; McCord, 1991; and Patterson, 1980). Our work contributes to this growing body of knowledge by examining the effect of punitive discipline by parents on juvenile delinquency.

The second area we explore relates to the effect of childhood and adolescent experiences on later adult outcomes. The idea that childhood experiences have important ramifications in later adult life is supported by a rich body of empirical research (e.g., Caspi, 1987; Franz, McClelland, & Weinberger, 1991; McCord, 1979; Robins, 1966). Surprisingly, this substantive area has been ignored by most criminologists, especially sociological criminologists. In our prior research (Sampson & Laub, 1990), we have demonstrated that antisocial behavior in childhood and early adolescence (e.g., juvenile delinquency, conduct disorder, persistent temper tantrums) is linked to later adult outcomes across a variety of life domains including behavior in the military, general deviance and criminality, economic dependency, educational attainment, employment history, and marital experiences. In this chapter, we explore the long-term effects of punitive discipline by parents on later crime.

The third area we explore is social control, especially punishment by the state. Most criminological studies have examined either informal social control (e.g., family and school) or formal social control (e.g., arrest and imprisonment) (see studies by Hirschi, 1969, and Smith & Gartin, 1989, for specific examples). The theoretical model we have developed in a larger work (Sampson & Laub, 1993) seeks to examine both. Following Elder (1975, 1985), we differentiate the life course of individuals on the basis of age and argue that the important institutions

247

of social control vary across the life course. In this chapter, we examine the long-term effects of punitive discipline by the state.

The longitudinal data we use come from the classic study by Sheldon and Eleanor Glueck, *Unraveling Juvenile Delinquency* (1950), plus follow-ups (see Glueck & Glueck, 1968). We turn next to a brief description of these data.

Description of the data

The Gluecks' prospective study of the formation and development of criminal careers was initiated in 1940 and involved a sample of 500 delinquents and 500 nondelinquents (officially defined). The delinquent sample contained persistent delinquents, white males, age 10 to 17, recently committed to one of two correctional schools – the Lyman School for Boys in Westboro, Massachusetts, and the Industrial School for Boys in Shirley, Massachusetts. The nondelinquent sample, also white males, age 10 to 17, was drawn from the public schools in the city of Boston. Nondelinquent status was determined on the basis of official record checks and interviews with parents, teachers, local police, social workers, recreational leaders, and the boys themselves. The Gluecks' sampling procedure was designed to maximize differences in delinquency and by all accounts appears to be successful; for instance, the average number of convictions in the delinquent sample was 3.5 (Glueck & Glueck, 1950).

These boys were also matched on a case-by-case basis according to age, ethnicity, general intelligence, and low-income residence – all classical criminological variables thought to influence both delinquency and official reaction. As to age, the delinquents averaged 14 years, 8 months, and the nondelinquents 14 years, 6 months, when the study began. With respect to ethnicity, one-fourth of both groups were of English background, another fourth Italian, a fifth Irish, less than a tenth old American, Slavic, or French, and the remaining Near Eastern, Spanish, Scandinavian, German, or Jewish. As measured by the Wechsler-Bellevue Test, the delinquents had an average IQ of 92 and nondelinquents 94. Finally, both the delinquents and nondelinquents grew up in lower-class neighborhoods of central Boston. These neighborhoods contained poverty, economic dependence, physical deterioration, and high rates of delinquency. Thus, both sets of boys grew up in similar high-risk environments with respect to poverty and exposure to delinquency and antisocial conduct.

A large amount of information on social, psychological, and biological characteristics, family life, school performance, work experiences, and other life events was collected on the delinquents and controls in the period 1940–1948. These data were collected through detailed investigations by the Gluecks' research team that included interviews with the subjects themselves and their families, employers, school teachers, neighbors, and criminal justice/social welfare officials.

The original sample was followed up at two different points in time – at age 25 and again at 32. This data collection effort took place from 1949 to 1965. As a result, extensive data are available for analysis relating to family life, employment history, military experiences, recreational activities, and criminal histories for matched subjects between the ages of 10 and 17, 17 and 25, and 25 and 32. Moreover, data are available for 438 of the original 500 delinquents (88%) and 442 of the original 500 nondelinquents (88%) at all three time periods (Glueck & Glueck, 1968). When adjusted for mortality, the follow-up success rate is approximately 92% – relatively high by current standards.

Key measures and methodological concerns

The two key measures we use in this paper are *father's erratic, harsh, and threatening discipline* and *mother's erratic, harsh, and threatening discipline*. Note that these discipline practices were not directly observed by the Gluecks' research team, but rather were inferred from the interview materials and the record checks previously mentioned. (For more details, see Glueck & Glueck, 1950, pp. 41–53.) These specific measures were constructed by summing three variables tapping the discipline and punishment practices of the mother and father. The first constituent variable concerns the use of physical punishment by the parent and refers to rough handling, strappings, and beatings eliciting fear and resentment in the boy – not to casual or occasional slapping that was unaccompanied by rage or hostility. The second constituent variable measures threatening and/or scolding behavior by mothers or fathers that elicited fear in the boy. The third component taps erratic and harsh discipline; that is, if the parent was harsh and unreasoning, vacillated between strictness and laxity and was not consistent in control, or was negligent or indifferent with regard to disciplining the boy (Glueck & Glueck, 1962, p. 220). Thus, the scales range from 1 to 4 and measure the degree to which parents used inconsistent disciplinary measures in conjunction with harsh, physical punishment and/or threatening or scolding behavior.

Some researchers have argued (e.g., Blumstein, Cohen, & Farrington, 1988, p. 66; McCord & McCord, 1959, p. 96) that the *Unraveling* data derived from the cross-sectional study suffer from "retrospective bias" in that the interviewers employed by the Gluecks to conduct the home investigations knew whether a family included a delinquent or nondelinquent sample member. Moreover, some of the questions in the home interview schedule relied on subjective ratings by the interviewers, and in certain instances, an evaluative coding scheme was utilized. Although a double-blind approach would have been the optimal design, it is important to reiterate that the Gluecks' strategy of data collection focused on multiple sources of information that were *independently* derived. Indeed, the Gluecks made use of detailed interviews with the boy chosen for the study, his parents, and his teachers. In conjunction with this home interview, the Gluecks' research team also conducted a field investigation by meticulously culling information from records of both public and private agencies that had any involvement with the family. The basic Glueck data, then, were the comparison, reconciliation, and integration of these multiple sources of data. In addition, information in the Glueck data that appears as subjective ratings by interviewers or that relies on evaluative coding schemes was, in fact, corroborated by specific accounts of behavior as recorded in the several sources of records examined and as gathered through self-reports during the home interview (see Vaillant, 1983, pp. 245–247).

Adult crime

From the detailed criminal history information collected by the Gluecks' research team, we created a variable assessing whether or not the subject had an official arrest during the follow-up periods (17 to 25 and 25 to 32). We also coded the criminal histories of each subject from age 32 until 45. A dichotomous variable was created to reflect an arrest for any crime in this period, excluding minor nonmoving auto violations (e.g., expired license/registration). These data came from the archives maintained by Dr. George E. Vaillant at Dartmouth Medical School and are based on official record searches in Massachusetts.

Empirical results: discipline in the family

In our earlier analyses of the cross-sectional data from the Gluecks' *Unraveling* study we found a strong positive effect of punitive discipline (i.e., erratic/harsh discipline) by both mothers and fathers on delinquency (whether measured by official records or unofficial boys', parents', and teachers' reports) (see Laub & Sampson, 1988; Sampson & Laub, 1993, for details). In this chapter, we ask a different question – What are the long-term effects for children and adolescents who experienced harsh physical punishment administered in an erratic manner by their parents?

In Table 15.1, we present data on the long-term relationship between punitive discipline and later crime. Examining the full sample, we see that there are strong relationships between punitive discipline in childhood and adolescence and arrests at ages 17 to 25, 25 to 32, and 32 to 45. However, when examined *within* the delinquent and control groups, these strong relationships for the most part disappear. These results suggest that adolescent delinquency mediates the long-term effect of family discipline on adult crime.

To explore this issue further, we performed a multivariate analysis that assessed the long-term independent effect of family discipline on later crime (see Sampson & Laub, 1993, for a full description of measures and analyses). Consistent with Table 15.1, the data showed that erratic parenting for both mothers and fathers had no effect on later crime once delinquency status and other control variables (e.g., supervision, early onset, parental rejection) were taken into account. More specifically, for both the delinquent and control group samples, unofficial delinquency had significant direct effects on arrest at ages 17 to 25, 25 to 32, and 32 to 45 (data not shown). On the other hand, family and individual-difference constructs generally had no effect on adult crime. Therefore, the major picture from the data is that

Table 15.1. *Long-term relationship between punitive family discipline in adolescence and later crime (percent arrested)*

| | Erratic/harsh discipline | | | |
| | Father's | | Mother's | |
Age	Low	High	Low	High
Full sample				
17–25	32	60*	34	60*
25–32	26	46*	27	47*
32–45	25	43*	23	46*
Delinquent sample				
17–25	73	77	79	75
25–32	61	61	60	61
32–45	52	56	45	59*
Control group sample				
17–25	17	24	17	26*
25–32	13	15	14	15
32–45	16	14	15	16

*$p < .05$.

the relationship of early family and child factors to adult crime is mediated by individual differences in adolescent delinquency.

Some researchers have argued that there are different sets of "causes" for participation in crime and continuation in offending (see Blumstein, Cohen, Roth, & Visher, 1986; Blumstein et al., 1988). For example, Farrington & Hawkins (1991) found that although troublesomeness at age 8 was predictive of participation in crime, this variable was not related to persistence in offending in adulthood. Similarly, Farrington and Hawkins (1991) found that low parental interaction, low commitment to school, and low verbal IQ in childhood were predictive of persistence in crime, but these variables were not the strongest predictors of participation. Our results seem to suggest that parental discipline is an important factor in explaining participation in crime as a juvenile, but not in understanding continuation in offending as an adult.

Discipline by the state

The next question is, What are the long-term effects of incarceration in custodial settings as a child or adolescent? By design, all of the delinquent subjects in the Gluecks' *Unraveling* study were incarcerated in either the Lyman School for Boys or the Industrial School for Boys at Shirley. The Lyman School was the first state reform school in the United States. George Briggs, the governor of Massachusetts, stated at the opening:

> Of the many and valuable institutions sustained in whole, or in part, from the public treasury, we may safely say, that none is of more importance, or holds a more intimate connection with the future prosperity and moral integrity of the community, than one which promises to take neglected, wayward, wandering, idle and vicious boys, with perverse minds and corrupted hearts, and cleanse and purify and reform them, and thus send them forth in the erectness of manhood and in beauty of virtue, educated and prepared to be industrious, useful and virtuous citizens. (Briggs, 1846, as quoted in Miller, 1991, p. 69)

Drawing on work by Miller (1991), McCord and McCord (1953), Ohlin, Coates, & Miller (1974), and an autobiography by a former Lyman inmate, Devlin (1985), one finds the reality of the Lyman School quite different from the lofty hopes expressed by Governor Briggs.

During the 1940s and 1950s (the time period of the Gluecks' study), the Lyman School was a large custodial institution containing 250 to 350 boys, primarily 13- to 15-year-olds. The institution was organized as a cottage system that was age segregated with houseparents. The structure of the institution was extremely regimented. For instance, inmates marched from their rooms to meals, and each day activities were segmented and marked by a series of bells and whistles. Credits were earned for privileges like cigarettes and ultimately parole. If an inmate misbehaved, staff could subtract any amount of credit from the boy's total. Physical punishment and verbal humiliations were common. For instance, boys were kicked in the rear for minor infractions like talking. Other physical punishments included hitting inmates with wooden paddles or straps on the soles of their bare feet. Cold showers were also used as a form of punishment and intimidation by the staff (see Miller, 1991, p. 96).

Most distressing were the unusual and downright cruel punishments imposed by the staff. For example, boys were forced to sit at their lockers for hours. Haircuts were also used as a form of punishment and punitive discipline. Jerome Miller, the former director of the Massachusetts Department of Youth Services, writes of staff reporting the need to "hit the little bastards for distance" (Miller, 1991, p. 94). Miller (1991, p. 94) goes on to describe "programs" that included "kneeling in a line in silence, scrubbing the floors with toothbrushes, or being made to stand or sit in odd, peculiarly painful positions." Along with these clearly "demeaning rituals," there were examples of sadistic discipline (e.g., having to drink from toilets or kneel for hours on the stone floor with a pencil under one's knees) (Miller, 1991, p. 95).

In this section we therefore focus on incarceration as a form of punitive discipline, especially on the length of confinement in juvenile and adult institutions. In the Gluecks' research design, all delinquent youths were incarcerated so there is no variation in the prevalence of institutionalization that can influence later development. There is, however, considerable variation among the delinquents in the *time* they served, not only in adolescence but in adulthood. For example, the average

Table 15.2. *Regression models predicting annualized frequency of crime per day free in adulthood: delinquent group* (n = 246)

Independent variable	Arrests per year free			
	Ages 17–25		Ages 25–32	
	β	*t* ratio	β	*t* ratio
Juvenile (age < 17)				
Arrests per year free	.24	4.31*	.22	3.56*
Unofficial delinquency	.14	2.67*	.10	1.88
Days incarcerated, age < 17	.04	0.75	−.06	−0.99
Young adult (ages 17–25)				
Exclusion risk	.43	8.03*	.24	4.19*
Income	.03	0.45	.01	0.23
Marriage	−.01	−0.14	.07	1.20
Commitment	−.01	−0.22	−.10	−1.61
Job stability	−.27	−4.57*	−.37	−5.75*
R^2		.41		.30

*$p < .05$.

time served during the juvenile period (up to age 17 in Massachusetts) was 553 days (about 18 months), though some individuals served about 4 months while others were incarcerated up to 7 years. To assess the relevance of incarceration, we calculated the actual number of days (not sentence length) each subject spent in a custodial institution as a juvenile (age < 17) and from 17 to 25 and 25 to 32.

As shown in our other work (Sampson & Laub, 1993), institutionalization was one of the two main factors explaining the likelihood that a delinquent youth would be excluded in the measurement of key social factors at the adult follow-up interviews. By examining the direct effects of incarceration on later crime, controlling for exclusion risk, we are in a position to separate the criminogenic effect of imprisonment from its role in sample selection.

The results shown in Table 15.2 are consistent in portraying the insignificant effects of juvenile incarceration on later criminal behavior. Consider first the results for crime frequency at ages 17 to 25 predicted by length of juvenile incarceration, controlling for criminal record (official and unofficial) and our social control dimensions. The standardized net effect of juvenile incarceration is insignificant and close to zero (.04). On the other hand, juvenile delinquency and exclusion risk have a positive effect, and job stability has a large negative effect ($\beta = -.27$, $p < .05$). Apparently, not only does juvenile incarceration have insignificant direct effects on later crime; its introduction to the models does not diminish the inhibitory effects of strong ties to work on adult crime.

A similar pattern develops when we consider the frequency of offending at ages 25 to 32 as a function of incarceration in adolescence. Namely, length of incarceration among those incarcerated as juveniles does not have a deterrent (or criminogenic) effect on later crime. Taken as a whole, Table 15.2 would seem to justify the conclusion that incarceration is unimportant in explaining crime over the life course. That is, it appears that in terms of its direct effects, length of incarceration is not a salient factor in the criminal careers of the Gluecks' sample.

However, the idea of cumulative continuity suggests a subtler effect – that adolescent delinquency and its negative consequences (e.g., arrest, official labeling, incarceration) "mortgage" one's future, especially later life chances molded by schooling and employment. In particular, there is theoretical support for hypothesizing that incarceration has negative effects on job stability and employment in adulthood (see esp. Bondeson, 1989; Freeman, 1987, 1992). Arrest and imprisonment are highly stigmatizing, and many jobs explicitly preclude the hiring of ex-prisoners (Glaser, 1969, pp. 233–238). As a result, those with lengthy incarceration records face structural impediments to establishing strong social ties to conventional lines of adult activity, regardless of their behavioral predispositions (see also Burton, Cullen, & Travis, 1987). By contrast, the absence or low frequency of institutionalization provides opportunities for prosocial attachments – especially at work – to emerge and solidify in adulthood.

In short, the logic of our theoretical perspective points to a possible *indirect* role of incarceration in generating future crime. To assess this possibility we examine the role of job stability at ages 17 to 25 and 25 to 32 as an intervening link between incarceration and adult crime. In doing so it is necessary to control for theoretically relevant factors in the etiology of job stability. As Gottfredson and Hirschi (1990) argue, those individuals with low self-control and tendencies toward crime are also same individuals likely to have unstable life histories in employment and other conventional lines of activity. Accordingly, we control for official arrest frequency, unofficial delinquency, and exclusion risk (i.e., sample selection bias).

Moreover, previous research (e.g., Robins, 1966; Vaillant, 1983) in conjunction with our own analyses (see Sampson & Laub, 1993) reveals the important role of drinking in understanding patterns of job stability. Heavy or abusive drinkers tend to either drift from job to job or be fired from their jobs at a rate much higher than nondrinkers. Excessive drinking during the same period that job stability is measured is thus also controlled, providing a very strict test for the independent effects of incarceration.

Table 15.3 shows that length of juvenile incarceration has a large negative effect on later job stability – regardless of prior crime, excessive drinking, and exclusion risk. Even though all the delinquent boys were incarcerated at some point, those incarcerated for a longer period of time had trouble securing stable jobs as they entered young adulthood as compared with delinquents with a shorter incarceration history. Since unofficial propensity to deviance, sample selection bias, drinking,

Table 15.3. *Regression model predicting job stability at ages 17 to 25: delinquent group* (n = 318)

Independent variable	Job stability	
	β	t ratio
Juvenile (age < 17)		
Arrests per year free	.01	0.20
Unofficial delinquency	.01	0.24
Days incarcerated	−.22	−3.86*
Young adult (ages 17–25)		
Exclusion risk	−.14	−2.75*
Excessive drinking	−.35	−6.58*
R^2		.20

*$p < .05$.

and prior criminal history are controlled (the latter influencing the length of confinement), it seems unlikely that this result is merely spurious.

Table 15.4 underscores the deleterious role that incarceration may play in developmental trajectories of employment in later periods of adulthood as well (ages 25 to 32). For comparative purposes the models in Table 15.4 examine incarceration length in *both* adolescence and young adulthood, controlling for juvenile crime and deviance, exclusion risk, and excessive drinking as a later adult. The data suggest that excessive drinking does indeed have a powerful concurrent effect on job stability ($\beta = -.39$). Still, length of incarceration in both adolescence and young adulthood has significant negative effects on job stability at ages 25 to 32 ($\beta = -.14$ and −.31, respectively). These results are noteworthy not only because confounding "propensity" factors are taken into account (e.g., crime and drinking), but also for the long-term negative consequences of juvenile incarceration independent of adult incarceration. It seems that the structural disadvantages accorded institutionalized adolescents are so great (e.g., through dropping out of high school, a record of confinement known to employers) that their influence lingers throughout adult development.

We extended this idea by considering the cumulative effect of incarceration from adolescence (age < 17) through the transition to young adulthood (ages 17 to 25). Despite this different model specification, the results painted the same general picture as Table 15.4 (data not shown). Drinking and exclusion risk significantly reduced job stability at ages 25 to 32. But so too did the cumulative experience of incarceration − as time served in juvenile and adult correctional facilities increased, later job stability decreased regardless of prior record, exclusion risk, and unofficial deviance.

Table 15.4. *Regression model predicting job stability at ages 25 to 32: delinquent group* (n = 355)

Independent variable	Job stability	
	β	t ratio
Juvenile (age < 17)		
Arrests per year free	.09	1.46
Unofficial delinquency	−.06	−1.23
Days incarcerated	−.14	−2.78*
Young adult (ages 17–25)		
Exclusion risk	.07	0.66
Days incarcerated	−.31	−2.74*
Later adult (ages 25–32)		
Excessive drinking	−.39	−8.32*
R^2		.30

*$p < .05$.

The data clearly suggest that looking only at the direct effects of official sanctions is misleading. Length of incarceration – whether as a juvenile or adult – has little direct bearing on later criminal activity when job stability is controlled. This does not imply unimportance, however, for our analysis suggests that the effect of confinement may be indirect and operative in a developmental, cumulative process that reproduces itself over time (see also Hagan & Palloni, 1990). Consistent with this theoretical idea of cumulative continuity and state (duration) dependence (Nagin & Paternoster, 1991), incarceration appears to cut off opportunities and prospects for stable employment later in life. And as already shown, job stability in turn has importance in explaining later crime. Therefore, even if the direct effect of incarceration is zero or possibly even negative (i.e., a deterrent), its indirect effect may well be criminogenic (positive) as a structural labeling theory would predict.

Conclusions

We derive three specific conclusions from our analyses and discussion. First, punitive discipline by parents is strongly related to delinquency. However, it is important to point out that other family variables (e.g., monitoring and supervision, attachment to children) are equally important in understanding delinquency. Therefore, we believe researchers need to consider a wide range of family factors including punitive discipline in their explanations of delinquent behavior.

Second, we found that in the Gluecks' data, delinquency *mediates* the effects of punitive discipline over the long term. In other words, even though erratic/harsh discipline increases delinquency and that in turn is strongly related to adult crime, once delinquency is controlled, the direct effect of erratic discipline on adult crime disappears. Our finding supports the idea that different factors may explain participation in crime and continuation in offending as an adult (see also Farrington & Hawkins, 1991). Clearly more research is needed to identify the specific determinants of participation versus persistence in criminal offending over the life course.

Third, and perhaps most interesting, punitive discipline by the state has important negative effects over the long term. Specifically, juvenile incarceration is strongly negatively related to job stability, which in turn has large negative effects on adult crime. As a consequence, juvenile incarceration has positive (criminogenic) long-term effects on adult crime.

In sum, these results strongly suggest the need to assess punitive discipline in the family *and* by the state in developmental or sequential probability models of crime and deviance over the life course (see Sampson & Laub, 1993). Stigmatizing and harsh punishment, by the family as well as the state, appears to backfire over the life course.

NOTE

This is a revised version of a paper presented at the Life History Research Society Meeting, May 1, 1992. The data utilized in this study are part of the Sheldon and Eleanor Glueck study materials of the Harvard Law School Library and are on long-term loan to the Henry A. Murray Research Center of Radcliffe College.

REFERENCES

Blumstein, A., Cohen, J., & Farrington, D. P. (1988). Longitudinal and criminal career research: Further clarifications. *Criminology, 26,* 57–74.

Blumstein, A., Cohen, J., Roth, J., & Visher, C. (Eds.). (1986). *Criminal careers and "career criminals."* Washington, DC: National Academy Press.

Bondeson, U. V. (1989). *Prisoners in prison societies.* New Brunswick, NJ: Transaction Books.

Burton, V., Cullen, F., & Travis, L. (1987). The collateral consequences of a felony conviction: A national study of state statutes. *Federal Probation, 51,* 52–60.

Caspi, A. (1987). Personality in the life course. *Journal of Personality and Social Psychology, 53,* 1203–1213.

Devlin, M. (1985). *Stubborn child.* New York: Atheneum.

Elder, G. H., Jr. (1975). Age differentiation and the life course. *Annual Review of Sociology, 1,* 165–190.

Elder, G. H., Jr. (1985). Perspectives on the life course. In G. H. Elder, Jr. (Ed.), *Life course dynamics* (pp. 23–49). Ithaca, NY: Cornell University Press.

Farrington, D. P. (1987). Early precursors of frequent offending. In J. Q. Wilson & G. C. Loury (Eds.), *From children to citizens: Vol. 3, Families, schools, and delinquency prevention* (pp. 27–50). New York: Springer-Verlag.

Farrington, D. P., & Hawkins, J. D. (1991). Predicting participation, early onset and later persistence in officially recorded offending. *Criminal Behaviour and Mental Health, 1,* 1–33.

Franz, C. E., McClelland, D. C., & Weinberger, J. (1991). Childhood antecedents of conventional social accomplishments in midlife adults: A 36-year prospective study. *Journal of Personality and Social Psychology, 60,* 586–595.

Freeman, R. (1987). The relation of criminal activity to black youth employment. *Review of Black Political Economy, 16,* 99–107.

Freeman, R. (1992, February). Crime and the employment of disadvantaged youth. Paper presented at the Urban Poverty Workshop, University of Chicago, Chicago, IL.

Glaser, D. (1969). *The effectiveness of a prison and parole system* (abr. ed.). Indianapolis, IN: Bobbs-Merrill.

Glueck, S., & Glueck, E. (1950). *Unraveling juvenile delinquency.* New York: Commonwealth Fund.

Glueck, S., & Glueck, E. (1962). *Family environment and delinquency.* London: Routledge & Kegan Paul.

Glueck, S., & Glueck, E. (1968). *Delinquents and nondelinquents in perspective.* Cambridge, MA: Harvard University Press.

Gottfredson, M., Hirschi, T. (1990). *A general theory of crime.* Stanford, CA: Stanford University Press.

Hagan, J., & Palloni, A. (1990). The social reproduction of a criminal class in working class London, circa 1950–1980. *American Journal of Sociology, 96,* 265–299.

Hirschi, T. (1969). *Causes of delinquency.* Berkeley: University of California Press.

Hirschi, T. (1983). Crime and the family. In J. Q. Wilson (Ed.), *Crime and public policy* (pp. 53–68). San Francisco: Institute for Contemporary Studies.

Laub, J. H., & Sampson, R. J. (1988). Unraveling families and delinquency: A reanalysis of the Gluecks' data. *Criminology, 26,* 355–380.

Loeber, R., & Stouthamer-Loeber, M. (1986). Family factors as correlates and predictors of juvenile conduct problems and delinquency. In M. Tonry & N. Morris (Eds.), *Crime and justice: An annual review of research* (pp. 29–149). Chicago: University of Chicago Press.

McCord, J. (1979). Some child-rearing antecedents of criminal behavior in adult men. *Journal of Personality and Social Psychology, 37,* 1477–1486.

McCord, J. (1991). Family relationships, juvenile delinquency, and adult criminality. *Criminology, 29,* 397–417.

McCord, W., and McCord, J. (1953). Two approaches to the cure of delinquents. *Journal of Criminal Law, Criminology, and Police Science, 44,* 442–467.

McCord, W., & McCord, J. (1959). *Origins of crime.* New York: Columbia University Press.

Miller, J. G. (1991). *Last one over the wall: The Massachusetts experiment in closing reform schools.* Columbus: Ohio State University Press.

Nagin, D. & Paternoster, R. (1991). On the relationship of past and future participation in delinquency. *Criminology, 29,* 163–190.

Ohlin, L. E., Coates, R. B., & Miller, A. D. (1974). Radical correctional reform: A case study of the Massachusetts Youth Correctional System. *Harvard Educational Review, 44,* 74–111.

Patterson, G. R. (1980). Children who steal. In T. Hirschi & M. Gottfredson (Eds.), *Understanding crime: Current theory and research* (pp. 73–90). Beverly Hills, CA: Sage.

Robins, L. (1966). *Deviant children grown up.* Baltimore: Williams & Wilkins.

Sampson, R. J., & Laub, J. H. (1990). Crime and deviance over the life course: The salience of adult social bonds. *American Sociological Review, 55,* 609–627.

Sampson, R. J., & Laub, J. H. (1993). *Crime in the making: Pathways and turning points through life.* Cambridge, MA: Harvard University Press.

Smith, D., & Gartin, P. (1989). Specifying specific deterrence: The influence of arrest on future criminal activity. *American Sociological Review, 54,* 94–105.

Vaillant, G. E. (1983). *The natural history of alcoholism.* Cambridge, MA: Harvard University Press.

16 Parental monitoring and peer influences on adolescent substance use

ANNE C. FLETCHER, NANCY DARLING, AND LAURENCE STEINBERG

Experimentation with drugs and alcohol often begins in early adolescence (if not sooner), with initiation rates for most substances dropping sharply after age 18 (Kandel & Logan, 1984). Use is heavier among males than females (Brook, Lukoff, & Whiteman, 1980; Kandel & Logan, 1984) and is most prevalent among white, middle-class adolescents (Gans, 1990), but drug use remains high among young people from all backgrounds. Indeed, experimentation with alcohol and other drugs is so common among today's young people that it is often considered normative.

Numerous studies have focused on understanding the factors that influence young people's patterns of drug use. Two domains of influence in particular have received a great deal of attention: the family and the peer group (Brook et al., 1980; Brook, Whiteman, & Gordon, 1983; Hawkins, Lishner, Catalano, & Howard, 1986).

With regard to the first of these domains, researchers have found that adolescents raised by authoritative parents are less likely to engage in substance use (e.g., Baumrind, 1989; Lamborn, Mounts, Steinberg, & Dornbusch, 1991). Authoritative parents are both responsive and demanding toward the adolescent. They are characterized by firm and consistent limit setting, but also by the respect with which they treat their adolescent and the warmth of the parent–child relationship.

Studies of selected aspects of authoritative parenting also have found significant relations between particular parenting practices and adolescent substance use. Brook and colleagues, for example, report that maternal affection is associated with lower rates of substance use and that paternal structure (as opposed to permissiveness) is also a factor in deterring drug and alcohol use (Brook, Whiteman, & Gordon, 1983). Other researchers have found that high levels of parental monitoring (i.e., knowing where children are and what they are doing) can insulate children and adolescents from a wide array of misbehavior, including alcohol and drug use (Steinberg, 1987; Snyder, Dishion, & Patterson, 1986).

Whereas parents have been seen as influencing adolescent drug use from a distance (either through socialization or through monitoring), it has long been believed that the most potent proximal influence on patterns of drug use in adolescence is that of peers. This belief stems from two observations. First, adolescents who use drugs or alcohol typically have friends who are users, whereas adolescents who are nonusers typically have friends who are not (Blount & Dembo, 1984; Hawkins et al., 1986; Huba, Wingard, & Bentler, 1979; Kandel, 1973, 1978; Needle et al., 1986). Although some of the observed similarity among friends in substance use patterns is due to selection (i.e., adolescents who are drug users seek out friendships with like-minded peers), studies show that peers influence each other's behavior above and beyond their initial similarity (Billy & Udry, 1985; Dishion, Reid, & Patterson, 1988; Kandel, 1978). Indeed, there is some evidence that for marijuana use the influence, or socialization effect, may slightly outweigh that of selection (Kandel, 1978).

A second reason for the presumed importance of peers as proximal influences on adolescent drug use is the observation that for most young people, drug and alcohol use occurs in social situations. To this end, studies have been conducted on the extent to which the socialization effect discussed previously is actually due to the coercive power of peer pressure (rather than, for example, mere imitation). Studies have shown that direct coercion to use alcohol and drugs does indeed exist within adolescent peer groups (at least in the contemporary United States), that coercion is more common among boys than girls (Brown, 1982; Brown, Clasen, & Eicher, 1986), and that coercion to use drugs and alcohol increases with age during the adolescent years (Brown, Clasen, & Eicher, 1986; Brown et al., 1986; Clasen & Brown, 1985). One interpretation of this age effect is that as adolescents near "adult" status, they exert more pressure on one another to engage in the "adult" activity of substance use. It is important to note, however, that several studies have found evidence of adolescents exerting pressure on their peers *not* to engage in drug and alcohol use or other types of misconduct, a finding which suggests that peer coercion may not always be toward behaviors that adults find undesirable (Brown, Lohr, & McClenahan, 1986; Clasen & Brown, 1985). Nevertheless, research does indicate that adolescents' drug use is influenced by exposure to drug-using friends and that one of the primary mechanisms through which this exposure operates is coercion.

Traditionally, parental and peer influences have been portrayed as oppositional throughout late childhood and adolescence, with parents socializing their children toward prosocial goals and peers acting coercively to undermine this influence (a portrayal that persists in most popular images of adolescent peer groups). More recently, however, some researchers have adopted a more complex, albeit nondynamic, perspective on parental and peer influences. For example, some studies attempted to estimate the contribution of peer influences after controlling for parental factors (e.g., Brook et al., 1983). Others recognized that the relative influences of parents versus peers varies with subject age and sex (e.g., Berndt, 1979). Still others sought to determine whether parental or peer influence was more potent under some circumstances than others (e.g., Hunter, 1984; Larson, 1972).

Studies of the relative potency of parental versus peer influence – even those that take into account the importance of situational and developmental factors – do not illuminate the processes through which parental and peer influences operate simultaneously, however. Indeed, only a handful of recent investigators have attempted to understand the dynamic interplay of parent and peer influence on adolescent deviance. Among the most popular of these models are those proposed by Patterson and colleagues (e.g., Dishion et al., 1988; Snyder et al., 1986). Briefly, Patterson's group has argued that ineffective parenting, especially ineffective parental monitoring, leads children to acquire poor social skills, which in turn leads to association with deviant peers in childhood and adolescence, and so to drug and alcohol use. In sum, parenting influences substance use through its effect on the child's peer group selection (Snyder et al., 1986). The purpose of the present study is to examine the joint influences over time of parental monitoring and peer influence on adolescent substance use. Our design overcomes several limitations inherent in previous research. First, because our data on peer drug use come from the adolescents' peers themselves (rather than from the target adolescents' perceptions of their friends' drug use), we have an estimate of peer coercion that is independent of the respondent's susceptibility to such coercion. Second, because we have data on adolescent drug use, peer drug use, and parental monitoring at two points in time, we are able to order these three variables temporally and better understand their dynamic interaction.

Limitations within the project design primarily involve our inability to obtain information about parental monitoring from parents themselves. Because our information on parenting practices comes through the eyes of adolescents, we can only ask whether youngsters who characterize their parents' monitoring in certain ways also report particular patterns of substance use. We recognize that it is also important to know whether parents' *actual* behavior toward their children is associated in similar ways with the outcome assessed. However, our position is that subjective and objective assessments of parental behavior each provide an important window on the child's experience in the family. In addition, the few studies that have correlated "objective" assessments of family life with both adolescents' reports of their parents' behavior and with their parents' reports suggest that adolescents, not parents, are more accurate (e.g., Schwartz, Barton-Henry, & Pruzinsky, 1985). This fact stands in contrast to studies of adolescent reports of their friends' drug use, which have been found to be less accurate than the reports of friends themselves (Bauman & Fisher, 1986).

Method

Sample

The present sample consisted of students at six high schools in Northern California and three in Wisconsin. Participants completed self-report questionnaires during three consecutive school years: 1987–88, 1988–89, and 1989–90. The information used in this study was drawn from the first 2 years of the project. Only those students completing questionnaires in both of the first 2 project years were considered in these analyses, and only those subjects providing full answers to questions needed for this study were retained. Of the approximately 10,000 students present in school at each time of testing, 6,494 provided data that were used in this study. This sample was diverse with respect to year in school (27% freshmen, 27% sophomores, 25% juniors, and 21% seniors) and ethnicity (65% European-American, 14% Asian-American, 12% Hispanic-American, 8% African-American, 1% Pacific Islander, and less than 1% each Native American and Middle Eastern). Measures of parental education showed the sample to be predominantly middle class or professional (4% lower class, 7% working class, 43% middle class, and 39% professional), although 7% of subjects did not provide information about their parents' education levels. The sample was 48% male and 52% female.

We employed a consent procedure that requested "active" informed consent from the adolescents, but "passive" informed consent from their parents. Fewer than 1% of the adolescents in each of the target schools had their participation withheld by their parents. Approximately 4% of students in attendance on the days of testing chose themselves not to participate in the study.

Measures

Parental monitoring. Parental monitoring was assessed by a monitoring questionnaire that has been shown to be an excellent predictor of delinquency among adolescent boys (Patterson & Stouthamer-Loeber, 1984). Students were asked to respond to five questions: "How much do your parents REALLY know . . . Who your friends are? Where you go at night? How you spend your money? What you do with your free time? Where you are most afternoons after school?" Adolescents responded on a 3-point scale, with 1 representing *Don't know,* 2 representing *Know a little,* and 3 representing *Know a lot.* Subjects were assigned a monitoring score equal to their mean response for these questions. Only subjects who responded to at least four of the five items were retained in analyses.

Substance use. Adolescent substance use was assessed using three questions asking subjects to report how often they had used alcohol excessively, smoked marijuana, or used a drug other than marijuana (such as "uppers" or cocaine) since the beginning of the school year. Subjects responded on a 4-point scale (1 indicating *Never,* 2 indicating *Once or twice,* 3 indicating *Several times,* and 4 indicating *Often*) to each item.

A substance usage typology was designed drawing on aspects of the works of both Shedler & Block (1990) and Baumrind (1991). Similar to these authors, we did not include cigarette smoking as a measure of substance use, as the use of cigarettes was legal for many of these adolescents, and tobacco is not considered to impair behavior and judgment as do drugs and alcohol. We considered both frequency and severity of drug use in constructing our typology. We also considered alcohol as an illicit substance for this age group, although experimentation with alcohol use was not considered to be as severe as experimentation with marijuana and other drugs. This decision was consistent with that reached by Baumrind and was based on the fact that within our sample a large number of adolescents reported experimentation with alcohol but not marijuana, while very few reported smoking marijuana but never experimenting with alcohol. Finally, our typology did not allow for differentiations within the "drug other than marijuana" category, as did Shedler and Block's. We consider this category to represent use of "hard" drugs such as amphetamines, cocaine, and heroin, although we recognize that use of such substances as cough medicine and inhalants may be improperly categorized as hard drug use. Such classifications should make our hypotheses less, not more, likely to be confirmed, and so should present no serious challenge to the results reported here.

Our original typology defined five categories of substance users/nonusers:

Category 1: nonusers. Subjects who indicated never having used alcohol, marijuana, or other drugs ($n = 3,181$).

Category 2: experimental alcohol users. Subjects who indicated that within the past year they had used alcohol excessively no more than several times, but had never experimented with marijuana or other drugs ($n = 1,263$).

Category 3: experimental drug users. Subjects who reported using marijuana or other drugs no more than several times, or both marijuana and other drugs once or twice each ($n = 1,141$).

Category 4: heavy alcohol or marijuana users. Subjects who reported using marijuana or alcohol to excess often ($n = 592$).

Category 5: heavy hard drug users. Subjects who reported using drugs other than marijuana often ($n = 317$).

These five categories of drug use were collapsed into three categories (nonusers, experimenters, and heavy users) for most analyses. This manipulation both made sense conceptually and added to the study's power, given the small number of subjects in some groups.

Measures of peer association and peer substance use. In each year of this study subjects were asked to provide the names of their five closest friends. Only those subjects who provided names of at least three friends who had also completed the survey at their school were retained for analyses in this part of the study. This requirement lowered the number of subjects retained in peer analyses to 4,757. It should be noted that subjects who did not name at least three friends differed from the retained subjects in their own substance use patterns, with those subjects who were eliminated showing heavier usage [$\chi^2(4, n = 43.55, p < .01$]. By matching the information provided by subjects on their friends' names and their friends' own self-reported substance use, we were then able to determine the peer group type of each subject. Peer groups were classified according to the substance use of their members, with member substance use classified as previously described:

Nonusers. Groups in which none of the identified friends reported any drug use.

Nonusers/experimenters. Groups composed of a combination of nonusers and experimenters with either marijuana or alcohol.

Mixed. Groups with at least one member from each of the substance use categories.

Experimenter/regular users. Groups with members who were experimenters with alcohol or marijuana and members who were regular users of one or both of these substances.

Regular users. Groups composed only of friends who were regular users of some substance.

Results

Preliminary analyses revealed that although substance use varied across ethnic and socioeconomic status (SES) groups and grades, the patterns of relations among the study variables were similar within each group. Accordingly, all results reported here were collapsed across these groups. Different patterns of relations were observed for boys versus girls, however, and all results are reported separately for each sex.

Parental monitoring and adolescent substance use

Time 1 monitoring and substance use. To establish the association of concurrent parental monitoring and adolescent substance use, mean parental monitoring scores were calculated for boys and girls classified in each substance use category at Time 1, and ANOVAs were performed to test the association. As expected, boys and girls who reported lower parental monitoring were more likely to be involved in substance use than were their peers [$F(4, 6489) = 153.34$, $p < .01$]. Interestingly, girls who were either nonusers or experimenting with alcohol or other drugs reported much higher levels of monitoring than similarly involved boys, but the monitoring levels of girls who were more heavily involved in substance use were comparable to those of heavy-drug-using boys [$F(4, 6484) = 2.78$, $p < .05$].

Time 1 monitoring and transitions in substance use from Time 1 to Time 2. To assess the influence of parental monitoring on changes in adolescent substance use between Time 1 and Time 2, adolescents were divided into the three previously described categories on the basis of their initial substance use: nonusers, experimenters, and regular or heavy users. Within each category, mean levels of Time 1 parental monitoring were calculated for those adolescents whose substance use was the same at Time 1 and Time 2, for those who became less involved in substance use, and for those who became more involved. Within each initial involvement group, *t* tests were conducted to examine whether mean levels of Time 1 monitoring discriminated between those whose substance use remained stable and those who had changed usage patterns. Monitoring means are reported in Table 16.1.

Table 16.1. *Mean T1 parental monitoring by T1 and T2 substance use*

| | T1 substance use | | | | | |
| | Nonusers | | Experimenters | | Heavy users | |
T2 substance use	M	SD	M	SD	M	SD
Boys						
Less involved	—	—	2.17 (121)	0.53	2.12** (71)	0.59
Stable	2.39** (656)	0.50	2.14 (302)	0.53	1.85 (90)	0.61
More involved	2.29 (177)	0.47	2.17 (121)	0.54	—	—
Girls						
Less involved	—	—	2.37* (137)	0.48	1.95 (56)	0.58
Stable	2.53** (788)	0.44	2.27 (390)	0.47	1.85 (85)	0.56
More involved	2.40 (194)	0.45	2.17 (78)	0.57	—	—

Note: Numbers in parentheses indicate sample size.
*$p < .05$; **$p < .01$.

Both boys and girls who experienced low parental monitoring were more likely to make the transition from being a nonuser at Time 1 to a substance user at Time 2 than were their more heavily monitored peers [boys: $t(831) = -2.42, p < .01$; girls: $t(980) = -3.56, p < .01$]. The relation between initial parental monitoring and changes in the substance use of adolescents who were already users was mixed, however, and differed depending on both initial level of involvement and gender. Specifically, boys who were heavy substance users at Time 1, but who reported relatively high parental monitoring, were more likely to decrease their substance use than were their less heavily monitored peers [$t(159) = -2.84, p < .01$]. However, parental monitoring did not predict which boys who were experimenting with substance use would stop using drugs and alcohol, versus which would go on to become heavy users. Among girls, however, parental monitoring predicted movement from experimenter to nonuser status [$t(525) = -2.41, p < .05$], but not from experimenter to heavy user status.

To summarize, high parental monitoring predicted which nonusers became users and which substance users became less involved (for boys who were heavy users and girls who were experimenters). Parental monitoring did not, however, predict which experimenters became heavy users.

Parental monitoring in the context of adolescents' peers

Similarity of Time 1 adolescent and peer substance use. As has been discussed, similarity in substance use by adolescents and their peers is typically attributed to both selection and socialization. We calculated the percentage of adolescents from each Time 1 substance use category who were members of each type of peer group. As expected, the more involved an adolescent was in substance use, the more likely it was that his or her peers were involved in substance use as well [boys: $\chi^2(8, n = 1816) = 519.26, p < .01$; girls: $\chi^2(8, n = 2448) = 717.31, p < .01$].

Time 1 monitoring and adolescent Time 1 substance use in the context of peers. To assess whether parental monitoring was equally effective in deterring adolescent substance use in different peer contexts, mean Time 1 monitoring levels were calculated for Time 1 nonusers, experimenters, and heavy users *within* each type of Time 1 peer group. Differences in the association of monitoring and substance use as a function of peer group affiliation were tested using a 3 (levels of substance use) × 4 (peer group types) ANOVA. Of primary interest in this analysis was whether the association between parental monitoring and adolescent substance use was equally strong when the adolescents' peers were all nonusers as when most of them were heavy users.

Among boys, higher parental monitoring was associated with lower reported substance use, controlling for peer groups [$F(2, 1564) = 34.50, p < .01$], and there was no indication that this relation varied with the adolescent's peer group type. Among girls, however, parental monitoring was more effective in preventing adolescent substance use in heterogeneous peer groups than in groups that were either primarily made up of heavy users or entirely made up of nonusers, [$F(6, 2105) = 2.17, p < .05$].

Finally, there was no independent association between parental monitoring and the substance use patterns of peers when adolescents' own substance use was controlled. This indicated that parental monitoring had no effect on whether an adolescent's peers were substance users, once the adolescent's own substance use was controlled. Thus, if monitoring was associated with peer group selection, it was through its impact on the individual adolescent's behavior.

Time 1 monitoring, peer substance use, and transitions in adolescent substance use from Time 1 to Time 2. A chi-square analysis was performed examining if the percentage of adolescents who made transitions in their substance usage patterns varied between peer group types. Results indicated that the extent to which peers were involved in substance use affected the likelihood that adolescents would change their own substance use. The more involved an adolescent's peers were in substance use, the more likely the adolescent was to begin using drugs or alcohol between Time 1 and Time 2 (see Table 16.2) [boys: $\chi^2(3, N = 558) = 43.71, p < .01$; girls: $\chi^2(3, N = 734) = 19.38, p < .01$]. As with parental monitoring, peers' substance use

Table 16.2. *Percentage of adolescents in each type of peer group making each transition*

	Nonuser to user (N = 54)	Experimenter to nonuser (N = 17)	Experimenter to heavy (N = 12)	Heavy to less heavy (N = 12)
Boys				
Users	5.8	47.1	25.0	—
Exp	29.5	29.7	23.4	58.3
Mixed	36.0	28.2	35.4	36.7
Exp/Reg	50.0	22.6	36.8	20.0
Girls				
Nonusers	11.6	44.1	17.4	—
Non/Exp	24.9	24.9	14.0	50.0
Mixed	27.3	23.2	17.9	39.5
Exp/Reg	33.3	15.6	26.9	25.6

also predicted boys' transitions from heavy user to experimenter status [$\chi^2(2, N=82)=8.46, p<.01$] and girls' transitions from experimenter to nonuser status [$\chi^2(3, N=449)=9.00, p<.01$].

To further investigate the effect of peer groups on changes in adolescent substance use, subjects were again divided into four groups based on their Time 1 and Time 2 substance use. MANOVAs were performed to predict transitions in substance use from Time 1 parental monitoring and peer group membership. Results indicated that when this control of monitoring was added, having many friends who were substance users made it more likely that boys would make the transition from nonuser to user status [$F(3, 495)=13.41, p<.01$] and from experimenter to heavy user status [$F(3, 240)=2.65, p<.05$]. The MANOVA also revealed that after controlling for Time 1 monitoring, having friends who were less involved in substance use also increased the likelihood that boys would move from being heavy substance users to lower levels of drug and alcohol involvement [$F(2, 66)=5.27, p<.01$]. Parental monitoring at Time 1 was not independently associated with these transitions. In other words, over time boys tended to move toward their peers in substance use, and these transitions were not influenced by parental monitoring.

For girls, the picture was somewhat different. Both low parental monitoring [$F(1, 668)=4.65, p<.05$] and greater peer involvement in substance use [$F(3, 668)=7.52, p<.01$] were independently associated with girls making the transition from substance nonusers to users. Low substance use by peers also increased the likelihood that adolescent girls would stop experimenting with substance use and revert to being nonusers [$F(3, 377)=2,85, p<.05$]. Neither parental monitoring nor substance use by peers predicted other transitions in substance use by girls, however. In other words, parents and peers helped determine girls' transitions from nonuser status, but not transitions from experimenter to heavy use status. For neither boys nor girls did the influence of peer groups on substance use transitions vary as a function of parental monitoring.

Discussion

The major findings of this study concern both the effects of perceived parental monitoring on adolescent substance use patterns and the effects of such monitoring in the context of coercion in the peer group. As is the case in other studies, we find that monitoring is negatively associated with levels of adolescent substance use for both boys and girls. Interestingly, although at most levels of substance use involvement girls report higher levels of parental monitoring than do their male counterparts, this sex difference becomes less evident at the highest levels of substance involvement. Heavy-drug-using girls report themselves to be monitored as poorly as are heavy-drug-using boys.

Previous research on parental monitoring and adolescent deviance has not been able to separate cause and effect. We were able to come closer in this longitudinal study. Our examination of the effects of perceived parental monitoring at Time 1 on adolescents' subsequent changes in drug and alcohol involvement suggests that high levels of parental monitoring do in fact discourage both boys and girls from beginning to use drugs. In addition, high levels of perceived monitoring also encourage boys who are heavily involved in substance use to lessen their involvement. Similarly, for girls, high levels of monitoring are influential in causing movement from experimental substance use to nonuser status. At the same time, it is worth noting that perceived parental monitoring is differentially effective at various levels of drug and alcohol involvement for boys and for girls. For boys, monitoring does not predict which adolescents will make transitions from experimenter status, and which directions such transitions will take. Among girls, however, parental monitoring does predict which experimenters will revert to nonuser status. It may be that moderate levels of drug and alcohol use are more socially acceptable among boys than among girls, and that girls are thus susceptible to parental intervention at an earlier stage in the development of substance use trajectories.

Considering peer context in addition to the effects of perceived parental monitoring on drug and alcohol use patterns complicates this picture further, however. Although high levels of reported monitoring are associated with lower levels of substance use in all peer groups, among girls monitoring is most effective in heterogeneous peer groups. The picture that emerges of girls is one of individuals poised to move in either direction in response to the coercion (in either direction) of their peers. In such a situation it may be that additional control provided by parents is enough to determine levels of subsequent drug use.

We also see, as have other researchers, that the more involved an adolescent's peers are in substance use, the more likely he or she is to make the transition into heavier substance use. Having peer groups who are less involved in substance use makes an individual less likely to move from nonuser status to involvement with drugs and alcohol. Among boys these effects are also evident in the transition from heavy use to lower levels of involvement, whereas among girls they are observed in transitions from experimenter status to lower levels of involvement. Again, it appears that different levels of substance use involvement are interpreted differently for boys and for girls. In this case, it may be that for girls being an experimenter is a less entrenched status, and they are therefore more easily moved out of this category.

The picture described here is further clarified by analyses that investigate the effects of monitoring controlling for peer coercion, and the effects of peer coercion controlling for monitoring. Boys appear to move toward their peers in transitions in substance use status. These transitions are apparently not influenced by levels of perceived parental monitoring. Girls, however, are influenced by both peer groups and parental monitoring in their transitions from nonuser status to greater involvement. We see that girls are then more susceptible to influences from the home than are their male counterparts, at least at this low level of substance use involvement.

The results reported here suggest that adolescent peer groups vary greatly in their involvement in substance use. While adolescents may be more heavily influenced by their peers than by their parents in the area of drug and alcohol involvement, it would be inappropriate to consider this influence as always negative. If an individual is involved with peers who do not use drugs and alcohol, he or she will not only be less likely to begin involvement, but may also be encouraged to reduce existing levels of substance use.

Although this study offers a very interesting picture of the relations among perceived parental monitoring, peer coercion, and adolescent substance use patterns, it does suffer from a number of limitations. First, the data available were derived from adolescents' self-reports. Although we were able to use data reported by the peers themselves to develop measures of peer group substance use (an advantage over many studies of peer influence and involvement), we were forced to rely on the adolescents themselves for reports of parental monitoring and subject substance use. We feel confident that the subjects in this project were reasonably accurate in their reports of drug and alcohol involvement. They were assured of confidentiality and were old enough to understand both the importance of the project and their option of refusing to participate. Furthermore, it is difficult to suggest a viable alternative to self-report of drug and alcohol use (McCord, 1990). In a normal high school population, no other method is reasonably available.

This project provides longitudinal data, but only over the course of one school year. While data from a longer time period would be valuable, it would also involve losing a larger number of subjects through graduation, school transfer, or failure to complete a questionnaire at one time period or another. We view the findings here as suggestive, however, and worthy of further investigation within a larger time frame.

The overall lesson of this study appears to be that parental monitoring *is* an appropriate strategy for parents attempting to deter adolescents from engaging in substance use. Strong parental monitoring helps to deter adolescents from using alcohol and drugs themselves and, as a consequence, prevents nonusing adolescents from associating with drug-using peers. Since it is these drug-using peers who are likely to pressure teenagers to initiate or elevate substance use, strongly monitored adolescents are, in essence, doubly protected from substance use involvement: they have the protective benefits of effective socialization in the family and they are less likely to find themselves in situations where they will be coerced to use drugs by their friends. Rather than view peer coercion to use drugs as a given that all adolescents inevitably encounter, our study suggests that some adolescents, by virtue of their family relationships, are more exposed to coercive influences – whether prosocial or antisocial – than are others.

NOTE

The study on which this report is based was supported by a grant to Laurence Steinberg and B. Bradford Brown from the U.S. Department of Education, through the National Center on Effective Secondary Schools, and a grant by the Spencer Foundation to Sanford M. Dornbusch and P. Herbert Liederman, at the Stanford Center for Families, Children, and Youth. Work on this paper was supported by a grant from the Lilly Endowment to Laurence Steinberg and by a grant from the William T. Grant Foundation to Laurence Steinberg and Nancy Darling. Address correspondence to the authors at the Department of Psychology, Temple University, Philadelphia, PA 19122. Portions of this chapter were presented at the meeting of the Society for Life History Research, Philadelphia, May 1, 1992.

REFERENCES

Bauman, K., & Fisher, L. (1986). On the measurement of friend behavior in research on friend influence and selection: Findings from longitudinal studies of adolescent smoking and drinking. *Journal of Youth and Adolescence, 15*, 345–353.

Baumrind, D. (1989). Rearing competent children. In W. Damon (Ed.), *Child development today and tomorrow* (pp. 349–378). San Francisco: Jossey-Bass.

Baumrind, D. (1991). The influence of parenting style on adolescent competence and substance use. *Journal of Early Adolescence, 11*(1), 56–95.

Berndt, T. J. (1979). Developmental changes in conformity to peers and parents. *Developmental Psychology, 15*(6), 608–616.

Billy, J. O. G., & Udry, J. R. (1985). Patterns of adolescent friendship and effects on sexual behavior. *Social Psychology Quarterly, 48*(1), 27–41.

Blount, W. R., & Dembo, R. (1984). Personal drug use and attitudes toward prevention among youth living in a high risk environment. *Journal of Drug Education, 14*(3), 207–226.

Brook, J. S., Lukoff, I. F., & Whiteman, M. (1980). Initiation into adolescent marijuana use. *Journal of Genetic Psychology, 137*, 133–142.

Brook, J. S., Whiteman, M., & Gordon, A. S. (1983). Stages of drug use in adolescence: Personality, peer, and family correlates. *Developmental Psychology, 19*(2), 269–277.

Brown, B. B. (1982). The extent and effects of peer pressure among high school students: A retrospective analysis. *Journal of Youth and Adolescence, 11*(2), 121–133.

Brown, B. B., Clasen, D. R., & Eicher, S. A. (1986). Perceptions of peer pressure, peer conformity dispositions, and self-reported behavior among adolescents. *Developmental Psychology, 22*(4), 521–530.

Brown, B. B., Lohr, M. J., & McClenahan, E. L. (1986). Early adolescents' perceptions of peer pressure. *Journal of Early Adolescence, 6*(2), 139–154.

Clasen, D. R., & Brown, B. B. (1985). The multidimensionality of peer pressure in adolescence. *Journal of Youth and Adolescence, 14*(6), 451–468.

Dishion, T. J., Reid, J. B., & Patterson, G. R. (1988). Empirical guidelines for a family intervention for adolescent drug use. *Journal of Chemical Dependency Treatment, 2*, 181–216.

Gans, J. (1990). *America's adolescents: How healthy are they?* Chicago: American Medical Association.

Hawkins, J. D., Lishner, D. M., Catalano, R. F., Jr., & Howard, M. O. (1986). Childhood predictors of adolescent substance abuse: Toward an empirically grounded theory. *Journal of Children in Contemporary Society, 18*, 11–48.

Huba, G. J., Wingard, J. A., & Bentler, P. M. (1979). Beginning adolescent drug use and peer and adult interaction patterns. *Journal of Counseling and Clinical Psychology, 47*(2), 265–276.

Hunter, F. T. (1984). Socializing procedures in parent–child and friendship relations during adolescence. *Developmental Psychology, 20*, 1092–1099.

Kandel, D. (1973). Adolescent marihuana use: Role of parents and peers. *Science, 181*, 1067–1070.

Kandel, D. B. (1978). Homophily, selection, and socialization in adolescent friendships. *American Journal of Sociology, 84*(2), 427–436.

Kandel, D. B., & Logan, J. A. (1984). Patterns of drug use from adolescence to young adulthood: I. Periods of risk for initiation, continued use, and discontinuation. *American Journal of Public Health, 74*(7), 660–666.

Lamborn, S. D., Mounts, N. S., Steinberg, L., & Dornbusch, S. M. (1991). Patterns of competence and adjustment among adolescents from authoritative, authoritarian, indulgent, and neglectful families. *Child Development, 62*, 1049–1065.

Larson, L. E. (1972). The influence of parents and peers during adolescence: The situation hypothesis revisited. *Journal of Marriage and the Family, 34*,(1), 67–74.

McCord, J. (1990). Problem behaviors. In S. S. Feldman and G. R. Elliott (Eds.), *At the threshold: The developing adolescent* (pp. 414–430). Cambridge, MA: Harvard University Press.

Needle, R., McCubbin, H., Wilson, M., Reineck, R., Lazar, A., & Mederer, H. (1986). Interpersonal influences in adolescent drug use – The role of older siblings, parents, and peers. *International Journal of the Addictions, 21*(7), 739–766.

Patterson, G., & Stouthamer-Loeber, M. (1984). The correlation of family management practices and delinquency. *Child Development, 55*, 1299–1307.

Schwartz, J., Barton-Henry, M., & Pruzinsky, T. (1985). Assessing child-rearing behaviors: A comparison of ratings made by mother, father, child, and sibling on the CRPBI. *Child Development, 56*, 462–479.

Shedler, J., & Block, J. (1990). Adolescent drug use and psychological health. *American Psychologist, 45*(5), 612–630.

Snyder, J., Dishion, T. J., & Patterson, G. R. (1986). Determinants and consequences of associating with deviant peers during preadolescence and adolescence. *Journal of Early Adolescence, 6*(1), 29–43.

Steinberg, L. (1987). Single parents, stepparents, and the susceptibility of adolescents to antisocial peer pressure. *Child Development, 58*, 269–275.

17 The relative importance of internal and external direct constraints in the explanation of late adolescent delinquency and adult criminality

MARC LE BLANC

This chapter focuses on social constraint. It analyzes coercive forces that operate as potential direct internal and external controls on individual criminal offending. Our study involves four categories of constraints to build an explanatory model of individual offending. These categories of constraint are formal and informal social reactions as direct external constraints and beliefs and perceived risk of punishment as direct internal constraints. In the literature there is neither a theory nor a study that considers simultaneously these four categories of constraint. Theories and studies look at one or, at most, two types of external or internal direct constraint. This chapter addresses two questions: Are internal constraints more important then external constraints for the explanation of adolescent and adult offending? Within internal and external constraints, which type of direct control is the most important predictor of offending?

Constraints

The following literature review introduces the 12 constructs used in our comprehensive constraint model.

External constraints

Thirty-six years ago, Nye (1958) clearly distinguished between formal and informal controls: "Restraint of the individual may be exercised by police and other designated officials, or entirely by disapproval, ridicule, ostracism, banishment, the supernatural, and similar techniques used by informal groups or by society as a whole" (p. 7). In Nye's definition of external constraint we find the formal social reaction perspective. Labeling theorists state that the imposition of the official label of *delinquent* following a criminal activity favors development of a delinquent self-

272

image and emergence of new and more serious forms of criminal activities. Regarding the behavioral effect of labeling, quantitative studies are far from conclusive. There is no strong connection between a delinquent label and subsequent offending if we consider only the label, the police contact, an arrest, or a conviction, and ignore its nature, severity, length, and so on. Studies like Gold (1970), Le Blanc and Fréchette (1989), and Wolfgang, Figlio, and Sellin (1972) have shown that the criminal activity of official delinquents is more frequent, more varied, and more serious than the offending of comparison groups of adolescents. However, formal processing appears more a selection artifact than a deviance-amplifying phenomenon, at least for official delinquency (Smith & Paternoster, 1990). In addition, there is no deterrence impact based on the severity of sanctions (Shannon, 1991). The impact of formal labeling on self-reported delinquency is small in cross-sectional research (Elliott & Ageton, 1980; Hindelang, Hirschi, & Weis, 1981; Junger-Tas & Junger, 1985; Palamera, Cullen, & Gersten, 1986; Williams & Gold, 1972). In addition, longitudinal research shows that the impact is either unclear (Jensen & Rojek, 1980; Junger-Tas & Junger, 1985; Thomas & Bishop, 1984), small (Farrington, 1977; Gold & Williams, 1969; Ray & Downs, 1986), decreases over time (Farrington, Osborn, & West, 1978), or does not sufficiently account for the stability of deviant behavior (Kaplan & Johnson, 1991). Smith and Gartin (1989) even show that arrest encourages the termination of the criminal career for novice offenders, while arrest significantly reduces future rates of offending for experienced offenders. These results, and others (see Shoemaker, 1990), show that formal sanctions produce deterrent effects on delinquency.

Social reactions are not only formal but also informal. Family informal control has long been studied, and its impact is well documented (see reviews by Loeber & Stouthamer-Loeber, 1986; Rollins & Thomas, 1979). Very low and very high levels of parental control are least effective. In consequence, strict, punitive, lax, and erratic disciplines produce conduct problems. Family control involves four components (Laub & Sampson, 1988; Le Blanc, 1992; Wells & Rankin, 1988) – normative regulation (rules decreed by parents), legitimacy of parental rules (and their fairness), supervision or monitoring, and discipline or punishment – as well as an indirect control dimension – attachment to parents or bonding. In these multivariate studies, if we statistically control attachment to parents and family context (family structure, marital relations, parental deviance, etc.), delinquency during adolescence depends on the direct parental control variables. However, indirect control variables, when compared with direct family control variables measured during adolescence, predict adult criminality more efficiently (Le Blanc, 1992).

Studies have also shown that disciplinary reactions by teachers and school authorities highly correlate with self-reported delinquency (Fréchette & Le Blanc, 1987; Malewska & Peyre, 1973; Schaber, Haussman, Beaufils, Boniver, & Kergen 1982). In addition, these reactions mildly associate with school involvement, school commitment, attachment to teacher, and belief in school rules (Le Blanc Valliéres, & McDuff, 1992). In the latter study, school disciplinary reactions display a direct and an indirect effect on self-reported delinquency. When adult criminality is predicted by informal school sanction variables and school-bonding variables, the former easily overrun the latter (Le Blanc, Vallires, & McDuff, 1993). In sum, the school domain rather than the family domain, and external constraint rather than indirect control, best explain adolescent delinquency and adult criminality.

Labeling and bonding theorists propose five constructs for external control: formal sanctions (arrest or court referral), family control in terms of regulations, supervision, discipline, and school control. However, they do not state all the pertinent relationships among these constructs. Our comprehensive control model undertakes this task. Only Thomas and Bishop (1984) compare one form of informal sanction (expulsion from the class and suspension from school) with one form of formal sanction (official contact with police and/or court). Their results show that, when prior self-reported delinquency is controlled, these two categories of sanctions account for only a 10% increase in variance in subsequent delinquency.

Internal constraints

Nye (1958) stated that "every society attempts to internalize its mores by integrating them into the developing conscience of the child. This control is both economical . . . and pervasive. . . . If it were entirely effective, other types of control would be unnecessary" (pp. 5–6).

Elaborating Nye's definition of direct internal constraint, Hirschi (1969) defines internal control as an attitude of respect toward the rules of society. He finds a relationship between beliefs and delinquency. Seventeen studies replicate this result (Kempf, 1993). Hirschi further defines adolescents' respect for the rules of society by using two constructs: legitimacy of the controlling institution's rules, particularly school, and legitimacy of parental rules. He also introduces techniques of neutralization borrowed from Sykes and Matza (1957). He shows that these techniques correlate with the delinquency, and replications are confirmatory (Caplan, 1978; Hindelang, 1973; Le Blanc, Ouimet, & Tremblay, 1988; Mannle & Lewis, 1979; Minor, 1981, 1985). Furthermore, Hirschi hypothesizes that beliefs result from deviant acts, and those beliefs, in turn, cause future deviance. In consequence, reciprocal causation describes the relation between beliefs and deviance. However, Matsueda (1989) challenges that hypothesis with measures of beliefs in honesty and of minor deviance. Church membership and attendance, belief in God and in an afterlife, as well as other religious beliefs inversely correlate with criminal behavior (Ellis, 1987) and drug use (Brownfield & Sorenson, 1991). In sum, five subconstructs represent the construct of belief according to Le Blanc and Caplan's (1993) formalization of Hirschi's theory: acceptance of the validity of legal rules, legitimacy of parental rules, legitimacy of school's rules, use of neutralization techniques, and religiosity.

According to bonding theorists the notion of belief defines direct internal control, while deterrence theorists propose the notion of perceived certainty and severity of sanctions for the same purpose. Perceptual deterrence theorists postulate an inverse relationship between the perceived certainty and severity of sanctions and self-reported offending. Cross-sectional studies support this hypothesis (Paternoster, 1987). However, panel studies find no, or at best very modest, evidence of a deterrent effect of either perceived certainty or severity of punishment (Meier, Burkett, & Hickman, 1984; Paternoster & Iovanni, 1986; Paternoster, Saltzman, Waldo, & Chiricos, 1983; Piliavin, Gartner, Thornton, & Matsueda, 1986; Schneider, 1990; Thomas & Bishop, 1984). Because of these results, authors suggested that for deterrence informal controls may be more relevant than formal controls (Nagin & Paternoster, 1989; Tittle, 1980). In sum, fear of sanctions has modest, if any, impact on delinquency.

In conclusion, bonding and perceptual deterrence theorists propose six constructs for direct internal constraint: perception of risks of sanction, moral beliefs, neutralization techniques, legitimacy of parental rules, parental moral beliefs, and religiosity. Only two studies consider the relationships among a few of these constructs. Minor (1977) integrates the bonding and deterrence perspectives when he considers beliefs in legitimacy of the law and fear of sanctions. He reports that beliefs display the strongest association with self-reported delinquency. Nagin and Paternoster (1991) looked simultaneously at belief, perceptions of risks of punishments, and informal sanctions (parental supervision and friends' approval) as explanations of self-reported delinquency. Their results favor moral beliefs over all other variables considered.

Constraints: a comprehensive perspective

Five sets of constructs were found necessary to build a comprehensive constraint model of offending. These major sets of constructs are internal and external direct constraints, self-reported and official offending, and structural and contextual factors. The internal constraint bloc contains parental beliefs in the validity of the law, adolescent beliefs in the legitimacy of parental regulations and in the moral validity of laws, perceptions of the risks of sanction, religiosity, and use of neutralization techniques to avoid culpability. The external constraint bloc includes parental approval of friends, imposition of regulations, use of disciplinary sanctions, and supervision, as well as adolescent experience of school disciplinary sanctions and reported police contacts. The offending bloc involves official juvenile and adult criminality, and self-reported juvenile and adult offending. Finally, the structural bloc includes parental deviance, socioeconomic status (SES), and family status.

Relationships between the constraint constructs and offending show that formal controls generally fail to amplify offending, while informal controls do. Beliefs in the validity of norms dominate perceptions of the risk of sanctions. In this chapter, we investigate simultaneously the relations within and among these categories of constraints as explanations of self-reported and official late adolescent delinquency and adult criminality.

Our comprehensive constraint model starts with some propositions from Durkheim (1934). Conformity requires the existence of common social norms. The enforcement of these norms is the result of disciplinary practices. In consequence, these practices are a necessary condition for learning norms. In this learning process, if children adhere to norms, sanctions are not necessary to guarantee conformity. The objective of the process of individual development is that legal norms are coercive forces for individuals by middle adolescence at the latest. Hirschi's (1969) bonding theory adopts the point of view that norms govern behavior, but it leaves aside formal sanctions. Hirschi defines four categories of bond: attachment, commitment, involvement, and belief. He proposes a significant explanatory role for beliefs in the legitimacy of the laws without accounting for relationships with the other components of the bond. The formalization of his theory by Le Blanc and Caplan (1993) establishes that interpersonal attachment supports the beliefs, and exposure to criminal influences distorts them. It follows from a bonding theory perspective that the major explanatory factors of late adolescent and adult offending will be from internal constraints, and within that domain beliefs will dominate other constructs.

If conformity, from early adolescence on, depends principally on internal constraints, we can expect that when adhesion to norms is fragile, particularly during late adolescence, external constraints will regulate the level of criminal activity. An individual not responsive to discipline will not integrate norms and as a consequence will be free to commit delinquent acts. Because of these offenses, he or she will be the object of successive informal and formal sanctions that will, in turn, support the continuation of his or her criminal activity. We suggest that labeling is the main constraint factor for continuation of delinquency, while tenuous belief is the major constraint factor of participation in crime (Loeber & Le Blanc, 1990).

We also expect that self-reported criminal activity should be more dependent on internal constraints, while official offending should be more contingent on external constraints. Loeber and Stouthamer-Loeber (1986, 1987) clearly show that external constraint variables more strongly correlate with official than with self-reported offending. Our own comparative analysis of family and school predictors of late adolescent and adult offending establishes that external constraint variables more strongly correlate with official than self-reported offending (Le Blanc, 1994). We expect that the constraint predictors of adolescent and adult criminal activity will be specific, and that within these categories, predictors will be particular for official and self-reported offending.

Finally, we propose that there are some structural variables that regulate the level of direct internal and external constraints. We anticipate that the family, SES, and parental deviance will only indirectly influence the level of criminal activity. Various studies observe this type of relation in the family system (Le Blanc, 1992) and in the school system (Le Blanc et al., 1992).

Data, measures, analysis

The sample of 1,611 boys is representative of the adolescent population in Montreal, including dropouts. At an average age of 14 (range, 12 to 16), subjects completed a self-administered questionnaire in public and private schools (Biron, Caplan, & Le Blanc, 1975, 1977). Two years later, the same questionnaire was readministered at home to a third of the original sample of 1,611 boys. The 458 boys who completed both questionnaires were compared with the rest of the original sample. Significant differences appeared on only 3% of the questions answered at time 1. To do this comparison, we used more than 50 questions concerning delinquent behavior, family life, school experience, and peers.

We constructed the internal and external constraint variables through item analyses. The usual criteria for item analyses are at least .10 correlation among the items of a scale, .30 correlation between an item and its scale, and .60 alpha. The questions operationalizing the constructs derived mainly from Hirschi's empirical verification of his theory (1969). Some questions emerge after a replication (Caplan & Le Blanc, 1985) or the formalization of his theory (Le Blanc & Caplan, 1993). Others come out of other studies. A sample of 6,604 female and male adolescents between the ages of 10 and 19 served for the item analyses. Each scale has sufficient reliability and excellent concurrent, discriminant, and predictive validity (Le Blanc, McDuff, & Fréchette, 1990). The 458 males used in this paper are a subgroup of these subjects. Since each scale does not have the same number of items, we calculated adjusted alpha for boys based on a scale of 12 items (see formula in Nunnally, 1967).

There are three structural variables: family SES, family status, and parental deviance. SES is a summary index based on occupational prestige, a classification of occupations based on schooling, and on receiving welfare or being unemployed. The highest score on this scale occurs when the parents have a low-prestige occupation and when they are out of the work force. Family status includes five indicators: family disruption, recency of disruption, mother working, size of family, and frequency of residential moving. The highest score occurs when all these indicators are present. A question concerning the father's alcohol use measures parental deviance.

There are five offending variables. Le Blanc & Fréchette (1989) present and analyze these variables at length. First, 21 questions on participation in fights, minor and major thefts, and vandalism in the preceding year measure prior delinquency. This scale includes serious crimes such as theft by breaking and entering, and seriously hurting someone during a fight (alpha .82). Second, the same scale measures late-adolescent self-reported delinquency. Third, the number of court convictions between 7 and 18 years of age measures adolescent official delinquency. Most of these court convictions happen at ages 16 and 17 (Le Blanc & Fréchette, 1989). Fourth, adult official criminal activity represents absence or presence of conviction for a criminal act while the 458 boys were between 18 and 32 years of age. The Canadian Criminal Code defines these acts. Ten percent of the 458 boys were convicted at least once, with a range of 1 to 32 convictions (see Le Blanc & Fréchette, 1989, for other statistical data on official criminal activity of the 1,611 boys). Fifth, a retrospective interview covering the period between ages 18 and 32 assesses adult self-reported criminal activity. This interview covers 16 types of offenses from minor thefts and frauds to serious assaults and thefts. With these types of offenses, we constructed a variety scale using the presence or absence of these types of criminal activity. At the average age of 32, we interviewed 309 of the 458 boys. Nine (2%) had died and we could not locate 58 (13%) others during a 2-year period; of the remaining 391 boys, 53 (14%) refused to participate and 29 (7%) were no longer living in the Province of Quebec. These 309 boys are not different from the rest of the 458 boys on the basis of their responses to the questionnaire during the period of adolescence: 67% of the 309 boys did not report participating in crime between 18 and 32 years of age, 31% report one type of offense, 2% report two types, and less than 1% report three or more. The analyses in this paper concerned 458 boys when adult official criminality is the dependent variable, and 309 boys when self-reported adult criminality is the dependent variable.

There are six external constraint variables. One variable, self-reported contact with police, represents a formal constraint (one question). Four variables from the family and one from the school domain represent informal constraints. The four family variables reported by adolescents are parental approval of friends (one question), regulations, supervision, and discipline. Regulations refer to the presence of rules decreed by parents concerning homework, meals, friends, and whereabouts (five questions, alpha .81). Supervision concerns the adolescents' perception of their parents' knowledge of where and with whom they are (two questions, alpha .95). Discipline refers to adolescents' reports of the types of punishment (quarrels, shouts, hits, restrictions of whereabouts, and unjust treatments, alpha .82) used by their parents. The last informal constraint variable refers to the presence of school disciplinary reactions. It is determined by three questions that assess school suspension, classroom expulsion, and constant checking by teachers (alpha .80).

Six variables explore the internal constraint domain. First, five questions measure beliefs or adhesion to norms. These questions assess the importance for the adolescent of respect of social norms concerning vandalism, shoplifting, use of drugs, going to school, and running away from home (alpha .89). Second, religiosity is evaluated with two questions about having and practicing a religion (alpha .70). Third, to measure the perceived risk of sanctions, we used five questions about the subjective probabilities of arrest for shoplifting, major theft, car theft, running away from home, and taking drugs (alpha .89). Fourth, one question is about the perceived legitimacy of parental rules. Fifth, two questions about denial of responsibility and one question about denial of the victim measure acceptance of neutralization formulas (alpha .88). The sixth variable is parental approval of deviance, as measured by the question, "Is it all right to get around the law if you can get away with it?"

Rankin and Wells (1988) show that the relationships between direct parental control variables and delinquency measures often depart from linearity. Their results indicate that curvilinear relationships are not substantial, even though a measure of nonlinear association (Eta) is greater for parental strictness than is a measure of linear association (Pearson *r*). We report similar observations concerning some of our family and school variables (Le Blanc, 1992; Le Blanc et al., 1992). Consequently, we verified linearity for all relationships. Results indicate that there was a departure from linearity for numerous relationships in the matrix, with correlation underestimated sometimes by half. Because many of our relationships depart from linearity without being U or inverse U shapes, we used Eta as the measure of association among all the variables. In addition, because of the absence of marked U shapes, we use the algebraic sign of the Pearson correlation because Guilford (1965) suggests that it is a good indication of the general trend in most circumstances. Eta serves also as a common base to start multivariate analysis with strictly comparable coefficients of correlation. One advantage of Eta is that it can precisely assess reciprocal relationships, and as a consequence, we can apply the interactional perspective proposed by Thornberry (1987, in press).

There are other reasons why we did not opt for alternatives such as the ones discussed by Judd and McClelland (1989). Adding curvilinear terms as additional independent variables would clutter the model. Another possibility would have been to transform monotonically the original variables. This method requires that we find the right transformation for each variable. We chose to use Eta to represent more exactly each relation between the variables and to compare them directly. In addition, our objective is not model verification but model building.

Rankin and Wells (1988) state that no multivariate statistical techniques are available for a matrix of Eta. Because of this situation, they propose to use ordinary multiple regression. We will follow them to assess which variables have a statistically significant direct relationship with each of the other variables in the model. We will also evaluate the proportion of variance explained in late adolescence delinquency and adult offending. We perform this operation for each of early and late adolescence variables by saturating the regression, that is, by including all the possible relations, and then performing a progressive elimination until the only variables left attained the $p = .002$ level.

Results

What is the relative importance of internal and external constraint variables in the prediction of offending?

Constraint variables explain a fair amount of variance of late adolescence and adult offending. Studies show that various control theory variables from the family and school domain can explain around 20% of the variance of adult self-reported or official offending (Jessor, Donavan, & Costa, 1991; Le Blanc, 1992, 1994; Le Blanc et al., 1992, 1993; Sampson & Laub, 1990). Internal and external constraint variables, without the consideration of any other well-known etiological variables, are not less efficient for the prediction of adult official criminality, with 24% of explained variance. However, constraint variables are less useful for the explanation of adult self-reported criminality, explaining only 12% of the variance. The proportion of variance explained increases from 7% by early adolescence constraint variables to 24% by late adolescence constraint variables. The reverse is true for adult self-reported criminality. When we use late instead of early adolescence constraint variables, the proportion of variance explained decreases from 13 to 8%. As shown by the Le Blanc and Fréchette data concerning this sample (1989), most of the juvenile convictions happened after the middle of adolescence. These results may indicate that adult convictions are the reflection of a cumulative labeling process. On the other hand, adult self-reported offending may be a consequence of a weaker bond to society, particularly during adulthood.

We can address these hypotheses by looking at the nature of the variables that best predict adult offending. Parental use of punishments (beta .14), boys' beliefs in the validity of legal norms (beta .31) during early adolescence, and those same beliefs (beta .28) during late adolescence best explain adult self-reported criminality. In addition, we can independently predict adult official criminality by self-reported delinquency during early adolescence (beta .26), by boys' beliefs at late adolescence (beta .32), and by juvenile convictions during adolescence (beta .8). When we use both sets of measures to predict adult offending, beliefs during early adolescence (beta .28) and perceptions of the risks of sanctions during late adolescence (beta .13) predict self-reported criminality, while beliefs during late adolescence (beta .32) and juvenile convictions (beta .28) predict adult official criminality.

Belief in the moral validity of legal norms appears to be the dominant variable. Belief overrides other internal direct constraint variables as well as all informal and formal external direct constraint variables. This relationship, established with cross-sectional data by Hirschi (1969) and replicated by others, is probably causal. It holds over time. It would be a long-standing predictor of offending because early adolescence belief is the best predictor of adult self-reported criminality. What is interesting about our results is that the importance of the beliefs replicates for official adult offending and for adult self-reported criminality in the same sample. As a consequence of the constraint variables, it is probably the only one that would stand a comparison with other bonding variables, such as attachment to persons, commitment to institutions, and involvement in activities.

Our results about self-reported and official criminality also support labeling theory. Even though the belief variable is dominant, there are some external direct constraint variables that contribute significantly and independently to the prediction of adult offending. Parental sanctions during early adolescence predict adult self-reported criminal activity, and juvenile convictions predict adult official criminality (from a labeling perspective, a conviction is a social reaction rather than the sign of a continuity in offending). These variables indicate that informal direct constraint is more significant for self-reported offending, while formal direct constraint is more important for official criminal activity. In addition, informal direct constraint variables, such as parental sanctions and supervision, correlate with adult self-reported criminal activity.

In sum, in the constraint domain at least, a mix of bonding and labeling theory seems a better explanation of adult offending. What is most interesting in our results is the continuity between informal controls and hidden offending, on one side, and formal sanctions and official criminal activity, on the other.

One variable absent from the list having a direct effect on adult offending is self-reported delinquency during adolescence. Its correlation with adult offending is important but it does not attain the chosen level of significance. This variable comes immediately after beliefs and external constraint variables in importance. In addition, this variable does not play a dominant role when only family (Le Blanc, 1992) or school (Le Blanc et al., 1992) variables are considered or when both were analyzed with adult offending (Le Blanc, 1994).

Early adolescence constraints, late adolescence delinquency, and juvenile convictions

Late adolescence self-reported delinquency has a large amount of variance accounted for (51%) by constraint variables. In turn, juvenile conviction, with 19% of explained variance, is in the range of explanation of adult offending. The level of variance explained for self-reported delinquency is comparable to figures reported by Elliott, Huizinga, & Menard (1989), Elliott, Huizinga, & Ageton (1985), Jessor et al. (1991), and Le Blanc et al. (1988) for more general models and by Le Blanc (1992; Le Blanc et al., 1993) for the family and school domain models.

There are many differences between the measures of late adolescence offending and between those of early and late adolescence when we consider the nature of the predictors. Concerning late adolescence self-reported delinquency, the early predictors are previous delinquency (beta .43), practice of religion (beta .18), and use of neutralization techniques (beta .16), while the later predictors are beliefs in the moral validity of laws (beta .50) and the imposition of school disciplinary sanctions (beta .34). Concerning late adolescent juvenile convictions, the early predictors are previous self-reported delinquency (beta .21), parental disciplinary sanctions (beta .17), and school sanctions (beta .16), while later predictors are moral beliefs (beta .22) and late adolescent delinquency (beta .19). What is also interesting in these results is that when we consider early and late adolescence variables simultaneously, an internal and an external direct constraint variable are the best predictors of juvenile offending: beliefs (beta .41) and school sanctions (beta .28) for late adoles-

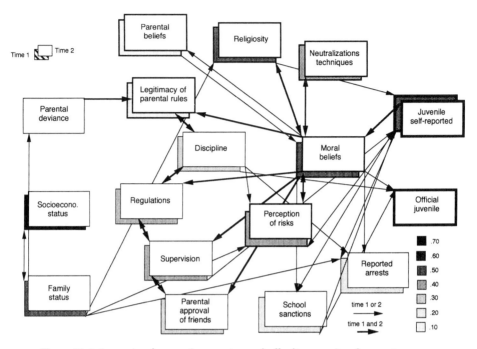

Figure 17.1. Internal and external constraints and offending, results of regressions.

cence self-reported delinquency; and school sanctions (beta .21) and beliefs (beta .19) for juvenile convictions. These results further confirm independent labeling and bonding effects on subsequent criminal activity.

There are a few specific differences between the nature of the predictors of late adolescence and adult offending. The main dissimilarities concern the role of previous delinquency. For adult offending, self-reported delinquency does not display an independent effect in five of the six regressions. The reverse is true for late adolescence self-reported and official criminal activity. In this case, we obtain an independent effect in four of the six regressions. Studies of adolescents support this role for previous self-reported delinquency (Blumstein, Cohen, Roth, & Visher, 1986; Elliott et al., 1985, 1989; Le Blanc et al., 1988). However, because delinquent acts are an epiphenomenon of adolescence, it is not surprising that self-reported delinquency is not a major predictor of adult offending.

The independent role of our four categories of internal and external direct constraints for the explanation of juvenile offending is established. Let's now investigate, for heuristic concerns, the patterns of the relationships among all the constraint variables. Five observations are worth mentioning when we plot all the independent effects of each of the early and late adolescence variables.

First, belief in moral validity of conduct norms is the central variable of the constraint domain. This variable relates to all the internal constraint measures and to five of the six external constraint variables. Only parental punishment does not correlate with beliefs. Belief in the validity of legal rules is then the organizing variable of the constraint domain. It is probably the only variable that can compete with other bonding constructs such as the attachment to persons and the commitment to institutions. Second, family constraint variables (supervision, regulations, discipline) reciprocally relate to each other. Third, there are many reciprocal effects among variables, particularly among family external constraint variables, among internal constraint variables (beliefs, neutralization, religiosity, perceived risks of arrest), and between beliefs and self-reported delinquency. Matsueda (1989) also observes these reciprocal relationships. He shows that the impact of minor forms of deviance on beliefs in honesty is more important than the impact of the beliefs on minor forms of deviance. Fourth, there are very few causal effects, that is, relationships between variables measured during early adolescence and ones assessed later. Fifth, there are only a few retroactive effects, that is, between self-reported delinquency and some internal and external constraint variables. Those retroactive effects are more numerous during early adolescence.

The results of the regressions are illustrated in Figure 17.1. It shows that internal and external constraint variables are significant explanations of late adolescence offending, and the belief in the moral validity of the law is the organizing variable of the constraint domain.

Discussion

Durkheim's distinction between conduct norms and discipline and Nye's classification of direct and indirect controls are the basis of our four categories of constraints: formal and informal social reactions as external constraints, and beliefs and perceived risk of punishment as internal constraints. We addressed two questions in this chapter. Are internal constraints more important than external constraints for the explanation of offending? Within internal and external constraints, which is the most important predictor of offending? We investigated these questions with four dependent variables: self-reported late adolescence delinquency and adult criminality and official juvenile and adult convictions.

Our results show that an attitude of respect toward the rules of society is the dominant predictor of the four types of offending; it is the most important force of restraint. Hirschi (1969) was right in proposing this construct for the explanation of adolescent conformity. However, this construct is generally left aside by most replications of Hirschi's theory. These replications concentrate on attachment and commitment as the most important elements of the bond to society (see Kempf, 1993). Also, belief in the validity of legal rules is, as in Farrington (1986), a good predictor of adult offending. Belief in the validity of conduct rules is also the organizing variable of the constraint domain. For adolescents, these beliefs are the main force of coercion when the temptation for offending is present.

While the bonding effect is the predominant one in our representative sample of males, there is also a labeling effect. External constraints display an independent effect on offending. Informal external constraints are triggering adolescent delinquency, while formal external constraints are encouraging adult criminality. Contrary to the bonding effect, the labeling effect varies with age and the measures of offending. There is clear continuity between formal processing during adolescence and the level of adult official criminality. In addition, there is continuity between informal parental and school sanctions during early adolescence and formal processing during late adolescence. Because of these results, we can think of labeling as a cumulative coercive process involving initial informal social reactions and then formal sanctions that eventually become continuous over time.

What is most interesting in our results is that the bonding effect is almost sufficient for the prediction of self-reported offending, while the labeling effect is essential for the prediction of official criminal activity. This observation is not surprising, since the correlation between official and self-reported offending, during adolescence and adulthood, is rather low in our sample. Criminal activity is always a response to tenuous beliefs, but formal social reactions are either a source of amplification or more probably a selection artifact (Smith & Paternoster, 1990).

In sum, the response to our first question is that internal constraints are the dominant coercive force for the explanation of late adolescence and adult criminal activity, while external constraints are secondary coercive forces. Within each of these types of constraints, what components are most compelling?

In the social reaction field, our data challenge Thomas & Bishop (1984), who found that formal sanctions are more important than informal sanctions. We find that adolescent self-reported offending is primarily a response to informal sanctions by parents and school authorities. Concerning adult official criminal activity, we confirm Thomas & Bishop (1984) regarding the importance of formal sanctions. In the internal constraint field, for every measure of criminal activity, beliefs surpass perceptual deterrence measures. We here replicate Meier and Johnson (1977) regarding marijuana use and Minor (1985) and Nagin and Paternoster (1991) regarding adolescent self-reported delinquency. We extend the observation to adult criminal activity.

In conclusion, constraint variables are competitive explanations of offending, since they account for a proportion of variance comparable to variables of other domains, such as family, school, and peers. What we must now test is how these constraint constructs behave when we consider all the possible direct and indirect control variables at the same time. In other words, which is most important for conformity: bonding or coercion? However, we know (Le Blanc, 1992; Le Blanc et al., 1993) that the external constraint variables of the family and school domains play an important role in the explanation of late adolescence and adult offending.

Attention should focus mainly on internal constraint variables, particularly beliefs. Minor (1985) indicates that constraint is a more proximal explanation of self-reported delinquency than is bonding. Withholding a positive or negative conclusion about the role of beliefs when compared with the role of a person's attachment, commitment, and involvement, we must remember that the measure of respect for the law is also an attitudinal measure of offending. This variable involves some items included in the self-reported delinquency scale. As in the case of measurement of delinquent peers, we could argue, with Gottfredson and Hirschi (1990), that there is a method overlap. The consistencies in our results with self-reported and official juvenile and adult offending do not militate for that explanation of the longitudinal relationship between beliefs and subsequent criminal activity.

NOTE

This research was funded by Le Conscil de la Recherche en Sciences Humaines du Canada. I thank Pierre McDuff for his help with data analysis. The author will provide data upon request.

REFERENCES

Biron, L., Caplan, A., & Le Blanc, M. (1975) *La construction de l'Echantillon, la cueillette des donneés et leur préparation.* Montréal: Groupe de recherche sur l'inadaptation Juvénile, Université de Montréal.

Biron, L., Caplan, A., & Le Blanc, M. (1977) La relanceé: Chantillonnage, cueillette et préparation des données. Montréal: Groupe de recherche sur l'inadaptation juvénile, Université de Montréal.

Blumstein, A., Cohen, J., Roth, J. A., & Visher, C. A. (1986). *Criminal careers and "career criminals."* Washington, DC: National Academy Press.

Brownfield, D., & Sorenson, A-M. (1991). Religion and drug use among adolescents: A social support conceptualization and interpretation. *Deviant Behavior: An Interdisciplinary Journal, 12,* 259–276.

Caplan, A. (1978). *A formal statement and extension of Hirschi's theory of social control.* Montréal: Groupe de recherche sur l'inadaptation juvénile, Université de Montréal.

Caplan, A., & Le Blanc, M. (1985). A cross-cultural verification of a social control theory. *International Journal of Comparative and Applied Criminal Justice, 9*(2), 123–138.

Durkheim, E. (1934). *L'éducation morale.* Paris: Alcan.

Elliott, D. S., & Ageton, S. (1980). Reconciling race and class differences in self-reported and official estimates of delinquency. *American Sociological Review, 45,* 95–110.

Elliott, D. S., Huizinga, D., & Ageton, S. S. (1985). *Explaining delinquency and drug use.* Beverly Hills, CA: Sage.

Elliott, D. S., Huizinga, D., & Menard, S. (1989). *Multiple problem youth: Delinquency, substance abuse, and mental health problems.* New York: Springer-Verlag.

Ellis, L. (1987). Religiosity and criminality from the perspective of arousal theory. *Journal of Research in Crime and Delinquency, 24,* 215–232.

Farrington, D. P. (1977). The effects of public labeling. *British Journal of Criminology, 17,* 112–125.

Farrington, D. P. (1986). Stepping-stones to adult criminal careers. In D. Olweus, J. Block, & M. R. Yarrow, *Development of antisocial and prosocial behavior* (pp. 359–384). New York: Academic.

Farrington, D. P., Osborn, S. G., & West, D. J. (1978). The persistence of labelling effects. *British Journal of Criminology, 18,* 177–184.

Fréchette, M., & Le Blanc, M. (1987). Délinquances et délinquants. Chicoutimi: Gatéan Morin.

Gold, M. (1970). *Delinquent behavior in an American city*. Belmont, CA: Brooks/Cole.

Gold, M., & Williams, J. R. (1969). The effect of "getting caught": Apprehension of the juvenile offender as a cause of subsequent delinquencies. *Prospectus, 3,* 1–12.

Gottfredson, M. R., & Hirschi, T. (1990). *A general theory of crime*. Stanford, CA: Stanford University Press.

Guilford, J. P. (1965). *Fundamental statistics in psychology and education*. New York: McGraw-Hill.

Hindelang, M. J. (1973). Causes of delinquency: A partial replication and extension. *Social Problems, 20,* 471–487.

Hindelang, M., Hirschi, T., & Weis, J. (1981). *Measuring delinquency*. Beverly Hills, CA: Sage.

Hirschi, T. (1969). *Causes of delinquency*. Berkeley: University of California Press.

Jensen, G. F., & Rojek, D. G. (1980). *Delinquency*. Lexington, MA: Heath.

Jessor, R., Donavan, J. E., & Costa, F. M. (1991). *Beyond adolescence, problem behavior and young adult development*. Cambridge University Press.

Judd, C. M., & McClelland, G. H. (1989). *Data analysis: A model comparison approach*. New York: Harcourt, Brace, Jovanovich.

Junger-Tas, J., & Junger, M. (1985). *Juvenile delinquency: The impact of judicial intervention*. The Hague: Research and Documentation Center, Ministry of Justice.

Kaplan, H. B., & Johnson, R. J. (1991). Negative social sanctions and juvenile delinquency: Effects of labeling in a model of deviant behavior. *Social Science Quarterly, 72,* 98–122.

Kempf, K. (1993). Hirschi's theory of social control: Is it fecund but not yet fertile? *Advances in Theoretical Criminology, 4,* 143–186.

Laub, J. H., & Sampson, R. J. (1988). Unraveling families and delinquency: A reanalysis of the Gluecks' data. *Criminology, 26,* 355–380.

Le Blanc, M. (1992). Family dynamics, adolescent delinquency and adult criminality. *Psychiatry, 55*(1), 336–353.

Le Blanc, M. (1994). Family, school, delinquency and criminality: The predictive power of an elaborated social control theory for male criminal behavior and mental health, *4*(2), 101–117.

Le Blanc, M., & Caplan, A. (1993). Theoretical formalization, a necessity: The example of Hirschi's bonding theory. *Advances in Theoretical Criminology, 4,* 329–431.

Le Blanc, M., & Fréchette, M. (1989). *Male criminal activity from childhood through youth: Multilevel and developmental perspectives*. New York: Springer-Verlag.

Le Blanc, M., McDuff, P., & Fréchette, M. (1990). *MASPAQ: Manuel sur des Mesures de l'Adaptation Sociale et Personnelle pour les Adolescents Québécois*. Montréal: Groupe de recherche sur l'inadaptation psycho-sociale chez l'enfant, Université de Montréal.

Le Blanc, M., Ouimet, M., & Tremblay, R. E. (1988). An integrative control theory of delinquent behavior: A validation, 1976–1985. *Psychiatry, 51,* 164–176.

Le Blanc, M., Valliéres, E., & McDuff, P. (1992). Adolescents' school experience and self-reported offending: A longitudinal test of a social control theory. *International Journal of Youth and Adolescence, 3*(3–4), 197–247.

Le Blanc, M., Valliéres, E., & McDuff, P. (1993). The prediction of male adolescent and adult offending from school experience. *Canadian Journal of Criminology, 35*(4), 459–478.

Loeber, R. & Le Blanc,, M. (1990). Toward a developmental criminology. In M. Tonry and N. Morris (Eds.), *Crime and justice: An annual review* (Vol. 12, pp. 373–473). Chicago: University of Chicago Press.

Loeber, R., & Stouthamer-Loeber, M. (1986). Family factors as correlates and predictors of juvenile conduct problems and delinquency. In M. Tonry & N. Morris (Eds.), *Crime and Justice: An Annual Review* (Vol. 7, pp. 29–150). Chicago: University of Chicago Press.

Loeber, R., & Stouthamer-Loeber, M. (1987). Prediction. In H. C. Quay (Ed.), *Handbook of juvenile delinquency* (pp. 325–382). New York: Wiley.

Malewska, H., & Peyre, V. (1973). Délinquance juvénile, famille, école et société en France et en Pologne. Vaucresson: Cujas.

Mannle, H. W., & Lewis, P. W. (1979). Control theory reexamined: Race and the use of neutralizations among institutionalized delinquents. *Criminology, 17*(1), 58–74.

Matsueda, R. L. (1989). The dynamics of moral beliefs and minor deviance. *Social Forces, 68*, 428–457.

Meier, R., Burkett, S. R., & Hickman, C. A. (1984). Sanction, peer and deviance: Preliminary models of a social control process. *Sociological Quarterly, 23*, 26–67.

Meier, R. F., & Johnson, W. T. (1977). Deterrence as social control: The legal and extralegal production of conformity. *American Sociological Review, 42*, 292–304.

Minor, W. W. (1977). A deterrence-control theory of crime. In R. F. Meier, *Theory in criminology: Contemporary views* (pp. 117–137). Beverly Hills, CA: Sage.

Minor, W. W. (1981). Techniques of neutralization: A reconceptualization and empirical examination. *Journal of Research in Crime and Delinquency, 18*, 295–318.

Minor, W. W. (1985). Neutralization as a hardening process: Considerations in the modeling of change. *Social Forces, 26*, 995–1019.

Nagin, D. B., & Paternoster, R. (1991). The preventive effects of the perceived risk of arrest: Testing an expanded conception of deterrence. *Criminology, 29*, 561–585.

Nunnaly, J. C. (1967). *Psychometric theory.* New York: McGraw-Hill.

Nye, F. I. (1958). *Family relationships and delinquent behavior.* New York: Wiley.

Palamera, F., Cullen, F. T., & Gersten, J. C. (1986). The effect of police and mental health intervention on juvenile deviance: Specifying contingencies in the impact of formal reaction. *Journal of Health and Social Behavior, 27*, 90–105.

Paternoster, R. (1987). The deterrent effect of the perceived certainty and severity of punishment: A review of the evidence and issues. *Justice Quarterly, 4*, 151–173.

Paternoster, R., & Iovanni, L. (1986). The deterrent effect of perceived severity: A reexamination. *Social Forces, 64*, 751–777.

Paternoster, R., Saltzman, L. E., Waldo, G. P., & Chiricos, T. G. (1983). Perceived risk and social control: Do sanctions really deter? *Law and Society, 17*, 457–479.

Piliavin, I., Gartner, R., Thornton, C., & Matsueda, R. L. (1986). Crime, deterrence and rational choice. *American Sociological Review, 51*, 101–119.

Rankin, J. H., & Wells, L. E. (1988). The effect of parental attachments and direct controls on delinquency. *Journal of Research in Crime and Delinquency, 27*(2), 140–165.

Ray, M. C., & Downs, W. R. (1986). An empirical test of labeling theory using longitudinal data. *Journal of Research in Crime and Delinquency, 23*, 169–194.

Rollins, B., & Thomas, D. (1979). Parental support, power, and control techniques in the socialization of children. In R. H. W. Burr, F. I. Nye, and I. Reiss (Eds.), *Contemporary theories about the family* (pp. 317–364). New York: Free Press.

Sampson, R. J., & Laub, J. H. (1990). Stability and change in crime and deviance over the life course: The salience of adult social bonds. *American Sociological Review, 55*, 609–627.

Schaber, G., Haussman, P., Beaufils, M., Boniver, M., & Kerger, A. (1982). Le poids de l'inadaptation en milieu scolaire dans le processus délinquantiel. Luxembourg: Fondation Universitaire Luxembourgeoise.

Schneider, A. L. (1990). *Deterrence and juvenile crime.* New York: Springer-Verlag.

Shannon, L. W. (1991). Changing patterns of delinquency and crime: A longitudinal study in Racine. Boulder: Westview Press.

Shoemaker, D. J. (1990). *Theories of delinquency: An examination of explanations of delinquent behavior.* New York: Oxford University Press.

Smith, D. A., & Gartin, P. R. (1989). Specifying specific deterrence: The influence of arrest on future criminal activity. *American Sociological Review, 54,* 94–105.

Smith, D. A., & Paternoster, R. (1990). Formal processing and future delinquency: Deviance amplification as selection artifact. *Law and Society, 24,* 1109–1131.

Sykes, G., & Matza, D. (1957). Techniques of neutralization: A theory of delinquency. *American Sociological Review, 22,* 664–670.

Thomas, C. W., & Bishop, D. M. (1984). The effect of formal and informal sanctions on delinquency: A longitudinal comparison of labeling and deterrence theories. *Journal of Criminal Law and Criminology, 75,* 1222–1245.

Thornberry, T. P. (1987). Toward an interactional theory of delinquency. *Criminology, 25,* 863–891.

Thornberry, T. P. (in press). Empirical support for interactional theory: A review of the literature. In J. D. Hawkins (Ed.), *Some current theory of crime and deviance.* Newbury Park, CA: Sage.

Tittle, C. R. (1980). *Sanctions and deviance: The question of deterrence.* New York: Praeger.

Wells, L. E., & Rankin, J. H. (1988). Direct parental controls and delinquency. *Criminology, 26*(2), 263–285.

Williams, J. R., & Gold, M. (1972). From delinquent behavior to official delinquency. *Social Problems, 20*(2), 209–229.

Wolfgang, M. E., Figlio, R. M., & Sellin, T. (1972). *Delinquency in a birth cohort.* Chicago: University of Chicago Press.

18 Negative social sanctions and deviant behavior: a conditional relationship

HOWARD B. KAPLAN AND KELLY R. DAMPHOUSSE

This chapter reports the results of a series of models that specify conditions under which the effect of negative social sanctions on deviant behavior (net of the effect of earlier deviant behavior on negative social sanctions and later deviant behavior) is relatively strong or weak.

Negative social sanctions from the labeling perspective

Social sanctions are reactions by others to the real or imagined behavior of an individual. The sanctions serve as either intended or perceived rewards/punishments for the behavior. The concept has been presented in sociological contexts as potentially powerful for understanding the processes underlying the continuation or escalation of deviant behavior. Two competing bodies of literature have developed that relate to the effect of punishment on behavior (Sherman & Berk, 1984). The deterrence literature hypothesizes that punishment deters people from repeating crimes for which they are punished. Labeling theory, on the other hand, fosters "the ironic view that punishment often makes individuals more likely to commit crimes because of altered instructional structure, foreclosed legal opportunities and secondary deviance" (1984, p. 261). The empirical support and theoretical basis of the labeling hypothesis (that individuals will engage in further deviance as a result of punitive response) have been evaluated extensively over the years.

Empirical support

Punitive social responses have been associated with subsequent acquisition of deviant identities and conformity to deviant roles. Farrington (1977) concluded that publicly labeled youths had higher self-reported delinquency scores than did the nonlabeled youths. More recently, Palamara, Cullen, and Gersten (1986) observed

289

that police and mental health intervention had both independent and interactive effects on increasing juvenile delinquency. They also noted that the effects varied according to the form of juvenile deviance (delinquency, anxiety, general psychological impairment) under consideration. Apprehended youths tended to commit more offenses subsequently than did the unapprehended controls (Gold, 1970; Gold & Williams, 1969; Gold, 1970). Compatible findings were reported also by Ageton and Elliott (1974), Klein (1974), Klemke (1978), O'Connor (1970), and Wheeler (1978).

However, other investigators have concluded that formal negative sanctions do not influence commitment to deviant careers (Gove, 1975; Hawkins, 1976; Hepburn, 1977; Wellford, 1975), do not influence variables that are hypothesized to mediate the relationship between sanctions and deviance (Foster, Dinitz, & Reckless, 1972), or do, indeed, deter rather than amplify deviance (Sherman & Berk, 1984). Thus, Foster, Dinitz, and Reckless (1972) failed to observe that apprehended boys perceived interpersonal difficulties associated with being apprehended. Sherman and Berk (1984), in a field experiment on domestic violence, found arrested subjects showed significantly less subsequent violence than did those not arrested.

The instances of failure to observe effects of negative sanctions may be accounted for by methodological problems including "poor matching of control subjects, inadequate adjustment or control for preintervention levels of delinquency or behavior impairment and the operationalization of 'secondary deviance' into criteria of questionable validity such as delinquency recidivism and school performance" (Palamara et al., 1986, p. 91). In any case, the numerous studies that report positive associations between negative social sanctions and amplified deviance suggest that at least under certain conditions, negative sanctions influence subsequent performance of deviant behavior. These findings were sufficiently encouraging to stimulate further research on the mechanisms that mediate the relationship between social sanctions and deviance.

Theoretical mediating variables

In the context of the theoretical formulation that guides the present analyses (Kaplan, 1972, 1975, 1980, 1982, 1984, 1986), personal and social consequences of negative social sanctions that adumbrate escalation or amplification of deviant behavior were interpreted as reflecting or influencing the deviant actor's (1) loss of motivation to conform to, and acquisition of motivation to deviate from, conventional norms, (2) association with deviant peers, and (3) reevaluation of deviant identities and behaviors.

Loss of motivation to conform to, and acquisition of motivation to deviate from, conventional norms. Negative social sanctions in responses to initial deviant responses increase the likelihood that the deviant actor will be publicly identified as deviant. The public identification has adverse social consequences for the deviant actor including exclusion from conventional groups. These consequences, secondary to the earlier punitive responses, also serve as negative social sanctions that signify and excite public identification of the person as deviant.

Negative social sanctions and social ostracism are intrinsically disvalued and reflect the deprivation of resources that are instrumental to the achievement of personal goals. Further, the associated deprivation of educational and employment opportunities, and of social cooperation in general (Link, 1982; Mankoff, 1971; Schwartz & Skolnick, 1962), impedes the achievement of other social values. The deprivations are exacerbated by the voluntary social withdrawal of the deviant actor out of fear of rejection and other maladaptive defensive maneuvers (Link, 1987).

The person's self-referent responses (self-perceptions, self-evaluation, self-feelings) to negative social sanctions influence his or her affective investment in the conventional order. The individual loses motivation to conform to conventional expectations because (1) the negative self-feelings, evoked by the self-devaluing experiences of being publicly identified and punished as a deviant, come to be associated with the conventional order and (2) the deviant actor anticipates that stigmatization as a deviant and concomitant exclusion from conventional society poses possible insurmountable barriers to reentry into conventional society and access to needed resources (including social acceptance itself). Deviant behavior is facilitated by the loss of motivation to conform to conventional expectations.

The person also acquires motivation to deviate from conventional norms. Deviation represents repudiation of the evaluative standards that the deviant actor associates with being stigmatized and deprived of future rewards. The motivation to deviate from conventional expectations increases the probability that the deviant actor in fact will become aware of and adopt deviant patterns not only because the deviant behavior represents a rejection of conventional patterns but also because the person continues to require fulfillment of personal needs through alternative mechanisms than the now rejected conventional patterns.

Association with deviant peers. Negative social sanctions increase association with deviant peers. The increased association with deviant peers is anticipated for several reasons (Akers, 1985; Farrell, 1989; Kaplan, 1984). First, the stigma that is secondary to negative social sanctions limits the opportunities for the deviant actor to interact with conventional people in conventional contexts. At the same time, the deviant actor recognizes the difficulty of reentry into conventional society as a result of becoming the object of formal and informal labeling (self-labeling). Consequently, the deviant actor decreases interaction in conventional spheres and, thus, increases interaction in deviant peer associations.

Second, certain social sanctions impose structural imperatives that require association with deviant peers. Most apparent are incarceration and expulsion or suspension from school, which constrains interaction with others to those who are similarly sanctioned. Third, negative social sanctions and their correlates influence the deviant actor's motivation to seek out deviant peer associations and to be receptive to such interactional opportunities. The achievement of deviant values and the consequent acceptance by deviant peers, as well as the associated symbolic rejection of conventional values, offers promise of enhanced self-attitudes.

Fourth, the publicly deviant actor is attractive to the deviant peers and may be recruited as part of their network. The recruitment is facilitated by the accessibility of the deviant actor secondary to being excluded from conventional society and by being amenable to overtures from deviant peers that results from the actor's motivation to forestall rejection by conventional others and enhance self-attitudes. The association with deviant peers has direct impact on the future performance of deviant behavior (Kaplan, Johnson, & Bailey, 1987).

Reevaluation of deviant identities and behaviors. Negative social sanctions cause the deviant actor to positively value deviant behaviors and identities. The person becomes attracted to deviant behavior for reasons related to the reduction of self-rejecting feelings and the affirmation of self-worth. First, the deviant actors evaluate deviant behavior and identities positively to "regain their identity through redefining normality and realizing that it is acceptable to be who they are" (Coleman, 1986, p. 225). Negative social sanctions influence self-conceptions of being the object of negative social sanction and of being one who experiences intrinsically and instrumentally disvalued outcomes such as loss of income and exclusion from conventional groups. Since positive responses from others and associated resources are among the evaluative standards of self-worth, negative social sanctions lead individuals to judge themselves negatively. Given the need to maintain one's self-esteem (Kaplan, 1986), the individual reevaluates the self-ascribed and other-ascribed deviant identities and behavior. The stigmatized social identity and the associated deviant acts are redefined as having positive value.

Second, the person comes to value deviant patterns and identities because they reflect achievable standards for positive self-evaluation that replace conventional standards that cannot be achieved because the negative social sanctions exclude the deviant actor from conventional circles and restrict access to resources.

Third, a commitment to deviant behavior and identities excuses conventional failure. The stigmatizing consequences of the negative social sanctions exacerbate the previous failures to conform to social expectations that have been implicated in the onset of the deviant behavior (Kaplan, 1980; Kaplan, Martin, & Johnson, 1986). By continuing to behave in a deviant fashion, and thereby continuing to evoke a labeling response, the individual can blame the label itself and excuses him- or herself by attributing failure to being socially stigmatized. (Whether or not the stigma is justified is irrelevant, although the implication, from the stigmatized person's perspective, is that it is not justified.) Further, the emotional commitment to deviant identity precludes the need to attempt to conform to conventional expectations, thereby forestalling further self-rejecting experiences and reinforcing the value of deviant behaviors and identities.

Fourth, the deviant actor values deviant activities and identities because they reflect or are instrumental in the achievement of conventionally valued ends. For example, unable to achieve material rewards by legitimate means, the person uses techniques of theft or fraud to gain these ends. Further, the deviant acts themselves may reflect conventionally valued ends, as when the successful performance of deviant acts provides the person with a sense of self-efficacy or when the performance of a particularly hazardous deviant act is interpretable as reflecting another valued end such as bravery.

Having transformed the value of deviant behaviors and identities from negative to positive, deviant actors are motivated to behave in ways that validate those identities. Once they come to value the identity, deviant actors are motivated to conform to its normative expectations so as to evaluate themselves positively.

On the basis of these considerations, we estimated a model in which negative social sanctions were specified to be a consequence of prior deviance and as having direct and indirect (via disposition to deviance and deviant peer associations) effects on later deviance. The model was estimated using LISREL VI on data from a three-wave panel of junior high school students. As expected, the interpolation of negative social sanctions partially decomposed the earlier observed effects of prior deviant behavior and increased the explained variance in later deviance (Kaplan & Johnson, 1991, p. 115). The specification of negative social sanctions as an in-·ervening variable constituted an elaboration of a previously estimated model. A further elaboration of the model estimated the theoretical basis for the hypothesized and observed direct effects of negative social sanctions on disposition to deviance and later drug use (Kaplan & Fukurai, 1992). These effects were hypothesized on theoretical premises relating to the effects of negative social sanctions on self-rejection and the effects of self-rejection on disposition to deviance and drug use, respectively. However, the mediating effect of self-rejection was not tested. This elaboration of the earlier model specified these intervening effects. It was hypothesized and observed that self-rejection would mediate and decompose the effects of negative social sanctions on disposition to deviance and drug use. These expectations were rewarded. Negative social sanctions had a significant and appreciable effect on self-rejection, which had a strong effect on disposition to deviance and a modest (but statistically significant) effect on drug use.

Theoretical moderating variables

The successful estimation of theoretically informed models that specify mediating variables between negative social sanctions and the escalation or amplification of later deviance (net of the influence of earlier deviance) lends a good deal of credibility to the labeling perspective. However, these analyses do not account for the numerous findings (only some of which may be accounted for by methodological differences or deficiencies) that failed to observe a labeling effect or the persistence of the deterrence hypothesis in the literature despite the lack of firm and consistent support (Piliavin, Thornton, Gartner, & Matsueda, 1986; Smith & Gartin, 1989). The differences in findings between the analyses conducted in our laboratory and those reported by others may be accounted for in part by the absence of conditions in some studies that are presumed to exist by those who expect that negative social sanctions in response to initial deviant acts will stimulate escalation or amplification of such acts. The relationship between being the object of negative social sanctions and the amplification of deviance may be conditional, for example, on the absence of commitment to conventional morality, perceptions of opportunities for benign outcomes of illicit occupations, and respect for such occupations (Piliavin et al., 1986). The acceptance or rejection of labeling (and, presumably, consequent deviant behavior) might be a function of such conditions as the defense mechanisms they employed, the degree of negative sanctions they received, and the environment in which the sanctions were administered (Covington, 1984). The deterrent or amplifying effect of punishment may depend on the stage of the deviant's career (Jensen, 1969; Packer, 1968; Smith & Gartin, 1989; Thorsel & Klemke, 1972). Populations in which a strong labeling effect is observed may be those characterized by the presence of certain of these conditions to the exclusion of other conditions. Populations characterized by other conditions may be those in which a weaker or nonsignificant labeling effect, or a deterrent effect, is observed.

Within the context of the theoretical framework that informs these analyses, a number of conditions are specified under which relatively strong and relatively weak labeling effects will be observed. A model is estimated for these specified (and their mutually exclusive) conditions in which being the object of negative sanctions is specified as influencing later deviant behavior net of the influences of earlier deviant behavior and exogenous sociodemographic variables. For the population at large, negative social sanctions are known to be the outcome of early deviance and the antecedent of later deviance. The positive effect of negative social sanctions on later deviance is expected to be weaker under certain conditions and stronger under other mutually exclusive conditions. The disposition to engage in deviance that is the outcome of negative social sanctions (mediated by alienation from conventional society, increased association with deviant peers, and the need to restore damaged self-esteem) should be weaker where the objects of negative social sanctions perceive that rewards are contingent on conforming behavior, are anxious about the consequences of risky behavior, are motivated to avoid negative interpersonal sanctions, are motivated to obtain conventional rewards (reflected in the need to restore or attain positive self-attitudes), and are subject to surveillance by agents of social control. Under mutually exclusive conditions the disposition to engage in deviant behavior is not constrained. The objects of negative social sanctions are not fearful of losing conventional rewards, are not anxious about risky outcomes, are not motivated to obtain conventional rewards or to avoid interpersonal sanctions, and do not perceive themselves as under surveillance.

Method

The analyses involve the estimation of a baseline structural model accounting for deviant behavior for different subpopulations characterized by mutually exclusive values of dichotomous variables that are expected to moderate the structural relationships using data from a three-wave panel. The structural model specifies the effect of negative social sanctions on later deviant behavior net of the effects of antecedent deviant behavior and sociodemographic factors on these constructs. The analyses examine the moderating influence of conditional values on the effects of being the object of negative social sanctions on later deviance by comparing the unstandardized structural effects across groups characterized by one or the other value for each dichotomous conditional variable.

Sample and data collection

The subject sample represents 50% of the students in the 36 junior high schools of the Houston Independent School District in 1971. The survey is a three-wave panel study beginning in 1971 (Time 1) and repeated in 1972 (Time 2) and 1973 (Time 3). The questionnaires generally were completed in class. Usable questionnaires were returned by 7,618 students (82%) at T1. A total of 3,148 students were present for all three administrations, constituting 41% of the usable sample interviewed at T1. Of these, 2,062 subjects provided data for all measures used in the baseline model. The numbers of subjects used in the conditional analyses depended on the distribution of responses to the conditional variables among the true–false or yes–no categories.

The effects of the appreciable sample attrition were evaluated by comparing the within-wave relationships among measurement variables at the first data collection for those subjects who were present at all three points in time and those who were not. Generally, the values in the two groupings were quite similar. Where differences were observed the coefficients were stronger for the latter group. This suggests that the results observed for subjects present at all three points were conservative and would have been even stronger had no sample attrition occurred (on the assumption that lagged relationships would have paralleled within-wave relationships). Caution dictates, however, not generalizing beyond the subjects present at all three test administrations.

The effects of missing data among those present at all three points in time were evaluated by comparing matrices using the listwise and pairwise options. Previous analyses have indicated that the two sets of matrices were quite comparable.

Latent constructs and measurement variables/baseline models

The baseline model specifies relationships among four exogenous sociodemographic variables used as control variables, with *deviant behavior* measured at T1 and T3 and *negative social sanctions* measured at T2.

Exogenous variables. Exogenous variables included *gender* (male = 1, female = 0), *race* (black = 1, nonblack = 0), *ethnicity* (Mexican-American = 1, non–Mexican-American = 0), and *father's education* (did not graduate elementary school = 1, some high school = 2, graduated from high school = 3, graduated from college = 4). If the subject had no father or did not know his level of education the data for mother's education were used.

Deviant behavior. Deviant behavior measured at T1 and T3 is conceptualized as any of a range of behaviors that reflect violation of conventional norms. This construct is difficult to operationalize since definitions of deviant behavior may vary for the several groups that comprise the inclusive society. Also, the subject's personal definition of the acts as deviant or not deviant may be at variance with the definition of others. For present purposes we simply assume that the behaviors we define as deviant would be so regarded by representatives of the more inclusive society. We also assume that our subjects share the more inclusive definitions of deviant behavior. This is somewhat justified since the subjects remained in school in their appropriate grades during the junior high school years.

Deviance is modeled as a latent construct indicated by three measures. Each of the measures reflects self-reports of engaging in at least one of several deviant responses that have prevalence rates falling within a narrow range. First, the grouping of seven least prevalent patterns (e.g., took things worth $50 or more that didn't belong to you; breaking and entering; participation in gang fights; vandalism) had prevalence rates between 5 and 9% and alpha coefficients of .55 and .74 for T1 and T3, respectively. Second, the grouping of six moderate prevalence items (e.g., carried a weapon; started a fistfight; stole things from a desk or locker at school; used drugs) had prevalence rates ranging between 12 and 17% and alphas of .55 and .67 for T1 and T3, respectively. Third, the grouping of six most prevalent patterns (e.g., stole things worth less than $2; smoked marijuana; skipped school without an excuse) had prevalence rates ranging between 24 and 28% and alphas of .52 and .65 for T1 and T3, respectively. Self-reports of deviance at T3 refer to behavior during the preceding year, with the exception of using wine, beer, or liquor more than two times, which refers to the preceding week. At T1 self-reports of deviant behavior refer to behavior during the preceding month with the exceptions of alcohol use (that, again, refers to the preceding week) and failing grades (that refers to the preceding 9-week period).

The three measures were created as dichotomies. Modeling the deviance construct in this fashion offers several advantages. First, each measure reflects engaging in some form of deviance (as opposed to none) rather than the amount of deviance (e.g., the number of acts over time). This is appropriate in a test of a model that purports to explain some form of deviant behavior from among the range of deviant acts that constitute violations of the normative expectations of specified membership groups. Second, each measure is defined in terms of behaving in any of a number of heterogeneous deviant ways. Again, this is appropriate in a test of theory that recognizes that deviant dispositions in a given social context may be expressed in any of a number of ways, the common defining element being the contravention of the group norms. Which of the several theoretically available deviant acts is adopted in fact is a function of more specific personal and situational constraints. To measure deviance in terms of more homogeneous indexes (e.g., stealing, violence) would decrease the likelihood of observing the expression of deviant responses (perhaps because of existing constraints against the acting out of these particular behaviors). Third, since the prevalence of deviant behaviors in each measure is roughly equal, the likelihood that any measure will be unduly weighted in favor of more prevalent items is precluded. This is important since either a successful or an unsuccessful test of theory might be conditional on the unique features of the more prevalent deviant patterns. In the case of moderate and severe forms of deviance the occurrence of at least one incident is taken as indicative of deviant behavior. Where behaviors are more prevalent, however, it is reasonable to think of an occasional performance as being incidental to deviant motivation. For this reason, in the relevant modes of deviance index we used two as the cutting point for indicating deviant behavior. The full-range scales of the three deviance measures correlated highly with the dichotomized scales (for the least, moderate, and most prevalent items, .76, .77, and .85, respectively).

Use of a general measure of deviance is warranted here since there is nothing in the labeling literature that requires that the stabilization of a deviant career be isomorphic with the initial deviance. Societal reactions to initial deviance may lead to the expression of alternative deviant forms depending on a number of situational contingencies. Palamara et al. (1986) observed (we believe, correctly) that many researchers involved in labeling research appear to accept the assumption of etiological specificity whereby the individual who is labeled as one who engages in a specific form of deviance will continue to behave according to that specific deviant pattern. However, in so doing, research may be precluded from observing important labeling effects on other modes of deviance. This may account, in part, for inconsistent conclusions in the literature regarding the effects of negative social sanctions on deviance.

Negative social sanctions. Negative social sanctions are measured by a single-indicator, three-item scale drawn from the second wave of the panel, T2. Since the items refer to experiences that occurred between the first two waves, the construct is modeled as occurring between T1 and T2 (as the consequence of T1 deviance and the precursor of T3 deviance). The three items refer to self-reports of the following experiences: suspended or expelled from school; had anything to do with the police, sheriff, or juvenile officers; and taken to the office for punishment. Negative social sanctions are conceptualized as responses by others to the behavior of the subject that, by the intention of the others or perception by the subject, serve as a punishment for the subject's behavior. The self-reports may reflect the true responses of others to the person's earlier deviance or the self-perceptions of being the object of rejection or punitive responses by others. In the former case the index is better interpreted as societal reaction. In the latter case the index is better interpreted as initial self-labeling as deviant that results from the perceived societal reaction. Since the two interpretations may be thought of as causally related (i.e., a societal reaction leads to self-labeling), we will interpret it as a higher order construct reflecting both phenomena.

Usually the assumption is made that a single indicator is measured without error. Given three repeated measures, however, the alternative assumption can be made that each time the variable is measured a fixed proportion of the score is "true" and the remaining nonzero variance is error. Using the technique described by Kessler and Greenberg (1981, p. 148), we estimated this proportion of true score and fixed the error term to its estimated value.

Conditional variables

Seventeen variables measured at T1 were selected to reflect conditions under which a positive effect of negative social sanctions on T3 deviant behavior was more or less likely to be observed. For each variable one of the yes–no or true–false dichotomous responses was expected to be a contingency for a stronger effect and the other mutually exclusive response was expected to be a condition for observing a weaker labeling effect (i.e., a positive effect of T2 negative social sanctions on T3 deviant behavior). The seventeen conditional variables, measured at T1, are presented in Table 18.1. The theoretical bases for their selection will be presented in conjunction with the presentation of the results.

Analysis

A baseline structural model (see Figure 18.1) was estimated for all of the subjects present at all three points in time who provided data for all of the variables. The same model was estimated for both mutually exclusive values for each of the 17 conditional variables. Thus, 35 models were estimated (the baseline plus 34 conditional values). The essential part of the analysis for present purposes was a comparison of the unstandardized effects of negative social sanctions on later deviant behavior of the subgroups defined in terms of the mutually exclusive response categories for each.

The baseline and conditional models were estimated using correlation and standard deviation matrices of self-reported variables as input to LISREL VII (Jöreskog

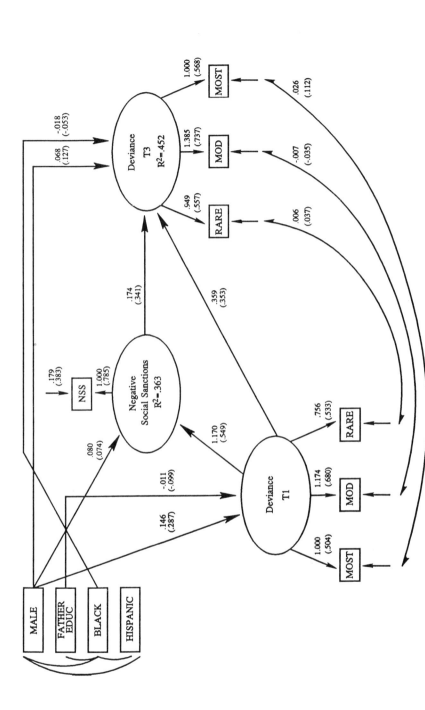

Figure 18.1. Baseline structural equation model with control variables. Standardized coefficients in parentheses. The measures of goodness-of-fit for the model are chi-square with 25 degrees of freedom = 47.94; the goodness-of-fit index = .996; adjusted goodness-of-fit index = .989; root mean square residual = .008; $N = 2,062$.

& Sörbom, 1989). This computer program provides maximum likelihood estimation (MLE) of model parameters that are specified as "free." Each model consists of measurement (observed) variables and latent constructs (unobserved variables). The latent constructs are theoretical variables among which there is a hypothesized causal structure. The measurement variables are specified as indicators of the latent constructs. The estimation of MLE models is made so that the factor loading and error terms along with the structural parameters form equations that can be used to predict each of the observed covariations among all variables. The adequacy of this simultaneous prediction of all effects can be used as a criterion for evaluating the model.

The model is estimated in conformity to the hypothesized structural effects. That is, it is assumed that all of the reliable variation between observed variables can be accounted for in terms of the theoretical variables. Any unique variation in any measurement variable is thus assumed to be uncorrelated, net of the sources of common variance, with any other measurement variable.

The baseline model specified direct positive effects of deviance at T1 on deviance at T3. Net of this effect, deviance at T1 was expected to have a positive effect on negative social sanctions, and negative social sanction was expected to influence later deviance (the labeling effect). That is, the mediating negative social sanctions would partially decompose the effect of early deviance on later deviance. Autocorrelated errors among the three repeated measures of deviant behavior were also specified. Finally, the four sociodemographic variables were allowed to correlate with each other and to freely influence the other three constructs.

Results and discussion

Baseline model

The parameter estimates for the measurement model, the "factor loadings," are considered reliable and valid indicators of the underlying latent construct. All loadings are large and the freely estimated parameters are highly significant. Whether judging by the ratio of chi square to degrees of freedom (47.97/25) or the goodness-of-fit index (.996), which is very near its maximum value of 1.0, the observed and theoretical models provide a good fit. As expected, negative social sanctions have a significant effect on later deviance net of the antecedent effects of early deviance and the exogenous factors on these constructs. The model is summarized in Figure 18.1.

Conditional models

The same model was estimated for both of the mutually exclusive response categories of each of the 17 conditional variables. The intercorrelations, means, and standard deviations for each of the items are presented in Table 18.1.

These conditional variables were selected on a face-value basis from self-reports at T1 to reflect various circumstances that theoretically would be expected to moderate the effects of negative social sanctions on deviance. Such variables include *anxiety* (Are you often troubled by your hands sweating so they feel damp and clammy?), *general sensitivity to the attitudes of others* (Do you become deeply disturbed when someone laughs at you or blames you for something you have done wrong?), *expectations of adverse consequences of wrongdoing* (My parents love me less when I am bad than when I am good), *motivation to achieve and/or attain or restore self-esteem* (I wish I could have more respect for myself; All in all I am inclined to feel I am a failure; I doubt if I will get ahead in life as much as I would really like; By my teacher's standards I am a failure; I certainly feel useless at times), *social control* (Do your parents get nervous when you are away from home?), *vulnerability to parental sanctions* (When my parents dislike something I do it bothers me very much; My parents pretty much agree about how I should be raised), *commitment to unconventional norms* (Most of the adults I know got what is important out of life without getting an education), and *expectations of social rejection* (For as long as I can remember, my parents have put me down; My parents are usually not very interested in what I say or do; My teachers usually put me down; My teachers are usually not interested in what I say or do; My teachers do not like me very much).

The data regarding the number of subjects, the unstandardized effects of early deviance and negative social sanctions on later deviance, the goodness-of-fit data, and the nature of the conditional variables for all 35 models tested are presented in Table 18.2. The table shows, for example, that the unstandardized effect of negative social sanctions (NSS) on deviance at T3 (D3) for the base model ($N = 2,062$) is 0.174, as exhibited in Figure 18.1. For respondents who reported they were often troubled by their hands sweating so that they felt damp and clammy ($n = 686$), the effect of negative social sanctions on deviance at T3 is 0.108. Conversely, for those who reported not having clammy hands ($n = 1,374$), the coefficient is 0.222, a significantly larger effect.

The data regarding the unstandardized effects of the exogenous variables on the main variables of interest and the autocorrelations are summarized in Table 18.3. The table shows, for example, that among respondents who feel as though they are failures, the unstandardized effect of male on deviance at T1 (M-DV1) is not significant (0.070). On the other hand, among those who did not feel like failures, the unstandardized effect of male on deviance at T1 (M-DV1) is significant (0.151).

Generally it was expected that under conditions indicating the absence of personal and social constraints against engaging in deviant behavior, the experience of negative social sanctions (and their sequelae) would be more likely to lead to deviant behavior and, under conditions indicating the presence of personal and social constraints against engaging in deviant behavior, the experience of negative social sanctions would be less likely to lead to deviant behavior. Consistent with this expectation for subjects who were *not* anxious, *not* sensitive to ridicule for wrongdoing, *not* expecting adverse consequences for wrongdoing (i.e., conditional love), *not*

Table 18.1. Correlation matrix, means, and standard deviations of the set of moderating variables ("yes" and "true" coded = 1 and "no" and "false" coded = 0)

	Clammy hands	Disturbed when laughed at	Parents love less when bad	More self-respect	Feel like a failure	Doubt I'll get ahead	By teacher's std./failure	Feel useless	Parents nervous/I'm away	Bothered/parents dislike/do	Parents agree how to raise me	Adults need no educ.	Parents put me down	Parents not interested	Teachers put me down	Teachers not interested	Teachers don't like me
Clammy hands	1.000																
Disturbed when laughed at	0.166	1.000															
Parents love less when bad	0.079	0.125	1.000														
Wish more re-spect for self	0.101	0.178	0.116	1.000													
Feel like a failure	0.116	0.155	0.156	0.179	1.000												
Doubt I'll get ahead	0.088	0.141	0.155	0.203	0.240	1.000											
By teacher's standard/failure	0.117	0.093	0.157	0.101	0.372	0.225	1.000										
Feel useless	0.174	0.194	0.123	0.210	0.166	0.210	0.135	1.000									
Parents ner-vous when I'm away	0.102	0.142	0.064	0.072	0.078	0.082	0.056	0.080	1.000								
Bothered when parents dis-like/I do	0.050	0.140	0.002	0.059	0.013	0.013	-0.036	0.098	0.077	1.000							
Parents agree how to raise me	-0.048	-0.027	-0.091	0.008	-0.113	-0.073	-0.126	-0.047	0.017	0.086	1.000						

Adults need no education	0.058	0.103	0.120	0.103	0.127	0.114	0.147	0.072	0.083	-0.019	-0.026	1.000					
Parents put me down	0.092	0.079	0.201	0.091	0.225	0.145	0.202	0.102	0.036	-0.040	-0.187	0.085	1.000				
Parents not interested	0.095	0.078	0.214	0.094	0.230	0.156	0.214	0.092	0.024	-0.034	-0.181	0.135	0.315	1.000			
Teachers put me down	0.093	0.113	0.149	0.094	0.239	0.171	0.356	0.114	0.054	-0.038	-0.140	0.119	0.238	0.259	1.000		
Teachers not interested	0.102	0.090	0.135	0.062	0.208	0.183	0.316	0.149	0.037	-0.036	-0.113	0.122	0.171	0.217	0.338	1.000	
Teachers don't like me	0.103	0.082	0.168	0.068	0.249	0.181	0.381	0.148	0.049	-0.050	-0.127	0.097	0.212	0.226	0.443	0.408	1.000
Mean	0.353	0.565	0.267	0.490	0.147	0.403	0.166	0.529	0.526	0.668	0.863	0.329	0.104	0.136	0.180	0.282	0.213
SD	0.478	0.495	0.442	0.499	0.354	0.490	0.372	0.499	0.499	0.470	0.343	0.469	0.305	0.342	0.384	0.450	0.409

Table 18.2. *Unstandardized effects for the core theoretical model by conditional variables*

Variable	N	DV1-NSS	DV1-DV3	NSS-DV3	χ^2	Goodness of fit	Adjusted goodness of fit	χ^2/df
Base model	2,062	1.170	0.359	0.174	47.94	0.996	0.989	1.92
Clammy hands								
Yes	686	1.285	0.377	0.108	27.64	0.993	0.981	1.11
No	1,374	1.116	0.355	0.222	37.61	0.995	0.987	1.50
Disturbed when laughed at								
Yes	1,023	1.172	0.337	0.146	35.04	0.994	0.984	1.40
No	870	1.175	0.340	0.245	39.89	0.992	0.978	1.60
Parents love me less when bad								
True	479	1.205	0.362	0.130	26.53	0.990	0.974	1.06
False	1,561	1.144	0.343	0.184	44.96	0.995	0.986	1.80
Wish more respect for self								
True	944	1.413	0.517	0.143	27.16	0.995	0.986	1.09
False	1,103	1.051	0.255	0.204	56.75	0.991	0.976	2.27
I feel like a failure								
True	215	1.955	0.935	−0.122*	16.16	0.987	0.965	0.65
False	1,832	1.093	0.328	0.205	48.40	0.995	0.987	1.94
I doubt I'll get ahead								
True	734	1.382	0.334	0.148	32.52	0.992	0.979	1.30
False	1,317	1.100	0.371	0.187	47.52	0.993	0.983	1.90
By teacher's std., I'm a failure								
True	197	1.962	0.386	0.080	43.65	0.961	0.897	1.75
False	1,841	1.098	0.359	0.190	42.32	0.996	0.989	1.69
I feel useless								
True	1,055	1.183	0.426	0.136	30.80	0.995	0.986	1.23
False	990	1.212	0.263	0.228	47.86	0.991	0.977	1.91

	N							
Parents nervous when I'm away								
True	1,019	1.357	0.371	0.154	36.36	0.994	0.983	1.45
False	1,031	1.018	0.343	0.195	28.86	0.995	0.987	1.13
Bothered/parents dislike what I do								
True	1,420	1.111	0.301	0.214	43.42	0.995	0.986	1.74
False	627	1.271	0.417	0.104	24.97	0.993	0.981	0.99
Parents agree how I should be raised								
True	1,796	1.162	0.329	0.194	43.71	0.996	0.988	1.75
False	240	1.291	0.402	0.035*	17.10	0.987	0.966	0.68
Adults need no educ. to get ahead								
True	573	1.144	0.312	0.176	29.31	0.991	0.976	1.17
False	1,474	1.180	0.387	0.158	48.41	0.994	0.984	1.94
Parents put me down								
True	172	1.162	0.258*	0.107	20.99	0.978	0.943	0.84
False	1,873	1.214	0.345	0.185	51.21	0.995	0.987	2.05
Parents not interested in me								
True	213	1.086	0.392	0.037*	43.14	0.966	0.910	1.73
False	1,840	1.178	0.336	0.196	56.11	0.994	0.985	2.24
My teachers put me down								
True	274	1.416	0.253*	0.095	31.96	0.980	0.947	1.28
False	1,771	1.089	0.388	0.184	46.43	0.995	0.987	1.86
Teachers not interested in me								
True	487	1.372	0.298	0.128	29.06	0.989	0.972	1.16
False	1,550	1.016	0.396	0.193	51.66	0.994	0.984	2.07
Teachers don't like me								
True	313	1.440	0.342	0.061*	35.42	0.980	0.947	1.42
False	1,736	1.111	0.348	0.205	40.33	0.996	0.989	1.61

Note: All paths are significant at $p < .05$, *except* where denoted by an asterisk. Differences between models for all NSS–DV3 paths are significant.

Table 18.3. *Unstandardized effects for the control variables (and the autocorrelated errors) on the core theoretical variables*

Variable	M-DV1	M-NSS	M-DV3	B-DV1	B-NSS	B-DV3	H-DV1	H-NSS	H-DV3	PE-DV1	PE-NSS	PE-DV3	Autocorrelated errors Most 1–most 3	Mod 1–mod 3	Rare 1–rare 3
Base model	0.146*	0.080*	0.068*	0.033	−0.018	−0.018*	0.010	−0.049	−0.006	−0.011*	−0.013	−0.004	0.026*	−0.007*	0.006*
Clammy hands															
Yes	0.130*	0.049	0.051	0.051	−0.044	−0.059*	−0.012	−0.166	−0.018	−0.010	−0.008	−0.005	0.018*	−0.007	0.004
No	0.146*	0.102	0.072	0.020*	−0.005*	−0.017	0.022	0.021	−0.008	−0.008*	−0.016*	−0.004	0.030*	−0.007	0.006*
Disturbed when laughed at															
Yes	0.147*	0.057	0.079*	0.021	0.067	−0.055*	−0.024	−0.075	−0.006	−0.012*	−0.014	−0.004	0.025*	−0.005	0.004
No	0.146*	0.150*	0.044	0.009	−0.110	0.019	0.025	0.020	−0.036	−0.009	−0.012	−0.006	0.028*	−0.010	0.010*
Parents love me less when bad															
True	0.123*	−0.041	0.066*	−0.005	−0.026	−0.034	−0.039	−0.223	−0.054	−0.007*	−0.014	−0.018	0.007	−0.009	−0.002
False	0.152*	0.117*	0.066*	0.037	−0.009	−0.033	0.033	0.019	0.002	−0.011*	−0.013	0.001	0.032*	−0.007	0.008*
Wish more respect for self															
True	0.128*	0.009	0.066*	0.038	−0.032	−0.028	−0.002	−0.094	−0.034	−0.010*	−0.013	0.001	0.031*	−0.015	0.009
False	0.167*	0.129*	0.062*	0.022	−0.003	−0.046*	0.020	0.010	0.023	−0.008	−0.015	−0.010*	0.024*	0.000	0.003
I'm a failure															
True	0.070	0.093	0.083*	−0.017	−0.057	−0.043	0.015	0.029	−0.036	0.000	0.003	−0.007	0.023*	−0.015	0.028*
False	0.151*	0.083*	0.068*	0.036*	−0.008	−0.032	−0.004	−0.044	0.001	−0.010*	−0.016*	−0.003	0.028*	−0.007	0.003
I doubt I will get ahead															
True	0.154*	0.032	0.064*	0.020	−0.022	−0.045	−0.008	−0.147	−0.026	−0.011*	−0.025	0.002	0.018*	−0.010	0.002
False	0.138*	0.103	0.074	0.040	−0.018	−0.024	0.012	0.020	0.007	−0.009	−0.007	−0.008	0.029*	−0.006	0.008
By teacher's std. I am a failure															
True	0.044	0.216	0.075*	0.013	−0.204	−0.002	−0.042	−0.011	−0.068	−0.006	−0.054*	0.002	0.005	−0.021	0.047
False	0.142*	0.082*	0.064*	0.034	0.008	−0.039*	0.007	−0.053	0.006	−0.010*	−0.008	−0.005	0.026*	−0.006	0.002
I feel useless															
True	0.151*	0.058	0.067*	0.061*	0.047	−0.036	−0.011	−0.060	0.012	−0.010*	−0.024*	0.002	0.031*	−0.006	0.005
False	0.141*	0.093*	0.066*	0.027	−0.084	−0.022	0.037	−0.032	−0.022	−0.011*	0.002*	−0.013	0.019*	−0.004	0.005

307

	C1	C2	C3	C4	C5	C6	C7	C8	C9	C10	C11	C12	C13	C14	C15
Parents nervous when I'm away															
True	0.122*	0.086	0.060*	0.018	-0.001	-0.026	-0.007	-0.082	0.001	-0.009*	-0.012	0.000	0.026*	-0.010*	0.004
False	0.175*	0.082	0.072*	0.044	-0.036	-0.038	0.013	0.030	-0.009	-0.008	-0.014	-0.010*	0.026*	-0.010	0.008*
Bothers/parents dislike what I do															
True	0.160*	0.094*	0.076*	0.047*	0.022	-0.030	0.000	-0.101	0.025	-0.014*	-0.016	-0.003	0.022*	-0.002	0.001
False	0.119*	0.049	0.057*	0.000	-0.085	-0.038	0.022	0.101	-0.060	-0.005	-0.003	-0.005	0.037*	-0.020*	0.015*
Parents agree how to raise me															
True	0.148*	0.074*	0.077*	0.038*	0.007	-0.039*	0.018	-0.038	-0.015	-0.011*	-0.015*	-0.006	0.028*	-0.007	0.007*
False	0.130*	0.141	0.024	-0.017	-0.236*	-0.012	-0.080	0.027	0.025	-0.009	0.014	0.004	0.017	-0.015	0.003
Adults need no educ. to get ahead															
True	0.129*	0.093	0.091*	0.022	0.010	-0.039	-0.002	-0.034	0.006	-0.006	0.007	-0.004	0.007	-0.010	0.013
False	0.146*	0.069	0.060*	0.023	-0.023	-0.025	0.012	-0.041	-0.017	-0.004	-0.026*	-0.005	0.034*	-0.008	0.003
Parents put me down															
True	0.098*	0.145	0.062	0.042	-0.153	0.037	0.006	-0.029	0.109	0.003	-0.041	0.015*	0.005*	0.006	0.009
False	0.147*	0.065	0.067*	0.030	-0.008	-0.040*	0.017	-0.046	-0.025	-0.010*	-0.008	-0.007*	0.028	-0.007	0.005
Parents not interested in me															
True	0.042	0.083	0.009	0.032	-0.007	-0.004	0.012	0.233	-0.040	-0.016	0.009	-0.013	0.011	-0.010	0.024
False	0.165*	0.071*	0.073*	0.025	-0.013	-0.038*	0.022	-0.070	0.003	-0.009*	-0.014*	-0.003	0.028*	-0.010	0.005
Teachers put me down															
True	0.071	0.068	0.062	0.004	-0.235*	-0.086*	-0.073	-0.074	-0.142	-0.007	-0.039	-0.014	0.015	-0.002	0.017
False	0.147*	0.089	0.065*	0.024	0.010	-0.028	0.026	-0.033	0.006	-0.012*	-0.009	-0.003	0.028*	-0.010	0.004
Teachers not interested in me															
True	0.155*	0.183*	0.042	-0.008	-0.153	-0.002	-0.070	0.115	-0.069	-0.014*	-0.019	-0.006	0.016*	-0.001	0.013
False	0.134*	0.060	0.073*	0.050*	0.032	-0.046*	0.047	-0.109	0.015	-0.007	-0.013	-0.003	0.029*	-0.010*	0.004
Teachers don't like me															
True	0.072*	0.115	0.008	-0.027	0.069	0.017	-0.117	-0.023	-0.058	-0.017*	0.005	-0.011	0.021*	-0.012	0.009
False	0.147*	0.079*	0.077*	0.041*	-0.022	-0.040*	0.029	-0.049	0.002	-0.009*	-0.017*	-0.002	0.026*	-0.008*	0.005

Abbreviations: M, male; B, black; H, Hispanic; PE, father's education.

* $p < .05$.

highly motivated to achieve or restore self-esteem, and *not* under strict parental control, the positive effect of negative social sanctions on later deviance was appreciably stronger than for the mutually exclusive groupings of subjects. Presumably, given the dispositions to engage in deviant behavior as a result of being the object of negative social sanctions for earlier deviance, the absence of personal and social constraints facilitated the performance of the deviant behaviors. In contrast, for people who *were* anxious, sensitive to ridicule for wrongdoing, expecting adverse consequences for wrongdoing, highly motivated to achieve or restore self-esteem, and under strict parental control, the effects of negative social sanctions on deviance (via alienation from the conventional world, increased association with deviant peers, and the need for self-approval) were sharply mitigated. Some of the same circumstances that mediated the effects of negative social sanctions on later deviance (observed in earlier studies) interacted with the administration of negative social sanctions and along with other conditions served to control the disposition to act out deviant behaviors. A particularly interesting model is provided by the subjects who agreed with the statement "All in all I am inclined to feel I am a failure." In this model the effect of negative social sanctions on later deviance not only is weakened, but is the only instance in which the effect is actually reversed (albeit not at a statistically significant level). That is, for these subjects, the administration of punishment for earlier deviance *deters* rather than *amplifies* or escalates later deviance (the labeling effect). Perhaps this variable captures both high motivation to achieve according to conventional standards and the need to restore self-esteem.

Considering items reflecting vulnerability to parental sanctions, it was observed that for subjects who endorsed the statements "When my parents dislike something I do it bothers me very much" and "My parents pretty much agree on how I should be raised," the effects of negative social sanctions on deviant behavior at T3 were appreciably stronger than for subjects who indicated these statements were false. These findings are interpreted as reflecting conditions under which negative social sanctions are particularly stigmatizing – that is, where the standards for disapprobation are clear and where it is important to the subjects that they be disapproved of – and that therefore stimulate deviant adaptations whether as expressions of resentment toward the conventional world or as alternative routes to the restoration of lost self-esteem. While it was equally reasonable to interpret the need for parental approval as a restraint against acting out deviant dispositions, the fact that this moderating variable did not influence the effect of sanctions on deviance in the same ways as being sensitive to ridicule for wrongdoing (discussed earlier) suggests that the interpretation in terms of stigmatizing conditions is viable.

Regarding commitment to unconventional norms, it was expected that the effect of negative social sanctions on later deviance would be stronger for those who endorsed the statement "Most of the adults I know got what is important out of life without getting an education" than for those who rejected the statement on the grounds that such sentiments would be supportive of dispositions to engage in deviant responses. The data supported this expectation, although the differences in the effects for the two models were quite small.

Regarding expectations of social rejection, subjects who were characterized by responses indicating the absence of social rejection were consistently more likely to manifest stronger positive effects of negative social sanctions on T3 deviant behavior; and for subjects characterized by responses indicative of rejection by parents and teachers, the effect of negative social sanctions tended to be much weaker. These items are interpretable in a number of ways. Social rejection indicators may suggest, as they did to us, the extreme stigmatization that might accompany being the object of negative social sanctions. By this interpretation, for subjects characterized by higher levels of social rejection, negative sanctions should have stronger positive effects on later deviance since these subjects would feel excluded from opportunities to restore self-esteem by conventional means. However, quite the reverse was observed. For subjects who *denied* being the object of rejection and disinterest by parents and teachers, the effects of negative sanctions on later deviance were *stronger* than for those who affirmed being the object of social rejection. The results were more compatible with three other related interpretations of these items. First, the denial of being the object of social rejection may indicate the absence of sanctions for deviance and, hence, the freedom to engage in deviant behavior in response to negative social sanctions without fear of reprisals. Second, being characterized by the absence of social rejection may imply full integration of the person in the conventional socionormative network. Therefore, being the object of negative social sanctions would be more stigmatizing than where expectation of conforming behavior was not as high. Consequently, the person would be more likely to experience the sequelae of negative social sanctions including deviant responses that reflect rejection of the conventional world that rejected him or her and more or less effective attempts to restore lost esteem through deviant patterns. Third, being the object of rejection by teachers and parents may imply the *need to conform* so as to gain their respect and attention. Hence, in response to negative social responses, subjects who are the objects of social rejection would be less likely to escalate deviant responses. This interpretation implies, further, that the subjects who are the object of social rejection nevertheless are emotionally tied to the conventional order for future gratification of personal values. This appears to be a reasonable assumption since all of the subjects were present for the in-school administrations at all three points in time. In any case, any or all of these interpretations of this set of conditional variables would be compatible with the observation that for subjects characterized by denial of social rejection, the effect of T2 negative social sanctions on T3 deviant behavior are appreciably stronger than they are for subjects affirming indicators of social rejection. Which, if any, of these interpretations hold remains to be determined.

Conclusion

The findings suggest a number of conditions under which the labeling effect will be observed to a greater or lesser degree and to some extent suggest certain conditions under which a deterrent effect of negative social sanctions will hold. At the same time these results may account for the inconsistencies in the literature by suggesting that theoretically implicit conditions for the two perspectives may hold in varying degrees in different studies. A number of the theoretically informed expectations were met in the present studies. Other findings, although statistically significant, were quite the reverse of what was hypothesized. It remains to be determined by future studies whether the guiding theoretical framework requires revision or whether the validity of certain of the conditional variables is problematic. It remains also for future studies to determine if combinations of the conditional variables impose a synergistic moderating effect on the generically observed positive effect of negative social sanctions for earlier deviance on the amplification or escalation of later deviant behavior.

REFERENCES

Ageton, S., & Elliott, D. (1974). The effect of legal processing on delinquent orientations. *Social Problems, 22,* 87–100.

Akers, R. L. (1985). *Deviant behavior: A social learning approach* (3rd ed.). Belmont, CA: Wadsworth.

Coleman, L. M. (1986). Stigma: An enigma demystified. In S. C. Ainley, G. Becker, & L. M. Coleman (Eds.), *The dilemma of difference: A multidisciplinary view of stigma* (pp. 221–232). New York: Plenum.

Covington, J. (1984). Insulation from labelling. *Criminology, 22*(4), 619–643.

Farrell, R. A. (1989). Cognitive consistency in deviance causation: A psychological elaboration of an integrated systems model. In S. F. Messner, M. D. Krohn, & A. E. Liska (Eds.), *Theoretical integration in the study of deviance and crime: Problems and prospects* (pp. 77–92). Albany: State University of New York Press.

Farrington, D. P. (1977). The effects of public labeling. *British Journal of Criminology, 17,* 112–125.

Foster, J. D., Dinitz, S., & Reckless, W. C. (1972). Perceptions of stigma following public intervention for delinquent behavior. *Social Problems, 20,* 202–209.

Gold, M. (1970). *Delinquent behavior in an American city.* Belmont, CA: Brooks/Cole.

Gold, M., & Williams, J. R. (1969). The effect of "getting caught": Apprehension of the juvenile offender as a cause of subsequent delinquencies. *Prospectus, 3,* 1–12.

Gove, W. R. (1975). *The labeling of deviance: Evaluating a perspective.* New York: Halstead.

Hawkins, G. (1976). *The prison: Policy and practice.* Chicago: University of Chicago Press.

Hepburn, J. R. (1977). The impact of police intervention upon juvenile delinquents. *Criminology, 15,* 235–262.

Jensen, G. F. (1969). Crime doesn't pay: Correlates of a shared misunderstanding. *Social Problems, 17,* 189–201.

Jöreskog, K., & Sörbom, D. (1989). *LISREL VII: User's reference guide.* Mooresville, IN: Scientific Software.

Kaplan, H. B. (1972). Toward a general theory of psychosocial deviance: The case of aggressive behavior. *Social Science and Medicine, 6,* 593–617.

Kaplan, H. B. (1975). *Self-attitudes and deviant behavior.* Pacific Palisades, CA: Goodyear.

Kaplan, H. B. (1980). *Deviant behavior in defense of self.* New York: Academic.

Kaplan, H. B. (1982). Self-attitudes and deviant behavior: New directions for theory and research. *Youth and Society, 14,* 185–211.

Kaplan, H. B. (1984). *Patterns of juvenile delinquency.* Beverly Hills, CA: Sage.

Kaplan, H. B. (1986). *Social psychology of self-referent behavior.* New York: Plenum.

Kaplan, H. B., & Fukurai, H. (1992). Negative social sanctions, self-rejection, and drug use. *Youth and Society, 23*(3), 275–298.

Kaplan, H. B., & Johnson, R. J. (1991). Negative social sanctions and juvenile delinquency: Effects of labeling in a model of deviant behavior. *Social Science Quarterly, 72*(1), 98–122.

Kaplan, H. B., & Johnson, R. J., Bailey, C. A. (1987). Deviant peers and deviant behavior: Further elaboration of a model. *Social Psychology Quarterly, 50*, 277–284.

Kaplan, H. B., Martin, S. S., & Johnson, R. J. (1986). Self-rejection and the explanation of deviance: Specification of the structure among latent constructs. *American Journal of Sociology, 92*, 384–411.

Kessler, R. C., & Greenberg, D. F. (1981). *Linear panel analysis: Models of quantitative change.* New York: Academic.

Klein, M. W. (1974). Labeling, deterrence, and recidivism: A study of police dispositions of juvenile offenders. *Social Problems, 22*, 292–303.

Klemke, L. W. (1978). Does apprehension for shoplifting amplify or terminate shoplifting activity? *Law and Society Review, 12*, 391–403.

Link, B. G. (1982). Mental patient status, work, and income: An examination of the effects of psychiatric label. *American Sociological Review, 47*, 202–215.

Link, B. G. (1987). Understanding labeling effects in the area of mental disorders: An assessment of the effects of expectations of rejection. *American Sociological Review, 52*, 96–112.

Mankoff, M. (1971). Societal reaction and career deviance: A critical analysis and introduction to the political economy of law enforcement. *Sociological Quarterly, 12*, 204–218.

O'Connor, G. G. (1970). The impact of initial detention upon male delinquents. *Social Problems, 18*, 194–199.

Packer, H. L. (1968). *The limits of the criminal sanction.* Stanford, CA: Stanford University Press.

Palamara, F., Cullen, F. T., & Gersten, J. C. (1986). The effect of police and mental health intervention on juvenile deviance: Specifying contingencies in the impact of formal reaction. *Journal of Health and Social Behavior, 27*, 90–105.

Piliavin, I., Thornton, C., Gartner, R., & Matsueda, R. L. (1986). Crime, deterrence, and rational choice. *American Sociological Review, 51*, 101–119.

Schwartz, R. D., & Skolnick, J. H. (1962). Two studies of legal stigma. *Social Problems, 10*, 133–142.

Sherman, L. W., & Berk, R. A. (1984). The specific deterrent effects of arrest for domestic assault. *American Sociological Review, 49*, 261–272.

Smith, D. A., & Gartin P. R. (1989). Specifying specific deterrence: The influence of arrest on future criminal activity. *American Sociological Review, 54*, 94–105.

Thorsel, B. A., & Klemke, Lloyd W. (1972). The labelling process: Reinforcement and deterrent. *Law and Society Review, 6*, 393–403.

Wellford, C. (1975). Labeling theory and criminology: An assessment. *Social Problems, 22*, 332–345.

Wheeler, G. R. (1978). *Counter-deterrence: A report on juvenile sentencing and effects of prisonization.* Chicago: Nelson-Hall.

V   Measuring and predicting in studies of coercion and punishment

19 Corporal punishment in everyday life: an intergenerational perspective

HÅKAN STATTIN, HARALD JANSON,
INGRID KLACKENBERG-LARSSON,
AND DAVID MAGNUSSON

Introduction

The influence of parents' disciplinary history on their everyday use of punishment of children has been the topic of much discussion. However, making generalizations on the basis of empirical investigations is limited by one or more of the following: (1) the focus has been on abuse rather than on both milder and stronger forms of punishment; (2) clinical groups or selected samples rather than representative samples have been used; and (3) data have often been taken from surveys rather than prospectively collected. The data to be presented here extend over a period of 25 years for a normal group of Swedish subjects and their parents, encompassing regularly collected information about parents' punishment of their children from infancy throughout adolescence, in addition to information about the parents' own punishment history, as well as the subjects' conceptions of their punishment history.

A review of the project

Grasping the course of development in different domains, as well as the impact of parental discipline, requires following an intact group of children over a long time. The planning of such a longitudinal study started in 1954 and was conducted at the Child Clinic at Karolinska Hospital in Stockholm (Karlberg et al., 1959; Klackenberg, 1981). The recruitment of subjects took place in Solna, one of the many communities around Stockholm. The community had an occupational distribution in keeping with that of Stockholm. Every fourth newly pregnant mother visiting the Solna prenatal clinic from April 1955 to April 1958 was asked to participate in the long-term developmental study. (In Sweden virtually all pregnant women receive regular care at prenatal clinics.) Of all mothers asked, only

315

3% refused the invitation. A pilot group of 29 children was added, bringing the total number of children in the study to 212, 122 boys and 90 girls. Comparisons in relevant variables – parents' socioeconomic status (SES), age, and marital status, as well as sibling order and childrens' gestational age and birth weight – have shown the subject sample to be representative of subjects in Swedish urban communities (Karlberg et al., 1968). The somatic development of the children in the cohort has been summarized in the form of growth charts of various body measurements (Karlberg, Taranger, Engström, Lichtenstein, & Svennberg-Redegren, 1976). They have been used as reference measures in daily child health and child clinical work in Sweden since 1973.

In accordance with the plans, the children were investigated six times during their first year (first week, and at the ages of 1, 3, 6, 9, and 12 months), two times during the second year (18 and 24 months), and thereafter annually up to the age of 18. Data were also collected at the ages of 21, 25, and 36 years. Up to the age of 18, so as to control for differences in chronological age, all subjects were tested as closely as possible to the age points referred to: the time limit for ages 3, 6, 9, and 12 months was ±2 weeks, while it was ±4 weeks for tests conducted at 18 months and thereafter.

Extensive information about the subjects has been collected during the years by means of somatic registrations, medical examinations, interviews, inventories, and ratings, objective tests, sociometric methods, and projective techniques. At each data collection the aim has been to be as thorough as possible in mapping of the subjects' somatic, psychological, and social development. This project is of particular interest in the context of generational effects because annual information about the parents' punishment practices exists for the child from age 6 months to 16 years and the validity of retrospective reports of childhood punishment histories can be ascertained.

Purpose of the study

There are ample reasons to believe that the learning situation with regard to parental discipline affects offsprings' punishment of their own children (Bandura, 1977) or, alternatively, that the home atmosphere with regard to discipline and parent–child relations tends to reproduce itself in the next generation. However, perhaps to the surprise of many, studies of normal samples on the intergenerational transmission of punitive practices do not strongly support this intergenerational effect. When parents are retrospectively asked about their histories of being punished, there is some evidence, albeit not particularly impressive, that their upbringing correlates with their discipline of their own children (Bronson, Katten, & Livson, 1959; Lefkowitz, Huesmann, & Eron, 1978; Straus, Gelles, & Steinmetz, 1980). The nature of the issue is such that only a prospective investigation, involving both parents and their offspring, can give accurate estimations of the effect of intergenerational transmission of punitive practices. So far, no longitudinal study has examined the role of parents' upbringing on the regular corporal punishment of their child at different ages. The focus of attention here is on the corporal punishment of children as it occurs in the everyday life of a representative sample. The specific research aims are (1) to examine the prevalence and incidence of parents' corporal punishment of the child from a very early age through adolescence, (2) to analyze the role of parents' histories of being disciplined and attitudes in the corporal punishment of their child at different ages, and (3) to study the correspondence between retrospective reports of parents' discipline with prospective parent reports of corporal punishment at different ages.

Data and design

To avoid a restricted analysis of whether corporal punishment per se in one generation can be traced to similar discrete behaviors in the next generation, different aspects of parental and child disciplinary issues are assessed. Thus, for parents, the influence of their histories of being disciplined and their disciplinary attitudes are both examined. There are ample reasons to believe that parents' attitudes with regard to strictness as well as their ability to cope with provocative child behavior determine the physical punishment of the child at different ages (see Belsky, 1984). Consequently, both aspects are analyzed here. To assess children's views of family discipline practices, data on how frequently they were physically punished by their parents as well as a broader picture of how they perceived their parents' demand for obedience and their rejecting attitudes have been captured.

The design of the study is summarized in Table 19.1. Under the heading Older Generation are the categories of parents' histories of being disciplined and parents' disciplinary attitudes. Two questions measure parents' histories: Were you struck (spanked) as a child? with replies of (1) never or almost never, (2) sometimes, or at times, and (3) frequently; Were you brought up more or less strict than people in general? with response categories of (1) more lenient, (2) about the same as others, (3) more strict, and (4) much more strict. The questions were asked of mothers when the child was 3 years old and of the fathers when the child was age 4.

Parents' disciplinary attitudes comprises two dimensions from Schaefer and Bell's Parental Attitude Research Instrument (Schaefer & Bell, 1958), which was answered separately by the mother and father when the child was 4 years of age. Two of the scales of this instrument that focused on disciplinary issues – *breaking the will* and *strictness* – were aggregated into one dimension, labeled *strict disciplinary attitude*. This attitude measure involves 10 items. Alpha reliability was .82 (mean interitem correlation = .32) for the items answered by the mother and .81 (mean interitem correlation = .31) for the items answered by the father. The second dimension comprises Schaefer and Bell's *irritability* factor. It is better described as *lack of tolerance for annoyance,* and comprises five items, such as (for the mother) "Children will get on any mother's nerves if she has to be with them all day," "Mothers very often feel that they can't stand their children a moment longer," and

Table 19.1. *Outline of the study and number of cases for different measures*

Older generation

Parents' histories of having been disciplined
Struck as a child (M: 207; F: 187)
Brought up strictly (M: 207; F: 186)

Parents' disciplinary attitudes
Strict disciplinary attitude (M: 202; F: 189)
Lack of tolerance for annoyance (M: 202; F: 189)

Prospective measures of physical punishment

Striking
6–24 months (M: 205; F: 198)
3–5 years (M: 199; F: 199)
6–8 years (M: 184; F: 178)
9–11 years (M: 184; F: 178)
12–14 years (M: 173; F: 169)
15 and 16 years (M: 179; F: 173)

Beating
3–5 years (with objects) (M + F: 199)
6–8 years (M: 198; F: 198)
9–11 years (M: 183; F: 178)
12–14 years (M: 187; F: 183)

Younger generation

Subject's disciplinary history
Struck as a child (M. report: 152; F. report: 148)
Parents: Demanding (M. report: 155; F. report: 154)
Parents: Rejecting (M. report: 155; F. report: 154)

"It's natural for a mother to 'blow her top' when children are selfish and de-manding." An alpha reliability of .71 (mean interitem correlation = .32) was obtained for this scale for mothers and a reliability coefficient of .82 (mean interitem correlation = .48) was obtained for fathers.

Parents' actual disciplinary practices, in terms of reported frequencies of milder and stronger corporal punishment – striking and beating – are aggregated over broader age spans (Figure 19.1). Questions about parental disciplinary methods were part of the annual interviews with mothers (up to child age 8) and part of questionnaires completed by mothers (from child age 9).

Information was collected on 19 occasions, from child ages 6 months to 16 years, about how frequently the parents struck their children. Information is also available from child ages 6 to 14 years about parents' beating of the child and from child ages 3 to 5 years and about whether the parents had used objects when punishing the child.

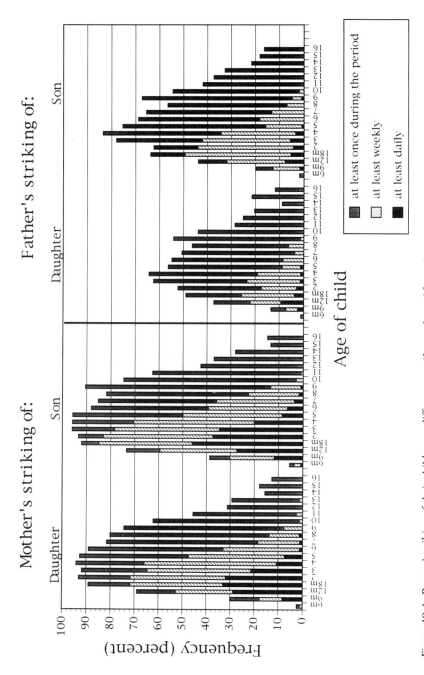

Figure 19.1. Parents' striking of their children at different ages (3 months to 16 years).

A potential limitation, which the present study shares with other studies in this area, is the lack of multiple informants for the measures of parents' discipline practices. Information reflecting the opinion of only one family member is sensitive to social desirability and response bias; the opinion of the mother need not coincide with that of others in the family. This limitation must be acknowledged.

Under the heading Younger Generation of Table 19.1 are measures of the subjects' retrospective accounts at age 25 of their own upbringing. There is empirical support for a connection between parental corporal punishment and emotional rejection of the child (see Herrenkohl, Herrenkohl, & Toedter, 1984; Herzberger, Potts, & Dillon, 1981; Sears, Maccoby, & Levin, 1957), so both measures have been used. The retrospective accounts include an interview question on frequency of corporal punishment (the same one as for the older generation, 21 years earlier) and two scales from a Swedish version of Roe and Siegelman's Parent–Child Relationship Questionnaire (Roe & Siegelman, 1963): *loving–rejecting,* with high values meaning high parental rejection, and *casual–demanding,* with high values signifying high parental demands on obedience. Each scale consists of 10 items measured on 4-point scales, and they are separately answered for the mother and the father. Subjects were instructed to think primarily about how they retrospectively perceived their parents when they were 12 years of age or younger. Alpha reliability was .82 (mean interitem correlation = .31) for the 10 items measuring mother's loving–rejecting attitude during upbringing, and .85 (mean interitem correlation = .37) for the 10 items measuring father's loving–rejecting attitude. The reliability coefficient was .83 for mother's demands for obedience (mean interitem correlation = .33) and .87 (mean interitem correlation = .39) for fathers.

In all analyses covering bivariate relationships, Pearson correlation coefficients have been computed, with one-tailed tests of significance. In the multivariate analyses, pairwise deletion of missing cases has been applied.[1]

Corporal punishment at different ages

Striking

Mothers were asked whether or not (and how often) they and their husbands struck (spanked, slapped) their children. For child ages 6 months to 9 years, the response categories were (1) never, (2) less than once per week, (3) once a week or more, (4) once or twice a day, (5) several times a day, and (6) on many occasions every day. Because of a lower incidence of striking older children, the response categories from the age of 10 were changed to (1) never, (2) seldom, (3) once a month or more, (4) once a week or more, and (5) daily.

Figure 19.1 shows the prevalence of striking at different ages. The overall height of the bars represents the proportion of mothers and fathers who reportedly had struck their children at least once. It makes a great difference whether we are talking about punishment of the son or the daughter and whether it is the father or the mother who administers the punishment. For this reason, the prevalence rates in Figure 19.1 are presented separately for daughters and sons, mothers and fathers.

Very similar developments over time appear for mothers' and fathers' striking of boys and girls; the main difference pertains to prevalence rates, with the highest being for mothers' striking their sons and the lowest for fathers' striking their daughters. As can be seen from Figure 19.1, the prevalence of striking rises quickly from the age of 6 months onward, reaching its peak at the age of 4 – both for mothers' and for fathers' striking of boys and girls. At this age almost all mothers and 75% of fathers reported that they had struck their children. Thereafter, there is a gradual decrease in striking through age 16 for both sexes.

Generally mothers, being together with the children much longer in the day than fathers, struck the child more often than did fathers. Paired-sample *t* tests revealed significant differences in rates of striking between mothers and fathers in all periods from ages 6 months to 11 years for both boys and girls (in most cases, $p < .001$). It might be noted that the decrease in striking is sharper for mothers than for fathers, so that in midadolescence the reported frequency of striking is about the same for both parents. In fact, paired-sample *t* tests showed a significantly higher striking rate for fathers than for mothers when the child was 15 years old.

Both parents, particularly fathers, tended to strike their sons more often than their daughters. Fathers' striking rates were significantly higher for boys than for girls on every test occasion from age 18 months to 7 years, at 9 years, and from 12 to 14 (in most cases, $p < .01$, at least). Mothers' striking rates were significantly higher for sons than for daughters at age 18 months, as well as at 3, 7, and 9 years.

Striking at least weekly is primarily concentrated in early childhood, reaching its peak for both boys and girls at age 18 months. Finally, at least daily striking is also concentrated at early ages of the child. Mothers' daily striking peaked at 18 months and was reported for 32% of daughters and 46% of sons. Fathers' daily striking peaked earlier – at 12 months and was recorded for 9% of daughters and 8% of sons.

Beating

For child ages 6 to 9, mothers were asked questions on whether or not they, or their husbands, had given the child a real beating. From ages 10 to 14, a frequency measure of mother's and father's beating of the child was obtained. Because information at the younger ages only concerned whether or not the mother or the father had given the child a real beating since the last visit to the clinic, only those data on whether the child had been beaten were employed. It should be added that in those cases where the mother reported that she (or her husband) had not struck the child, the interviewers did not specifically ask the question about beating in the age period 6 to 9 years. With knowledge about how often beating of the child but not striking occurred in the older ages, it can be estimated that the effect of the underreporting of beating from ages 6 to 9 is very small.

To some extent the age-related trend for beating is similar to that for striking,

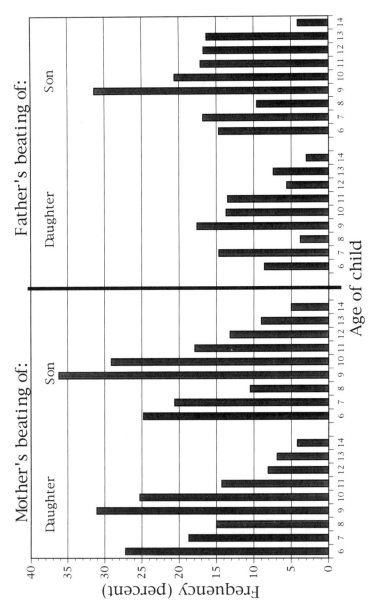

Figure 19.2. Parents' beating of their children at different ages.

the overall tendency being a gradually declining prevalence from childhood to adolescence. As can be seen from Figure 19.2, a considerably lower proportion of both parents beat their children in adolescence as compared with late childhood. Another similarity between the two punishment measures is that more mothers than fathers were reported to have beaten their children, especially daughters. A significantly higher proportion of mothers than fathers had given the daughter a real beating at ages 6, 8, 9, and 10 ($p < .05$, at least). Fewer significant differences were found for parents' beating of their sons. A significantly higher proportion of mothers than fathers who had beaten their sons emerged only at age 6. The reverse tendency was true in early adolescence, such that at age 13 a higher proportion of fathers than mothers were reported to have given the son a real beating.

Some differences regarding the development over time of beating should be noted in comparison with the trend for striking. In contrast to the gradually declining rate of striking the child after age 4, a peak at age 9 can be observed in the case of beating. At this age, 32% of girls were reported to have been given a real beating by their mother and 18% by their father. Of the boys, 36% had been beaten at least once by their mothers and 32% by their fathers at this age. There is no clear-cut age-related trend before age 9. With respect to mothers' beating of the child, there was a decrease between ages 6 and 8 (around the time when school starts to take care of the children during the day), but this was not the case for fathers' beating.

Because systematic information about beating was not available before age 6 and after age 14, we hesitate to say anything more definitive about when in development beating is most prevalent. Actually, data on beating from age 5 years (not reported in Figure 19.2) was collected by some interviewers (but not all). At least for males, these data suggest about the same high prevalence of maternal beating as was the case at age 9. Among the 84 males with information about parents' beating, 32 (38%) had been beaten by their mother at this age and 22 (26%) by their father. Among the 60 females, 11 (18%) had been beaten by their mother and 10 (17%) by their father.

Finally, for ages 3 to 5 years, the reported use of objects, for example, a rod, in punishing the child was recorded. A total of 27 mothers (13.2%) and 1 father were reported to have used objects when hitting the child.

Temporal stability of parental punishment

The temporal stability of parents' corporal punishment of their children over the years of upbringing was calculated. Relatively high stabilities for striking were found between the six age periods described in Table 19.1. The average correlation coefficient between adjacent periods was .55 ($p < .001$; range .45 to .62) for mothers' striking, and .59 ($p < .001$; range .42 to .66) for fathers' striking. Similar temporal stabilities between adjacent age periods were calculated for beating. For the three age periods, the average period-by-period correlation coefficient was .41

for mothers' beating of the child ($p < .001$) and .53 for fathers' beating ($p < .001$). These analyses reveal rather substantial longitudinal stabilities for the two measures of child punishment.

If the mother reported punishing the child in one age period, the chances were also high that the father was reported to punish the child during the same period. The correlation between fathers' and mothers' striking, averaged over the six age periods, was .61 ($p < .001$; range .54 to .69). The equivalent coefficient for beating was .54 ($p < .001$; range .40 to .63).

Cumulative prevalence rates of striking and beating. To obtain some grasp of the prevalence of corporal punishment over the total time period covered by the study, cumulative prevalence rates from age 1 to 16 for striking, and from age 6 to 14 for beating were calculated. Such analyses ideally require data for each individual at each age, a requirement that could not be met here without losing a considerable number of cases. However, with a limited number of missing observations per individual, there was a rationale for the following procedure. In the case of striking, all individuals who remained in the project sample and were tested at age 16 were selected for the analysis; for beating, those individuals who had been tested up to age 14, at least, were all selected. For individuals who had not been tested on a particular occasion, no striking or beating on a particular occasion was imputed. Of course, such a procedure leads to an underestimation of the "true" cumulative prevalence rate, and the underestimation will be greater the larger the number of such assignments made. However, given that there were a limited number of missing observations (6.1% of observations for striking and 5.2% for beating) the cumulative prevalence rates give reasonable estimates, albeit somewhat lower, than with complete information.

The results for striking showed, first and foremost, that there was not a single subject in the cohort who did not report being struck by his or her mother or father on at least one test occasion from age 1 to 16. In fact, maternal reports of having struck the child were made on 10 out of the total 16 test occasions for the average girl and on 11 occasions for the average boy (8 for girls and 9 for boys when it concerned fathers' striking). Thus, mothers of the average subject reported having struck their child more than every second time they were interviewed at the clinic.

A large majority of the children in the younger cohort had been given a real beating at least once between ages 6 and 14; 68% of females and 71% of males had been given a real beating at least once by their mother, 68% of females and 67% of males by their father. There were only minor sex differences with regard to having been beaten per se. However, the greater the number of years beating was recorded, the more often it concerned boys.

The role of parental characteristics in the corporal punishment of children

We have come to the main analyses, namely, (1) the impact of parents' disciplinary histories and attitudes on their corporal punishment of the child at different ages, and (2) the validity of retrospective reports of corporal punishment. A starting point for these analyses is the existence of marked sex differences in overall intergenerational patterns. The impact of the mother's history of being disciplined is strikingly different from the father's. The retrospective reports of the subjects in the younger generation differ between males and females. For this reason, the results will be presented separately for each sex and for mothers and fathers.

The impact of maternal characteristics

The role of the mother's history of being disciplined and disciplinary attitudes in her corporal punishment of the child is shown in Figure 19.3 for daughters and in Figure 19.4 for sons. The significant bivariate correlations are marked by arrows.

Consider first the impact of maternal characteristics for corporal punishment of

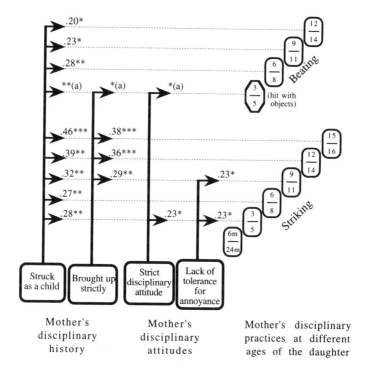

Figure 19.3. The role of the mother's history of having been disciplined and disciplinary attitudes for the punishment of her daughter.

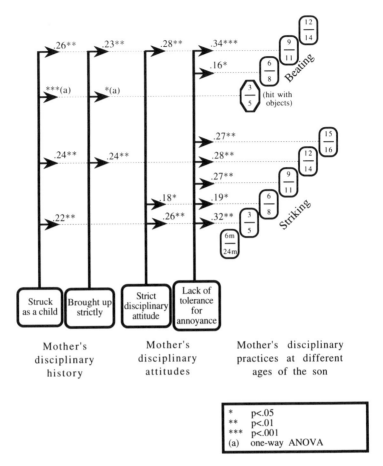

Figure 19.4. The role of the mother's history of having been disciplined and disciplinary attitudes for the punishment of her son.

daughters. As can be seen from Figure 19.3, how often the mother reported that she was struck as a child was significantly related to her reported punishing of her daughter over almost all the age periods covered – regarding both striking and real beating. There were also significant relationships (1) between the strictness of the mother's disciplinary upbringing and her striking of the daughter from age 9 to 16, and (2) between being brought up strictly and using objects in punishing from ages 3 to 5.

It should be observed in Figure 19.3 that the relation between the mother's own history of being struck and striking of her daughter tended to increase as the daughter grew older. Another way to illustrate this developmental tendency is reported in Figure 19.5.

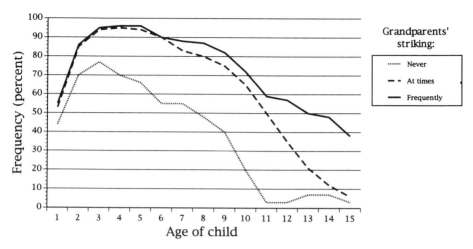

Figure 19.5. Mothers' striking of girls in relation to grandparents' striking.

Figure 19.5 shows the proportion of reports of striking at different ages of the child in three groups of mothers: those who reported being punished frequently, at times, or never. The great majority of mothers struck their daughters at a very early age, with few differences between mothers who had been struck frequently or infrequently by their own parents. With the increasing age of daughters, a higher proportion of the mothers who never had been struck, or who had been struck more sporadically, stopped punishing their daughters corporally, in comparison with the mothers who had themselves been frequently punished. When daughters were age 15, almost 40% of mothers who had been struck frequently as children still struck their daughters, whereas only a small proportion of the mothers who had been struck less frequently by their parents, or not at all, struck their daughters at this age.

In addition, we want to draw attention to the linkage between the mother's history of being punished and her use of objects when hitting her child from age 3 to 5. Figure 19.6 shows the findings for both girls and boys.

We now turn our attention to the impact of maternal characteristics for the corporal punishment of sons (see Figure 19.4). While being struck as a child had the most consistent relationship with the mother's striking of her daughter at different ages, her lack of tolerance for annoyance was the prime prognostic variable for the striking of her son at all age periods covered.

Also, mother's history of having been struck, the strictness of her upbringing, and her own strictness regarding the disciplining of her children were related to punishing her son during one or another age period. However, the latter relationships need to be qualified in some respects. Despite significant correlations with striking, these measures interacted with the mother's tolerance for annoyance in

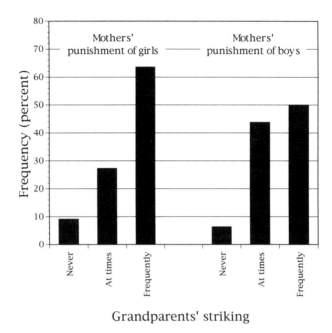

Grandparents' striking

Figure 19.6. Mothers' use of objects in punishment in relation to grandparents' striking.

almost all cases. This is illustrated in Figure 19.7, which shows the simultaneous impact of the mother's history of having been struck and her tolerance for annoyance on beating her son at ages 9 to 11.

It can be seen from Figure 19.7 that the impact of the mother's history of having been struck is detectable in the case of the group of mothers with a low tolerance for annoyance, but not for those with an intermediate or high tolerance for annoyance.

To summarize the prospective analysis, the main findings regarding the future impact of the mother's history of having been disciplined and disciplinary attitudes are the consistent relationship between how frequently she was struck and the striking of her daughter at different ages, and that between her lack of tolerance for annoyance and the striking of her son.

The impact of paternal characteristics

Compared with the case of the mother, the father's history of having been disciplined and disciplinary attitudes had comparatively less impact on his punishment of the child (see Figures 19.8 and 19.9).

Having been struck frequently as a child or having been brought up strictly was significantly related to the father's striking of his daughter at an early age. Beyond this, there were only a few significant associations between measures of the father's

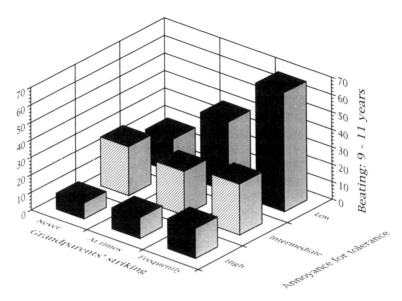

Figure 19.7. The mother's beating of her son at ages 9 to 11 as a function of her tolerance for annoyance and her own parents' striking.

history of having been disciplined and disciplinary attitudes and the punishment of his daughter. Also, as is shown in Figure 19.9, there was very little impact of the same paternal characteristics on the father's punishment of his son at different ages.

A multivariate approach to prospective analyses of corporal punishment

To study the combined effects of parents' history of having been disciplined and disciplinary attitudes on the punishment of their children at different ages, a set of multiple regression analyses was conducted. The prospectively collected measures of parental striking and beating during each of the age periods covered served as dependent variables, and multiple correlation coefficients were calculated from the parental data, with struck as a child, brought up strictly, strict disciplinary attitude, and lack of tolerance for annoyance as independent variables. The analyses address the question: To what extent can we predict parents' striking and beating of their children at different ages from knowledge of the parents' history of being disciplined and their disciplinary attitudes? The results of these analyses for each age period and aggregated over the entire study period are shown in Table 19.2.[2]

It is obvious from Table 19.2 that only very limited statistical predictions of the father's corporal punishment can be made from his history of having been disciplined and disciplinary attitudes. The prediction is more powerful in the case of the mother's corporal punishment, the highest linear composite being for her striking

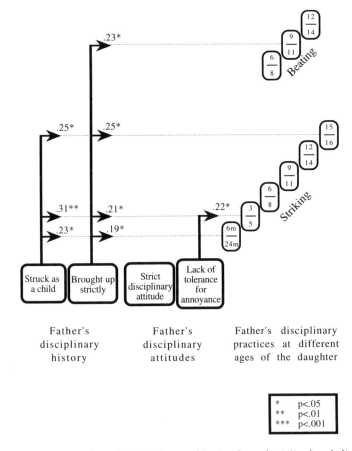

Figure 19.8. The role of the father's history of having been disciplined and disciplinary attitudes in the punishment of his daughter.

of her daughter in adolescence, with multiple correlations around .50. For girls, the multiple correlation for the mother's striking of children, aggregated over the six age periods, was .53 ($p < .001$); for boys, it was .42 ($p < .001$). The average multiple correlation coefficient for the mother's beating of children was somewhat lower, .38 ($p < .05$) for girls and .34 ($p < .01$) for boys.

Father: independent punitive agent or vicarious punisher for the mother?

A salient finding in the preceding section with regard to the intergenerational continuity of punishment is the relatively consistent impact of the mother's history

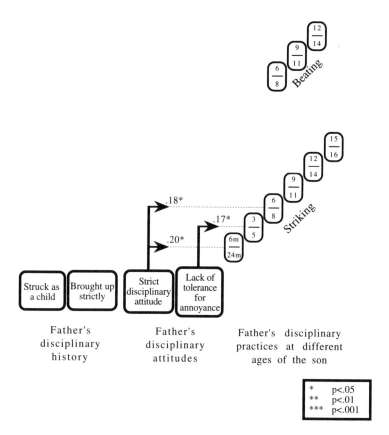

Figure 19.9. The role of the father's history of having been disciplined and disciplinary attitudes in the punishment of his son.

of punishment and disciplinary attitudes on the striking of children at different ages, but the lack of such a systematic impact in the case of fathers. Appreciable differences between fathers' and mothers' punishment of their children were also detectable in the findings presented earlier. In particular, the prevalence of striking and beating of children was generally higher for mothers than for fathers, particularly in childhood years. That mothers punish their children more often than fathers has been frequently reported in earlier longitudinal studies (Bronson et al., Livson, 1959; Lefkowitz et al., 1978). Despite these differences, the father's punishment of the child cannot be seen as separate from the mother's punishment. Earlier in this study, correlations between mothers' and fathers' punishment of children over different age periods were found, with an average magnitude of .61 for striking and .54 for beating. How can these two findings be reconciled? There is both a

Table 19.2. *Multiple correlation coefficients for striking and beating the child at different ages with the prospective measures of the parents as independent variables*[a]

	Struck by mother		Struck by father	
	Girls	Boys	Girls	Boys
Striking				
6–24 months	.20	.29*	.27	.19
3–5 years	.39**	.41***	.38*	.20
6–8 years	.31	.25	.11	.19
9–11 years	.45**	.30	.16	.06
12–14 years	.48**	.37**	.21	.16
15–16 years	.52***	.34*	.17	.17
Total period	.53***	.42***	.22	.12
Beating				
6–8 years	.33	.22	.18	.12
9–11 years	.27	.43***	.22	.19
12–14 years	.39*	.19	.21	.14
Total period	.38*	.34**	.21	.14

[a] Independent variables: struck as a child, brought up strictly, strict disciplinary attitude, and lack of tolerance for annoyance.
*$p < .05$; **$p < .01$; ***$p < .001$.

differential impact of maternal and paternal characteristics on their corporal punishment of children *and* a rather strong correlation at different ages between fathers' and mothers' punishment of children.

If the interpretation that fathers tend to support the mother's role as the primary disciplining agent and to act as vicarious punisher on behalf of the mother is correct, then one would expect that different types of maternal disciplinary issues would have a stronger impact on fathers' actual use of punishment than the same issues would have for fathers themselves. Indeed, this seems to be the case.[3] For example, fathers' striking (and beating) of their daughters from early childhood to adolescence produced significant correlations with how frequently mothers had been struck, but not with how frequently fathers themselves had been struck. However, mothers' striking (and beating) of daughters was more strongly related to their own history of having been struck than to the fathers'. For fathers' punishment of their sons, the correlations with both the fathers' and mothers' own history of having been struck were both low and insignificant.

To make a more comprehensive examination of the proposition that maternal characteristics are involved in the father's punishment of the child, the following procedure was adopted. A multiple regression analysis was performed with the father's striking of the child (aggregated over all years) as the dependent variable. First, the father's striking was regressed on the four measures of the father's history of having been disciplined (struck as a child, brought up strictly) and disciplinary attitudes (strict disciplinary attitude, lack of tolerance for annoyance). Then, in the same equation, the father's striking was regressed on the same four measures for the mother.

After the paternal characteristics entered the equation, how frequently the mother had been struck emerged as a further statistically significant predictor ($t = 3.22$, $p < .01$). Similar analyses were conducted for the father's beating of the child. Also in this analysis, maternal characteristics had an independent impact on the father's frequency of beating over and above the paternal characteristics. After the measures of paternal characteristics entered the equation, the mother's lack of tolerance for annoyance was found to be a significant predictor of the father's beating ($t = 2.26$, $p < .05$).

Similar analyses for the mother's striking and beating were conducted. In no case did paternal characteristics predict maternal punishment of children above and beyond the prediction offered by maternal characteristics. Taken as a whole, these analyses support the notion that the father's punishment should be viewed to a substantial extent as supportive of the mother's disciplining of the child.

A multivariate approach involving the child's conduct problems

Only a few characteristics of parents have been factored into the analyses of their use of corporal punishment, and many other factors must be accounted for to explain more fully the rate of punishment across different ages. The child's behavior, evidently, is one such factor. Due to space limitations, only brief information involving child's conduct problems will be presented.

At the repeated interviews, the mother was asked about the child's disruptive behavior at home. A broad, age-appropriate measure of conduct problems (including oppositional behavior, violation of rules at home, and aggressive conduct) was formed on each data collection occasion from 6 months to 16 years. For example, this measure at age 6 covered the following questions, rated on 5-point scales: "Does he usually obey at once?" "Is he/she defiant when being rebuked?" "Can you trust him/her not to do things which he/she should not do?" "Does he/she break things willfully?" "Does he/she get really furious?" "Does he/she quarrel to have his/her way?" "Does he/she strike back when siblings or other children set about him/her?" "If you (mother) tell him/her off, does he/she seem to mind?" "Does he/she have a hot temper against siblings or other children?" "Is he/she disobedient on purpose?" At age 12 the conduct problems measure included the following questions, rated on 5-point scales: "Does he/she usually obey at once?" "Is he/she defiant when being rebuked?" "Can you trust him/her not to do things which he/she should not do?" "Does he/she break things willfully?" "Does he/she quarrel to have his/her own way?" "Does he/she enjoy a rough and tumble?" "If you (Mother) tell him/her off, will he/she do the same thing again the same day?" "If Father tells him/her off, will he/she do the same thing again the same day?" "Does he/she stay out without your permission?" "Is he/she disobedient on purpose?" "Does he/she tell fibs to get out of trouble?" "Does he/she take things he/she knows he/she should not have?" and "Does he/she get really furious?" Alpha reliabilities for different age periods averaged .82 (range .68 to .91). Analyses of sex differences in the manifestation of conduct problems revealed significantly stronger evidence of conduct problems among boys than among girls from age 6 to 12.

The average correlation across the different age periods (from 6 months to 16 years) between the mother's punishment of the child and the child's conduct problems was .40 ($p < .001$) for both boys (range .34 to .53) and girls (range .31 to .48). From age 6 months to 16 years, an aggregated measure of mothers' striking correlated with an aggregated measure of the daughters' conduct problems at .51 ($p < .001$) and at .55 ($p < .001$) for sons. The same correlation with fathers' striking was .39 ($p < .001$), for daughters and .48 ($p < .001$) for sons. Apparently, and not surprisingly, striking of children is quite highly correlated with parental perceptions of the children's conduct problems. Similar broad correlational analyses for the parents' beating of children were performed. The aggregated measure of mothers' beating of children age 6 to 14 correlated at .29 ($p < .01$) with an aggregated measure of daughters' conduct problems and at .28 ($p < .01$) for sons. The same correlations for fathers' beating were .28 ($p < .01$) for daughters and .39 ($p < .001$) for sons.

Do the magnitudes of the correlations between the perceived child conduct problems and parents' use of punishment match the magnitudes of the effects of parents' histories of being disciplined and disciplinary attitudes on the use of corporal punishment? The measures were commensurate for mothers. However, children's conduct problems generally had more impact on fathers' physical punishment of children than the combined effect of the fathers' own histories of having been disciplined and disciplinary attitudes.

In our earlier examinations of the antecedents of the parents' corporal punishment of the child, the results were found to differ according to the sex of both the child and the parent. Having observed the influences of maternal upbringing and disciplinary attitudes on the physical punishment of the child, a key question is whether these maternal characteristics have an impact on the mother's corporal punishment of the child over and above the effect of the child's conduct problems.

This issue was examined using partial correlations. When the child's conduct problems were partialed out (aggregated measure from the age of 6 months to 16 years), the former correlation of .43 ($p < .001$) between how frequently the mother had been struck as a child and her striking of the daughter (aggregated over the same ages) was slightly reduced to .42 ($p < .001$). A similar analysis of the mother's beating of her daughter reduced the size of the correlation from .34 ($p < .001$) to .31 ($p < .01$), that is, after the daughter's conduct problems were partialed out. Thus, in the case of girls, the mother's punitive upbringing had an impact on her striking and beating of her daughter that was independent of the daughter's conduct problems.

A similar partial correlation analysis was conducted to examine the influence of the mother's lack of tolerance for annoyance on her striking and beating of her son, controlling for the son's conduct problems: the former correlation of .40 ($p < .001$) for striking was reduced but still significant ($r = .31$, $p < .001$); for beating the correlation was reduced from .28 ($p < .001$) to .22 ($p < .01$).

The important conclusion to be drawn from these analyses is that maternal characteristics – punitive upbringing and disciplinary attitudes – have an influence on the mother's striking of her child over and above the child's conduct problems. In the case of girls, this is indicative of physical punishment in one generation having a direct impact on the next.

Finally, to account more fully for individual differences with regard to parents' corporal punishment, involving aspects of *both* the parents *and* the children, a further set of multiple regression analyses was carried out. Independent measures in these analyses were the four measures of the father's and mother's upbringing and disciplinary attitudes and the child's conduct problems from age 6 months to 16 years. The dependent variables (treated separately) were the parents' striking and beating of the child. The multiple correlations were of .67 ($p < .001$) for the mother's striking of her daughter, and .61 ($p < .001$) for the striking of her son, .44 ($p < .05$) for the father's striking of his daughter and .48 ($p < .001$) for the striking of his son. With beating the child as the dependent variable, the multiple correlations were .44 ($p < .01$) for the mother's beating of her daughter, .39 ($p < .01$) for beating her son, .32 (ns) for the father's beating of his daughter, and .39 ($p < .01$) for beating his son. In summary, as seen from the joint magnitudes of the effects of factors related to both parents and children on corporal punishment, the predictive power is greatest in the case of the mother's striking, accounting for 37 to 45% of the variance. For the father's striking and both parents' beating, the combined effect of the parental and child measures was less powerful.

The validity of self-reported parental discipline

The extent to which reports given by the subjects at adult age (on their parents' corporal punishment practices and demands for obedience/attitudes of rejection) covary with parental reports is shown next. Figure 19.10 concerns females' retrospective reports of maternal discipline, while Figure 19.11 is for males. The significant bivariate correlations are depicted as arrows.

With respect to the retrospective accounts at adult age of the females in the younger generation, recalling having been struck frequently was significantly associated with the prospective measures of maternal striking during several age periods, and with beating from age 12 to 14. Retrospective reports of the mother's rejection and demands for obedience were also significantly associated with the prospective punishment measures for some age periods, particularly from age 6 on.

With respect to the retrospective reports at adult age of men in the younger generation, one finding attracts attention: recalling being struck as a child by the

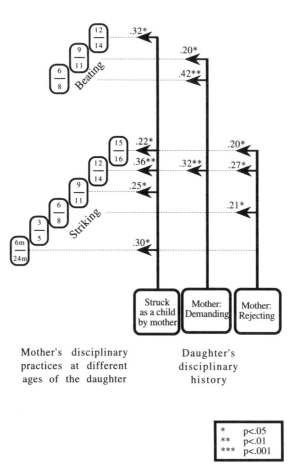

Figure 19.10. The relationships between daughter's retrospective account of maternal discipline and prospective measures of the mother's punishment at different ages.

mother was not significantly related at any age to the recorded, prospective measures of corporal punishment at different ages. Rather, it was the son's retrospective accounts of his mother's rejections and demands for obedience that tended to be associated with the recorded maternal striking and beating at different ages (at similar ages for both reports of maternal rejection and demands for obedience).

The relationships between the retrospective reports of paternal discipline and the prospective measures of the father's striking and beating the child at different ages are shown in Figure 19.12 for females and in Figure 19.13 for males.

Looking at the retrospective reports of the females in the younger generation (Figure 19.12), significant correlations were obtained between recalling being struck by the father and recorded paternal striking between ages 9 and 16. Recall-

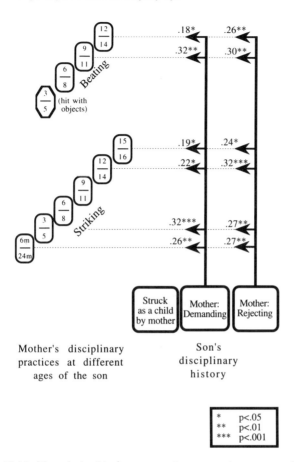

Figure 19.11. The relationship between son's retrospective account of maternal discipline and prospective measures of the mother's punishment at different ages.

ing the father as demanding obedience was significantly related to recorded striking for two age periods, but was particularly associated with the father's beating of the daughter at age 6 to 11. Retrospective accounts of the father's rejections were also significantly associated with recorded paternal striking and beating in several age periods.

As also shown in Figure 19.13, all three aspects of the son's recall of paternal discipline were related to recorded striking and beating by the father at different ages. With few exceptions, recalling being struck as a child by the father and remembering the father as demanding obedience were significantly correlated with recorded paternal striking from age 3 to 16 and beating from the age of 6 to 14. Recalling the father as having an attitude of rejection was also significantly associ-

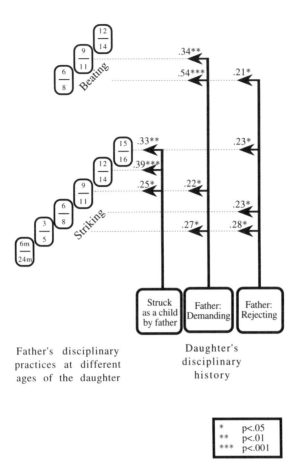

Figure 19.12. The relationships between daughter's retrospective account of paternal discipline and prospective measures of the father's punishment at different ages.

ated with recorded paternal striking from age 3 to 14, and with beating from age 12 to 14.

A multivariate approach to the validity of self-reported parental discipline

To what extent can we retrospectively account for parents' corporal punishment of their children at different ages when using *all of the information* on parental authority and punishment obtained from the children at adult age? Because retrospective reports are much relied upon in research on the intergenerational impact of punishment, it is of interest to examine in greater detail the extent to which subjects' global construction of their punishment history has an overall correlation with

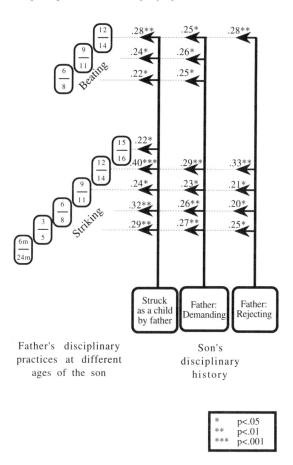

Figure 19.13. The relationships between son's retrospective account of paternal discipline and prospective measures of the father's punishment at different ages.

prospectively collected information on parents' corporal punishment of their children. For this reason, one set of our multivariate analyses was designed to retrospectively "predict" parents' striking and beating of their children at different ages from the memories that the now-adult subjects had of their parents' discipline. In these analyses the prospectively collected measures of parental smacking and beating for each of the age periods served as dependent variables, and the retrospective reports at 25 years of age – struck as a child, parent: demanding, and parent: rejecting – as independent variables. The results of these analyses are presented in Table 19.3.

One conclusion to be drawn from the coefficients in Table 19.3 is that retrospective reports of the subjects do not, in most cases, account for sizable proportions of recorded parental striking and beating at different ages. The magnitudes of the

Table 19.3. *Multiple correlation coefficients for striking and beating the child at different ages, with measures of the subjects' retrospective accounts of their disciplinary history as independent variables*[a]

	Struck by mother		Struck by father	
	Girls	Boys	Girls	Boys
Striking				
6–24 months	.42**	.33*	.14	.08
3–5 years	.11	.35*	.35*	.33
6–8 years	.21	.16	.26	.35*
9–11 years	.27	.18	.31	.28
12–14 years	.45**	.33*	.39*	.43**
15–16 years	.36*	.24	.42**	.27
Total period	.36*	.34*	.34*	.38**
Beating				
6–8 years	.46**	.15	.55***	.27
9–11 years	.30	.34*	.33	.29
12–14 years	.40*	.30*	.06	.35*
Total period	.42**	.30*	.39*	.34*

[a] Independent variables: struck as a child, parent: demanding, and parent: rejecting.
*$p < .05$; **$p < .01$; ***$p < .001$.

coefficients vary greatly between age periods. Subjects' recall of their mothers' discipline was most strongly related to mothers' striking in the earliest age period and in adolescence. With one exception, the multiple correlations for maternal beating at different age periods were in the range .30 to .46. Also regarding subjects' recall of fathers' discipline, the coefficients vary considerably, from a low of .08 for the striking of boys in the earliest age period to a high of .43 at ages 12 to 14. Considerable variation in the size of the coefficients are also revealed for fathers' beating at different ages, at least of their daughters; from a coefficient of .55 at age 6 to 8 years to .06 for age 12 to 14. Over the total period covered for striking and beating, the retrospective reports accounted for around 12 to 14% of the variance in recorded striking and for 9 to 18% of the variance in recorded beating.

For the analyses covering the entire age period, retrospective reports of how frequently the parents had struck the subjects was the strongest "predictor" of recorded parental striking. This was true for both males and females, with one exception. In the case of the retrospective reports of males, the mother's demands for obedience was the strongest predictor of recorded maternal striking over the entire period.[4] With respect to recorded maternal beating, the strongest predictor was the recall of the mother's demands for obedience for females and recall of the rejection for males. As to recorded paternal beating, the father's demands for obedience was the strongest predictor of the retrospective measures for both males and females.

Summary and conclusions

Some features that differentiate the present study from earlier research in this area should be highlighted. First, the sample of subjects consisted of a nonclinical group and their parents, which was followed over a longer period of time than that which has been reported in earlier research on intergenerational effects. Because the group of subjects was a representative sample of subjects in Swedish urban communities, the prospects for generalizing from the findings are good. Second, the annual collection of information on parents' use of punishment in the everyday life of the child has presented a more detailed view of the occurrence of striking and beating of the child at different ages than has previously been possible; moreover, the overall prevalence of physical punishment has been examined in greater depth. Third, because both data on actual disciplinary practices and the subjects' recollections of parental disciplinary practices are available, the design has provided opportunities to examine the relationship between prospective and retrospective measures of corporal punishment.

The first conclusion that can be drawn from the results is that corporal punishment is not an uncommon phenomenon. Striking and beating the child seem to have been part of child rearing in most families with children born in the fifties. According to parental reports, 100% of the children in our cohort had been slapped or spanked on at least one occasion up to the age of 16. For the average child, maternal striking was reported at more than half of the annual tests. Even daily striking, especially at an early age, took place for a substantial proportion of the subjects. At age 18 months, the peak for maternal daily striking, 32% of the females and 46% of the males were struck at least daily by their mothers. More serious forms of corporal punishment were also common in the study group. Almost 70% had been given a real beating at least once between ages 6 and 14. In the light of the "normality" of striking and beating in this Swedish cohort, it is of interest to compare these findings with those in other countries.

In their national survey of U.S. family violence, Straus, Gelles, and Steinmetz (1980) interviewed about 1,400 parents in intact families with a child between 3 and 17 years of age. They reported that 73% of the interviewed parents admitted having made use of some type of violence in their discipline of the child, and 71% had slapped or spanked the child on one or several occasions. It is likely that even these high prevalence rates are an underestimate, since basic data consisted of retrospective reports made on only one occasion. Memory lapses concerning specific instances and other factors contribute to lowering the prevalence rate. If data had been available as regularly as was the case for the present study, it is likely that only a tiny minority of children who had never been physically punished in childhood or adolescence would have appeared in a representative population (see Sears, Maccoby, & Levin, 1957).

Several previous studies on attitudes toward corporal punishment indicate that milder forms of such punishment are not something condemned by parents; rather, they are approved as a legitimate means of setting bounds on the child's behavior. In Straus et al.'s survey, three out of four parents felt that slapping and spanking a 12-year-old was normal, necessary, and acceptable. At the same time, we have to recognize that a strong repressive element is involved in much corporal punishment. This is illustrated, for example, in the following extreme remarks made by mothers in our repeated interviews: "They should be punished so it hurts," "She needs a lot before she gets the message," "A couple of times we have had to do everything we could to break him, so that he should not have his own way," "This spring he was beaten up several times, and at that time we really had to prove who was in charge."

The occurrence of corporal punishment is highly dependent on the child's age. Striking was most prevalent at an early age in our sample, the peak at age 4 for both the father's and the mother's striking of sons and daughters. The peak age for the *regular* use of striking was even earlier: weekly striking of the child was concentrated at toddler age and culminated at 18 months for both mothers and fathers; daily maternal striking peaked at 18 months, and daily paternal striking at 12 months (see Klackenberg-Larsson & Stensson, 1970, for further information on striking at early ages in the case of the present subjects). The strong concentration of more regular use of corporal punishment at toddler age probably can be explained by the children's increased activity, disobedience, and anger at this age, which interferes with ordinary life at home.

The findings with regard to parental disciplinary practices obtained here also correspond to the results reported in the Straus et al. U.S. survey in other respects. In both studies, boys were corporally punished more frequently than were girls. Mothers also reported physically punishing the child more frequently than did fathers. This difference is presumably related to the amount of time mothers and fathers spend with their children.

Looking simultaneously at the sex of the parent and of the child, the present findings show the highest incidence of corporal punishment to be the mother's discipline of her son and the lowest to be the father's discipline of his daughter. Also, a considerably lower incidence of discordant father–daughter relations than of other types of parent–child discord was found at different ages by Stattin and Klackenberg (1992) for the present sample of subjects.

In summary, our findings and those obtained in the Straus et al. (1980) U.S. survey show clear resemblances, indicating a certain cross-national invariance of punitive practices. At the same time, one should not overstate this similarity. The present results are bound to a certain culture with specific influencing characteristics. Although the rearing environment with respect to parent–child relations for Swedish and U.S. urban children is similar in some respects, there are also differences. These have been discussed and empirically examined in several studies (e.g., Intons-Peterson, 1988; Stattin & Magnusson, 1990, 1991).

With regard to intergenerational transfer of physical punishment, the mother's history of having been struck, in particular, was related to her corporal punishment of her children. For both boys and girls, how frequently the mother had been struck as a child was also related to hitting the young child with an object of some kind. Perhaps the most conspicuous finding with regard to the mother's punishment of the child concerned the different correlates for the punishment of her son and daughter. The mother's own history of punishment was the most important predictor of her striking and beating her daughter, while her lack of tolerance for annoyance was the main predictor for her punishment of her son at different ages.

One reasonable interpretation of this is that the different correlates with regard to the sex of the child reproduces differences in the manifestation of conduct problems between boys and girls. The relationship between broad measures of conduct problems during the different age periods and the mother's corporal punishment was around .40 for both boys and girls. Stronger evidence of conduct problems among boys than among girls was found in the age range 6 to 12 years. The differences in conduct problems between boys and girls might be one explanation for the finding that a measure reflecting coping was the strongest correlate of punishment of the son, whereas aspects covering the mother's history of being disciplined was the major correlate of the punishment of her daughter.

Because parents' use of corporal punishment is largely dependent on the child's behavior at home, analyses were undertaken to examine whether the maternal correlates of corporal punishment of the child still had an impact on the physical punishment of the child after controlling for individual differences in the children's conduct problems. After partialing out individual variations with regard to child conduct problems the mother's own history of having been struck still had a significant impact on the striking (and beating) of her daughter, as did the mother's lack of tolerance for annoyance on the striking (and beating) of her son. Apparently, maternal characteristics have an impact on the mother's punishment of the child even when the effects of the children's conduct problems are controlled for.

A further comment should be made concerning the lack of an impact of the father's history of having been disciplined and disciplinary attitudes on physical punishment of the child. The hypothesis was advanced that paternal punishment should to some extent be regarded as an extension of the mother's punishment. This was supported by the data. The father's disciplinary practices at different child ages were more connected with the disciplinary practices that the mother reported to have existed in her home than with the disciplinary practices that existed in the father's home. No impact of the father's own physical punishment on the mother's corporal punishment of the child was detected. In essence, part of the father's punishment of the child functions as an extension of the mother's disciplinary practices, but not the other way around. This finding is consistent with the widespread observation that the father is called in by the mother to help her discipline the child. It should be added that before this finding is more firmly established, independent measures of paternal punishment should be obtained (rather than maternal reports of the father's punishment of the child).

One has to be cautious about drawing too firm conclusions about the relationships between parents' own histories of having been disciplined and their corporal punishment of the child. Parents' reports of their upbringing with regard to physical punishment were retrospective reports. They partly reflect the actual state of affairs with regard to discipline in the grandparents' home, but the extent to which they represent a totally accurate picture is less clear.

Many have issued warnings against the use of retrospective reports of parental behavior (e.g., Halverson, 1988; Ross & Conway, 1986; Yarrow, Campbell, & Burton, 1970), but such data are widely used for generating hypotheses and also for drawing tentative conclusions on causation (McCrae & Costa, 1988). Because many of the conclusions concerning the disciplinary influences of one generation onto the next have been drawn from retrospective data, it is vital to examine the validity of such reports of corporal punishment. Our data point to limited correspondence between what the subjects remembered about their parents' use of discipline and the prospectively collected parent report measuring physical punishment. The retrospective "predictions" of parents' striking and beating during upbringing from the prospective accounts of parental discipline were modest, with multiple correlations in the range .30 to .40.

On the other hand, retrospective reports may measure distinct aspects of the mother–child relation at early age. Janson (1992), in a study of the validity of retrospective reports of mother–child relations for the present sample, with retrospective measures similar to those used in this study, reported that adult subjects' recollections of the mother's warmth correlated significantly with psychologists' ratings of the mother's warm attitude toward the child at age 4, but not with psychologists' ratings of the mother's discipline at the same age. The reverse was true for the retrospective reports at adult age of the mother's demands for obedience; significant correlations were found with psychologists' ratings of the mother's discipline at age 4, but not with ratings of her warm attitude toward the child at this age. Consequently, retrospective reports of particular kinds of parent–child relations may be regarded as gross generalizations of such constructs, without, however, capturing much of the variance in the measure in interindividual comparisons. This is in line with the conclusion drawn by Yarrow, Campbell, and Burton (1970).

No linkage between males' recall of the mother's striking and beating and the prospectively collected measures for maternal corporal punishment in childhood and adolescence was found. However, significant relationships turned up for the retrospective male reports of the mother's demands for obedience and her attitude of rejection toward the child. Thus, recall of specific behaviors did not correlate with the earlier factual data for these behaviors; broader discipline measures were more appropriate indices of what had occurred earlier in the family. This can be taken as an example of what Yarrow et al. (1970) have termed the "halo effect" – remembrance of general conditions without specific examples of these.

Finally, we want to draw attention to some facets of the results reported here that might prove fruitful for the development of future hypotheses. The most salient finding was the differential role played by the mother's and father's upbringing and disciplinary attitudes in their physical punishment of their children, as well as the differential effects with respect to the sex of the child. Future research must address the widely different correlates of punitive practice that appear for father–son, father–daughter, mother–son, and mother–daughter relations. Second, the restricted and simplistic analysis of whether physical punishment in one generation is directly transmitted to the next has to be replaced by a broader consideration of which aspects of parent–child relations in one generation tend to be relevant for aspects of punitive practices in the next. As many others have advocated (e.g., Starr, MacLean, & Keating, 1991), there is a need in both retrospective and prospective analyses to consider a broad range of operating factors. As was documented here, personal characteristics of the parents can be stronger prognostic factors for corporal punishment in everyday life than the parents' reports of prior experiences of being punished. Moreover, from a retrospective point of view, the best correlate of corporal punishment at different ages may not be the retrospective report of the frequency of such practices.

In terms of linear predictions, the limitations of a main-effects analysis with regard to the issue of intergenerational continuity has to be recognized. Statistical linear predictions of parents' corporal punishment of the child at different ages showed that measures of the parents' own histories of being punished and their disciplinary attitudes only accounted for about 25% of the variance. (When the children's conduct problems also entered the equation, the ability to predict increased, such that the total set of independent measures accounted for 45% of the variance in the mother's striking of the daughter (37% for the son) over the total period from 6 months to 16 years.)

One further issue merits consideration. Due to space restrictions, the primary aim of the report was to examine the role played by a few parental characteristics in the corporal punishment of the child, without conducting detailed analyses of the everyday family dynamics underlying the impact of such characteristics on corporal punishment at different ages or of intervening factors. For an exhaustive understanding of the determinants of everyday physical punishment, it is necessary for the macrosocial and microsocial ecological setting, the family climate, and both the parents' and the children's behaviors to all be brought into the picture. Such analyses are to be further undertaken within the framework of the research program.

NOTES

This chapter was prepared as part of the longitudinal Solna Study, led by the first author. It is a condensed version of a larger manuscript that can be obtained from Håkan Stattin,

Department of Psychology, University of Stockholm, S-106 91, Stockholm, Sweden. The research was supported by funds from the Swedish Council for Social Research.

1 The bivariate correlations have been recalculated with Spearman rank correlations. A very similar pattern of results is obtained using Spearman correlations rather than product moment correlations.

2 In this aggregation over all ages, individuals were excluded if data were missing from more than two of the six age periods for striking or more than one of the three age periods for beating.

3 Fathers' striking of their daughters from early childhood years to adolescence (aggregated from 6 months to 16 years) correlated more highly with how frequently the mother herself had been struck ($r = .32$, $p < .001$) than with how frequently the father himself had been struck ($r = .17$, ns). The father's beating of his daughter from ages 6 to 14 correlated more highly with how frequently the mother had been struck ($r = .23$, $p < .05$) than with how frequently the father had been struck ($r = .06$, ns). By contrast, the mother's striking of her daughter was more strongly related to her own history of having been struck ($r = .43$, $p < .001$) than to the father's history of having been struck ($r = .16$, ns). Also, the mother's beating of her daughter correlated more highly with her own history of having been struck ($r = .34$, $p < .001$) than with the father's ($r = .05$, ns). Regarding the punishment of the son, there were significant correlations between the mother's striking and beating of her son and her own history of having been struck ($r = .17$, $p < .05$; $r = .19$, $p < .05$; respectively) but not with the father's history ($r = .14$, ns; $r = .11$, ns; respectively).

4 The strongest single predictor of the mother's recorded striking for females was being struck as a child by the mother (beta $= .31$), and for males it was the mother's demands for obedience (beta $= .28$). The strongest predictor of the father's recorded striking was being struck as a child by the father both for males and females (beta $= .25$ and $.31$, respectively). The strongest predictor of the mother's recorded beating for females was her demands for obedience (beta $= .37$), and for males it was her rejections (beta $= .25$). The strongest predictor of the father's recorded beating was his demands for obedience for both males and females (beta $= .38$ and $.30$, respectively).

REFERENCES

Bandura, A. (1977). *Social learning theory*. Englewood Cliffs, NJ: Prentice-Hall.

Belsky, J. (1984). The determinants of parenting: A process model. *Child Development, 55,* 83–96.

Bronson, W. C., Katten, E. S., & Livson, N. (1959). Patterns of authority and affection in two generations. *Journal of Abnormal and Social Psychology, 58,* 143–152.

Halverson, C. F., Jr. (1988). Remembering your parents: Reflections on the retrospective method. *Journal of Personality, 56,* 435–443.

Herrenkohl, E. C., Herrenkohl, R. C., & Toedter, L. J. (1984). Perspectives on the intergenerational transmission of abuse. In D. Finkelhor, R. J. Gelles, G. T. Hotaling, & M. A. Straus (Eds.), *The dark side of families: Current family violence research* (pp. 305–316). Beverly Hills, CA: Sage.

Herzberger, S. D., Potts, D. A., & Dillon, M. (1981). Abusive and nonabusive parental treatment from the child's perspective. *Journal of Consulting and Clinical Psychology, 49,* 81–90.

Intons-Peterson, M. J. (1988). *Gender concepts of Swedish and American youth*. Hillsdale, NJ: Erlbaum.

Janson, H. (1992). How valid are retrospective reports of mother–child relations? An analysis of the affective and dominance dimensions. Unpublished manuscript. Department of Psychology, University of Stockholm.

Karlberg, P., Klackenberg, G., Engström, I., Klackenberg-Larsson, I., Lichtenstein, H., Stensson, J., & Svennberg, I. (1968). The development of children in a Swedish urban community: A prospective, longitudinal study – Parts I–VI. *Acta Paediatrica Scandinavica Supplement, Whole No. 187.*

Karlberg, P., Klackenberg, G., Klackenberg-Larsson, I., Lichtenstein, H., Svennberg, I., & Wallgren, A. (1959). A longitudinal study of children's biological development in a modern city community. *Acta Paediatrica Supplement, 118,* 126–127.

Karlberg, P., Taranger, J., Engström, I., Lichtenstein, H., & Svennberg-Redegren, I. (1976). The somatic development of children in a Swedish urban community: A prospective longitudinal study. *Acta Paediatrica Scandinavica Supplement* (Whole No. 258).

Klackenberg, G. (1981). The development of children in a Swedish urban community: A prospective longitudinal study. In S. R. Mednick & A. E. Baert (Eds.), *Prospective longitudinal research: An empirical basis for the primary prevention of psychosocial disorders* (pp. 212–215). Oxford University Press.

Klackenberg-Larsson, I., & Stensson, J. (1970). Physical punishment of small children. Unpublished manuscript. Department of Psychology, University of Stockholm.

Lefkowitz, M. M., Huesmann, L. R., & Eron, L. D. (1978). Parental punishment. *Archives of General Psychiatry, 35,* 186–191.

McCrae, R. R., & Costa, P. T. (1988). Recalled parent–child relations and adult personality. *Journal of Personality, 56,* 417–434.

Roe, A., & Siegelman, M. (1963). A parent–child relations questionnaire. *Child Development, 34,* 355–369.

Ross, M., & Conway, M. (1986). Remembering one's own past: The construction of personal histories. In R. M. Sorrentino & E. T. Higgins (Eds.), *Handbook of motivation and cognition: Foundations of social behavior* (pp. 122–144). New York: Guilford.

Schaefer, E. S., & Bell, R. Q. (1958). Development of a parental attitude research instrument. *Child Development, 29,* 339–361.

Sears, R. R., Maccoby, E. E., & Levin, H. (1957). *Patterns of child rearing.* Evanston, IL: Row, Peterson.

Starr, R. H., MacLean, D. J., & Keating, D. P. (1991). Life-span developmental outcomes of child maltreatment. In R. H. Starr and D. A. Wolfe (Eds.), *The effects of child abuse and neglect: Issues and research* (pp. 1–32). London: Guilford.

Stattin, H., & Klackenberg, G. (1992). Discordant relations in intact families: Developmental tendencies over 18 years. *Journal of Marriage and the Family, 54,* 940–956.

Stattin, H., & Magnusson, D. (1990). *Pubertal maturation in female development.* Hillsdale, NJ: Erlbaum.

Stattin, H., & Magnusson, D. (1991). Stability and change in criminal behavior up to age 30: Findings from a prospective, longitudinal study in Sweden. *British Journal of Criminology, 31,* 327–346.

Straus, M. A., Gelles, R., & Steinmetz, S. (1980). *Behind closed doors: Violence in the American family.* New York: Anchor.

Yarrow, M. R., Campbell, J. D., & Burton, R. V. (1970). Recollections of childhood: A study of the retrospective method. *Monographs of the Society for Research in Child Development, 35* (Serial No. 38).

20 Coercive family process and delinquency: some methodological considerations

JACQUELINE BARNES-McGUIRE AND FELTON EARLS

Introduction

Social scientists have underscored the role of the family in the origins of child behavior problems, suggesting the importance of lack of parental involvement or overt neglect (McCord, 1991), inadequate supervision (Patterson, DeBaryshe, & Ramsey, 1989), parental rejection or hostility (Rohner, 1980), aversive discipline such as nagging or scolding (Patterson, 1986), and parent–child separation (Bowlby, 1944). A strict, punitive style, nagging and scolding, or erratic behavior have been pinpointed as probably the most relevant aspects, particularly in studies of aggression, delinquency, and other externalizing behavior problems (Burt, 1925; Loeber & Stouthamer-Loeber, 1986; McCord, 1988; Patterson, 1986).

While it is compelling to hypothesize that a child's experiences within the family are relevant to the development of delinquency and antisocial behavior, there is increasing interest in a broader focus, incorporating the contextual framework in which a family is placed (Melton, 1992; Sampson, 1992; Tonry, Ohlin, & Farrington, 1991). To study the influence of community variation on family characteristics, samples need to be drawn from a number of different communities and in sufficient numbers that there is individual variation within and between communities. However, there are methodological issues in studying large samples.

Much of the key research on the effect of coercive interactions within the family has been derived from relatively small-scale investigations using detailed observations of parent–child interactions (Dowdney Skuse, Rutter, & Mrazek, 1985; Patterson, 1982). Observations appear to be the most effective technique (Maccoby & Martin, 1983), although disciplinary exchanges are generally not as easily or reliably observed as is positive behavior. Patterson has shown that observer ratings may be more effective than detailed counts of behaviors, while interviews are the least valid (Capaldi & Patterson, 1989).

The second methodological issue relates to the utility of methods and theories for studying minorities and families living in urban disadvantage. It is possible that theoretical constructs used to explain the development of aggression or other antisocial behavior may not be relevant to families different from those involved in much of the early research. Wilson (1984) suggests that much of the research on family relationships in black families is based on the mistaken assumption that the culture, class, and values of the white majority and the black minority are equivalent. Ogbu (1985) has argued that there is no universally "correct" style of child rearing and that theories about the competence of African-American children should not be derived from studies of dissimilar populations. He suggests that disadvantaged black families may need to use strategies very different from those used by middle-class parents in suburban white contexts – physical punishment to encourage early emotional independence, and an emphasis on aggression and fighting back in play to ensure self-reliance. This style of child rearing may be perceived as coercive. Knowing the norms of white, suburban, middle-class families, neither parent nor child may want to admit to coercive and aggressive parenting that could result in cultural differences in responding to questionnaires. Ogbu's idea that strict or harsh strategies are the most effective to prepare children for their environment has been questioned (Bronfenbrenner, 1985). However, there is no doubt that few measures of parenting have been standardized with African-American or Hispanic families.

Finally, at least two family members are relevant to coercive processes, either of which could be the informant, and in large-scale research there is often only one informant. In studies reviewed by Loeber and Stouthamer-Loeber (1986), 18 out of 23 were questionnaire- or interview-based with one informant from the family, 3 out of 23 asked both parents but not the child, and only 2 out of 23 gained information from parent and child. The issue of multiple informants has been raised in relation to child psychiatric diagnosis (Reich & Earls, 1987; Zarin & Earls, 1993). However, when a dyadic relationship is being described, validity of one informant becomes even more controversial and increases the need for measures that are psychometrically robust.

The research reported in this paper is part of the planning for the Program on Human Development and Criminal Behavior (PHDCB) (Earls, 1991; Earls & Reiss, 1993; Tonry et al., 1991). The program's agenda is to evaluate the contribution of individual characteristics, family relationships, social context, and community variables to the development of conduct disorder, delinquent behavior, and criminality in both males and females. The sample will include subjects from urban communities of different socioeconomic status, will be ethnically diverse, and will include many families that differ from the nuclear family structure (Earls, 1991).

In preparation for the PHDCB, a review was made of questionnaires and other techniques that incorporated discipline and hostility or rejection. A number of criteria were considered when selecting instruments, the major ones being relevance to different ethnic groups, differing family structures, and a wide age range of children, as well as suitability for large-scale population research. Other criteria were ability to discriminate "deviance" in family relationships, low cost in terms of subject time, and low cost for scoring and data preparation. Finally, instruments needed to have good reliability including for test and retest and demonstrated validity, preferably with a diverse sample.

Only 9 of the 17 questionnaires selected for detailed review had test–retest data, but more importantly only 2 stated that some African-American families had been included in the reliability and validity trials: the Parent Practices Scale (Strayhorn & Weidman, 1988) and the Child Abuse Potential Inventory (Milner, 1980). Eleven of the remaining 15 instruments gave no information on race in descriptions of samples used in measure development, and 4 stated that samples were white.

A small number of the most promising instruments were included in pilot studies: the Conflict Tactics Scale (CTS; Straus, 1979), the Family Environment Scale (Moos & Moos, 1981), the Parental Acceptance–Rejection Questionnaire (PARQ; Rohner, 1990), Parental Attitudes Toward Childrearing (Easterbrooks & Goldberg, 1984), and Raising Children (Greenberger, 1988). We have been investigating ways to integrate open-ended techniques into epidemiological work, so that the quantitative information from questionnaires can be supplemented with qualitative, potentially explanatory information. To this end, the Five Minute Speech sample (FMSS; Magaña et al., 1986) was also selected.

The FMSS is a brief method for finding out about the quality of the parent–child (or any dyadic) relationship, derived from work on "expressed emotion" (Brown & Rutter, 1966; Leff & Vaughn, 1985). The scoring provides an overall rating of high or low expressed emotion (EE) and subdivides into critical comments (CC) and emotional overinvolvement (EOI). Although originally designed for use in studies of the prognosis of individuals with schizophrenia, the FMSS has more recently been used to clarify the relationship between family interactions and child hyperactivity (Marshall, Longwell, Goldstein, & Swanson, 1990), oppositional defiant and obsessive compulsive children (Hibbs et al., 1991), children with depressive disorder (Asarnow, Goldstein, Tompson, & Guthrie, 1993), and in a community study of psychiatric disorders in preadolescents (Stubbe, Zahner, Goldstein, & Leckman, 1993).

A major focus of our pilot studies was to establish test–retest reliability for the measures and to determine their relevance to a multiethnic sample living in an urban environment, with the aim of creating a culture-sensitive, cost-effective measurement strategy for this high-risk domain. All the measures were shown to have adequate test–retest reliability with a sample of this nature. For the Raising Children instrument (Greenberger, 1988) and the PARQ (Rohner, 1990), scales depicting harsh or coercive behavior tended to be the most consistent. Test–retest correlations for the three Raising Children subscales were .60 (firm control), .77 (lax control), and .91 (harsh control). For the PARQ the values were .66 (warmth), .68 (neglect), .67 (rejection), and .78 (aggression/hostility). While test–retest results from the CTS were also within acceptable limits, the subscale with the least consistency was the one that is the most relevant to coercion, physically violent discipline (reasoning, .80; verbal aggression, .79; physical violence, .42). This was in part due to the infrequency with which many of the items were endorsed, but it was also clear on examination of the individual items that a substantial minority of respondents gave affirmative answers on one occasion and at the other administration did not acknowledge use of the strategy.

The CTS has been used with large samples of parents, covers constructs that are key to the development of conduct problems and delinquency, and is cost effective to use, even when administered as an interview rather than a questionnaire. We consequently wanted to examine further its utility and to develop a research strategy that would combine established structured methods with contextual, qualitative information to enhance the validity of information for families from a variety of backgrounds.

In this chapter we report on the relationship between the FMSS, the CTS, and some other questionnaire measures with two samples drawn from predominantly urban and minority areas.

Method: Sample 1

Subjects

Parents were approached in four elementary schools within a part of Boston characterized by economic disadvantage and large concentrations of ethnic minorities. A special education school that provides for children with behavioral, emotional, or learning difficulties such that they cannot be adequately served within their own school systems was also included. Thirty mothers were contacted through community schools and 10 through the special education source.

The majority of the mothers (25, 63%) were living in single-parent households and their mean age was 34 (range 23 to 47). The target child's age ranged from 3 to 14 years (mean 8.5). Most of the mothers were African-American (13, 33%) or Hispanic (18, 45%), and a third (14, 35%) used Spanish as their first language. Almost two-thirds (24, 60%) had been born within the United States, with a substantial minority (12, 30%) born in Puerto Rico. Many (24, 60%) were unemployed and living in disadvantaged circumstances.

Measures

The Parental Acceptance–Rejection Questionnaire (PARQ; Rohner, 1990) includes 60 statements about parent–child relationships, with a 4-point Likert response scale ranging from "Almost always true of me" to "Almost never true of me." In addition to a total score, representing acceptance–rejection, there are four subscales:

warmth (20 items), aggression or hostility (15 items), neglect (15 items), and rejection (10 items). Reliability is reported in terms of internal consistency, with a median Cronbach alpha of .91 (range .86 to .95).

Raising Children (Greenberger, 1988; Greenberger & Goldberg, 1989) is a scale that reflects three dimensions from Baumrind's (1967) model of parenting: authoritarian ("Harsh control"), authoritative ("Firm/responsive control"), and permissive ("Lax control"). It contains 39 (13 per subscale) statements about raising preschool age children, with a 7-point Likert response scale from "Strongly agree" to "Strongly disagree." Reported consistencies are harsh control, .72; firm control, .69; and lax control, .60.

The Conflict Tactics Scale (CTS) was developed to give information on intrafamily conflict and violence (Straus, 1979). Each of 19 items is considered in turn as a possible tactic that has been used in the past 12 months, when the respondent was having difficulty with the child in question. The 6-point scale indicates frequency, ranging from "Once" to "More than 20 times." *Physical force* includes items such as "slapped or spanked him/her" and "Threatened him/her with a knife or gun," *verbal aggression* includes swearing and making spiteful remarks, and *reasoning* involves behavior such as discussing issues calmly with the child. Internal consistencies, based on a national survey, range from .50 to .76 for reasoning (3 items), .77 to .88 for verbal aggression (5 items), and .62 to .88 for physical force (10 items).

The PARQ has a Spanish translation available. The three remaining questionnaires were translated into (Puerto Rican) Spanish, and then translated from Spanish back to English to ensure that the meaning of questions had been maintained. The resulting questionnaires were then checked by a third individual for grammatical and spelling errors.

For the Five Minute Speech Sample (FMSS; Magaña et al., 1986) the parent is asked, "Tell me about (child) and how the two of you get along together." They are instructed to speak for 5 minutes and told they will not be interrupted. The speech is tape recorded, and the resulting description is examined for content that is critical or hostile, and for indications of emotional overinvolvement between parent and child. Criticism (CC) can be scored from the initial statement made (e.g., "About Joey, well he's a kid that, his mood changes very badly"), by describing a negative relationship between parent and child (e.g., "David and I don't get along because he sees things one way and I see things the other way"), or by direct statements of criticism, reflecting that the behavior elicits critical emotion in the parent (e.g., "He's just a loner and that's something that I don't like"). Emotional overinvolvement (EOI) is evidenced by statements indicating extreme sacrifices made by the parent (e.g., "I would spend my last cent to make sure that Julie leads a happy life"), excessive comments about the child's good qualities (e.g., five or more remarks in the 5 minutes such as: "He's extremely intelligent"), or explicit statements expressing love for the child.

A family history interview was also conducted and a number of open-ended questions were asked concerning what constitutes a good or bad parent, whether their ethnic background influenced their parenting, what was good or bad about their neighborhood, and how conditions for parenting had changed since they were themselves children.

Procedure

Families were interviewed on three occasions. During the first visit, open-ended questions were asked and a family history and the FMSS were completed. On the second and third visits the structured questionnaires were administered and then repeated two to three weeks subsequently to establish test–retest reliability (McGuire & Earls, 1993). The FMSS was repeated on the second visit to establish reliability (McGuire & Earls, in press).

All measures were completed in the presence of the interviewer, who encouraged questions about their content and any unfamiliar words or concepts. Help with reading was given when necessary, but the majority of the mothers completed the measures themselves. One exception was the CTS, which was administered as an interview.

Method: Sample 2

Subjects

Families were contacted by random household sampling in one census tract in an impoverished section of Boston. When an appropriate family with at least one child under the age of 18 was located, an interview lasting about 10 minutes was completed. Six months later an attempt was made to recontact the original sample of 101 families. It was possible to locate 71, and hour-long interviews were conducted (Earls, McGuire, & Shay, 1994).

The respondents were predominantly female (65, 91%) and the majority were mothers (55, 78%). The remainder included fathers (5, 7%), grandparents (7, 10%), and other relatives such as aunts (4, 5%). The mean age of the target child (the youngest in the home) was 4.7 years (range 3 months to 18 years). The mean age of the remaining 60 children was 5.6 years. About half had English as their primary language (37, 52%), while a large proportion (24, 34%) spoke Cape Verdean Portuguese. The remainder spoke Spanish (7, 10%) or Haitian Creole (2, 3%). The majority (45, 64%) had been born outside the United States, either in Cape Verde (28, 39%), the West Indies (11, 16%), or Puerto Rico (6, 9%). Nearly a quarter of the sample (16, 22%) had been born in or around Boston, with smaller numbers coming from the southern United States (7, 10%) or other regions (3, 4%).

Measures

Raising Children (Greenberger, 1988) and the CTS (Straus, 1979) were used to assess methods of discipline. The FMSS was also given, as was a modified form of the *Simcha-Fagan Neighborhood Questionnaire* (Simcha-Fagan & Schwartz, 1986) to gain information on perceptions of the neighborhood. It had four subscales that describe community involvement in the neighborhood, the extent of crime and other dangers within the environment, the quality of life for parents and children, and the extent of social contacts with neighbors. The *Parental Bonding Instrument* (PBI; Parker, Tupling, & Brown, 1979) was included to investigate parents' feelings toward their own mothers. It includes 25 statements about maternal behavior, to which respondents agree or disagree, which constitute two scales: care and warmth, and overprotection.

Open-ended questions in the interview addressed differences between respondents' own childhoods and their current circumstances, whether ethnic status influenced their parenting, what were the good and bad aspects of their neighborhood, and how they would improve the neighborhood to make it a better place to bring up children. Since almost all respondents with children under 1 year of age received scores of zero, they were omitted from analysis of the CTS.

Procedure

All structured questionnaires and the FMSS were administered during one interview. Questions were read aloud to the respondents, and the interviewer completed the response sheets. Given the multilingual nature of the families living in the area and problems with making written versions of languages that are predominantly oral rather than visual (Haitian Creole, Cape Verdean Creole), no attempt was made to produce different versions of the scales in each of the languages that would be encountered. The interviewers were multilingual and presented the questions to the informants in the preferred language, translating as they administered the interview.

Results

Respondents in Sample 1 reported significantly more use of both reasoning and verbal aggression on the CTS than did the parents in Sample 2 (reasoning: means 10.0, 6.4, $t = 4.13$, $p < .001$; verbal aggression, 6.9, 3.6, $t = 3.09$, $p < .05$). There was a trend in the same direction for use of physical violence (means: 5.8, 4.1, $t = 1.86$, $p < .10$). Looking at the individual items there was a pattern throughout for more of the respondents in Sample 2 to state that they never used each behavior.

For example, more than three-quarters said that they never "threatened to hit their child" compared with less than half of Sample 1. Nearly a third of Sample 1

Table 20.1. *The relationship between critical comment (CC) on the FMSS and coercive discipline on the Conflict Tactics Scales (CTS)*

	High CC	Borderline CC	Low CC	Pearson Correlation
Sample 1				
n	11	6	21	—
Verbal aggression, CTS	9.6	5.5	6.0	.28
				$p < .10$
Physical violence, CTS	8.0	6.7	4.3	.45
				$p < .01$
Sample 2				
n	6	6	42	—
Verbal aggression, CTS	10.5	2.0	2.2	.50
				$p < .001$
Physical violence, CTS	13.8	4.7	2.2	.62
				$p < .001$

reported that they threatened between 3 and 10 times, and one-tenth described a greater frequency (chi-square $= 19.66$, 3 df; $p < .01$). A similar pattern can be seen for "Push, grab or shove the child" (chi-square $= 12.07$, 3 df; $p < .01$). Other items such as "Hit the child with something" and "Do or say something spiteful" showed comparable, but nonsignificant trends in the same direction.

The informants born in Cape Verde reported significantly less verbal aggression (mean 0.7, with a potential maximum of 30) than those born in the West Indies (mean 4.0; $t = 3.11$, $p < .01$), Puerto Rico (mean 5.3; $t = 3.29$, $p < .01$) and those born within the northeastern United States (mean 6.6; $t = 3.17$, $p < .01$) or the South (mean 5.0; $t = 1.76$, $p < .06$).

For use of physical violence, the trend was the same, but comparisons did not reach significance. The mean value for parents born in Cape Verde was 2.5 (maximum value 40), compared with values ranging from 4.0 to 5.8 for the other cultural groups (see Earls, McGuire & Shay, 1994, for more discussion of these results).

The pattern of responding to the FMSS was similar to that for the CTS: 27% of Sample 1 had high critical expressed emotion, compared with 11% of Sample 2. However, there was no overall significant effect. Nor was the level of criticism related significantly to place of birth, with the exception that those born within the northeastern United States were slightly overrepresented (33% of the high-criticism group, 22% of the two samples). The relationship between responses on the CTS and the FMSS was significant within each sample but the effect was clearer in Sample 2. Table 20.1 shows the mean amount of verbal aggression and physical

Table 20.2. *Correlations between critical comment (CC) on the FMSS and items from the Conflict Tactics Scales (CTS)*

CTS item	Sample 1	Sample 2
Insult, swear at child	.14	.47
Sulk	.39	.22
Stomp out of room	.29	.33
Cry	.39	.15
Say spiteful things	.21	.44
Threaten to hit child	.28	.29
Throw things	.43	.49
Throw objects at child	.12	.03
Push, grab, shove	.21	.67
Slap, spank	.26	.52
Kick, bite, punch	.15	.34
Hit with something	.17	.48
Beat up	.30	.27

violence for those rated high, borderline, or low on expressed critical comments (CC). In all cases the high-CC group has the greatest use of coercive methods, and the low group the least.

Looking at the individual items of the CTS, many showed significant correlations with the criticism rating (see Table 20.2). The strongest effect, across Samples 1 and 2, was for "throwing objects" (.43 and .49, respectively, $p < .001$). Other items that were significantly related to CC in Sample 2 included "Pushing or shoving the child" (.67, $p < .001$), "Hitting them with something" (.48, $p < .001$), "Insulting or swearing at the child" ($r = .47$, $p < .001$), and "Saying something spiteful" ($r = .44$, $p < .001$).

The Raising Children scale was used in both studies, and in neither did the level of expressed criticism have any relationship to any of the subscales (harsh, firm, or lax control). The PARQ (used only in Sample 1) was related in the expected direction in that aggression/hostility and rejection were related (aggression means: high or borderline $= 27.7$, low $= 23.5$, $t = 2.08$, $p < .05$; rejection means: high or borderline $= 17.09$, low $= 14.4$, $t = 2.01$, $p < .05$), while warmth and neglect were not.

In Sample 2, more criticism was evident when less social support was reported ($r = -.29$, $p < .03$), and there was a trend for the level of criticism to be related to perceiving the neighborhood as more dangerous ($r = .23$, $p < .10$). Criticism was not related to a sense of belonging to the neighborhood, to the quality of the environment as a place to live or to raise children, or to perceptions of respondents' own childhoods, in terms of lack of maternal care or maternal overprotection, as identified by the "care warmth" and "overprotection" scales of Parental Bonding instrument.

Discussion

The relationship between the measures could be interpreted as some sign of validity for each, in that parents who reported problems, annoyance, dissatisfaction, and hostility on the FMSS were also more likely to describe the use of coercive and violent techniques of control. This is particularly important information if reliance is to be placed on measures such as the CTS, asking directly about specific abusive and power-assertive behaviors, as a main source of information about discipline.

The lower rate of responding in Sample 2 may have been related to the differences in procedure between the two samples. In Sample 1, rapport had been established during the first visit with the completion of open-ended questions and a family history. Even prior to the first meeting, there had been some telephone discussion about the interviews and the topics to be covered. The CTS was not given until the second meeting. In Sample 2, the CTS questions were asked in an interview after an unknown interviewer made contact by door-to-door canvassing. However, there were other differences between the samples, such as their ethnic composition. A large percentage of Sample 2 had recently immigrated to the United States, and we were interested to find that place of birth was related to the use of coercive disciplinary practices, with immigrants from Cape Verde reporting less coercion. What cannot be known for certain from this study is whether the instrument itself elicits more information from some groups than others, or whether there were substantive differences between the Cape Verdeans and other residents in their use of coercive language as a control technique.

The FMSS may be seen as an alternative technique, particularly if informants are hesitant to report maladaptive parenting. A fairly neutral, open-ended question is able to elicit not only quite detailed comments about difficulties in coping with a child, but also explicit statements about the use of physical discipline. For example, one Jamaican-born father talked about his 15-year-old son this way:

He tends to do better when you talk to him, because he is very afraid of flogging, you know, he doesn't like to get flogged . . . but he is not a type of person that if you talk to him and if you promise to flog him, he would call the police, he is not a guy like that, you know. . . . I have to do what I want done, then you know they (Brian and his brother) are fun about it and they try their best, because I am behind them with a stick, you know.

One Cape Verdean mother talked about her son, aged 7, similarly:

He is naughty, I talk to him until I get tired and I spank him. He runs, sometimes he comes to me to say that he is my first child and I should not spank him. He goes on like that, and I say that sometimes we spank children without reason.

In addition, the content of the FMSS can be used to make more integrated conclusions about the relationship between child characteristics, family behavior, and the wider community context. For example, a mother born in the rural South reported in response to the CTS that she uses coercive discipline with her 14-year-old son. However, within the more open-ended format of the FMSS she described how she became a mother when she was 15 years old as well as the problems and positive aspects of their relationship as a consequence, and also explained the use of regular physical control in relation to her anxiety about gangs in her neighborhood:

He is not a bad kid. He likes, you know, he just likes playing with me too much and it aggravates me. I love him though. If I had the chance to do it again I would do it again. Since I was a young mother, for when I had him I was 15 years old, when I had him. And he grew up with me so like sometimes he sees me fairly like a sister to him instead of a mother. Sometimes he had to get back on the track and realize that I'm his mother or he gets his behind kicked. Point blank, because he knows I'll tear his behind — when he comes in late I go look for him, because I tell him there are these gangs out here, people like to be in gangs.

This type of remark would most likely be elicited during an in-depth interview about parenting, but the issues brought up within 5 minutes seem to be both varied and pertinent to understanding the development of problem behavior. It may provide a cost-effective way to add qualitative detail and context to epidemiological studies, and the critical expressed emotion score could be an important indicator of risk for behavior problems, although this remains to be established.

One of the respondents cited previously referred to his son "not going to the police," and it was clear from responses to other questions during the interview that some parents had mixed feelings about the influence that social services and the police had on their style of parenting. This view corresponds to Ogbu's (1985) idea that some parents raising children in disadvantaged urban areas may think that severe discipline is the most effective way of helping their children cope with the hostile environment within which they reside. In responding to an open-ended question on the changes in how they and their children were raised, remarks such as the following were made by a number of parents:

My parents are from Cape Verde where parents have more freedom to educate their children. Here if you spank your children, the children themselves are told to call the police. That is why there is so much crime, because the children can do whatever they feel like doing. My own children are small now, but I feel like they will be doing the same when they grow up if I do not control them.

Parents now do not have the control over their children. It is all against the parents. When you go to court the judge will tell you if you touch those children. . . . The old days it was the other way around. There is no opportunity for the parents to set an example for the children.

In Haiti one can spank the children in order to educate them. Here they can dial 911. And children more listen to everyone. Here they don't listen even to their parents. More respect for other people. (In Haiti) Anybody can speak to children in order to reproach them; here it is not possible.

These types of sentiment were more frequently, but not exclusively, expressed by parents who were first-generation immigrants. These individuals were open to us about their feelings, but thoughts such as these may be representative of many more parents who did not state them explicitly. A resentful attitude toward constraint on the type of discipline that is permitted or accepted within a society, or a specific community, may influence responses to direct questions about whether respondents "hit their child with an object" or "beat them up." This issue is not exclusive to questionnaires. Any interaction with parents is influenced by their expectations of what the researcher (or clinician) expects them to say, or hopes they will not say. However, highly structured techniques are more vulnerable to bias of this nature.

In research that aims to describe the family environment and distinguish coercive interactions, cultural norms and community variation in norms must play a critical role in choosing measures and interpreting the results. Establishing sound psychometric properties of instruments with families of ethnic minority status goes some way toward addressing this issue. However, more work is necessary if the study of families in large populations is to have the same clarity and utility with which small-scale research has been conducted.

REFERENCES

Asarnow, J. R., Goldstein, M. J., Tompson, M., & Guthrie, D. (1993). One-year outcomes of depressive disorders in child psychiatric in-patients: Evaluation of the prognostic power of a brief measure of expressed emotion. *Journal of Child Psychology and Ps* ... , 34(2), 129–138.

Baumrind, D. (1967). Child care practices anteceding three patterns of preschool behavior. *Genetic Psychology Monographs, 75*(1), 43–88.

Bowlby J. (1944). Forty-four juvenile thieves: Their characters and home-life. *International Journal of Psychoanalysis, 25,* 1–57.

Bronfenbrenner, U. (1985). Summary. In M. B. Spencer, G. K. Brookins, & W. R. Allen (Eds.), *Beginnings: The social and affective development of black children* (pp. 67–73). Hillsdale, NJ: Erlbaum.

Brown, G. W., & Rutter, M. L. (1966). The measurement of family activities and relationships. *Human Relations, 19,* 241–263.

Burt, C. (1925). *The young delinquent.* New York: Appleton.

Capaldi, D., & Patterson, G. (1989) *Psychometric properties of fourteen latent constructs.* New York: Springer-Verlag.

Dowdney, L., Skuse, D., Rutter, M., & Mrazek, D. (1985). Parenting qualities: Concepts, measures and origins. In J. Stevenson (Ed.), *Recent advances in developmental psychopathology* (pp. 19–42). Oxford: Pergamon.

Earls, F. (1991). Not fear, nor quarantine, but science: Preparation for a decade of research to advance knowledge about causes and control of violence in youths. *Journal of Adolescent Health, 12,* 619–629.

Earls, F., McGuire, J., & Shay, S. (1994). Evaluating a community intervention to reduce the risk of child abuse: Methodological strategies in conducting neighborhood surveys. *Child Abuse and Neglect, 18,* 473–486.

Earls, F., & Reiss, A. J. (1993). *Breaking the cycle: Predicting and preventing crime.* Unpublished manuscript.

Easterbrooks, M., & Goldberg, W. (1984). Toddler development in the family: Impact of father involvement and parenting characteristics. *Child Development, 55,* 740–752.

Greenberger, E. (1988). New measures for research on work, parenting, and the socialization of children. Unpublished manuscript. Irvine, CA: Program in Social Ecology.

Greenberger, E., & Goldberg, W. (1989). Work, parenting and the socialization of children. *Developmental Psychology, 25,* 22–35.

Hibbs, E. D., Hamburger, S. D., Lenane, M., Rapoport, J. L., Kruesi, M. J. P., Keysor,

C. S., & Goldstein, M. J. (1991). Determinants of expressed emotion in families of disturbed and normal children. *Journal of Child Psychology and Psychiatry, 32*(5), 757–770.

Leff, J. P., & Vaughn, C. (1985). *Expressed emotion in families: Its significance for mental illness.* New York: Guilford.

Loeber, R., & Stouthamer-Loeber, M. (1986). Family factors as correlates and predictors of juvenile conduct problems and delinquency. In M. Tonry & N. Morris (Eds.), *Crime and justice* (Vol. 7, pp. 29–149). Chicago: University of Chicago Press.

Maccoby, E. E., & Martin, J. (1983) Socialization in the context of family: Parent–child interaction. In P. H. Mussen (Ed.), *Handbook of child psychology* (Vol. 5, pp. 1–101). New York: Wiley.

Magaña, A., Goldstein, M., Karno, M., Miklowitz, D., Jenkins, J., & Falloon, I. (1986). A brief method for assessing expressed emotion in relatives of psychiatric patients. *Psychiatry Research, 17,* 203–212.

Marshall, V., Longwell, L., Goldstein, M. J., & Swanson, J. M. (1990). Family factors associated with aggressive symptomatology in boys with attention deficit hyperactivity disorder: A research note. *Journal of Child Psychology and Psychiatry, 31,* 629–636.

McCord, J. (1988). Parental behavior in the cycle of aggression. Meeting of the Society for Life History Research on Psychopathology (1984, Baltimore, MD). *Psychiatry, 51*(1), 14–23.

McCord, J. (1991) Questioning the value of punishment. *Social Problems, 38*(2), 167–179.

McGuire, J., & Earls, F. (1993). Exploring the reliability of measures of family relations, parental attitudes, and parent–child relations in a disadvantaged minority population. *Journal of Marriage and the Family, 55,* 1042–1046.

McGuire, J., & Earls, F. (in press). Research note: The test–retest stability of the Five Minute Speech Sample in parents of disadvantaged, minority children. *Journal of Child Psychology and Psychiatry.*

Melton, G. B. (1992). It's time for neighborhood research and action. *International Journal of Child Abuse and Neglect, 16,* 909–913.

Milner, J. S. (1980) *The child abuse potential inventory: Manual.* Webster, NC: Psytec Corporation.

Moos, R., & Moos, B. (1981). *Family environment scale manual.* Palo Alto, CA: Consulting Psychologists Press.

Ogbu, J. U. (1985). A cultural ecology of competence among inner-city blacks. In M. B. Spencer, G. K. Brookins, & W. R. Allen (Eds.), *Beginnings: The social and affective development of black children* (pp. 45–66). Hillsdale, NJ: Erlbaum.

Parker, G., Tupling, H., & Brown, L. B. (1979). A parental bonding instrument. *British Journal of Medical Psychology, 52,* 1–10.

Patterson, G. (1982). *Coercive family process: A social learning approach.* Eugene, OR: Castilia.

Patterson, G. R. (1986). Performance models for antisocial boys. *American Psychologist, 41*(4), 432–444.

Patterson, G. R., DeBaryshe, B. D., & Ramsey, E. (1989). A developmental perspective on antisocial behavior. [Special issue] Children and their development: Knowledge base, research agenda, and social policy application. *American Psychologist, 44*(2), 329–335.

Reich, W., & Earls, F. (1987). Rules for making psychiatric diagnoses in children on the basis of multiple sources of information: Preliminary strategies. *Journal of Abnormal Child Psychology, 15*(4), 601–616.

Rohner, R. (1980). Perceived parental acceptance–rejection and children's personality and behavioral dispositions: An intracultural test. *Behavior Science Research, 15,* 81–88.

Rohner, R. (1990). *Handbook for the study of parental acceptance and rejection.* Unpublished manuscript. Storrs, CT: Center for the Study of Parental Acceptance and Rejection.

Sampson, R. J. (1992). Family Management and Child Development: Insights from Social Disorganization Theory. In J. McCord (Ed.), *Facts, Frameworks, and Forecasts: Advances in Criminological Theory* (Vol. 3, pp. 63–93). New Brunswick, NJ: Transaction Press.

Simcha-Fagan, O., and Schwartz, J. (1986). Neighborhood and delinquency: An assessment of contextual effects. *Criminology, 24,* 667–703.

Straus, M. (1979). Measuring intrafamily conflict and violence: The Conflict Tactics (CT) Scales. *Journal of Marriage and the Family, 41,* 75–88.

Strayhorn, J., & Weidman, C. (1988). A parent practices scale and its relation to parent and child mental health. *Journal of the American Academy of Child and Adolescent Psychiatry, 27,* 613–618.

Stubbe, D. E., Zahner, G. E. P., Goldstein, M. J., & Leckman, J. F. (1993). Diagnostic specificity of a brief measure of expressed emotion: A community study of children. *Journal of Child Psychology and Psychiatry, 34*(2), 139–154.

Tonry, M., Ohlin, L. E., & Farrington, D. P. (1991). *Human development and criminal behavior.* New York: Springer-Verlag.

Wilson, M. N. (1984). Mothers' and grandmothers' perceptions of parental behavior in three-generational black families. *Child Development, 55,* 1333–1339.

Zarin, D. A., & Earls, F. (1993). Diagnostic decision making in psychiatry. *American Journal of Psychiatry, 150*(2), 197–206.

21 Sex roles as coercion

ALEX E. SCHWARTZMAN, PIERRETTE VERLAAN,
PATRICIA PETERS, AND LISA A. SERBIN

Sex roles are a coercive aspect of socialization to the extent that conditions of restraint or domination define them, and explicit or implicit threat or force molds their assimilation. Inequities in opportunity by virtue of gender identity alone qualify as instances of restraint; and sex role assimilation in a climate of threat or force is coercive by definition. In this chapter, normative sex role development is examined as a source of coercion, and psychiatric disturbance is examined as the effect of excessive coercion modulated by sex role expectations. We treat childhood aggression and withdrawal first as dimensions of social interaction that are implicated in normative sex role socialization. In this context, we examine childhood peer relations, parental approval, and later personality functioning. We then treat aggression and withdrawal as psychiatric risk factors that signal extremes of coercive sex role socialization, as well as examine sex differences in later psychiatric disorders from this perspective.

Peer aggression and withdrawal

Sex differences in children's peer-directed aggression and social withdrawal vary as a function of the form and context of the behavior (Frodi, Macaulay, & Thorne, 1977; Huston, 1983). Physical and instrumental forms of aggression are more frequently observed among boys than girls (Bjorkquist, Lagerspetz, & Kaukiainen, 1992; Serbin, Marchessault, Peters, McAffer, & Schwartzman, 1993), and the openly fearful, avoidant behaviors are more frequently observed among girls than boys (Maccoby & Jacklin, 1974). Inequities in sex role sanctions and constraints have a bearing on the behaviors themselves and also on how those behaviors are perceived (Condry & Ross, 1985; Fagot & Hagan, 1985; Hersberger & Teunen, 1985; Huston, 1983; Maccoby & Jacklin, 1974). Peer nominations of children are of interest in the latter context because they afford the opportunity to track developmentally the influence of sex role expectations on peer perceptions of children's social interactions, particularly their aggressivity and withdrawal. The question of interest here is whether the perceptions of children mirror the conventional sex role expectations of the adult culture by the time they reach adolescence. We examined the peer nomination data of the Concordia Longitudinal Study (Ledingham, 1981; Schwartzman, Ledingham, & Serbin, 1985) toward this end.

As a starting point for the Concordia Study, a large sample of French-speaking school children ($N = 3,648$) had been screened for aggression and withdrawal in 1977–78. The children were in Grades 1, 4, and 7 at the time of data collection, and the schools they attended served a population that was largely working class. The children received a French translation of the peer nomination sociometric, the Pupil Evaluation Inventory (PEI; Pekarik, Prinz, Liebert, Weintraub, & Neale, 1976). The PEI consists of three subscales of items drawn from a large pool of behavior descriptors that had been factor analyzed for *aggression, withdrawal,* and *likeability.* Evidence obtained in earlier phases of the Concordia Study attests to the PEI's robust psychometric properties (Ledingham, Younger, Schwartzman, & Bergeron, 1982; Moskowitz, Schwartzman, & Ledingham, 1985; Serbin, Lyons, Marchessault, Schwartzman, & Ledingham, 1987).

We reexamined the peer nomination data to compare the attributions of male and female raters. The original screening procedure had the children nominate up to four male and four female classmates in separate sequences on each behavior descriptor. This method of screening permitted analysis of the mean number of nominations boys and girls at each grade level received from male and female peers on each of the three PEI subscales. Table 21.1 lists by sex of the peer rater and target child the mean number of nominations on the aggression and withdrawal subscales in Grades 1, 4, and 7. Inspecting the column means by pairs downward permits comparison of boys and girls as peer raters at each grade level; appraisal of the row means, left to right, permits comparison of boys and girls rated by male peers in the first row, and by female peers in the second row at each grade level. The number of significant sex differences in each age group either downward for raters or left to right for targets can be readily gleaned from the number of superscripts that are not identical.

It can be seen from Table 21.1 that significant differences between male and female raters declined in number from Grade 1 to Grade 7. Four were evident in the Grade 1 group, two in the Grade 4, and one in the Grade 7. Comparisons of column means in the Grade 7 group indicate that, as raters, both sexes agreed in their perceptions of the magnitude of aggressivity in boys and withdrawal in both boys and girls. They differed, however, on the extent of aggression they attributed to girls. Male peers attributed more aggressivity to girls than did their female peers. Evident in these data was the perception of withdrawal in a conventional sex role context by both the male and female raters; that is, girls were seen as more withdrawn than boys. Also evident was the discordance between the sexes in their perceptions of girls' aggressivity. The question here was whether the boys and girls

Table 21.1. *Mean number of peer nominations on the Peer Evaluation Inventory aggression and withdrawal scales*

Rater	PEI aggression, target child		PEI withdrawal, target child	
	Boy	Girl	Boy	Girl
Grade 1[a]				
Boy ($n = 558$)	15.9[b]	15.2[b]	8.2[b]	8.9[c]
	(13.5)	(14.9)	(5.6)	(6.8)
Girl ($n = 555$)	16.8[c]	13.7[d]	9.0[c]	7.9[bd]
	(16.3)	(13.7)	(6.8)	(5.6)
Grade 4				
Boy ($n = 619$)	34.6[b]	27.3[c]	9.1[b]	9.6[bc]
	(35.0)	(33.6)	(8.3)	(8.9)
Girl ($n = 675$)	41.7[d]	26.0[c]	10.1[c]	9.6[bc]
	(44.5)	(31.5)	(9.3)	(8.4)
Grade 7				
Boy ($n = 647$)	30.4[b]	27.5[b]	9.2[b]	10.6[c]
	(33.9)	(43.1)	(11.0)	(12.1)
Girl ($n = 594$)	30.0[b]	24.0[c]	9.2[b]	11.0[c]
	(36.3)	(32.7)	(12.3)	(12.8)

Note: Numbers in parentheses are standard deviations.
[a] PEI abbreviated for Grade 1 children.
[b,c,d] Different superscripts indicate pairs of means significantly different at $p < .05$.

were attending to the same aspects of aggressive behavior in rating their male and female peers.

To clarify this aspect of the findings, we tagged the PEI aggression items that differentiated boys from girls in terms of the number of nominations received from male and female peers. The results indicated that boys received either more or the same number of nominations as did girls from male and female peers alike on all 20 PEI aggression items. Thus, although it was possible to generate a male profile of aggression, that is, items that were most frequently attributed to boys by both male and female raters, we could not catalogue a distinctively female counterpart. Instead, we delineated a profile of aggression items that were "gender neutral." These were the items that drew an equivalent number of frequent endorsements from both sexes and were directed as often at girls as at boys.

Table 21.2 lists the items of the male profile and the gender-neutral profile. The male aggression profile underlines public, disruptive behavior perceived as intrusive, uncontrolled, and immature by peers. The gender-neutral aggression profile singles out behaviors that can be perceived as hostile or domineering. The data are

Table 21.2. *Peer Evaluation Inventory aggressive behavior items*

Discriminating items for sex differences (male profile)
Those who can't sit still
Those who play the clown and get others to laugh
Those who make fun of people
Those who bother people when they are trying to work
Those who don't pay attention to the teacher
Those who want to show off in front of the class

Nondiscriminating items for sex differences (gender-neutral profile)
Those who act stuck-up and think they are better than everyone else
Those who start a fight over nothing
Those who tell other children what to do
Those who give dirty looks

---

consistent with evidence of sex differences in the manifest expressions of aggression, as well as cross-sex similarities in the motives and negative affect that prompt the aggressive acts (Cummings, Pillegrini, Notarius, & Cummings, 1989).

Returning to the question posed earlier, Grade 7 male and female raters were similar in their perceptions of aggression in boys because both sexes were likely to be endorsing the manifestly aggressive behaviors of the male profile. These were the behaviors that, as noted previously, were in fact more frequent in boys than girls. In evaluating girls for aggressivity, it was the gender-neutral aggression items that were more relevant for peer endorsement. These were the behaviors that were found to be equally frequent in girls and boys. Hence, any sex difference in the perception of gender-neutral aggression would likely have stemmed from rater bias rather than from a sex difference in the frequency of the aggressive behaviors themselves. In this instance, the attributions of female raters were tilted more in the direction of the male and female sex role stereotypes of the culture regarding aggression than were those of male raters.

In checking further on other possible sources of discrepancy between male and female peer perceptions of aggression in girls, we focused on the importance boys and girls attach to particular aggressive behaviors in each sex. We ranked the PEI aggression items for frequency of endorsements directed at target girls by male and female raters separately. Meaningful rank differences between the sexes were few. Both the girls and boys, however, appeared to place more stress on the behaviors that risk social censure from peers. Peer approval was examined further as a factor influencing peer evaluation.

Peer approval

To assess the role of approval in peer evaluations of children's aggression and withdrawal, we examined the relationship between PEI likeability, our index of

Table 21.3. *Correlations between PEI likeability (L) and PEI aggression (A) and withdrawal (W)*

	Rater–target			
	Boy–boy	Girl–girl	Girl–boy	Boy–girl
Grade 4				
n	619	675	619	619
L with A	−.223*	−.198*	−.230*	−.083
L with W	−.105	−.192*	−.044	−.053
Grade 7				
n	647	594	594	594
L with A	−.094	.041	.129*	.125*
L with W	.063	−.016	.116*	.224*

*Significant at $p < .001$.

peer approval, and PEI aggression and withdrawal in the Grade 4 and Grade 7 children. The nomination data were analyzed as a function of the sex of the peer rater and the sex of the target child. Grade 1 children were not included because the PEI likeability subscale had been considerably shortened for this age group to ensure comprehension.

The results of correlational analysis (see Table 21.3) indicated that high aggressivity in Grade 4 boys and girls was associated with low approval from same-sex peers. Withdrawal was also negatively linked with approval from same-sex peers, but more prominently so for girls than for boys ($p < .05$). Approval from other-sex peers was not a significant factor in this age group, except for aggression in boys; that is, boys who were more aggressive received less approval from their female peers.

The picture was considerably different in the Grade 7 sample. The negatively toned peer evaluations of children's aggression and withdrawal in Grade 4 shifted to a positive view of these behaviors in Grade 7; and the relevance of same-sex peer opinion for the 10-year-old was replaced by the significance of other-sex peer opinion for the young teenager. In addition, males in the Grade 7 sample registered a differential preference for girls who were withdrawn as opposed to aggressive ($p < .05$), whereas girls in this age group did not favor either behavior stance more than the other in their male peers.

These data underscore the negative valence of aggression in the male peer's evaluations of 10-year-old boys, and the negative valence of both aggression *and* social withdrawal in the female peer's evaluations of 10-year-old girls. A broader spectrum of social interaction in girls appears to fuel the potential for rejection by same-sex peers at this stage of their social development. The data on the 13-year-olds point to a change in the valences of aggressivity and withdrawal between age

10 and puberty as the salience of other-sex approval increases. We might expect this period of adjustment to be more taxing for girls than boys because of the negative connotations of both behavioral styles for girls at the start of the adjustment process.

Item analyses of the Grade 4 data provide grounds for the assumption. Correlations of the individual items of the PEI's aggression and withdrawal subscales with each of the five items of its likeability subscale were computed according to the sex of the rater and target, summed, and then ranked for negativity. There were three sex differences in rater behavior that pointed to a more critical social scrutiny of peers – female peers in particular. More aggressive and withdrawn behaviors were implicated in the negative evaluations of 10-year-old girls; same-sex friendships were more closely linked with their likeability; and withdrawal among girls was more closely linked with the risk of rejection by female peers. Boys and girls in this age group, however, singled out the same behaviors that were most likely to invite peer rejection. These were, in effect, the behaviors listed earlier as part of the male profile of aggressivity. None was a component of the gender-neutral profile.

Taken together, these findings suggest that peer approbation of children's social interactions facilitates the entrenchment of sex roles that allow for aggression in males. Although it is evident from the data that 10-year-old boys who engage in frequent acts of coercive aggression are likely candidates for peer rejection, gender-neutral aggressivity and withdrawal in this age group appear to jeopardize the social status of boys among their male peers less than do the same behaviors in girls among their female peers. The implication of peer sanctions in a broader array of social behaviors in girls would be expected to sharpen their social sensibilities and peer conformity incentives to a larger extent relative to boys – in effect, to prime girls more than boys to seek peer approval. Hence, we would expect girls as they approach their teens to strive for the now socially more desirable withdrawn behavioral style in their heterosexual peer interactions. In sum, the sequence of adjustments in the socialization of aggression and withdrawal channeled by childhood peer sanction appears more complex and demanding for women than men. Sex role maturation calls for shifts of valence primarily in the domain of aggression for the young boy and in the domain of withdrawal as well as aggression for the young girl.

Parent approval

We have collected evidence that suggests that parent-sanctioned aggression and withdrawal also present more of a developmental challenge for girls than boys. In a study of parent characteristics and their adolescent children's social competence (Beaudet & Schwartzman, 1987), parents of a representative subsample of the Concordia Study's research population received an abbreviated version (Wynne & Gift, 1978) of the Expressed Emotion Index developed by Brown and Rutter (1966). Mothers and fathers in separate, consecutive interviews were asked to describe their child and the parent–child relationship. A 5-minute speech segment of the parent's response was recorded and analyzed for frequency of positive and negative comments. The abbreviated version has been shown by its authors to capture the essential affective flavor of the original procedure. A negative comment is typically followed by many others, as is a positive comment. For the purposes of the present report, it was possible to use one negative *or* one positive comment in a speech sample as the criterion for assignment of sons and daughters to mother-negative, mother-positive, father-negative, and father-positive categories with little classificatory overlap of children in either the mother or father groups.

We treated these categories as bivariate indicators to analyze the relationship of parent attitude to the PEI measures of male and gender-neutral aggression and withdrawal. Of 174 couples interviewed, 169 described their adolescent children (79 boys, 90 girls; mean age 15.6 years) in either a negative or positive context. The category father-negative was dropped because, interestingly enough, there were too few fathers who described their children, male ($n = 5$) or female ($n = 1$), in negative terms. A separate multivariate analysis of variance (MANOVA) for sons and for daughters in each of the three remaining parent groupings was conducted, with the mean number of nominations received from classmates on the three PEI measures serving as the dependent variables. If the multivariate effect was significant, a stepdown analysis of variance (ANOVA) assessed the contribution of the individual dependent variables for each significant main effect.

The results revealed that boys who prompted negative comment from their mothers ($n = 14$) differed from those who did not [Hotellings $F(3, 75) = 3.62$, $p < .02$]. The contribution made by male aggressivity in childhood was significant [Roy-Bargman stepdown $F(1, 77) = 8.17$ $p < .01$]; male aggressivity was higher in the group receiving maternal criticism ($M = 37.9$ vs. 19.2). No other comparison in the male sample was significant in either the mother or father data sets, although childhood withdrawal tended to be more prevalent in mother-positive sons ($n = 17$). By contrast, girls prompting negative comment from mothers ($n = 11$) could not be distinguished from other girls on any of the three indicators; and those positively viewed by mothers ($n = 18$) *or* fathers ($n = 17$) differed from the rest of the female sample [mothers: Hotellings $F(3, 86) = 2.95$, $p < .05$; fathers: Hotellings $F(3, 86) = 3.76$, $p < .01$]. Mother-positive daughters were perceived by childhood peers as more aggressive on the male profile [Roy-Bargman stepdown $F(1, 88) = 4.66$; $p < .05$; $M = 27.3$ vs. 14.9] and the gender-neutral profile [Roy-Bargman stepdown $F(1, 87) = 4.11$; $p < .05$; $M = 22.1$ vs. 9.5]; father-positive daughters, however, were perceived as significantly more withdrawn [Roy-Bargman stepdown $F(1, 86) = 9.76$, $p < .01$; $M = 29.4$ vs. 18.2].

The main feature of the findings on adolescent boys was the likelihood of maternal disfavor as a sequel of elevated aggressivity in childhood, although it is possible that maternal disfavor preceded the aggression. The main feature of the findings on adolescent girls was the divergence in the behavioral antecedents of parental approval. Relevant and positive for mothers was childhood aggression;

relevant and positive for fathers was childhood withdrawal. Taken together, the parent and peer data portray more coherence for boys than girls in the sanctions and sex role expectations associated with the aggression–withdrawal spectrum of behavior.

Personality traits in early maturity

The question prompted by the peer and parent findings was whether the sex differences in sanctions and sex role expectations signify vulnerability among girls to a range of normative developmental challenges that is broader than that which boys are likely to encounter as they move from childhood to maturity. This issue was addressed in a study conducted by Leung and Schwartzman (1991). Its purpose was to examine sex differences in personality formation as outcomes of normative sex role constraints on children's aggressivity and withdrawal. A subsample (117 boys, 113 girls) representative of the older children of the Concordia Study provided the data. The children were in Grades 4 and 7 at the time of screening on the PEI and they completed the Eysenck Personality Questionnaire (EPQ) 13 years later when they were, on average, 24 years of age (range 23 to 27). Separate canonical correlational analyses of the PEI aggression and withdrawal factor scores and the EPQ data were performed for males and females. The results (see Table 21.4) indicated that childhood aggression and withdrawal could be modeled largely on an extraversion–introversion dimension of personality functioning in the male sample. There was little shared variance with the EPQ factors of neuroticism and psychot-

Table 21.4. *Canonical correlations between peer-rated childhood social behaviors and self-rated adulthood personality traits*

Variable	Male sample ($n = 117$) Variate 1	Female sample ($n = 113$) Variate 1	Variate 2
Childhood behaviors			
Aggression	.88	−.16	.99
Withdrawal	−.78	.99	−.06
Adulthood personality traits			
Psychoticism	.28	−.10	.87
Neuroticism	−.11	−.01	.69
Extroversion	.95	−.93	.00
Eigenvalue	.35	.21	.12
Percent	96.04	63.73	36.27
Canonical R	.51***	.42***	.33**
Canonical R^2	.26	.17	.11

**$p < .002$; ***$p < .001$.

icism. A two-variate model, however, was required to accommodate the PEI–EPQ relationships observed in the female sample. Withdrawal in childhood for the women, as in the men, was associated with introversion in early maturity. Aggression in childhood was associated primarily with adult neuroticism and psychoticism. The results were consistent with the tenor of the peer and parent findings. The challenge of acquiring a repertoire of aggressive behaviors that is consonant with sex role expectations appears more burdensome for girls than boys, rendering them more vulnerable to a broader range of adjustment problems than boys.

Psychiatric outcomes in early maturity

Conditions that place a child at risk for psychiatric disturbance are likely to be amplified by normative sex role pressures. If girls are more susceptible to these pressures, as the above data indicate, we should expect the sex difference to be reflected in more psychiatric vulnerability among girls than boys. Specifically, we expected that girls who are both frequently aggressive *and* frequently withdrawn would be prone to a broader range of psychiatric disorders than their male counterparts. In addition, we expected sex role norms to have a bearing on psychiatric outcome: the aggressive and aggressive-withdrawn boys more than the girls of these groups would be susceptible to the externalizing disorders, and the withdrawn and aggressive-withdrawn girls more than the boys of these groups would be at risk for the internalizing disorders. The Concordia Study's follow-up research program provided data that were pertinent to the question of sex differences in the diversity and form of psychiatric disorder.

To qualify as psychiatric risk factors, children's aggression and withdrawal were treated as polarities of an approach–avoidance axis in the Concordia Study. There is ample evidence of the clinical significance of frequent aggressive and withdrawn behaviors in screening children for emotional problems (Achenbach & Edelbrock; 1984; American Psychiatric Association, 1987). Children who participated in the 1977–78 PEI screening program were assigned to four groups on the basis of the number of nominations they received from classmates on the PEI aggression and withdrawal subscales described earlier. For purposes of group assignment, the raw nomination scores were adjusted for class size, age, and sex-normative aggression and withdrawal (see Ledingham, 1981, for a detailed description). The aggressive group consisted of children who were above the 95th percentile on the PEI aggression scale and below the 75th percentile on the withdrawal scale; the withdrawn group consisted of children above the 95th percentile on withdrawal and below the 75th on aggression; the aggressive-withdrawn group contained those who were above the 75th percentile on both factors; the control group were those registering scores between the 25th and 75th percentiles. Essentially, then, the Concordia Study was designed to follow groups of children who were at psychiatric risk because they were frequently aggressive, frequently withdrawn, or frequently both aggressive *and* withdrawn.

The work we describe concerns a selected subsample of participants of the Concordia Study now in early adulthood [$n = 211$ men, 227 women; mean age = 23 years (range 18 to 27 years)] who were seen in the laboratory for extensive assessment. They constituted a representative 25% of the 1,770 children selected for follow-up in 1978 with respect to peer classification group, sex, and grade level. A French version of the Structured Clinical Interview for DSM-III-R (Non-patient Form, SCID-R; Spitzer, Williams, Gibbon, & First, 1988) was administered to the laboratory sample after it had been checked for interrater reliability. Kappas for Axis I and Axis II disorders ranged from .73 to 1.0. Two experienced clinicians who had been trained to administer the French SCID-R and who were blind to the classification group status of participants alternated in the conducting of psychiatric interviews. Interviews were videotaped with the participants' consent to facilitate diagnostic evaluation and reliability checks.

To obtain estimates of risk for psychiatric disorder, relative risk ratios (RR) were computed that compared by sex each of the three target groups with the control group on age-adjusted lifetime and current prevalence rates of Axis I and Axis II DSM-III-R psychiatric disorders. Current prevalence refers to the presence of a disorder within the past month. The relative improvement over chance (RIOC) statistic (Copas & Loeber, 1990) was calculated for the statistically significant risk ratios. The RIOC is a measure of improvement in prediction over chance accuracy expressed as a percentage of its theoretical maximum and is, essentially, a summary estimate of predictive sensitivity and specificity. Table 21.5 lists by sex and peer classification group the psychiatric disorders for which lifetime and current RRs were significant ($p < .05$). Listed are the RR, the prevalence rates of the target group and the control group (% TG/% CG), and the RIOC estimate for each disorder.

It is evident from Table 21.5 that the range of psychiatric diagnoses eliciting significant lifetime RRs was broader in the women than the men of the sample. It was the women of the aggressive-withdrawn group who accounted for the sex difference in diagnostic diversity. These findings are consistent with the assumption that the more burdensome normative demands of sex role development augment girls' vulnerabilities to psychiatric disturbance. The influence of sex role norms was also evident. Only boys of the aggressive and aggressive-withdrawn groups were at risk for antisocial personality, and only girls of the withdrawn and aggressive-withdrawn groups were susceptible to simple or social phobia.

Early adult psychiatric status as indexed by current prevalence rates of disorder was of interest because it could be compared with the sample's adjustment in adolescence indicated by the lifetime rates of disorder. The psychiatric disorders that elicited significant current RRs (see Table 21.5) remained consistent with conventional sex role expectations. Prevalence rates for cocaine and cannabis abuse were again elevated in males of the aggressive and aggressive-withdrawn groups; and phobias remained more common in females of the withdrawn group. Childhood withdrawal, however, now appeared as a risk factor for social phobia in the males as

Table 21.5. *Rates of psychiatric disorder, risk ratios (RR), and relative improvement over chance (RIOC) by sex and peer classification group*

Sex	Disorder	RR	% TG/% C[a]	RIOC
Lifetime rates				
Females				
Aggressive	Histrionic	9.6	15/1	60
Withdrawn	Simple phobia	4.5	21/4	40
	Social phobia	9.0	7/1	60
Aggressive/withdrawn	Histrionic	8.7	12/1	58
	Cannabis	2.3	21/9	19
	Cocaine	3.3	18/6	29
	Simple phobia	2.9	12/4	25
	Social phobia	8.7	6/1	58
Males				
Aggressive	Antisocial	4.3	36/8	33
	Histrionic	4.5	14/3	34
	Cannabis	2.0	50/24	31
	Sedatives	8.9	14/1	54
	Cocaine	7.4	46/6	48
Aggressive/withdrawn	Antisocial	3.2	24/8	23
	Sedatives	6.0	8/1	41
	Cocaine	3.7	20/6	27
Current rates				
Females				
Withdrawn	Simple phobia	2.8	21/4	26
	Social phobia	4.5	5/0	40[b]
Aggressive/withdrawn	Simple phobia	2.4	12/4	19
	Depression	8.7	6/1	58
Males				
Aggressive	Cannabis	6.0	41/7	42
	Cocaine	8.9	23/1	54
Withdrawn	Social phobia	4.5	5/0	40[b]
Aggressive/withdrawn	Cannabis	5.3	32/7	37
	Cocaine	7.5	16/1	47

[a] Target group/control group.
[b] Males and females combined because of low rates.

well as the females; and the mixed pattern of childhood aggression and withdrawal now emerged as a risk factor for depression in the girls. The developmental challenges of early maturity appear to increase the risk for internalizing disorder in men with childhood histories of withdrawal, and in women with childhood backgrounds of frequent aggression and withdrawal. Follow-up studies of the risk sample in the future will provide opportunities to track the impact of the continuing interplay of sex role norms, developmental challenge, and psychiatric vulnera-bility on the form, onset, and course of psychiatric disorders at later developmental time points.

Conclusions

We have drawn on findings of the Concordia Study in support of the proposition that sex roles can be coercive and inimical to well-being. Children's evaluations of one another are increasingly influenced by the adult culture's traditional sex role expectations as they advance to adolescence. These expectations translate themselves into peer conformity pressures in line with the sex role skills that the culture designates for men and women. Our focus, in the data reviewed, was on the relation between interpersonal competence and the sex role expectations of peers and parents. Girls in our culture, we suggest, are confronted with a more complex developmental task than are boys in assimilating the traditional sex role norms that pertain to aggressivity and withdrawal in their peer and parent relations. The role constraints of the culture regarding aggression and withdrawal are less restrictive and more consistent for boys in comparison with those that girls experience in their social development. In line with this perspective, our prospective data trace a more extensive developmental profile of adjustment issues and psychiatric disorder in girls than in boys.

It is the case, however, that the domains of competence designated by the culture for males are also a source of coercion that can be inimical to personal adjustment. The culture traditionally expects more from males than females in the roles of achiever, provider, and protector; and boys are vulnerable to the emotional toll of these expectations. Technological, occupational, and social changes in the last century have blurred or erased much of the traditional divisions of labor that have shaped the culture's sex roles. In effect, we are left to wonder whether the emotional costs of an obsolete and potentially coercive code of sex role norms can be justified.

NOTE

We are grateful to the Conseil Québécois de la Recherche Sociale, Quebec, the National Health Research and Development Program of Health and Welfare, Canada, and the Na-tional Institute of Mental Health, United States, for their support of the Concordia Study. We thank the Concordia project staff members for their assistance in data collection and analyses, and Claude Senneville, in particular, for his invaluable coordination and manage-ment of a complex data bank. We deeply appreciate the cooperation of the study's partici-pants, whose continuing interest and involvement make our longitudinal study possible.

REFERENCES

Achenbach, T. M., & Edelbrock, C. S. (1984). Psychopathology of childhood. *Annual Review of Psychology, 35,* 227–256.
American Psychiatric Association. (1987). *Diagnostic and statistical manual of mental disorders* (3rd rev. ed.). Washington, DC: American Psychiatric Association.

Beaudet, J., & Schwartzman, A. E. (1987, June). *Parental affective attitudes and children's atypical social behaviors.* Paper presented at the 48th Annual Meeting of the Canadian Psychological Association, Vancouver, BC.

Bjorkquist, K., Lagerspetz, K. M., & Kaukiainen, A. (1992). Do girls manipulate and boys fight? Developmental trends in regard to direct and indirect aggression. *Aggressive Behavior, 18,* 117–127.

Brown, G. W., & Rutter, M. (1966). The measurement of family activities and relationships: A methodological study. *Human Relations, 19,* 241–263.

Condry, J., & Ross, D. (1985). Sex and aggression: The influence of gender label on the perception of aggression in children. *Child Development, 56,* 225–233.

Copas, J. B., & Loeber, R. (1990). Relative improvement over chance (RIOC) for 2×2 tables. *British Journal of Mathematical and Statistical Psychology, 43,* 293–307.

Cummings, E. M., Pillegrini, D. S., Notarius, C. I., & Cummings, J. S. (1989). Children's responses to angry adult behavior as a function of marital distress and history of interparental hostility. *Child Development, 60,* 1035–1043.

Fagot, B. I., & Hagan, R. (1985). Aggression in toddlers: Responses due to assertive acts of boys and girls. *Sex Roles, 12,* 341–351.

Frodi, A., Macaulay, J., & Thome, P. R. (1977). Are women always less aggressive than men? A review of the experimental literature. *Psychological Bulletin, 84,* 634–660.

Hersberger, S. D., & Teunen, H. (1985). "Snips and snails and puppy dog tails": Gender of agent, recipient, and observer as determinants of perceptions of discipline. *Sex Roles, 12,* 853–855.

Huston, A. C. (1983). Sex typing. In E. M. Hetherington (Ed.), P. H. Mussero (Series Ed.), *Handbook of child psychology: Vol. 4, Socialization, personality and social development* (pp. 387–468). New York: Wiley.

Ledingham, J. E. (1981). Developmental patterns of aggressive and withdrawn behavior in childhood: A possible method for identifying preschizophrenics. *Journal of Abnormal Child Psychology, 9,* 1–22.

Ledingham, J. E., Younger, A. E., Schwartzman, A., & Bergeron, G. (1982). Agreement between teacher, peer and self ratings of children's aggression, withdrawal and likability. *Journal of Abnormal Child Psychology, 10,* 363–373.

Leung, F., & Schwartzman, A. E. (1991). *Peer-rated childhood social behaviors as predictors of self-rated adulthood personality traits: A 14-year follow-up study.* Unpublished manuscript.

Maccoby, E. E., & Jacklin, C. N. (1974). *The psychology of sex differences.* Stanford, CA: Stanford University Press.

Moskowitz, D. S., Schwartzman, A. E., & Ledingham, J. (1985). Stability and change in aggression and withdrawal in middle childhood and adolescence, *Journal of Abnormal Psychology, 94,* 30–41.

Pekarik, E. G., Prinz, R. J., Liebert, D. E., Weintraub, S., & Neale, J. M. (1976). The pupil evaluation inventory: A sociometric technique for assessing children's social behaviour. *Journal of Abnormal Child Psychology, 4,* 83–97.

Schwartzman, A. E., Ledingham, J., & Serbin, L. A. (1985). Identification of children at risk for adult schizophrenia. *International Review of Applied Psychology, 34,* 363–380.

Serbin, L., Lyons, J., Marchessault, K., Schwartzman, A. E., & Ledingham, J. (1987). An observational validation of a peer nomination technique for identifying aggressive, withdrawn and aggressive-withdrawn children. *Journal of Consulting and Clinical Psychology, 55,* 109–110.

Serbin, L. A., Marchessault, K., Peters, P., McAffer, V., & Schwartzman, A. E. (1993). Patterns of social behavior on the playground in 9–11 year old girls and boys: Relation to teacher perceptions and to peer ratings of aggression, withdrawal and likability. In C. Hart (Ed.), *Children on playgrounds* (pp. 162–183). Albany: State University of New York Press.

Spitzer, R. L., Williams, J. B. M., Gibbon, M., & First, M. B. (1988). *Structured clinical interview for DSM-III-R – Patient version (SCID-NP)*. New York: Biometrics Research Department, New York State Psychiatric Institute.

Wynne, L. C., & Gift, T. (1978, April). *Brief speech samples as an analogue of expressed emotion*. Paper presented at the National Mental Health Workshop on Methods for the Study of Intrafamilial Stress in Schizophrenia, Washington, DC.

Name index

Achenbach, T. M., 12, 13, 31, 128, 129, 131, 132, 135–7, 166, 178, 218, 226, 370, 373
Ageton, S. S., 101, 103, 230, 233, 243, 273, 281, 285, 290, 310
Ainley, S. C., 310
Ainsworth, M. D. S., 169, 170, 172, 178
Akers, R. L., 291, 310
Albin, J. B., 10, 32
Aldrich, J. H., 65, 76
Allen, V. L., 138
Allen, W. R., 359, 360
Allison, P. D., 109, 122
Altmann, S., 87, 102
Amberson, T. G., 167, 179
Ambramowitz, A. J., 199, 210
American Psychiatric Association, 40, 57, 370, 373
Ames, C., 212
Ames, R. E., 212
Anderson, G., 10, 27, 28, 31, 32
Anderson, K. E., 31, 107, 121
Anderson, L. M., 199, 201, 209, 210
Andrews, B., 34, 36, 57
Angleitner, A., 137
Anglin, T. M., 102
Anthony, E. J., 124, 137
Arend, R., 170, 179
Aristotle, 2, 5
Arthur, J., 10, 32
Arthur, M. W., 106, 109, 121
Asarnow, J. R., 350, 359

Asher, S. R., 183, 185, 195, 196, 213, 215, 218, 227, 228, 230, 243
Askenasy, A. R., 63, 76
Avgar, A., 158, 163

Babigian, H., 198, 211
Baert, A. E., 347
Bailey, C. A., 292, 311
Baldwin, D. V., 106, 107, 114, 121, 123
Baltes, P. B., 153
Bandura, A., 85, 102, 199, 210, 316, 346
Bank, L., 81, 90, 92, 94, 98, 102, 104, 165, 179, 230, 231, 243
Banville, P., 150, 153
Bareuther, C. M., 209, 211
Barling, J., 33, 57, 106, 122, 198, 211
Barnes, J., 217, 218, 227
Barton-Henry, M., 261, 271
Bates, J. E., 3, 124–7, 129, 137, 138, 184, 196
Bauman, K., 261, 270
Baumrind, D., 12, 16, 28, 31, 259, 262, 263, 270, 352, 359
Beamesderfer, A., 170, 178
Beaudet, J., 367, 374
Beaudin, L., 11, 16, 31, 32
Beaufils, M., 273, 287
Beck, A. T., 170, 178, 179
Becker, G., 310
Behar, L. B., 200, 201, 210
Belding, M., 183, 196

Subject index